HOMER'S *ODYSSEY* AND THE NEAR EAST

The *Odyssey*'s larger plot is composed of a number of distinct genres of myth, all of which are extant in various Near Eastern cultures (Mesopotamian, West Semitic, Egyptian). Unexpectedly, the Near Eastern culture with which the *Odyssey* has the most parallels is the Old Testament. Consideration of how much of the *Odyssey* focuses on non-heroic episodes – hosts receiving guests, a king disguised as a beggar, recognition scenes between long-separated family members – reaffirms the *Odyssey*'s parallels with the Bible. In particular this book argues that the *Odyssey* is in a dialogic relationship with Genesis, which features the same three types of myth that comprise the majority of the *Odyssey*: theoxeny, romance (Joseph in Egypt), and Argonautic myth (Jacob winning Rachel from Laban). The *Odyssey* also offers intriguing parallels to the Book of Jonah, and Odysseus' treatment by the suitors offers close parallels to the gospels' depiction of Christ in Jerusalem.

BRUCE LOUDEN is Professor in the Languages and Linguistics Department at the University of Texas at El Paso. His previous books are *The* Odyssey*: Structure, Narration, and Meaning* (1999) and *The* Iliad*: Structure, Myth, and Meaning* (2006).

HOMER'S *ODYSSEY* AND THE NEAR EAST

BRUCE LOUDEN

CAMBRIDGE
UNIVERSITY PRESS

University Printing House, Cambridge CB2 8BS, United Kingdom

One Liberty Plaza, 20th Floor, New York, NY 10006, USA

477 Williamstown Road, Port Melbourne, VIC 3207, Australia

314-321, 3rd Floor, Plot 3, Splendor Forum, Jasola District Centre, New Delhi - 110025, India

79 Anson Road, #06-04/06, Singapore 079906

Cambridge University Press is part of the University of Cambridge.

It furthers the University's mission by disseminating knowledge in the pursuit of education, learning and research at the highest international levels of excellence.

www.cambridge.org
Information on this title: www.cambridge.org/9781108730136

© Bruce Louden 2011

This publication is in copyright. Subject to statutory exception and to the provisions of relevant collective licensing agreements, no reproduction of any part may take place without the written permission of Cambridge University Press.

First published 2011
First paperback edition 2018

A catalogue record for this publication is available from the British Library

Library of Congress Cataloging in Publication data
Louden, Bruce, 1954–
Homer's *Odyssq* and the Near East / Bruce Louden.
p. cm.
Includes bibliographical references and index.
ISBN 978-0-521-76820-7
1. Homer. Odyssey. 2. Mythology in literature. 3. Greek literature - Relation to the Old Testament. 4. Bible. O.T. – Extra-canonical parallels. 5. Mythology, Greek – Comparative studies. 6. Mythology, Middle-Eastern – Comparative studies. I. Title.
PA4167.L67 2010
883'.01 – dc22   2010041674

ISBN 978-0-521-76820-7 Hardback
ISBN 978-1-108-73013-6 Paperback

Cambridge University Press has no responsibility for the persistence or accuracy of URLs for external or third-party internet websites referred to in this publication, and does not guarantee that any content on such websites is, or will remain, accurate or appropriate.

Contents

Acknowledgements		*page* vii
	Introduction	1
1	Divine councils and apocalyptic myth	16
2	Theoxeny: *Odyssey* 1, 3, 13–22, and Genesis 18–19	30
3	Romance: The *Odyssey* and the myth of Joseph (Gen. 37, 39–47); Autolykos and Jacob	57
4	*Odyssey* 4: Helen and Rahab (Josh. 2); Menelaus and Jacob (Gen. 32:22–32)	105
5	*Odyssey* 5: Ogygia and creation myth; Kalypso and Ishtar	124
6	*Odyssey* 6–8, 10–12, 13.1–187; Genesis 28–33; Argonautic myth: Odysseus and Nausikaa/Kirke; Jason and Medea; Jacob and Rachel	135
7	Odysseus and Jonah: sea-monsters and the fantastic voyage	164
8	The combat myth: Polyphêmos and Humbaba	180
9	*Catabasis*, consultation, and *the vision*: *Odyssey* 11, 1 Samuel 28, *Gilgamesh* 12, *Aeneid* 6, Plato's *Allegory of the Cave*, and the Book of Revelation	197
10	Thrinakia and Exodus 32: Odysseus and Moses, the people disobey their leader and rebel against god	222
11	The suitors and the depiction of impious men in wisdom literature	244

12	Odysseus and Jesus: the king returns, unrecognized and abused in his kingdom	258
13	Contained apocalypse: *Odyssey* 12, 13, 22 and 24; Exodus 32 (and Gen. 18–19)	283
	Conclusion	314

Bibliography   330
Index locorum   345
Subject index   353

Acknowledgements

I want to thank Mark Smith for acquainting me with David Carr's *Reading the Fractures of Genesis*, James Lipinti for calling Kenton Sparks' *Ancient Texts for the Study of the Hebrew Bible* to my attention, and one of the referees for Cambridge University Press for suggesting I read N. J. Lowe's *The Classical Plot and the Invention of Western Narrative*. Robin Lane Fox's *Travelling Heroes* was called to my attention too late for me to refer to it at this time.

A few sections of this work were earlier presented before the following audiences:

    I presented portions of Chapter 9 at a meeting of the University of Texas at El Paso Philosophy Club in November 2006;

    portions of Chapter 4 as a paper at the April 2007 meeting of the Classical Association of the Middle West and South (CAMWS) in Cincinnati;

    portions of Chapter 10 as a paper at the April 2008 meeting of CAMWS in Tucson.

I thank those audiences for hearing me out and providing feedback, and those organizations for hosting me.

I want to thank Michael Sharp for his help and encouragement.

Lastly, I want to thank James Joyce for getting me started on all this.

Introduction

Why a new study of the *Odyssey*? Lowe, in his analysis of classical plot types in Western literature, revises Northrop Frye's (1976) claim for the Bible's pre-eminence as most influential text, replacing it with the *Odyssey* (2000: 129):

> A generation ago, it hardly seemed controversial to declare that "western literature has been more influenced by the Bible than by any other book". Yet already this is looking less true, and perhaps it never was. In the forms and media of popular fiction, at least, the pagan influence of the *Odyssey* has always been incomparably more alive. Now, as the traditional borders between high and low culture seem to be opening permanently to traffic, that persistent influence is more visible than ever.

Lowe argues for its pre-eminence not only as a paradigm for later narrative, but for its command of an unprecedented variety of narrative types (128):

> [T]he *Odyssey* is the most encyclopaedic *compendium* of technical plot devices in the whole of ancient storytelling, and one of the most dazzling displays of narrative fireworks anywhere in literature.

I will also look at the *Odyssey* as a "compendium of plot devices," if from another perspective: how it combines distinct narrative types, or different genres of myth.

Lowe divides Western literature into two subdivisions, a major key, first present in the *Odyssey*, and a minor key, first present in the *Iliad* (2000: 128), a neat correction of the usual bias that assigns greater importance to tragedy. In his major, Odyssean, key, the protagonist has greater control, makes decisions consistent with those forces that govern the protagonist's world, whereas in his minor, Iliadic, key, those forces are beyond the protagonist's control. Agreeing with Lowe's claims for the *Odyssey* as paradigmatic for Western culture, I will slightly problematize its Western-ness by considering its relationship with his and Frye's other paradigmatic text, the Bible.

GENRES OF MYTH

What does it mean to say that the Odyssey is an epic? What is an epic? Myths employ traditional components, verbal formulas, motifs, and type-scenes, such as divine councils, or a host receiving a guest. Traditional types of characters, such as heroes, gods, prophets, and patriarchs, are also constituent elements of myth. Specific genres of myth are also recurring elements of a mythology. By a genre of myth I mean that myths can be seen as falling into, or existing, in specific categories, each usually consisting of a few interconnected type-scenes. Audiences, performers, and cultures, in a certain sense, acquire an understanding of a "template" of the respective genre of myth, to which some individual modifications, local details, accrue, to make a given instance of the genre fit into a specific context. A few such genres are well known: *creation myth*, depicting the creation of mortals, gods, or the earth, as in the *Enuma Elish*, the Sumerian *Enki and Ninmah*, the Babylonian *Adapa*, Genesis 1 – 6: 4, Hesiod's *Works and Days* (47–174), Ovid's *Metamorphoses* (1.5–88), Milton's *Paradise Lost* (5–6), and the like. *Theoxeny*, when a host receives a stranger who is really a god in disguise, ending favorably, with Nestor (*Odyssey* 3) and Abraham (Genesis 18; cf. Ovid, *Fasti* 5.493–544), or ending with the destruction of those who violate hospitality (*Odyssey* 1, 17–22, Genesis 19, *Metamorphoses* 8. 611–724), has been explored by Reece (1993: 10, 47–57, 181–7).

This study argues that the *Odyssey*'s larger plot combines several distinct genres of myth (eighteen, by my count), including *theoxeny* (explored in Chapter 2), *romance* (Chapter 3), *creation myth* (Chapter 5), *combat myth* (Chapter 8), and *catabasis* (Chapter 9). For those genres that lack established names, I have put forth simple descriptive titles, *Sea-monsters and the fantastic voyage* (Chapter 7), *The king returns, unrecognized and abused in his kingdom* (Chapter 12). I will establish and analyze these and the other genres of myth that together make up the *Odyssey* by demonstrating that the same genres are also extant in Near Eastern mythic traditions.

Three studies, exploring common ground between the Old Testament and various Near Eastern cultures, use similar approaches to those I employ here. Sparks' *Ancient Texts for the Study of the Hebrew Bible: A Guide to the Background Literature* (2005) is a study of genre, a comparative, cross-cultural exploration of the different forms of narrative the OT employs, much as I will do for the *Odyssey*. In one chapter Sparks compares hymns, prayers, and laments in Mesopotamian, Egyptian, Hittite, and Ugaritic texts, while in another he notes parallels between apocalyptic myths from Mesopotamian, Egyptian, Persian, and Greek sources. He offers a nuanced discussion of genre theory (1–18), including a typology of different perspectives on what constitutes genre (generic matrix, intrinsic genre, and analytical genre), a dichotomy of how new genres are formed (generic assimilation and generic extension), and a typology of cultural diffusion, forms of intercultural transmission of genres.

Carr's *Reading the Fractures of Genesis: Historical and Literary Approaches* (1996: 16) explores the transmission history of Genesis. Briefly noting how the composer of the Old Babylonian *Gilgamesh* epic linked together previously separate narratives depicting Gilgamesh doing this and that to form the complete tale that the epic presents, Carr invokes this model to consider the formation of Genesis. First noting how the Deuteronomist source "itself refers repeatedly to independent source documents upon which it depends" (1996: 17), he finds evidence for the sources behind the other two principal strands previously identified by biblical commentators, the Yahwist and Priestly (P) layers, particularly the latter. He demonstrates how Israelite culture joined together originally separate accounts, Mesopotamian creation and apocalyptic flood myths, independent story cycles about Jacob, on the one hand, and Joseph on the other, by linking them all together under the larger rubric of promise-covenant narratives (1996: 48, 79, 81–5, 154–5, 204–8, 210, 222, 226–34). The Abraham narratives, later than those of Jacob and Joseph, provide the model for the larger "promise" framework. The editors/redactors make occasional insertions and changes in the earlier Jacob and Joseph traditions so they conform to the pattern the Abraham narratives establish (1996: 203):

In summary, I will be arguing for a model of an originally separate, but not independent P source, a source written in constant relation to non-P material (=dependent), but designed to stand separate from and over against it (=originally separate). If this model is accurate, then the final form of Genesis is the product of a remarkable intertextual move. It is the compositional interweaving of an originally separate P source with the non-P material it was originally designed to replace.

There is much here relevant to my consideration of the *Odyssey*'s structure. I will argue that Genesis shares more genres of myth in common with the *Odyssey* than does any other ancient narrative. Carr's theory on its formation, *mutatis mutandis*, can serve as a hermeneutic for understanding how the *Odyssey* may have come together.

The essays John J. Collins collects in *The Encyclopedia of Apocalypticism; Volume 1: The Origins of Apocalypticism in Judaism and Christianity* (2000) explore a variety of apocalyptic myths in considerable detail, breaking them down into different subtypes (see especially VanderKam [2000]), showing the different components that together make up this well-known mythic type (Clifford [2000]). A fourth book, N. J. Lowe's *The Classical Plot and the Invention of Western Narrative* (2000), though it does not engage Near Eastern mythic traditions, offers germane observations about the *Odyssey* and Homeric epic, and has much to say about genre, and the comparative neglect of Books 1–4 and 13–24, relevant to Chapters 2–3, and 11–13 of this study.

My work has techniques and objectives in common with these studies, though I developed my method independent from them (nor should these authors be held accountable for possible shortcomings in this work).[1] As in Sparks (2005), much of my discussion is comparative, and those mythic traditions offering the closest parallels to the *Odyssey*, employing the same genres of myth, are the same as his *comparanda* for OT myth: Mesopotamian (whether Sumerian, Akkadian, or Babylonian), Egyptian, Ugaritic, and occasional other Near Eastern cultures. Like Carr does for Genesis, I consider how the *Odyssey* joins together separate, smaller types of narrative, and how it may have imposed changes upon them, to form its larger plot. As some of the essays in Collins, I analyze the smaller components that together constitute a specific genre of myth, such as apocalyptic myth. Like that of Lowe, this study considers the entire *Odyssey*, not just Books 5–12 (or 9–12). In terms of labels, my work, like these four, applies comparative typological and structuralist perspectives.

Consideration of other examples of the mythic genres the *Odyssey* employs is significant for several reasons. A non-Homeric instance of one of the *Odyssey*'s genres helps demonstrate the genre's existence, and helps us interpret how the genre functions within the *Odyssey*. Each separate instance of a genre elucidates the others. Lowe (2000: 55) notes how awareness of a narrative's genre increases an audience's understanding:

> One of the distinctive qualities of *genre* is that it allows a common rule-system to be assumed across a whole corpus of texts. A reader familiar with a system of genre conventions will not need to have the rulebook spelled out within any particular text, any more than Italian-speakers need to consult a grammar every time they engage in conversation . . . There is no such thing as a narrative innocent of genre.

The parallels, and divergences, between different instances of a given genre of myth reveal what is most traditional or most expected for that mythic type, how a given instance conforms or innovates.

---

[1] See Louden (2006: 149–285; 1999: 70–2, 95–9) for earlier instances of the approach used in the present work.

Sparks, in his study of parallels between Near Eastern and OT myth, quotes Ricoeur (2005: 8) on how awareness of genre helps an audience interpret a narrative:

In the words of P. Ricouer [*sic*], genre functions "to mediate between speaker and hearer by establishing a common dynamics capable of ruling both the production of discourse as a work of a certain kind and its interpretation according to rules provided by the genre."

The process I follow through much of this work, noting parallel instances of the *Odyssey*'s genres of myth, using them to better understand it, and the other narratives, is what Sparks calls *analytical genre* (2005: 10):

[W]e must deliberately compare problem texts with others in the hope that this will help us understand what is unclear. This grouping of similar texts creates an *analytical genre*, a class of texts that serve our comparative purposes by helping us adjust our generic expectations, which may either be broadened or narrowed, depending on the situation.

Sparks compares the result of using analytical genre to Chomsky's notion of literary competence (2005: 12), gaining "a familiarity with the ancient context," that in Sparks' case approximates that of those who compiled/composed/edited the Old Testament. Sparks concludes (2005: 18), "In sum, good interpretation must consider the modal traits of a composition."

My study demonstrates that the genres of myth that comprise the *Odyssey* are also extant in Near Eastern cultures, often in *Gilgamesh*, but most frequently in OT myth. Why do commentators usually omit consideration of the substantial parallels between Homeric and OT myth?[2] Modern audiences may, even without realizing, project their beliefs onto how they read ancient texts. Given the long dominance of Christianity and Judaism in the West, a majority of modern Western audiences, whether consciously or unconsciously, may, on the basis of their faith, regard biblical and Homeric narratives as opposites, seeing the former as "true" or "real," but the latter as "false," "unreal," or "fictional." Intentionally or unintentionally, faith has erected a wall between the study of the two narrative traditions. I ask readers, therefore, to consider the parallels I adduce, and the arguments proposed concerning them, as objectively as possible.

The Near Eastern parallels also serve as a challenge to the theory that Homeric epic descends from an Indo-European prototype, or largely

---

[2] Taylor (2007: 1–36) is a recent exception.

reflects or conforms to an Indo-European inheritance. Though Greek is certainly an Indo-European language, and Homeric epic may very well retain *some* motifs from an Indo-European inheritance, the unproven assumption that it is largely or primarily Indo-European has, in my view, hindered study of arguably deeper and more numerous parallels Homeric epic exhibits with Near Eastern myth and epic. My study challenges the Indo-European paradigm and would replace it, at least in part, with another. As I hope to demonstrate, the genres of myth, the narrative vehicles the *Odyssey* employs to depict Odysseus' arc from Troy to his recognition scene with Laertes, are closer to those in several Near Eastern traditions, and suggest extensive interaction with non-Indo-European Near Eastern cultures.

West's recent survey, *Indo-European Poetry and Myth* (2007), offers a good test for my thesis. Having read this study after my own was largely finished, I remain firmly convinced that, though Indo-European and Near Eastern myth employ many of the same motifs, the specific *combinations* of motifs that comprise the genres of myth in the *Odyssey* have more in common with Near Eastern myth than with Indo-European. I posit five areas as offering the most fruitful overlap between Near Eastern and Indo-European myth. One is the structure of hymns. West's analysis of *Rig Veda* 2.15.1–9, a hymn to Indra (2007: 314), has several elements in common with some of the Psalms, and I suspect this could be a productive area for research. Near Eastern and Indo-European myth both make central use of divine councils (on Indo-European use see West, p. 151). In a future study I will consider whether the specific subtypes analyzed and explored here common to Homeric epic and Near Eastern myth are also extant, say, in Sanskrit epic. West reviews the evidence that in Indo-European pantheons the sky father figure and the god of thunder were originally two separate gods, though Greek myth combines the two in Zeus (2007: 238–9). The same is also true in Ugaritic myth where El, the sky father, and Baal the storm god, are separate figures. Classical Indian myth, especially dramas such as Kalidasa's *Shakuntala*, employs a form of romance close to that considered here in the *Odyssey* and the myth of Joseph (Gen. 37, 39–47). The hero's interactions with the gods are again quite close in Near Eastern and Indo-European myth.

My study would also challenge another dominant paradigm, the assumption that the *Iliad* provides the best context for understanding the *Odyssey*. The majority of Homeric criticism and commentary, I suggest, employs an *Iliad*-centered paradigm, either explicitly or implicitly, for interpreting the *Odyssey*. According to this rarely questioned model, the *Odyssey* was composed with the *Iliad* as its main backdrop; an episode in the *Odyssey* functions more as an inter-textual comment on an episode in the *Iliad* rather than serving its own integral function within the *Odyssey* itself. In my analysis the two Homeric epics are composed of almost entirely different genres of myth. While the *Iliad* employs such mythical genres as *siege myth, the king who quarrels with his prophet, god sends the king a deceiving spirit, aristeiai,* and *theomachy*,[3] perhaps only in Book 22, and part of 21, does the *Odyssey* employ subgenres of myth also found in the *Iliad*. Only here does Odysseus engage in the kinds of acts one might expect from an *Iliad*-based perspective. Though both epics feature divine councils, they employ different subtypes (excepting *Il.* 7.445–64, where the *Iliad* uses the *Odyssey*'s main type).[4] The presence of the same genres in various Near Eastern traditions, many of which predate Homeric epic, suggests that not only does Near Eastern narrative offer a more germane context for interpreting the *Odyssey*, in many respects, but that the *Odyssey* may just as well be responding to Near Eastern mythic traditions as to the *Iliad*.[5]

MYTH AND EPIC

I define myth as, *a sacred, traditional, narrative, that depicts the interrelations of mortals and gods, is especially concerned with defining what is moral or ethical behavior for a given culture, and passes on key information about that culture's traditions and institutions*.[6] My definition should be thought of as applying best to ancient Near Eastern texts including *Gilgamesh*, the *Enuma Elish*, and other Mesopotamian narratives, the Ugaritic *Kirta*, and *The Aqhat*, the Bible, especially the OT, European epics including the *Odyssey, Iliad, Argonautica,* and *Aeneid*, Hesiod, Greek tragedy, the *Mahabhârata* and the *Ramâyana*, and some later epics, such as *Beowulf* and *Paradise Lost*. This list should not be taken as a value judgment privileging or validating one myth over another, but a natural grouping of texts that bear close relations to each other, texts that can provide contexts for each other, and may have genetic relations with each other.[7]

Lowe, much as I define myth as illustrating "what is moral or ethical behavior for a given culture," stresses the *Odyssey*'s central moral concerns (2000: 140–1):

---

[3] For fuller analysis of the principal genres of myth that make up the *Iliad*'s plot, see Louden (2006: Chapters 5 and 6).
[4] Discussion below in Chapters 1 and 13.
[5] The *Iliad*-centered bias reflects the prejudice that tragedy is more important or instantiates a greater seriousness than romance.
[6] Cf. Louden (2006: 9), and Kirk (1974: 27).
[7] For a very different, more inclusive definition of epic, see Martin (2005).

[T]he three great Odyssean principles that will become virtual constants of the rule-system of classical narrative: that crime brings inevitable punishment, brain is intrinsically stronger than brawn, and trespass on another's property is an invariably fatal violation . . . any mortal contempt for divine status or authority – invariably brings retribution, whether on the ogre Polyphemus, the beggar, Irus, or even (in his blasphemous final outburst to the blinded giant) Odysseus himself . . . To a great extent, the narrative roles of the human players themselves are straightforwardly defined in terms of these moral laws.

I define epic not as a *type* of myth, such as "heroic myth," but as a *framework that can contain within it any other kind of myth, but which features a heroic protagonist and heroic modality, depicts that hero's close interaction with the gods, and through his dilemmas, explores some of the meanings of mortality, what it means to have to die.*[8]

Let us partly apply this definition to *Gilgamesh*, which, as is commonly understood (e.g., Carr 1996: 16), combines a number of originally separate narratives, distinct genres of myth. To insert the character Enkidu into its narrative, and to account for his character's unique qualities, the *Gilgamesh* epic employs a version of *creation myth*. It depicts the gods creating Enkidu in the same way creation myths depict the creation of the first mortal: fashioned from clay or earth, formed not as an infant, but as an adult male, living away from human culture in a pastoral environment, and so forth, very much as Genesis 2:4–3:24. Like *Gilgamesh*, the *Odyssey* also incorporates creation myth, or at least some key facets of it, though for a very different purpose: to depict Odysseus' circumstances on Ogygia with Kalypso (explored in Chapter 5).

Though Mesopotamian and Egyptian myths afford parallels with the genres of myth the *Odyssey* employs, OT myth is the Near Eastern tradition with the greatest number of relevant parallels (as I argue is also true of the *Iliad*; Louden 2006: Chapters 5 and 6). OT myth not only has affinities with epic (Yadin), but draws on it as a source, as Sparks notes (2005: 302; cf. Niditch 2005):

[E]pic and legend appear to have been prominent among the sources used by Israelite historians . . . the Hebrew Bible may allude to such sources when it refers to the "Book of Jashar" (Josh. 10:13; 2 Sam. 1:8) and to "the Book of the Wars of the Lord" (Num. 21:14), and scholars have long suspected that remnants of the Hebrew epic tradition are preserved in poems such as the Blessing of Jacob (Gen. 49), the Song of Miriam (Exod. 15), the Oracles of Balaam (Num. 24), the Blessing of Moses (Deut. 33), the Song of Deborah (Judg. 5), and the lament over Saul and Jonathan (2 Sam. 1). There can be no doubt that poetic narrative sources existed

---

[8] As also given in Louden (2006: 6).

in ancient Israel; that these were substantial epic works in the Homeric sense is only an educated guess.

This study will more frequently adduce parallels from OT myth than from other Near Eastern traditions. Though some readers may not be used to thinking of OT, let alone New Testament, narratives as *myth*, the examples adduced from those two collections do conform to my definition (*sacred, traditional, narrative, that depicts the interrelations of mortals and gods, is especially concerned with defining what is moral or ethical behavior for a given culture*).

OT myth's relevance is evident in the close parallels three well-known myths offer to the *Odyssey*. Joseph, separated from his brothers and father for virtually the same length of time Odysseus is away from Ithaka, meets with them unrecognized, submits them to various painful tests, before revealing his identity to them. The recognition scenes serve as the climax to his narrative, as do Odysseus' recognition scenes with Penelope and Laertes. The parallels suggest a highly developed form of *romance*, with intricate recognition scenes, is a mythical genre common to both Greek and Israelite culture, as explored in Chapter 3. Odysseus' crew, confined on Thrinakia for a month, in revolt, sacrificing Helios' cattle in a perverse ritual, offers extensive parallels to the Israelites' revolt against Moses, and perverse worship of the gilded calf in Exodus 32. The myths of Jonah and Odysseus suggest that Greek and Israelite culture both have a genre of myth we might think of as the *fantastic voyage*.

As these examples indicate, very different types of myths are used to depict the various stages of Odysseus' larger narrative trajectory from Troy to Ithaka. Gaining an understanding of how these smaller units function helps reveal how the *Odyssey* as a whole functions, how it ties together distinct mythic types into a large, smoothly functioning composite. Many of the genres of myth in the *Odyssey*, such as *theoxeny*, challenge usual assumptions of what constitutes an epic. For the greater part of nine books (14–22) Odysseus, to all outward appearances, is a beggar, associating with lowly slaves, abused, unrecognized in his own kingdom – unexpected behavior for an epic hero. The *Odyssey* establishes its central concern with non-heroic genres of myth in the *Telemachy* (Books 1–4), which especially explores hospitality myth. Here the focus is first on Telemachos' observance of the sanctity of hospitality, and the suitors' thematic violation of the same (Book 1). Later the patriarch Nestor offers exemplary hospitality to Telemachos, now a guest, and to the disguised Athena (Book 3), furthering the *Odyssey*'s use of non-heroic genres of myth. In these ways and others the *Odyssey* has more in common with Genesis and parts of the gospels (see Chapters 9, and 11–12 of this study) than with most heroic myth, or the *Iliad*.

WHY THE *ODYSSEY* EXHIBITS EXTENSIVE PARALLELS WITH NEAR EASTERN MYTH

As I will argue, the parallels are far too frequent and close (differences in tone and narrative agendas notwithstanding) for coincidence. The similarities between Greek and Near Eastern myth suggest some form of diffusion. I assume that each tradition, Homeric or Near Eastern, learned or acquired a "template" of the respective genre of myth, to which each culture then made some modifications, added more local details, to make it fit into the specific context in which that culture now employed it. The *Odyssey*, for instance, uses theoxeny as episodes in the lives of warriors, Odysseus, Nestor, and Telemachos, whereas OT myth employs theoxeny as episodes in the lives of patriarchs, Abraham and Lot. Because of the different type of characters featured, the respective instances have different modalities. The warrior Odysseus himself carries out the destruction of the suitors, as demanded by Athena, whereas in Genesis 19 destruction rains down from the sky. My analyses do not depend on verbal echoes between the different forms of the same myth. Rather, the genre of myth exhibits parallels at a morphological level, different instantiations using the same themes and type-scenes, if differing in some details.

The likeliest scenario for cultural diffusion is Greek contact with Phoenician culture, whether in ancient Syria, on Cyprus, or in the Greek world.[9] Ongoing archeological research affirms how close ties were at times between Greeks and various Near Eastern peoples, the Phoenicians in particular. Since the Greeks obtained their alphabet from the Phoenicians (see Teodorrson: 2006: 169–72, and Powell 2002: 99–108, for recent discussions), and Greek myth assigns key roles to Phoenicians (Cadmus, most importantly), it is likely that the two cultures also engaged in *exchanges of narratives*, or specific genres of myth, as well.[10]

Sparks (2005: 4) delineates four types of dispersion:

---

[9] Note the prominence of Sidonia, a Phoenician city, at *Iliad* 6.289–91; cf. Proclus' account in the *Cypria*, and Apollodorus, *Epitome* 3.4. See also the background information on Agamemnon's corselet as a gift from a Cyprian king, *Iliad* 11.19–28. I make a few additional comments in the Conclusion.

[10] The *Odyssey* makes many references to Phoenicians or Phoenician culture: 4.83–4, 618; 13.272, 285; 14.291; 15.118, 415, 419, 425, 473; cf. *Iliad* 6.290–1; 23.743–4.

At least four basic types of diffusion are distinguishable: *direct connection* (A is dependent upon B), a *mediated connection* (A knows about B from source C), a *common source* (A and B utilized a common source, C), and a *common tradition* (A and B have no immediate connections but participate in a common tradition).

Since we lack surviving texts of Phoenician myths, other than the brief account by Philo of Byblos, we must extrapolate on the basis of Ugaritic myths, which offer significant common ground with Homeric epic (Louden 2006: Chapter 7), and references to Canaanite religion in the OT. Evidence is rarely if ever sufficient to argue for *direct connection* between Greek and another Near Eastern culture. My default position is that, owing to the greater antiquity of some Near Eastern cultures, particularly the greater antiquity of their familiarity with writing, both Greek and OT myth probably reflect influence from an earlier Near Eastern source, whether Ugaritic, Mesopotamian, Egyptian, or some other. An indirect relationship between a Greek and Israelite genre of myth could result from either the third or fourth of Sparks' types, *common source*, or *common tradition*. Thus parallels I adduce between the *Odyssey* and OT myth might typically imply that both Greek and Israelite culture are drawing on earlier Near Eastern instances of the same genre of myth. I do *not* believe, as a reviewer (West, E. 2008: 313) of my second book (Louden 2006) suggested, that Greek myth was influenced by OT myth. In that book as well as this, the main reason I adduce OT myths is because their parallels provide a tool for our understanding and interpretation of Homeric epic.

There are, however, significant complications, and exceptions to consider. Greek myth is best understood as having a *dialogic* relationship with Near Eastern myth, and a particularly close and multifaceted relationship with OT myth, however mediated. Responsible reading of the OT in accurate translation reveals Israelite culture was not monotheistic as early as modern audiences might assume. The Israelites were fully polytheistic at an earlier period, and only gradually, over centuries, probably not until some point during the Babylonian captivity, did a majority of their culture convert to monotheism (cf. Smith 2001). For the lengthy period in between, Israelite culture is best viewed as monolatrous, worshipping a single god, but assuming that other gods exist whose worship was forbidden. In their earlier polytheistic period the Israelites worshipped the pantheon of Ugaritic deities, evident in the frequent mention in OT myth of El, Asherah, and Baal, in particular. Whenever *any* of these gods is mentioned, their entire pantheon is implicitly invoked. Study of Ugaritic myth, *The Baal Cycle*, the *Aqhat*, and the *Kirta*, clarifies the functions of several of the Ugaritic gods, El, Asherah, Baal, Anat, Yam, and Mot, all of whom are mentioned in OT myth, and is quite relevant to Homeric epic. The Ugaritic pantheon, particularly interaction between the different gods, has been singled out as the pantheon most like the Homeric Olympians (Louden 2006: Chapter 7, cf., Morris 1992, 1995).

Recent work on the OT has dramatically brought forward the dates for when the texts reached a form like that which we have. Though the OT contains units of considerable antiquity, the larger narratives were edited, rewritten, redacted, at much later times, when influence between the two cultures may well be from Greek to Israelite culture. If we consider how widespread were Greek language and culture during the time in which OT narratives reached their final form, and how comparatively limited was the use of Hebrew, the likelihood that OT writers were influenced by Hellenistic culture, rather than the other way around, increases considerably. I will occasionally suggest, then, that a Greek instance of a specific genre of myth not only predates an Israelite instance of the same mythic genre in the OT, but that the OT myth is reacting to, possibly even adapting, a Greek myth.[11]

Greek myth should be seen in a dialogic relation with Near Eastern myth, with influence running in both directions, during several different eras. Yadin argues that 1 Samuel's account of David and Goliath's duel, as we have it, is written in reaction to Homeric epic. Summarizing other scholarship on the episode at 2 Samuel 21:19, where Elhanan slays Goliath, Yadin argues that this is the earlier passage, that the story was later appropriated by the David tradition (2004: 376). Since the version of the episode is significantly shorter in the Septuagint, scholars see the Masoretic Text as a later expansion, reflecting the influence of Homeric epic. Yadin notes the significant expansion of Greek culture into the Near East when the OT was taking shape (2004: 381):

At the middle of the sixth century the Greeks stood at the end of a century and a half of intensive colonization... Greek colonies dotted the eastern Mediterranean coast... a strong presence along the Phoenician coast and in parts of Palestine.

Yadin thus argues that the close parallels between David and Goliath's duel and several of those in the *Iliad*[12] are neither coincidence nor evidence that both separately depict a historical reality (2004: 386–7),

---

[11] The Book of Jonah is a likely instance of an OT narrative influenced by Greek myth (discussion in Chapter 7).
[12] On which, see Louden (2006: 172–6).

David's victory over Goliath... [t]he parallels to Homeric epic are not... evidence of the antiquity of these elements, but of the familiarity of the redactor with Greek culture... the battle of David and Goliath is best read with the *Iliad* as its intertext.

I will argue that sections of Genesis and Jonah, and those parts of the gospels that depict Jesus' entrance into Jerusalem and his treatment there, exist in a similar relationship with the *Odyssey*.

Interconnections between Homeric epic and older Near Eastern myth and epic necessarily involve the additional complication of *written* texts possibly influencing an oral tradition. If the parallels I argue for are valid, we need to consider the form in which Greek culture came into contact with Near Eastern myth and epic. Since many Near Eastern myths and epics were fixed in written form long before Homeric epics were, it is possible that Greek culture encountered versions of *Gilgamesh* or Ugaritic or Phoenician myths in public performance or recitation, or as fixed, written texts.[13] If so, such contact problematizes the generally accepted theory of the oral genesis of Homeric epic.[14] The converse is also likely, as Yadin argues. If OT composers were influenced by Greek myth, it is likely that they encountered the myths in written form. Since Greek culture also impacts the OT through the Septuagint, since Jews of the period knew Greek, were part of Hellenistic culture, to some degree, and probably could not help but be exposed to some forms of Greek myth, I will therefore often give passages of OT myth in Greek from the Septuagint. Doing so sometimes makes the parallels between the *Odyssey* and OT myth even closer, and, since the authors of the gospels read the OT in Greek and quote from the Septuagint, also makes parallels between the *Odyssey* and NT myth more immediate.

Every individual motif that makes up the *Odyssey* is traditional; each of the genres of myth it uses is also a traditional type extant elsewhere. But the *Odyssey* is a unique combination of these traditional narrative types. Three particular genres of myth provide its larger overarching framework, *theoxeny*, *romance*, and *Argonautic myth* (analyzed respectively in Chapters 2, 3, and 6). These three types bind the various parts of the epic together, and

---

[13] For recent discussion and some conjectures, see Teodorsson (2006: 166–9).

[14] Cf. Malkin (2008: 266–7): "It may be possible to suggest that the very idea of writing down a great epic could also have come from the Near East, where epic poetry was being written long before the Greeks had thought of using the alphabet to write down the Homeric epics. The Gilgamesh epic is, of course, the most familiar, but closer to the region of Greek-Phoenician acculturation oral Ugarit epics were being written down as early as the fourteenth century along the coast of Syria opposite Cyprus... The Near Eastern evidence of written epic and other poetry as early as the third millennium B.C. is still in need of reassessment by classicists, who... have not yet recognized how much they have to learn from Near Eastern studies about the development of epic tradition."

constitute the majority of its plot. Theoxeny particularly provides the main framework for depicting events involving the suitors. Argonautic myth on the other hand serves as a template for much of Books 6–12: Odysseus away from Ithaka. Several episodes in these books offer different "refractions" of the basic situation depicted in Argonautic myth: the wandering hero meets an unmarried female and is compelled to perform labors by her hostile father. Romance is the mythic genre that restores Odysseus to Ithaka, and reunites him with family members.

OT myth is also composed of traditional, recurring elements. Almost every detail in the narratives as we have them is a generic motif. OT myth also employs genres of myth extant elsewhere (see Speiser 1962: liv and ff. on the Mesopotamian texture of the Genesis narratives; Sparks [2005] throughout). We need look no further than Genesis to find theoxeny (Gen. 18–19: Abraham, Lot), romance (Gen. 37, 39–47: Joseph in Egypt), and Argonautic myth (Gen. 28–33: Jacob winning Rachel), the same three mythic genres that comprise much of the *Odyssey*'s plot. As is well known, the myth of the Flood, Genesis 6:5–8:22, comes from an earlier Mesopotamian version, whether that in *Gilgamesh*, or an earlier, independent version. Other OT narratives also draw on traditional myths that predate the OT versions.

If Genesis is the book of OT myth with the most parallels with the *Odyssey*, Jacob is the character that participates in the greatest number of genres of myth found in the *Odyssey*. Parallels and differences between Jacob and Homeric protagonists illustrate a key difference between the respective mythic traditions. The *Odyssey* has heroes, warriors, kings, and their families as its protagonists and central characters, whereas Genesis, employing many of the same genres of myth, has patriarchs and their families as its protagonists. Menelaus wrestles with Proteus, as Jacob does with Yahweh (Gen. 32:22–32); Nestor hosts a positive theoxeny as Abraham does in Genesis 18; Telemachos hosts a negative theoxeny as Lot does in Genesis 19; Odysseus' recognition scenes closely parallel Joseph's in Genesis 43–5. Genesis shares considerable parallels with the *Odyssey* because the Torah offers large-scale parallels, wandering and return, a *nostos*, sometimes put forth as a generic classification for the *Odyssey*.

My view of the Homeric gods is close to Allan's recent study (2006). He convincingly undermines long-held assumptions that the Homeric Olympians in the *Odyssey* are incompatible with those in the *Iliad* in their sense of justice, or that in both epics we should see them as amoral. Though he does not consider the Near Eastern texts with which we are here concerned, my own conclusion is that Homeric epic maintains very similar notions of justice, reward, and punishment, as does OT myth (though I leave further discussion to specific instances in the various chapters). When contemporary commentators argue that a specific act by a Homeric god is immoral or amoral, they do not place the act within an *ancient* context to see whether or not in other cultures of the same period, such as OT myth, a god behaves in the same manner, with a sense of justice perhaps equally at odds with modern notions. I will argue that Yahweh's destruction of *all* the inhabitants of Sodom and Gomorrah, or having the Israelites slay each other in Exodus 32 until over 3,000 die, are at least as problematic as Poseidon's destruction of the Phaiakian crew in *Odyssey* 13.

CHAPTER I

Divine councils and apocalyptic myth

After a short proem (*Od.* 1.1–10), and brief transition, the *Odyssey*'s first scene is a divine council on Mount Olympos (*Od.* 1.26–96). I define a divine council simply as *a conversation between two or more gods, often a large assembly of them, usually with the chief god presiding, usually concerned with the myth's protagonist.* Since they depend on the presence of more than one god, divine councils are a naturally polytheistic genre, and also occur outside of epic.[1] They are often considered a type-scene, but I here treat them as a genre of myth because in the *Odyssey* they trigger, manage, or conclude, larger blocks of narrative. Since divine councils come in only a few basic types, a typology of the specific subtypes is useful. Having determined which subtype a given divine council belongs to, we can then place it in a larger context of similar scenes, each of which helps demonstrate how instances of that subtype typically function. Our context for analyzing the *Odyssey*'s divine councils will be the divine councils in *Gilgamesh*, the Ugaritic myths, the *Iliad*, Hesiod, and Old Testament myth.[2]

In most Greek or Near Eastern heroic myths three gods typically define the parameters of a hero's career.[3] The three gods are each associated with a specific type-scene through which they demonstrate and act out their specific relationship with the hero. The sky father, Zeus, in Homeric epic, judge and ruler of the cosmos, supports the hero and guides his destiny by *presiding* over divine councils involving the hero, rather than personally intervening on his behalf. A mentor god defends and advises the hero, speaks on his behalf at divine councils, and personally appears to him in *theophany*. A third god places obstacles in his path, speaks against him at divine councils, and causes the deaths of others around the hero, *a divine wrath*. The three gods suggest a legal configuration in which the

---

[1] They are also common in creation myths, particularly in theomachies occurring before mortals have yet been created, on which see Louden (2006: 212–25).
[2] For a brief discussion of divine councils in Indo-European myth, see West (2007: 150–1).
[3] See fuller discussion in Louden (2005: 90–4), from which this has been adapted.

sky father is judge, the mentor god a defense attorney, and the wrathful god a prosecuting attorney. The three typical functions, and the gods who serve them, are already visible in *Gilgamesh*. Anu is the sky father who presides over divine councils, and supports Gilgamesh but does not appear to him in person. Shamash, the sun god, also alluded to in OT myth,[4] is the mentor god who appears face-to-face before Gilgamesh in theophany, advises him, and speaks on his behalf in divine councils (George 2003: V.1, VII.1). When Gilgamesh rejects her advances, Ishtar develops a divine wrath against him, speaks against him at a divine council (George 2003: VI.81–114), and causes Enkidu's death. In the *Odyssey* Zeus presides over divine councils that focus on Odysseus, and supports his return. Athena, his mentor, speaks on his behalf at divine councils, appears to him in theophany, and advises him how to proceed (*Od.* 13.221–440). Poseidon develops a wrath against him because of the Polyphêmos episode. I call this traditional divine configuration *the epic triangle*.

Though many gods are often said to be present at a divine council, only two usually speak in any given instance. In Mesopotamian myth a full divine council was thought to include fifty-seven gods.[5] A Homeric divine council on such a scale opens Book 20 of the *Iliad*, at which the narrator specifies that all the rivers and nymphs were present (*Il.* 20.4–32). But in spite of the plentiful attendance, only two gods, Zeus and Hera, actually speak. The two gods who speak up at a divine council tend to be two of the three deities that comprise the epic triangle. Thus most divine councils, Homeric and other, consist of a dialogue between the sky father and either the mentor god or the god with a divine wrath. This simple distinction, whether the divine council features the sky father speaking with the mentor god or the wrathful god, subdivides divine councils into two basic types. Any given divine council either concerns the gods acting on behalf of the hero, as the mentor god advocates, perhaps righting a wrong which he suffers, or it is concerned with the gods acting against him, as the wrathful god desires, often resulting in the death of others around him.

The *Odyssey*'s first divine council, programmatic for the entire epic, depicts the sky father conversing with the mentor god. Though all the Olympians except Poseidon are said to be present (*Od.* 1.26–7), the council is a dialogue between Zeus and Athena (*Od.* 1.32–95). In what is probably

---

[4] The place name Bethshemesh, mentioned some twenty times in the OT, literally means "Temple of the Sun," and reflects worship, if in an earlier era, of the same god as in *Gilgamesh*, on which see Boling (1982: 60).
[5] Mullen (1980: 175).

an instance of ring composition, the *Odyssey*'s last divine council features the same two gods, Zeus and Athena (*Od.* 24.472–86). In the divine council that separates the *Telemachy* from the rest of the epic, and serves as fanfare as the narrative is about to turn its focus to Odysseus (*Od.* 5.3–42), though all the gods are again said to be present (*Od.* 5.3), and Zeus presides as usual, only he and Athena have speaking parts (*Od.* 5.5–42). Hermes is addressed but does not take part in the dialogue.

This specific subtype of divine council that opens the *Odyssey*, between the sky father and the mentor god, is common in Near Eastern epic and myth. In the Ugaritic epic, the *Aqhat*, the war and storm god Baal converses with El, the sky father, asking him to grant offspring to Danel (Corpus des tablettes cunéiformes alphabétiques [CTA] 17.i.16–27). From the perspective of Greek myth, El combines the functions and characteristics of Zeus, who presides over divine councils, and Kronos, a less dynamic, more aged figure. In helping bring about the birth of Aqhat, Danel's son, Baal clearly acts as the mentor god for the protagonist. The Ugaritic myth *Kirta* features a similar scene, in which again Baal intervenes with El in a divine council to get the sky father to help Kirta obtain offspring (CTA 15.ii.11–28).[6] In *Gilgamesh*, Enkidu dreams of a divine council (*Gilgamesh* Vii.i, Dalley 1991: 83–4) in which Shamash, the sun god who serves as mentor to Gilgamesh, speaks on his behalf with Anu, who presides over the divine councils, and with Ellil, a god whose functions are difficult to determine.

The opposite, complementary, subtype of divine council, which depicts the sky father conversing with the god who has a divine wrath against the hero, occurs three times in the *Odyssey*, and is also extant in Near Eastern myth. This subtype generates greater drama because it usually precipitates some form of apocalyptic destruction. I define an apocalypse as a genre of myth in which *a god, angry at mortals' disrespect, destroys them in large numbers* (explored in Chapters 10 and 13). *Gilgamesh* offers a paradigmatic instance of this subtype, and its link with apocalyptic destruction, in the dialogue between Ishtar and Anu, *Gilgamesh* VI.iii–iv (Dalley 1991: 80–1; VI.81–114 in George [2003]). When Gilgamesh rudely rejects her offer of marriage (discussed in Chapter 5), an enraged Ishtar goes to her father Anu, threatening to raise the dead so they eat the living, unless he allows her to use the Bull of Heaven to kill Gilgamesh. If she were to descend to the underworld and release the dead,[7] they would soon outnumber the

---

[6] Mullen (1980: 245–52) compares the two scenes.
[7] As Dalley notes (1991: 129, n. 62), Ishtar makes the same threat in the *Descent of Ishtar*, as does Ereshkigal in *Nergal and Ereshkigal*.

living, resulting in a large level of destruction, a full-scale apocalypse. But Anu mediates her wrath, talking her down to a lower level of destruction. Concerned that the Bull would cause seven years of drought for Uruk, he hesitates. But Ishtar assures him that she has stockpiled grain,[8] and he relents. When she does send the Bull of Heaven down, several hundred people still die (600 or 1,200), but far fewer than would have been the case if she had followed through on either of her two other options.

Anu's mediation of Ishtar's wrath in this council implies three possible degrees of apocalypse, presented in descending order. Ishtar's initial threat to unleash the dead so that they eat the living would probably result in the destruction of all or most human life, a full-scale apocalypse:

> If you don't give me the Bull of Heaven ...
> I shall set my face toward the infernal regions,
> I shall raise up the dead and they will eat the living,
> I shall make the dead outnumber the living!
> *Gilgamesh* VI.iii[9]

Full-scale apocalypse is also extant in Noah's flood (itself modeled on the earlier Mesopotamian myth of Utnapishtim/Ziusudra), and Hesiod's earlier races (of Gold, Silver, and the first Bronze race).

Anu's concern that the Bull would cause seven years of famine in Uruk, which would perhaps destroy the population, represents a middle degree of apocalypse, the destruction of an entire city,

> On no account should you request the Bull of Heaven from me!
> There would be seven years of chaff in the land of Uruk.
> *Gilgamesh* VI.iii

This middle degree, the destruction of a whole city (often leaving a lone survivor, "the one just man," discussed in Chapter 13), is the most common degree of apocalypse in ancient myth, manifest not only here in Anu's concern for Uruk, but in the myth of Troy, in the myth of Sodom and Gomorrah, in Ovid's Baucis and Philemon (*Metamorphoses* 8), in Poseidon's initial wish to punish the entire city of the Phaiakians (*Od.* 13.152), and in many others (cf. *Works and Days* 240–1; discussion at Louden 2006: 227–9).

Anu here mediates Ishtar's wrath, persuading her to adopt the lowest of the three levels of apocalyptic destruction. Her subsequent annihilation of

---

[8] Cf. Joseph planning ahead for Egypt's famine, Genesis 41:25–57, and his earlier dream of seven gaunt cows devouring seven fat ones, Genesis 41:1–4. We consider the myth of Joseph at length in Chapter 3.
[9] Unless noted otherwise, translations of *Gilgamesh* are by Dalley (1991).

several hundred people instead of the majority of the race, or the whole city, is a significantly lower degree of destruction, which I call a *contained apocalypse*. The *Odyssey* is structured around three contained apocalypses: Helios' destruction of the crew at Thrinakia (*Od.* 12.376–419), Poseidon's petrifaction of the Phaiakians' ship (instead of their whole city, *Od.* 13.125–64), and Athena's direction of the destruction of the suitors (*Od.* 13.393–5, 22.205–309). Contained apocalypses in other traditions include Exodus 32 (discussed in Chapter 10), and several briefer instances in Numbers 11, 14, 16, and 25.

Three of the *Odyssey*'s divine councils are the same specific subtype as that between Ishtar and Anu (*Gilgamesh* VI.iii–iv, Dalley 1991: 80–1; VI.81–114 in George [2003]). Zeus, the sky father, similarly mediates and adjudicates the complaints of three different wrathful gods, talking each one down from a threat of greater destruction to a contained apocalypse. Each such scene concludes the respective sequence of the narrative pattern (Aiaian, Scherian, Ithakan) in which it occurs (discussion in Louden 1999: 69–72, 96–103). In Book 12 Helios, angered because Odysseus' crew have plundered his sacred cattle (discussion in Chapter 10), threatens to descend to the underworld and upset the basic cycle of human life, much as Ishtar:

> If then they will not requite me with just recompense for my cattle,
> I will go down into Hades and shine among the dead.[10]
>
> *Odyssey* 12.382–3

Like Ishtar's threat to descend and release the dead, Helios' shining in the underworld would similarly invert the order of the cosmos, and, by withholding his beams from the earth's surface, threaten all mortals' existence. Demeter's threat to stop all crops from growing, until Zeus intervenes and mediates (*Homeric Hymn to Demeter* 310–13), is another instance of the same level of threatened destruction. Zeus, much as Anu with Ishtar, carefully talks Helios down from his threat of full-scale apocalypse, to the destruction of only the crew, those who actually violated the sacred, interdicted, cattle:

> Helios, truly shine for the immortals
> and for mortals on the grain-giving earth.
> But I will cleave their ship with a silver lightning bolt.
>
> *Odyssey* 12.385–8

Zeus mediates the wrathful god's destruction from a full apocalypse to the crew members of one ship, a contained apocalypse.

---

[10] Unless otherwise noted, translations of Homeric epic and Hesiod are my own.

In Book 13, a wrathful Poseidon, angered that the Phaiakians have given Odysseus safe passage back to Ithaka, threatens to destroy not only the crew who ferried him home, but the entire Phaiakian city:

> Now, in return, I wish to smite the very beautiful ship
> of the Phaiakians, as it returns from its escort
> on the misty sea, that they cease, and halt their conveyance
> of mortals, and I would obliterate their city with a great mountain.
>
> *Odyssey* 13.149–52

As with Helios, Zeus, acting quickly to prevent the larger level of destruction Poseidon threatens – in this case the middle degree of apocalypse, destruction of a whole city – guides him to the lesser level, a contained apocalypse:

> Oh good brother, this is what seems best to me,
> when everyone from the city beholds the ship
> driving by near the land, turn her into a stone
> like a ship so all the people marvel;
> but don't obliterate the city with a mountain.
>
> *Odyssey* 13.154–8

This council features the usual underlying reason for the angry god's divine wrath, a perceived lack of respect by mortals. As the council opens Poseidon complains:

> Zeus Father, no longer will I have any honor among
> the immortal gods, when mortals honor me not at all.
>
> *Odyssey* 13.128–9

His complaint resembles Ishtar's first words to Anu:

> Father, Gilgamesh has shamed me again and again!
> Gilgamesh spelt out to me my dishonor,
> My dishonor and my disgrace.
>
> *Gilgamesh* VI.iii 15–17

Both wrathful gods are angry at a perceived lack of respect (cf. Poseidon's complaint at *Il.* 7.446–53). Zeus ensures that both Helios and Poseidon receive honor and respect, convincing each to contain his wrath and lessen his destruction (*Od.* 12.385–8, 13.140–5).

The *Odyssey*'s final divine council (*Od.* 24.472–86) also belongs to this same subtype, if somewhat modified. As is clear from her remarks at *Od.* 13.393–6 and much earlier (*Od.* 1.227–9), Athena is the wrathful god in the Ithakan sequence, her wrath directed at the suitors, not at Odysseus, as Helios' against the crew, and, after Zeus' mediation, Poseidon's at the

Phaiakian crew.[11] Though Poseidon is thematically wrathful at Odysseus through the first twelve-and-a-half books, his wrath is redirected against the Phaiakian crew after they ferry Odysseus home. Each of the *Odyssey*'s three sequences (Ithakan: Books 1–4, Book 13.188 through to end of Book 24; Scherian: Books 6–8, 9–12, 11.333–84, 13.1–187; and Aiaian: Books 9–12) leads up to and concludes with a contained apocalypse, though each one does so by employing a different genre of myth (discussed in Chapters 2, 6, 10, and 13).

In Book 24 Athena asks Zeus if he will provoke further violence, or put an end to the fighting (*Od.* 24.473–6). Since Athena's wrath only pertained to the suitors, she has no desire for further destruction. Therefore, there is little need for Zeus to mediate here since the destruction she desires has already occurred, the contained apocalypse that is Athena's direction of Odysseus slaying the 108 suitors and their henchmen. Zeus, having sanctioned the destruction that has already taken place, directs her to prevent additional violence. Though the details differ somewhat from the other scenes discussed above, the divine council validates the lower degree of destruction, as do the other instances. It is thus this lowest degree of divine destruction, contained apocalypse, with which the *Odyssey* is concerned, in the slaying of the suitors, and the two parallel episodes, the destruction of Odysseus' crew off Thrinakia, and the destruction of the Phaiakian crew off Scheria. The *Iliad*, by contrast, works toward the middle degree of apocalypse, the destruction of an entire city, which, in Homeric epic, only Zeus can validate, not a wrathful god such as Poseidon, Helios, or Athena.[12]

The *Iliad* nonetheless has one instance of the same subtype of divine council, especially like that at *Odyssey* 13.127–58, with Zeus again mediating a wrathful Poseidon, again angry over a perceived lack of respect (*Il.* 7.443–63). Noting that the Greeks did not sacrifice to the gods when they built the wall to defend the ships, Poseidon complains that mortals will forget how he and Apollo built the walls of Troy. Reassuring him of his respect among the gods, Zeus bids him to obliterate the wall, but to wait until after the war is concluded to do so (*Il.* 7.459–63). In so doing, Zeus prevents destruction on a larger scale, which would have included extensive loss of life. This divine council also concludes the first of the *Iliad*'s three sequences (Books 1–7), as do each of the three parallel instances in the *Odyssey* under consideration (*Od.* 12.376–88, 13.127–58, 24.472–86).[13]

---

[11] See discussion in Chapter 2.   [12] See discussion in Louden (2006: 228–35).
[13] See Louden (1999: 23–5, 69–72, 78, 95–103) on how this subtype of divine council concludes each of the *Odyssey*'s three sequences of the narrative pattern.

Divine councils and apocalyptic myth 23

Ugaritic myth, the *Iliad*, and OT myth also have instances of divine councils between the sky father and a wrathful god that do not lead to apocalyptic destruction, but to the death of a *single* mortal. In both the *Aqhat* and the *Baal Cycle*, the war goddess, Anat (see Louden 2006: 240–85 on her parallels with Athena), angrily confronts her father, Anu, in divine councils. In the *Aqhat*, Anat covets a bow that the god Kothar (Hephaistos' counterpart) has made for the title character. In exchange for the bow she offers Aqhat eternal life, the companionship of the gods, but he refuses her offer, insulting her in a scene reminiscent of Gilgamesh's rejection of Ishtar (VI.i–iii) and Diomedes' criticism of Aphrodite (*Il.* 5.348–51).[14] Incensed, Anat goes to El, and asks for and receives his permission to cause Aqhat's death (CTA 17.vi.46–18.i.19). The *Iliad* has a close parallel in Athena's divine council with Zeus (*Il.* 22.166–86) in which she obtains permission to cause Hektor's death. In the *Iliad* Athena serves as mentor god for Akhilleus, but as wrathful god for Hektor.[15] In both myths the final comments by El and Zeus are quite close:

> Lay hold of what you desire, carry out what you wish,
> The one who gets in your way may be struck down.
> CTA 18.i.18–19

> Act as your purpose would have you do, and hold back no longer.
> *Iliad* 22.186[16]

It is not often realized that OT myth contains many divine councils, a natural consequence of the Israelites' earlier centuries of polytheism before they converted to monotheism.[17] Many OT myths thus employ genres and motifs common to polytheistic mythic traditions, showing parallels with other West Semitic traditions, such as Ugaritic, as well as with Mesopotamian, and Egyptian. Consequently divine councils are not infrequent, especially in Genesis, Psalms, and the prophetic books.[18] Those in Genesis are clear, if abbreviated: the expulsion from Eden (Gen. 3:22), "The man has become like one of us," and the Tower of Babel (Gen. 11:7),[19]

---

[14] See discussion in Louden (2006: 261–9).
[15] On which, see Louden (2005: 92–6, and 2006: 241–3).
[16] For further comparison of the two scenes, see Louden (2006: 266–8).
[17] "[T]his monotheism emerged only midway through Israel's history. It was heir and reaction to a long tradition of Israelite polytheism": Smith (2001): 17.
[18] E.g. Job 15:8; Psalms 82:1, 89:5–7; Isaiah 14:12–14; Jeremiah 23:18; Daniel 7:9–10; Zechariah 3:1–10; *et al.* See discussion in Miller (1973: 66–74), and Mullen (1980: 118–19, 155–60, 192, 209–44).
[19] On Genesis 3:22 and 11:6–7 as abbreviated forms of a divine council, see Carr's comment (1996: 238) on the latter, "it is the first time after Gen 3:22 that God uses the first person plural to talk to the divine council."

"Come, let us go down there and confuse their language."[20] Though no one dies, god's deliberate confusion of mortals resembles a contained apocalypse. Athena similarly incapacitates the suitors in *Odyssey* Book 2, and the angels strike the mob with temporary blindness in Genesis 19 (both discussed in Chapter 2), episodes connected with subsequent apocalyptic destruction. But those most like Homeric divine councils are in Job and 1 Kings. 1 Kings 22:19–22 features a divine council quite close to Agamemnon's dream at *Iliad* 2.5–34.[21] While two episodes at the beginning of Job share features with that at *Odyssey* 1.27–95, as well as with those just noted between El and Anat (*Aqhat* CTA 17.vi.46–18. i.19), and Zeus and Athena (*Il.* 22.17–86).

As at *Odyssey*. 1.27–95, though many immortals are described as being present, only two speak in the first divine council in Job:

The day came when the members of the court of heaven took their places in the presence of the Lord, and the Adversary, Satan, was among them. The Lord asked him where he had been. "Ranging over the earth," said the Adversary, "from end to end." The Lord asked him, "Have you considered my servant Job? You will find no one like him on earth, a man of blameless and upright life, who fears God and sets his face against wrongdoing." (Job 1:6–8)

OT myth's emerging monotheism forces alterations on the traditional epic triangle. While Satan clearly occupies the function of the wrathful god,[22] Yahweh's position suggests a combination of both the sky father and the mentor god. Like the *Odyssey*'s first divine council, this serves to focus the narrative on the myth's mortal protagonist, but it is Yahweh himself who does so, whereas at *Odyssey* 1.480, it is Athena who first raises the topic of Odysseus, suggesting Yahweh's attitude toward Job is that of the mentor god. But Yahweh's concluding comment is essentially the same tag line El says to Anat, and Zeus to Athena (*Il.* 22.186), as he gives Satan free rein to do almost anything he wants to Job, "Very well," said the Lord, "All that he has is in your power, but you must not touch him" (Job 1:12), the sky father's presiding role.

Much as the *Odyssey* presents a second divine council very like the first (*Od.* 5.3–43), the Book of Job has a second divine council very like its first (Job 2:1–7). Again, the only speakers are Yahweh, who voices his support

---

[20] Unless otherwise noted, all OT translations are from Suggs (1992).
[21] Discussion in Louden (2006: 163–7).
[22] Note Suggs' comment, "Heb. 'the satan,' accuser, apparently a legal term" (1992: 511). Thus Satan here conforms nicely to our argument that the wrathful god also resembles a prosecuting attorney.

for Job, suggesting the traditional functions of both a mentor god and the sky father, while Satan presses Yahweh to let him oppress Job in stronger fashion (Job 2:4–5). Again the council concludes with a variation of the same tag line we have seen three earlier times (*Aqhat* CTA 18.i.18–19, *Il.* 22.186, Job 1:12), "The Lord said to the Adversary, 'So be it. He is in your power, only spare his life'" (Job 2:6). There is a further unexpected link between Job and the *Aqhat*. Aqhat's father is Danel, who is himself mentioned in OT myth as an example of the righteous man. Twice in Ezekiel Danel and Job are paralleled, along with Noah, as key instances of this type, "Even if these three men, Noah, Daniel, and Job, were there, they would by their righteousness save none but themselves" (Ezek. 14:14, 14:20, cf. Ezek. 28:3).[23]

This same specific subtype, a divine council between the sky father and a wrathful god who plans sufferings for a *single* mortal, occurs again in the *Iliad* in Agamemnon's narrative about the goddess Ate. The king of Mycenae describes a divine council between Zeus and Hera (*Il.* 19.100–13), in which she thwarts his designs for Herakles, causing a life of struggles and agony for Zeus' special son. Though the scene omits the usual tag line, the overall dynamic is clearly the same. Zeus has given permission for the wrathful god to cause sufferings for the protagonist of the myth (Herakles). But in a key variation Zeus is unaware that he gives Hera license to cause horrible sufferings for Herakles (as Anat did for Aqhat, Satan for Job, and Athena for Hektor), a replay of Hera's deception of him in Book 14 of the *Iliad* (Chapter 6 notes parallels with Rebecca's deception of Isaac). The closest to this subtype in the *Odyssey* is not a divine council, but Poseidon's soliloquy when he sees Odysseus crossing the sea by raft (*Od.* 5.286–90, 377–9), the epic's only divine monologue. The sea god announces his intent to harass Odysseus just short of killing him (*Od.* 5.286–90), which, as he is fully aware, he is not permitted to do. The upshot is thus quite close to Satan harassing Job. Neither Poseidon nor Satan is allowed to kill their hated mortal, as do Anat and Athena (*Il.* 22.186).

OT myth also features divine councils that lead to apocalyptic destruction, but with a radical innovation. In Exodus 32 and in Genesis 18, OT myth has two beings debating the severity of imminent apocalyptic destruction. But instead of two gods, the "divine councils" are between Yahweh and Moses (Exod. 32), and Yahweh and Abraham (Gen. 18). In Exodus 32,

---

[23] This same figure remains active into later periods of OT myth, heavily adapted into the Daniel of the Book of Daniel, anachronistically set in a much later period, the Babylonian captivity.

when the Israelites rebel during Moses' absence, and turn to other gods, Yahweh wants to destroy them all.

> The Lord said to Moses, "I have considered this people, and I see their stubbornness. Now, let me alone to pour out my anger on them, so that I may put an end to them and make a great nation spring from you." Moses set himself to placate the Lord his God: "Lord," he said, "why pour out your anger on your people, whom you brought out of Egypt with great power and a strong hand? . . . Turn from your anger, and think better of the evil you intend against your people." . . . So the Lord thought better of the evil with which he had threatened his people. (Exod. 32:9–14)

Moses, in talking Yahweh out of enacting a large-scale apocalypse against the Israelites, replays the same dynamic we have seen three times in the *Odyssey* (*Od.* 12.376–88, 13.127–58, 24.472–87), in *Gilgamesh* (*Gilg.* VI.iii–iv), and in the *Iliad* (*Il.* 7.443–63), the specific subtype of divine council in which Zeus talks a wrathful god down from full apocalyptic destruction (Helios), or from destruction of a whole city (Poseidon), to a lesser degree of violence, a contained apocalypse.

The dialogue between Moses and Yahweh is clearly a modified divine council, in which a mortal, a patriarch and prophet, serves in place of a god.[24] Having Moses act in a role traditionally assigned to a god is thus a radical innovation. But in an even more surprising innovation, it is Yahweh who serves the traditional function of the angry lesser god, while Moses serves the function elsewhere given the sky father, to mediate and adjudicate the concerns of the wrathful, lesser god. We return to this episode and compare it to events on Thrinakia in Chapters 10 and 13.

A similar episode concludes Genesis 18. Here, in a dialogue with Abraham, Yahweh threatens to destroy the entire cities of Sodom and Gomorrah. Abraham proceeds in much the same way as Moses in Exodus 32, getting Yahweh to agree to spare the cities if he can find first fifty, but eventually ten, righteous men (Gen. 18:23–32). The dynamic is the same. Their dialogue is clearly adapted from traditional divine councils, the same subtype we have observed in the *Odyssey* (*Od.* 12.376–88, 13.127–58, 24.472–87) and *Gilgamesh* (*Gilg.* VI.iii–iv). The dialogue features the same radical innovation seen in Exodus 32: it is Abraham who attempts to mediate, the

---

[24] See Hauge, "But a corresponding parallelism between YHWH and Moses is reflected in this episode" (2001: 266–7); "Moses . . . has been assigned a role which transcends the level of a human being" (311–12); "He can be presented as the substitute of the divine actor" (313). Though Hauge's remarks given here are prompted by other episodes in Exodus, Leviticus, and Numbers, they pertain equally well to Exodus 32.

usual role of the sky father, while the wrathful Yahweh is in the traditional role of the lesser god. The outcome is different, however. Yahweh goes ahead with the destruction of the entire cities, the usual, middle level of apocalypse, not the contained apocalypse noted in all five other instances. We reconsider the episode from additional perspectives in Chapters 2 and 13.

The *Odyssey*'s opening divine council also, if indirectly, points to a contained apocalypse. Zeus specifically convenes the council to air his complaint about humans:

> For shame, how mortals blame the gods!
> For they say evils come from us, when they themselves,
> through their own recklessness, suffer pains beyond their share.
>
> *Odyssey.* 1.32–4

Though he makes the complaint, Zeus neither expresses any animus, nor recommends that the gods initiate events against mortals, but merely comments on a general human failing. The *Atrahasis* offers a loose parallel. Six hundred years after their creation mortals have become so numerous, and their noise so great, that the god Ellil complains at a divine council, which he has apparently convened:

> He addressed the great gods,
> "The noise of mankind has become too much,
> I am losing sleep over their racket.
> Give the order that *suruppu*-disease shall break out."
>
> *Atrahasis* I.vii (Dalley translation)

Unlike Zeus, Ellil immediately initiates a plan to act on his complaint, and destroy mortals in doing so.

Athena, the only other speaker at the divine council, responds to Zeus' complaint about mortals' irresponsibility, strongly concurring:

> Our father, son of Kronos, highest of the lords,
> to be sure, he, at least, lies in fitting destruction.
> So let any other perish who would accomplish such acts!
>
> *Odyssey* 1.45–7

Athena's "such things" (τοιαῦτά γε) refers to Aigisthos' exploits, that he slew Agamemnon and "wooed" Klytaimnestra, though Hermes had earlier warned him not to (*Od.* 1.37–9). Divine interdictions, a god commanding a mortal *not* to do something, are often pivotal occasions in myth.[25] Mortals

---

[25] On the *Odyssey*'s use of divine interdictions in general, see Louden (1999: 15–16, 18–20, 92–5, 97–102, 128–9). We consider them in our analysis of events on Thrinakia in Chapter 10.

are typically unable to uphold them, as is the case with Aigisthos. Zeus uses Aigisthos for a specific instance of behavior to illustrate a larger pattern of mortals' conduct; Athena applies his consequent death to a larger body of mortals, "So let any other perish who would accomplish such acts!" She affirms Zeus' complaint, and clearly predicts the death of the suitors by so doing.[26] They will execute both categories of Aigisthos' wrongdoing: they are wooing a married woman; they will attempt to kill Telemachos, and then Odysseus. The destruction of all 108 suitors and their retinue constitutes another contained apocalypse.

For the rest of the divine council Athena plays her usual role as Odysseus' advocate and mentor. Though she agrees with Zeus' paradigm of human irresponsibility, Odysseus clearly does not fit it, and she briefly lashes out at Zeus, "Why then do you hate him so much, Zeus?" (*Od.* 1.62). In the *Aqhat*, Baal, who serves as the mentor god for Danel (and Aqhat), has a similar scene with El (CTA 17.i.16–34), and makes a similar complaint, "Art thou indifferent to Dan'el, the Rapian?" Like Athena's scene with Zeus, this divine council occurs close to the beginning of its narrative, and establishes the sky father's supportive relationship with the designated characters, Danel and Odysseus.

The *Odyssey*'s first divine council also has additional parallels with one in the *Aqhat* (CTA 17.i.16–27) and one in the *Kirta* (CTA 15.ii.11–28). All three belong to the same subtype, the sky father in dialogue with the mentor god; all three focus on the hero's son. After disabusing Athena of the notion that he hates Odysseus, Zeus reveals that Poseidon's wrath is responsible for Odysseus' failure to return home, but that now he will have to yield to the other Olympians, who all support Odysseus' return (*Od.* 1.63–79). Athena will go to see Telemachos, to give him confidence, that he may earn fame (*Od.* 1.88–95). The *Aqhat* opens with Danel praying for a son, while the *Kirta* begins with the title character yearning for an heir. In the *Odyssey*, Telemachos is a young man, but was an infant when his father last saw him, twenty years before. The *Aqhat* quickly switches its focus from Danel to his son, Aqhat, who remains the poem's mortal protagonist. Like the *Aqhat* the *Odyssey* quickly turns its focus to the hero's son, by way of the divine council (*Od.* 1.88–95). The parallel focus on the hero's son in the *Aqhat* and *Kirta* suggests that the *Telemachy*, sometimes thought a later

---

[26] Cf. S. West (1988: 80), "Athena's imprecation foreshadows the death of the suitors"; (78) "Here too the fate of Aegisthus foreshadows that of the suitors, who similarly ignore divine warnings." Cf. Lowe (2000: 140–1) "Zeus's chosen illustration is the recurrent exemplum of Aegisthus, whose career of crime and punishment is a template for that of the suitors."

addition to the *Odyssey*, may be more traditional, part of the epic longer than thought.

To sum up our discussion, epics such as *Gilgamesh*, the *Iliad*, the *Aqhat*, the *Kirta*, and the *Odyssey*, tend to have two main subtypes of divine councils. No matter how many other immortals are said to be in attendance, the sky father figure is in dialogue either with the mentor god (Athena in *Odyssey* 1 and 5, Shamash in *Gilgamesh*, Baal in the *Aqhat*), or the wrathful god (Helios in Book 12 of the *Odyssey*, Poseidon in Book 13, Athena in Book 24). Divine councils between the sky father and the mentor god tend to begin large actions, and occur, fittingly near the beginning of an epic (*Od.* 1.32–95, *Aqhat* CTA 17.i.16–27, cf. *Aen.* 1.223–97). The opposite type, divine councils between the sky father and the wrathful god, tend to conclude large actions, even whole sequences of an epic (as is the case at *Od.* 12.377–88, 13.128–58, 24.472–86; *Il.* 7.446–63; cf. *Aen.* 12. 791–842), often resulting in apocalyptic destruction.

Given Athena's importance in divine councils with Zeus in the *Odyssey* (*Od.* 1.32–95, 5.3–42, 24.472–86; cf. *Il.* 8.5–40, 22.166–85), it is worth noting that *Gilgamesh*, the *Aqhat*, the *Baal Cycle*, the *Iliad*, and the *Odyssey* (and the *Aeneid*) all have father-daughter divine councils (*Gilgamesh*: Anu, Ishtar; the *Aqhat*: El, Anat; *Baal Cycle*: El, Anat; *Iliad*: Zeus, Athena; *Odyssey*: Zeus, Athena), which may be more than mere coincidence.[27] In many ways Athena's relationship with Zeus resembles Anat's relationship with El. In particular Athena often gets her way with Zeus in divine councils, as Anat does with El.[28]

---

[27] Though Ishtar is not Anu's daughter in all traditions, she is in *Gilgamesh*.
[28] On Athena's angry exchanges with Zeus in the *Iliad* as particularly close to Anat's with El, see Louden 2006: 248–51.

CHAPTER 2

Theoxeny
Odyssey 1, 3, 13–22, and Genesis 18–19

Hospitality myth in general, and theoxeny in particular, is one of the two main types of myth that provide the *Odyssey*'s larger overarching structures.[1] While romance forms the *Odyssey*'s outermost frame, and provides its ending (the recognition scenes with Penelope and Laertes, Books 23–4), theoxeny forms the frame directly within, providing the epic with its other climax, the destruction of the suitors in Book 22. I define hospitality myth simply as *a mortal host entertaining or receiving a guest (usually a stranger of unknown identity) into his dwelling.* Most of Books 1, 3–4, 9–10, 14–15, and 17–22 (with shorter treatments in Books 7–8), are detailed presentations of hospitality myth. The anthropologist Pitt-Rivers is one of many to assert the centrality of hospitality in the *Odyssey* (1977: 94), "Indeed the whole work may be viewed as a study in the law of hospitality."

Hospitality is sacred. Both the *Odyssey* (*Od.* 9.270–1; 14.283–4, 14.389, 17.155; cf. 3.346) and the *Iliad* (13.624–5) declare Zeus its special guardian. As Bolin notes (2004: 39–40, 48), hospitality resembles sacrifice in being similarly grounded in reciprocity, as in the formula, *do ut des,* "I give, that you may give." Though written about Genesis 18–19, Bolin's comments about the dynamics of hospitality in ancient cultures are equally applicable to Homeric episodes, and worth noting at length (2004: 45):

Hospitality was the creation of a temporary patronage relationship with the host as patron and the guest as client. The motivation behind offering hospitality to a stranger lay in the increased honor one had in assimilating a potential threat into the community by asserting one's superiority over the newcomer. Guests played their role in this arrangement by acceptance of the offered hospitality. The practical benefit of this arrangement was that it defused a confrontational moment with the potential for violence. Reciprocity was essential to the arrangement's success.

[1] Reece (1993: 190–1): "By far the most pervasive type-scene in the *Odyssey* is the hospitality scene... Such hospitality scenes make up a large part of the narrative of the *Odyssey*... the *Odyssey* may be regarded as a sequence of hospitality scenes."

Hosts honored guests by extending favor and protection in order to increase their own honor. Guests accepted the honor of the host and, in doing so, added to the host's honor as patron. For either party to be denied its due in the relationship created the situation of injustice.

In hospitality myths the gods monitor these relationships to redress wrongs committed against either party, guest or host.

Why does the *Odyssey* employ hospitality myth so frequently? Several different factors encourage this mythic type. Polyphêmos' curse specifies that Odysseus will return home late, with difficulty, in someone else's ship (*Od.* 9.534–5; cf. Teiresias' and Kirke's prophecies, *Od.* 11.114–15, 12.141). The curse (chronologically earlier than the rest of the poem, except for brief retrospective accounts such as *Od.* 19.393–466) thus dictates that Odysseus will be destitute, a wanderer. As a wanderer, Odysseus is thrust into a dependent role, relying on the hospitality of those to whose shores he now comes. Odysseus' own violation of hospitality in his encounter with Polyphêmos (*Od.* 9.216–32)[2] helps bring about his transformation into a wanderer. Since much of the *Telemachy* thematically parallels Odysseus' own wanderings,[3] the prominence of hospitality scenes with the father prompts related episodes featuring the son. Wandering also looms large as a theme in romance, where, typically, the protagonist undergoes a drastic reversal of fortune or status into a state of dependence (explored in Chapter 3). Episodes of hospitality also provide a means for demonstrating Zeus' thesis on mortals' irresponsibility in the opening divine council. The suitors, in their continual violation of hospitality, will conform to the pattern Zeus figures in Aigisthos, mortals who ignore warnings from the gods, and ignore the consequences of their own actions.[4]

Theoxeny is the specific subset of hospitality myth in which, unknown to the host, his guest (*xenos*) is a god (*theos*) in disguise. The *Odyssey* has an unnamed suitor define the mythic type when Antinoös strikes the disguised Odysseus:

Antinoös, it is not well that you struck the unfortunate wanderer; you are accursed if somehow he is one of the heavenly gods, since the gods do go about the cities, seeming like strangers from other parts, taking on all sorts of forms, witnessing both the arrogance (ὕβριν) and good behavior of men. (*Odyssey* 17.483–7)

---

[2] On which, see Reece (1993: 143).
[3] E.g., Austin (1975: 78): "The Telemachy, reduced in scale to adapt to the capabilities, age, and character of its central figure, is a parallel of the action in Books 5 to 13."
[4] Cf., Cook (1995: 27): "Homer's compositional technique: structural and verbal parallels allow the fate of one character or group to provide tacit commentary on that of another."

The passage not only defines what theoxeny is, but evokes the term, since the unnamed suitor here juxtaposes the words for gods and guests, θεοὶ ξείνοισιν, *theoi xeinoisin* (*Od.* 17.485). Though the *Odyssey* initiates its first theoxeny when Athena appears as Mentes (*Od.* 1.105), it saves its explicit definition of the type for Antinoös' shocking act, behavior even other suitors find offensive. Theoxeny as a genre of myth explains why hospitality is sacred: *any* guest could be a god in disguise. The *Odyssey* uses both kinds of myth, hospitality and theoxeny, to gauge its characters, as indices of their morality.[5] Hospitable characters are moral and pious; those who violate hospitality not only act incorrectly, but offend the gods.

Theoxenies come in two opposite subtypes. When a disguised god comes among mortals to test their hospitality, they either pass the test, or they fail it. The situation allows no gray area, no middle ground. I use *positive theoxeny* to denote a community correctly observing hospitality, and *negative theoxeny* for a community that violates hospitality. In both kinds of theoxeny the host is hospitable. It is the response of his surrounding community that radically differs. Instances of negative theoxeny are more dramatic, prompting more intense narratives, usually segueing directly to an apocalypse (Ovid, *Metamorphoses* 8.611–724, Genesis 19, Nonnus, *Dionysiaca* 18.35). The *Odyssey* initiates a negative theoxeny as soon as Athena appears among the suitors as Mentes (*Od.* 1.105). Athena's wrath against the suitors for violating hospitality in her presence takes up roughly one third of the epic (Books 1, 13.376–96, 17–22). As often for Homeric epic,[6] Old Testament myth, in Genesis 18–19, offers the closest non-Greek parallels for the *Odyssey*'s use of theoxeny.

Both the *Odyssey* and Genesis nuance their presentations of theoxeny by also presenting *positive* theoxenies. When Telemachos visits Nestor in Book 3, Athena accompanies him in the form of Mentor (*Od.* 3.31–384), making the episode a theoxeny. Nestor and all his people observe correct hospitality. Genesis 18, when Abraham and Sara receive the disguised angels as guests, is also a fully developed theoxeny in which all the mortals behave as they should. By giving examples of positive and negative theoxenies in close proximity, the *Odyssey* and Genesis demonstrate to their audiences how theoxeny works, allowing the stark difference in outcomes between the two types to emerge with greater clarity. Positive theoxeny demonstrates how hospitality is supposed to function, the rewards in store for those who correctly uphold it. Ovid also has narratives of each type: positive, the

---

[5] Race (1993: 82) "the treatment of a guest or suppliant is the touchstone of every character's ἦθος in the *Odyssey*." Cf. Bolin (2004: 48): "Those who show hospitality, that is, give their guests what they deserve, are rewarded; those who do not show justice to their guests are rightfully punished."
[6] For examples and discussion of parallels between the *Iliad* and OT myth, see Louden (2006: 149–239).

myth of Hyrieus (*Fasti* 5.493–544); and negative, the myth of Baucis and Philemon (*Metamorphoses* 8.611–724). We will consider negative theoxeny first, since it comes first in the *Odyssey* and has far greater impact on its plot than positive theoxeny.

NEGATIVE THEOXENY: *ODYSSEY* 1, 13, 17–22, AND GENESIS 19

As noted in Chapter 1, the suitors' death is implied in Athena's remark about Aigisthos' death in the opening divine council, "So may any other perish who would accomplish such acts!" (*Od.* 1.45–7). Neither Athena nor Zeus mentions the suitors' violation of hospitality. Athena's stated purpose for coming to Ithaka is to prompt Telemachos to become a hero (*Od.* 1.88–95). However, as soon as she appears in Ithaka in the guise of Mentes, the *Odyssey* initiates its first theoxeny. As at *Odyssey* 17.485, Athena, a *theos*, appearing as a *xenos* (εἰδομένη ξείνῳ: *Od.* 1.105), not only starts the mythic genre, but evokes its name as well. *Xenos* (Homeric *xeinos*) has a variety of meanings: a stranger (not from around here), a guest, and a host. Mentes is a stranger, unknown in Ithaka. She will claim that her father was Odysseus' host on an earlier occasion (*Od.* 1.187–8, 257–64), invoking the other meanings latent in *xenos*. Upset that a guest would have to stand, waiting to be seated (*Od.* 1.118–20), Telemachos is first to notice her. Greeting her, he takes her by the hand, and seats her, while attendants bring water for washing, food, and drink (*Od.* 1.121–43). He has already passed the test, implicit in any theoxeny, offering commendable hospitality to the disguised god. But since the host demonstrates his hospitality in both subtypes of theoxeny, this episode could still go either way.

What tilts this episode into a *negative* theoxeny is the suitors' behavior, Athena's reaction to it, and the implied violence in her anecdote about Odysseus' visit to her father's house. Before his guest says anything, Telemachos raises the suitors as a topic of concern several times. When he seats her, he selects a secluded spot, lest his guest be disturbed by their uproar (*Od.* 1.133), since they are overbearing (ὑπερφιάλοισι: *Od.* 1.134), implying violence and insolence (S. West 1988: 93).[7] Telemachos complains that they feast on his goods without recompense (*Od.* 1.159–65). Even his initial frustration that a guest would have to stand and wait (*Od.* 1.119–20) indirectly suggests concern over the suitors' behavior while a guest is present (S. West 1988: 97).

---

[7] Though 1.132–4 are the narrator's remark, see de Jong (2001: 22) on how they are "focalized" around Telemachos.

The disguised Athena asserts that she and Odysseus were ξεῖνοι... πατρώϊοι, "paternal guest-friends" (*Od.* 1.187), later specifying that he visited her father seeking a poison to put on his arrows (*Od.* 1.257–64). When he failed to obtain the poison from another man, Athena/Mentes claims her father, fond of Odysseus, gave him the poison he sought. Commentators have focused too much on whether or not Athena invents this unusual story,[8] and too little on its thematic function in the *Odyssey*'s plot. While the unusual detail helps validate her claim about Odysseus' visit by conjuring up specific circumstances, it also evokes a violent undercurrent. What would Odysseus' purpose be in applying poison to his arrows?

Sandwiched between the two brief accounts of Odysseus' visit to her father's house is Athena's reaction to the suitors, the most important detail in the episode. Noting their continual feasting, she wonders what occasion prompts it:

How reckless they seem to me, feasting in their arrogance (ὑβρίζοντες) throughout the palace! Should a righteous man come among them he'd be outraged, seeing their many disgraceful acts! (*Odyssey* 1.227–9)

While her assessment helps strengthen her bond with Telemachos, establishing her as a father figure (as his own reaction implies: *Od.* 1.307–8), the audience recognizes a far more serious consequence. Central to the workings of theoxeny, either positive or negative, is the irony that results from the host being unaware of his guest's divine identity, which the audience fully perceives.[9] "Mentes'" remarks are thus not merely the sympathetic observations of a family friend, but the judgment, even the doom (in that word's older sense) of a god in whose presence the suitors have violated a sacred institution. Athena now has a divine wrath directed against them, until their destruction is accomplished.

Only after her judgment on the suitors does "Mentes" give Telemachos the provocative details about Odysseus seeking poison for his arrows (*Od.* 1.257–64). She prefaces mention of the poison with a wish to see Odysseus now as he was then, fully armed, with helmet, shield, and two spears (*Od.* 1.256). Just before seeing Mentes, Telemachos was fantasizing about

---

[8] E.g., S. West (1988: 107). I would parallel it with Athena's claim at *Odyssey* 15.16–23, also made to Telemachos, that Penelope is eager to marry Eurymakhos, which Hoekstra, rightly in my view, regards as "a white lie on the part of Athena" (232).

[9] Cf. Bolin (2004: 45): "Dramatic irony is created in that the hearers are aware that the hospitality of the unwitting but good-hearted hosts is really an ideal example of divine service."

his father returning, scattering the suitors (*Od.* 1.115–17). The juxtaposition of his mental picture with Mentes' arrival suggests that Telemachos will associate Mentes' visit with his father. When Athena suggests a violent potential in Odysseus, armed with two spears, seeking poison for his arrows, she points, if indirectly, to his slaying of the suitors,[10] the contained apocalypse that this negative theoxeny, the suitors' violation of hospitality, now moves toward. Odysseus will be armed with two spears when he goes against the suitors (*Od.* 22.101, 125, though this is standard equipment for the Homeric warrior). While in Book 1 the violence is only implied, when Odysseus first returns to Ithaka, Athena demands such destruction, declaring she expects "his immense floor to be splattered with the suitors' blood and brains" (*Od.* 13.395).

This prefigured violence, the eventual result of Athena's wrath against the suitors, is suggested even earlier in the description of her spear as she prepares to descend from Olympos,[11]

> She took up her stout spear, furnished with a sharp bronze point,
> heavy, great, and strong, with which she subdues the ranks
> of heroes, those at whom she of the mighty father is angered.
>
> *Odyssey* 1.99–101

As Walsh shows (2004: 23–9, 50, 52–3, 79, 97, 101), the verb used here of Athena's anger, κοτέω, denotes long-term anger, especially the kind of divine wrath that figures in an apocalypse. Nowhere in the *Odyssey* or *Iliad* does Athena actually wield her spear against mortals (though she does wound Ares with it: *Il.* 21.406). But in each epic she is angry at a group of heroes, the Trojans, collectively, in the *Iliad*, and, as a result of their own actions in Book 1, the suitors in the *Odyssey*. In each epic, at the same respective point, she aids the protagonist as he uses his spear against each poem's primary antagonists, Akhilleus against Hektor (*Il.* 22.325–7), and Odysseus against the suitors (*Od.* 22.262 and ff.). This is another aspect of Athena's function as mentor to the hero: she aids him in his greatest battles, as Shamash aids Gilgamesh against Humbaba (*Gilg.* V.i–ii; V.137–47 in George [2003]). Accordingly, both Homeric epics employ the tableau-like description of Athena taking up her spear,[12] to figure, in a kind

---

[10] S. West (1988: 89): "In this episode we may also see a foreshadowing of the later part of the poem, when Odysseus himself appears as a stranger in his own home."

[11] Cf. de Jong (2001: 18): "The ominous overtones of the description of the spear also alert the narratees to the fact that her rousing of Telemachus is the first step on the road toward Odysseus' revenge, which will take the form of a battle."

[12] Cf. *Il.* 5.746–7, 8.390–1.

of shorthand, the outcome of each narrative, the protagonists defeating their antagonists, aided by an eager Athena.[13]

NEGATIVE THEOXENY IN GENESIS 19

Since, as Book 1 prefigures, Odysseus will carry out the destruction of the suitors, the *Odyssey* puts full development of its negative theoxeny on hold until he returns to Ithaka. Before considering how the *Odyssey* resumes this thread, we first explore negative theoxeny in OT myth, the destruction of Sodom and Gomorrah. Genesis 19, in its close parallels, provides a context for interpreting the *Odyssey*. The myth begins, as does the negative theoxeny in *Odyssey* 1, by depicting the immortals' arrival to the city that is to be tested. There are two immortals in Genesis 19,[14] both unnamed angels. As Telemachos sits apart from the suitors in Book 1, Lot initially sits by the city gate, apart from the other inhabitants. Lot, like Telemachos, is first to see the strangers, and rises to greet them. Offering hospitality, he persuades them to come to his house, bathe their feet, and spend the night. After he serves them a meal, and has clearly passed the implicit test imposed on the host, a mob of men of all ages gathers around his house. This is essentially the point at which the *Odyssey* has interrupted the progress of its negative theoxeny. There are clear parallels in the roles played by Athena and the two angels, by Telemachos and Lot, and especially close, by the suitors and the mob.

Since Genesis is not using its negative theoxeny as part of a heroic epic whose protagonist is far from home, it has no need to delay or interrupt its conclusion, as does the *Odyssey*. It seems likely, then, that the *Odyssey* is innovating, both in interrupting its theoxeny, and pausing for such a great length before concluding it. In this respect the *Odyssey*'s complex manipulation and placement of the genres of myth is more reminiscent of Ovid's techniques for interweaving myths in the *Metamorphoses* than what we might expect of an epic rooted in oral tradition. Following the *Odyssey*'s model, we interrupt our consideration of Genesis 19's negative theoxeny, to resume it, as does the *Odyssey*, after first exploring the opposite type, positive theoxeny.

POSITIVE THEOXENY: ODYSSEY 3 AND GENESIS 18:1–15

In Book 1, Athena instructs Telemachos to go to Pylos to see if Nestor knows of Odysseus' whereabouts (*Od.* 1.284). Athena, now in the guise

---

[13] On Athena's thematic association with bloodthirsty violence in Homeric epic, see Louden 2006: 257–61.
[14] Cf., two immortals, Jupiter and Mercury, do the testing in Ovid's negative theoxeny, *Meta.* 8.626–7.

of Mentor, provides a ship (*Od.* 2.287) and crew, and accompanies him, thereby turning a hospitality scene into a theoxeny, though not often noted as such.[15] When they arrive Nestor is leading 500 of his people in a lavish offering to Poseidon, the largest-scale sacrifice in the poem. Though busy with this enterprise, the Pylians graciously receive the two unexpected guests. Nestor's son Peisistratos is first to see them, taking them to seats next to Nestor himself to partake of the feast (*Od.* 3.34–9). Peisistratos continues exemplary hospitality by asking "Mentor," that is Athena, to make the prayer accompanying the sacrifice, telling her, "all men need the gods" (πάντες δὲ θεῶν χατέουσ᾽ ἄνθρωποι: *Od.* 3.48), the epic's simplest statement of piety. Such sentiments typify the episode, and positive theoxenies. A pleased Athena goes on to make the prayer, with irony typical of theoxeny, "so she prayed but she herself was bringing everything to completion" (*Od.* 3.62).

Peisistratos' piety is also implicit acknowledgement that Nestor raised him and his brothers to be so. Nestor's piety and exemplary hospitality establish him as a highly moral man.[16] Commentators rightly emphasize how Nestor's own family members perform tasks for the guests that are elsewhere performed by servants.[17] It is more typical of theoxeny than of hospitality myth that family members perform the main duties.[18] The pious Nestor reasons that since Athena used to aid Odysseus at Troy she might now do the same for Telemachos:

> If only gray-eyed Athena might wish to love you
> as she then deeply cared for renowned Odysseus
> in the land of the Trojans, where we Achaians suffered pains.
> For never have I seen the gods openly display their love
> as when Pallas Athena then openly stood by him.
>
> *Odyssey* 3.218–24

In irony more typical of the *Odyssey*'s later books (14–21), where characters think about and discuss, but cannot recognize the disguised Odysseus before them, Nestor correctly reasons that Athena *could* help Telemachos,

---

[15] E.g., Reece's otherwise detailed analysis (1993: 59–66) does not recognize the episode as a theoxeny. De Jong (2001: 16) classifies the episode as a "god meets mortals scene," a much broader grouping that does not distinguish hospitality from other forms of encounters (along with *Od.* 1.96–324, 2.267–97, 382–7; 3.1–485; 7.18–81; 8.193–200; 10.277–308; 13.221–440; 16.155–77; 22.205–40; 24.502–48).
[16] S. West (1988: 160): "It is surely significant that Telemachus finds Nestor engaged in sacrifice; Nestor's piety... is thus established from the outset"; Reece (1993: 59): "Nestor is exceptionally pious."
[17] Reece (1993: 66): "In Sparta, heralds, servants, and handmaids attend to the guests; in Pylos, these duties fall on members of Nestor's family."
[18] But cf. Akhilleus, *Iliad.* 9.196–222.

though unaware she is actually doing so.[19] Nestor honors the gods in exactly the ways that myths portray the gods as expecting mortals to act.

Irony of a more comic sort appears in Telemachos' reaction to Nestor's observation. In one of the *Odyssey*'s most humorous scenes, with the disguised Athena looking on, Telemachos (with the audience well aware of her extensive aid to him), refutes Nestor, denying the goddess would help him. "Mentor" firmly corrects him:

> *Telemachos*, what sort of word has escaped the fence of your teeth?
> Easily a god, should he wish, can save a man, even *from a distance*.
> *Odyssey* 3.230–1

Athena playfully underscores her point with wordplay on his name, Telemachos, "Fighter from a distance.'" The first component, *têle-*, "distant," is the same as the antepenultimate word of the next line, *têlothen*, "from a distance"; "Even from a *distance* a god can save a man, oh 'Fighter from a *distance.*'"[20] As comparison with Genesis 18 will show, positive theoxenies include humorous interaction once the host has demonstrated his piety.

Genesis features a positive theoxeny in Abraham's hospitable reception of the angels (Gen. 18:1–15), a close parallel to Nestor and Athena in *Odyssey* 3. As at Pylos, each detail of Abraham's reception of his disguised divine guests is a generic, traditional, motif, extant in other narratives. Yahweh and two angels, in the form of unnamed men, appear to Abraham as he sits outside his tent (Gen. 18:1–2).[21] As soon as he sees them Abraham approaches[22] (cf. Peisistratos in *Odyssey* 3, and Telemachos in Book 1), and extends hospitality.[23] Offering water to wash their feet, cakes, a (sacrificed) calf, curds and milk, Abraham himself waits on them while they eat (Sara prepares the cakes).[24]

Having easily passed the hospitality test, Abraham receives a blessing and prophecy. Yahweh, or an angel, says he will come back in a year and Sara will have given birth to a son, an instance of Reece's motif *XIV. Visitor pronounces a blessing on the host*. The blessing functions similarly to Athena saying the prayer in the sacrifice to Poseidon, after having first blessed Nestor and his sons (*Od.* 3.57). In doing so, she enacts two of Reece's

---

[19] On the irony, see Dekker (1965: 94–7) and Fenik (1974: 158).
[20] The pun is thematic in the *Odyssey*, also found at 15.10, 17.251–3; discussion in Louden (1995: 37–9).
[21] A referee points out a parallel at Herodotus 6.35–6, where Miltiades, while sitting on his porch, extends hospitality to two strangers (the Dolonci) who pass by.
[22] Speiser (1962: 129): "*he rushed*. No exertion, even on behalf of total strangers, is too much where hospitality is concerned."
[23] Reece (1993: 6–7) has these as elements VII. Reception, a, Host catches sight of the visitor, d, Host approaches the visitor, g, Host bids the visitor welcome, as they occur in Homeric epic.
[24] *Ibid.* these are elements XVIII, IX. a. b. Cf. Ovid, *Metamorphoses* 8.611–724, and Philemon and Baucis themselves waiting on the disguised Jupiter and Mercury.

elements, *XV. Visitor shares in a libation or sacrifice*, and *XIV. Visitor pronounces a blessing on the host*. But Sara, eavesdropping, laughs at the seeming absurdity of her giving birth at such an advanced age (Gen. 18:12). Yahweh subsequently corrects her, "Is anything impossible for the Lord?" (Gen. 18:14). His doing so is the same motif as Athena correcting Telemachos ("Even from a distance a god can save a man," *Od.* 3.230–1). Both Telemachos, in refusing to believe that Athena would help him, and Sara, by not believing the guest's claim that she will bear a son, imply limits on the gods' powers. Each god is quick to disabuse the doubter, without becoming wrathful. What each character refuses to believe (that Athena would help Telemachos, that Sara would bear a son) is something the god gives because the hosts have earlier earned a boon by their exemplary hospitality.

Both positive theoxenies employ wordplays on proper names at this point. Sara's laughing is an apparent allusion to a folk etymology associating the name Isaac with a verb of laughing and smiling, as Speiser notes on Genesis 17:17 (1962: 123: "Heb. *yishaq*, play on 'Isaac'").[25] In each case the wordplay is connected with the character being corrected, Sara and Telemachos. Sara's laughter at the divine prediction is mentioned four times (Gen. 18:12, 13, and twice in 15). In both instances the wordplay is on the name of the son of the hero (Isaac, son of Abraham, Telemachos, son of Odysseus), and is thematic, occurring in several passages.[26]

The parallels in their receptions of the divine guests reveal additional links between the hosts, Nestor and Abraham. Abraham is the first of a series of patriarchs in Genesis, including Jacob and Joseph. Just before the positive theoxeny, Yahweh defines Abraham as such a figure:

I shall make you father of many nations. I shall make you exceedingly fruitful; I shall make nations out of you, and kings shall spring from you. (Genesis 17:5–6)[27]

Genesis 18 initiates Abraham as patriarch by highlighting the dramatic birth of his first son. Until Abraham has legitimate male offspring he cannot be the patriarch Yahweh has declared. Indeed, there would be no Old Testament without the birth of this son. The OT authors thus dramatically highlighted the story of Isaac's birth by setting it within a

---

[25] Cf. Speiser (1962: 131): "this vivid sketch has been colored, at least in part, by the supposed origin of the name Isaac... This is what J's play on the verb *shq* plainly implies... That neither J's etymology nor P's happens to be right is beside the point, since the underlying cultural context had been lost in the meantime."

[26] Such wordplays on proper names, or folk etymologies, are common in both mythic traditions. E.g., Jacob to Israel (Gen. 32:28), Moses (Exod. 2:10), Gideon as Jerubbaal (Judg. 6:32), Odysseus (*Od.* 19.406–9). For further discussion of instances in Homeric epic, see Louden 1995.

[27] For a close, but non-Homeric, Greek parallel, see Athena's prophecy about Ion, Euripides, *Ion* 1574–94.

positive theoxeny, a genre of myth that underscores Abraham's respect for god, showing he deserves to be the patriarch he will now become.

Nestor, too, is such a figure, if on a slightly smaller scale. He leads a highly moral community, having reached an age and fathered offspring to a degree that establish him as a patriarch, the same mythic type as Abraham in OT myth.[28] Both men are preternaturally old. Telemachos refers to Nestor having ruled over three generations of men (*Od.* 3.245; cf. *Il.* 1.250–2), and describes his appearance as like an immortal (*Od.* 3.246, literally, like one who is "deathless," ἀθάνατος). Two of Nestor's most frequent epithets in Homer are γεραιός "old," and γέρων "old man." Abraham is ninety-nine years old shortly before the episode (Gen. 17:1). Both men are leaders of peoples or clans (cf. Nestor's epithet "shepherd of the people" [*Od.* 3.469, 15.151, 17.109; *Il.* 2.85, 10.73, 23.411, cf. 9.81]).[29]

The numerous parallels between the two episodes reveal that Greek and OT myth each adapted the same specific subgenre of myth, positive theoxeny with a number of highly specific shared elements. The host in both narratives is a patriarch, who has or will have many sons, and holds sway over whole peoples. Both narratives employ thematic wordplays on the name of the protagonist's son. The key difference is Peisistratos' prominence in *Odyssey* 3, and Sara's in Genesis 18. With no son yet born, Sara is the only other family member who could figure in the narrative, and consequently functions much like Peisistratos in *Odyssey* 3.

It is worth briefly noting Ovid's positive theoxeny (*Fasti* 5.493–544). Three immortals, Jupiter, Neptune, and Mercury, come to Hyrieus, who owns a small farm, greets them, and offers them hospitality (*Fasti* 5.494–502). While he heats two pots of food, he serves them wine. But after Hyrieus has served the disguised Neptune, the sea god declares that the next cup will go to Jupiter. After the meal, when Jupiter asks what he desires, Hyrieus responds "a son," though he is not married (*Fasti* 5.523–30). Jupiter and the other two gods then take the hide of the sacrificed ox and... Ovid doesn't say. Claiming he is ashamed to, he continues that the gods buried the reeking hide in the earth, and ten months later, a son was born. Gantz (1993: 273) assumes that "they cover it with their semen." Others think the gods urinate on it, with which the son's name, Orion, has been associated as a folk etymology. In spite of the bizarre method of conception, the tale parallels much of Abraham's in Genesis 18. In both

---

[28] Cf. S. West (1988: 158): "this patriarchal family"; and Reece (1993: 62, n. 3): "Nestor der Patriarch, Menelaos der Weltmann."

[29] Dee (2000: 299).

positive theoxenies the host wishes for a son (cf. the Ugaritic myths *Aqhat* and *Kirta*). In each case a miraculous conception occurs as reward for the host's correct hospitality. An apparent wordplay on the son's name may occur, as in both other positive theoxenies.

THE *ODYSSEY*'S INNOVATION ON THEOXENY

Theoxeny is not typically a heroic genre of myth. Lot, Hyrieus, and Baucis and Philemon[30] are not heroic characters: good, moral people, yes. The *Odyssey* innovates considerably in increasing theoxeny's potential for heroic action, making it more suitable for epic. The suitors' destruction, inevitable once Athena witnesses their desecration of hospitality, is postponed until Odysseus' return to Ithaka. In Genesis 19, by contrast, Sodom and Gomorrah are destroyed the night they violate hospitality (cf. *Metamorphoses* 8.689–97). But in the second half of the *Odyssey*, Odysseus himself plays the role normally played by the outraged immortal. Substituting for a god, Odysseus will act as the instrument of Athena's divine wrath against the suitors.[31] The suitors' destruction will be a heroic act or labor, not rained down from heaven, as in Genesis 19 and Baucis and Philemon (*Metamorphoses* 8.689–97).

When Odysseus returns to Ithaka, after his recognition scene with Athena (*Od.* 13.221–86),[32] the goddess and the hero plot strategy against the suitors. Though their meeting is portrayed as a joint deliberation (*Od.* 13.373, 376, 439), it is Athena who declares what his course of action will be, and how he is to proceed. He is to keep everyone in the dark (*Od.* 13.308–9), implicitly even Penelope and Laertes. In essence Athena initiates another genre of myth, *The king returns, unrecognized and abused in his own kingdom* (*Od.* 13.309–10, analyzed in Chapter 12), in her general statement that "he must endure many pains in silence, accepting violence from men" (ἀλλὰ σιωπῇ / πάσχειν ἄλγεα πολλά, βίας ὑποδέγμενος ἀνδρῶν). Her declaration resembles prophecies of Christ treated with abuse in the gospels (e.g., Matt. 16:21: πολλὰ παθεῖν; Luke 18:32). She specifies that he is to make trial of his wife (σῆς ἀλόχου πειρήσεαι: *Od.* 13.336), but relays this in a way making it difficult to tell if she means such is Odysseus' manner, or that this is her plan. He will have an impenetrable disguise (literally "disfigured" ἀεικέλιος: *Od.* 13.402), and implicitly be a *xeinos*, stranger/guest, used of the disguised Odysseus a few lines later

---

[30] For fuller discussion of Baucis and Philemon, see the final chapter.
[31] Cf. Reece (1993: 182–5). [32] Discussed in Chapter 3 as part of romance.

(*Od.* 14.56). His first move will be to stay with the swineherd, and test him (ἐξερέεσθαι: *Od.* 13.411).

Duals, the grammatical number between singular and plural, help emphasize how the *Odyssey* transforms theoxeny into a more heroic genre of myth than is usual. The close teamwork of hero and god is expressed grammatically: they are yoked in several words in the dual number (τὼ δὲ καθεζομένω, φραζέσθην, τώ γ᾽ ὥς βουλεύσαντε, διέτμαγεν: *Od.* 13.372, 373, 439). Homeric epic marks the climax of each poem with this same construction; duals are also used of Athena and Akhilleus as he is about to face Hektor (*Il.* 22.216: νῶϊ, 22.218: δηώσαντε).

In a further index of this heroic modality, Odysseus asks Athena to stand by him in ways similar to the beginning of an *aristeia* (*Od.* 13.387). The *Iliad* initiates an *aristeia* by having a god, most frequently Athena, put *menos*, "battle might" (or a close equivalent, *tharsos* and *kratos*), in the best of the Achaians (*Il.* 5.1–2, 19.47–54, cf. 19.37).[33] Odysseus, conforming to the *Iliad*'s convention, asks Athena to put *menos* in him (μένος πολυθαρσὲς ἐνεῖσα: *Od.* 13.387), and to stand beside him (πὰρ δέ μοι αὐτή στῆθι). OT myth has a parallel conception of Yahweh infusing "spirit" in a hero before his great battle (Josh. 1:5, 5:13–14; Judg. 3:10, 6:12–14, 6:34, 11:29, 13:25, 14:6, 14:19, 15:14). Shamash's relationship with Gilgamesh is perhaps the earliest such depiction of this special relationship between the hero and his mentor god.[34] Athena affirms that she will stand by him (*Od.* 13.393–4), as she earlier defined their relationship (ἥ τέ τοι αἰεὶ / ἐν πάντεσσι πόνοισι παρίσταμαι: *Od.* 13.300–1). Taken together, the two passages suggest a core conception of god and hero working as partners.

What emerges from the scene in Book 13, then, is a striking interweaving of the roles of Athena and Odysseus for the remainder of the poem. The goddess defines Odysseus as her own counterpart (*Od.* 13.296–9), each as master of disguise and deception. Her subsequent agenda calling for Odysseus to be in disguise turns much of the second half of the *Odyssey* into a *virtual* theoxeny, in which Odysseus now serves as the god in disguise, testing the hospitality of the Ithakans.

But perhaps the most striking element in Athena's plans for the suitors is her declaration that she expects Odysseus' "immense floor to be spattered with the suitors' blood and brains" (*Od.* 13.395). Her graphic, violent intent resembles the traditions of Anat, a West Semitic virgin war goddess, worshipped by Phoenicians, and Egyptians under the Ramesside Pharaohs.

---

[33] Discussion in Louden (2006: 18–19).
[34] See Ellil's comment to Shamash, "you accompanied them daily, like one of their comrades" (*Gilg.* VII.i; p. 84 Hittite insertion in Dalley [1991]).

The Homeric Athena has much in common with Anat.[35] OT myth's conception of a wrathful Yahweh has similarly graphic passages (e.g., Jer. 46:10; Isa. 34:2–4, 6), none more so than this exchange between Isaiah and Yahweh,

> Why are your clothes all red,
> like the garments of one treading grapes in the winepress?
> ... I trod the nations in my anger,
> I trampled them in my fury,
> and their blood bespattered my garments
> and all my clothing was stained ...
> I stamped on peoples in my anger,
> I shattered them in my fury
> and spilled their blood over the ground.
>
> (Isaiah 63:2–3, 6)

Athena's vivid declaration that she expects the floor to be "spattered with the suitors' blood and brains," sounds some of the same notes as Isaiah's wrathful Yahweh. Her final words include a prophecy of the suitors' destruction (*Od.* 13.427–8).

RESUMPTION OF THE *ODYSSEY*'S NEGATIVE THEOXENY

When the disguised Odysseus stays with Eumaios, as Athena directs, the *Odyssey* initiates not only a hospitality myth, but a *virtual* theoxeny, as noted above. Eumaios is the good host within the impious community. He has the same low economic means as Baucis and Philemon, and prefigures Christianity's concern with similar types. A herdsman, Eumaios, is in charge of Odysseus' swine herds, the males of which currently total 360 (*Od.* 14.20). The number suggests thematic parallels with the cattle of Helios on Thrinakia, which are 350 in number (*Od.* 12.129–30). Both numbers figure the days in a year, and may reflect Indo-European material. In the *Rig Veda* cows are likened to rays of the sun or dawn.[36] On Thrinakia, Helios' herds are an extension of himself, an embodiment of the sun with its roughly 360 days (further discussion in Chapter 13). The corresponding numbers imply parallels between the suitors' violation of Odysseus' herds and the crew's of Helios'. The suitors plundering the flocks Eumaios oversees instantiates the *Odyssey*'s thematic concern with improper consumption, the medium through which its characters display their lack of self-control.[37] As the crew perished, destroyed by the gods for

---

[35] See Louden (2006: Chapter 7).   [36] E.g., *RV* 1.92.1–4, 12, 14.
[37] On which see Louden (1999: 14, 31–40, 79, 94, 139n. 16, 142n. 68).

consuming Helios' herd, so will the suitors, who command the sacrifice of another of Eumaios' herd (*Od.* 14.26–8).

Approaching the enclosure around Eumaios' quarter, the disguised Odysseus is threatened by two hounds. Within the virtual theoxeny, a level of violence is threatened against the disguised guest similar to that directed against the angels in Genesis 19. Intervening to call off his hounds, Eumaios passes the initial hospitality test, calls Odysseus *xeinos* (*Od.* 14.56–7), as Telemachos did Athena (*Od.* 1.123), and ushers him in, offering a full meal, which he himself prepares. In these particulars, the episode suggests not only a hospitality scene, but a theoxeny. The rest of Books 14–16 employ other genres of myth and are less concerned with theoxeny. Telemachos' reception of the fugitive prophet Theoklymenos (*Od.* 15.223–86) has much in common with the cycle of myths associated with the prophets Elijah and Elisha (1 Kgs. 17–19, 21; 2 Kgs. 1–8). Odysseus' recognition scene with Telemachos (*Od.* 16.156–320) will be considered in Chapter 3 as romance. But in Book 17 the *Odyssey* offers its most overt treatment of theoxeny.

BOOK 17, THE *ODYSSEY*'S KEY PRESENTATION OF "VIRTUAL" NEGATIVE THEOXENY

Though Melanthios' assault (*Od.* 17.204–54) does not technically fall under the rubric of theoxeny, since the outdoor setting allows for neither host nor guest, the episode uses several motifs that recur when Antinoös hurls his stool at Odysseus, serving as transition into the *Odyssey*'s crucial virtual negative theoxeny. Telemachos having gone ahead to meet with Theoklymenos and Penelope, Eumaios leads the disguised Odysseus to the palace. Before they reach it, they arrive at a fountain where Ithakans draw their water, with an altar of the nymphs, so wayfarers can sacrifice (*Od.* 17.210–1). Into this sacred site, comes the goatherd Melanthios, driving his goats to provide dinner for the suitors. Unprovoked, he insults and verbally abuses them (*Od.* 17.217–32), claiming Odysseus will spoil the suitors' feasts. Not content with verbal abuse, he strikes Odysseus, kicking him in the hip (*Od.* 17.233–34). Eumaios here resembles Lot, who passed the hospitality test, but is unable to shield his divine guest from the mob's violence. In response Eumaios calls on the nymphs of the fountain to make Odysseus return, a god leading him, to scatter Melanthios' arrogant (ὑβρίζων: *Od.* 17.245) glories. In wishing a god would lead Odysseus home, Eumaios adapts Melanthios' earlier remark (*Od.* 17.243: ἀγάγοι δέ ἑ δαίμων responds to 17.218: ἄγει θεός) that the gods see to it that "like leads like." In irony very like that in Nestor's positive theoxeny, who correctly intuits that Athena *could* aid Telemachos, Eumaios wishes for *precisely what is happening*, though he cannot perceive that it is.

When Odysseus enters the palace unaccompanied (after Eumaios has gone in), Telemachos has a meal set out for him (as he did for Athena in Book 1). But then Athena has him go among the suitors to test which are reasonable and which are lawless (*Od.* 17.360–3). In doing so she defines theoxeny, or, with Odysseus substituting for a god, what we are calling virtual theoxeny.[38] She specifies that a *negative* theoxeny is underway, "but even so, she was not going to save any of them from destruction" (*Od.* 17.364). Russo notes the apparent discrepancy (1992: 38), "we may wonder why she encourages Odysseus to search for the distinction in the first place." But this misses the point. Athena has earlier witnessed their violations of hospitality in Book 1, abuses that, within a theoxeny, merit their destruction. In the other negative theoxenies, Genesis 19, and Baucis and Philemon, there are no survivors except the hosts (and their families). In allowing the suitors another chance, though they will again fail, Athena repeats her method from Book 2.[39] She directs Telemachos to hold an assembly even though it will be unsuccessful, the suitors easily thwarting his requests. But it is important that the assembly is held, that Telemachos publicly airs his complaints. It is equally important that the door remain open for the suitors to leave in Books 17–22, even if none does so. Both Telemachos' assembly in Book 2 and Odysseus' testing in Books 17–21 help legitimize the suitors' destruction, in addition to the divine justice with which a theoxeny is overtly concerned.

Following Athena's directive, Odysseus begs from the suitors, initially meeting with success from several (*Od.* 17.365–8, 411–13), until Melanthios tells Antinoös about Eumaios bringing him to the palace. Antinoös, much as Melanthios just before, then berates (νείκεσσε) the swineherd, and calls Odysseus a spoiler of feasts (δαιτῶν ἀπολυμαντῆρες: *Od.* 17.377 = 17.220). The audience knows he and the suitors are the spoilers of feasts, as Athena earlier observed (*Od.* 1.227–9). Ironically furthering this unintended point, Antinoös now hurls a footstool at Odysseus. The *Odyssey* teasingly extends this key moment by having Odysseus approach Antinoös and speak with him after he first hints at his intentions with the footstool (*Od.* 17.409–10), but before he throws it (*Od.* 17. 462–3). Though the

---

[38] Cf. Russo (1992: 38): "Homer is invoking an old folk-tale motif, in which a king (or deity) goes about in disguise to find out who is loyal (or reverent) among his subjects."

[39] We return to this issue at greater length in Chapter 11 where we compare Yahweh hardening the heart of Pharaoh.

tale Odysseus tells him resembles that which he earlier told Eumaios,[40] the different context gives it another purpose and meaning. Intended to provoke sympathy when told to Eumaios, the tale now serves as a warning, an exemplum for Antinoös, that Zeus can suddenly snatch wealth and power away (especially *Od.* 17.424–6, 437–9). Refusing to give the beggar anything, Antinoös hurls his footstool, striking Odysseus in the shoulder. As with Melanthios in the sacred grove, Odysseus withstands Antinoös' blow without flinching.[41]

It is at this point, Antinoös striking the disguised Odysseus, that the *Odyssey* defines theoxeny in the shocked reaction of an unnamed suitor:

> Antinoös, it is not well that you struck the unfortunate wanderer;
> you are accursed if somehow he is one of the heavenly gods,
> since the gods do go about the cities, seeming like strangers
> from other parts, taking on all sorts of forms,
> witnessing both the arrogance (ὕβριν) and good behavior of men.
>
> *Odyssey* 17.483–7

The remark also confirms that the episode is a *virtual* theoxeny, with Odysseus as a stand-in for a god.

Antinoös' outrages do not stop here. After striking Odysseus, he threatens to torture or mutilate him (*Od.* 17.479–80). The threat resembles Laomedon's threats to disfigure Apollo and Poseidon (*Il.* 21.455). Though the *Iliad*'s elliptic references to this myth do not allow us to be certain, in Apollodorus' account it is clear that Apollo and Poseidon had assumed human form in order to test Laomedon's arrogance (II.5.9).[42] Antinoös aligns himself not only with Laomedon, but with some of the worst offenders in Hades, those eternally punished for committing offences against the gods. His violence, and threats of worse physical abuse of a *xeinos*, reveal that the crisis is even more advanced, has reached a more critical stage than the threats of the mob in Genesis 19. Here, the mob, in the form of the suitors, has already taken over the palace, has committed violence against "the disguised god," and, though reminded of the consequences of such acts, threatens to commit further atrocities.

ATHENA AGAINST THE SUITORS, THE ANGELS AGAINST LOT'S MOB

In Genesis 19 the angels strike the mob with blindness to prevent them from harming Lot's guests or family (Gen. 19:11). Since the actual destruction

---

[40] See Russo (1992: 39–40) on the similarities and differences.
[41] Russo (1992: 41) notes the parallel between *Odyssey* 17.463–4 and 17.234–5.
[42] For fuller discussion, see Louden (2006: 183–5, 216).

of the mob will come later, this earlier episode serves as an anticipatory echo of the mob's eventual destruction. The angels prevent the mob from acting against the host and his guests by disabling them with blindness. Westerman (1994: 302) assumes a temporary incapacity is intended, rather than a permanent loss of sight, adducing the parallel when Elisha asks Yahweh to immobilize the armed forces of Aram (2 Kgs. 6:18), "Strike this host, I pray, with blindness," yet their sight is restored shortly afterward.[43] Twice in the *Odyssey* Athena acts against the suitors in a similar manner, temporarily disabling them, anticipations of their eventual destruction, the requisite climax of a negative theoxeny. In Book 2, his crew and ship ready to visit Nestor and Menelaus, Athena helps Telemachos leave in secret by incapacitating the suitors:

> She went on her way, into the house of godlike Odysseus
> and there she drifted a sweet slumber over the suitors,
> and struck (πλάζε) them as they drank, and knocked the goblets from
>   their hands.
>
> *Odyssey* 2.394–6

This is equivalent to what the angels do to the mob: both acts provide for the safety of the respective hosts, Lot and Telemachos, by disabling the respective mobs. The *Odyssey* uses the verb *plazo* (πλάζω), "strike, drive," of the gods acting against mortals in much the way that the angels do against Lot's mob. The verb is used several times of the wrathful Poseidon driving Odysseus on the high seas (*Od.* 1.74–5, 5.388–9, and, by implication, 1.2), expressing his wrath against Odysseus.[44] The *Odyssey* also uses *plazo* to depict Athena as the god wrathful against the suitors.

Athena incapacitates the suitors a second time, again articulated by the verb *plazo*. Like the angels against the mob, this is Athena's penultimate move against the suitors, both episodes occurring just before the apocalyptic destruction that concludes each negative theoxeny:

> In the suitors Pallas Athena
> stirred up uncontrollable laughter, and addled (παρέπλαγξεν)
>   their thinking,
> Now they laughed with jaws that were no longer their own.
> The meat they ate was splattered with blood; their eyes were
>   bursting
> full of tears, and their laughter sounded like lamentation.[45]
>
> *Odyssey* 20.345–9

---

[43] Cf. Speiser (1962: 139–40): "immediate, if temporary, loss of sight."
[44] Discussion in Louden (1999: 81–7).
[45] We consider the passage at greater length in Chapter 13.

SEXUAL RELATIONS: LOT'S MOB AND THE SUITORS

Having established specific parallels between some of Athena's interactions with the suitors and the angels' with the mob, we now consider other parallels between the two myths as a corrective to a prominent misreading of Genesis 19. Though popular culture assumes Genesis 19 is a condemnation of homosexuality, responsible reading of the text and understanding of theoxenic myth reveal that the story is not about sexual preference, nor is the offence that brings on their destruction even a sexual act. The wrongdoing for which the two cities are destroyed is attempted violence against guests, the same reason for which Athena directs the destruction of the suitors.

After Lot receives his guests hospitably, and all prepare for sleep, a mob of men, young and old, surround the house, and demand to have sex with Lot's guests. Since Athena departs after she has finished speaking with Telemachos, such a scene could not occur in the *Odyssey*. But as soon as she has left, Antinoös presses Telemachos for details about his unknown guest:

> But I wish to ask you, best of men, about the stranger,
> where is this man from, of what land does he claim
> to be, where is his race and fatherland . . . ?
> How quickly he departed, dashing off, and he did not wait
> for us to know him. Truly he was not mean to look at.
>
> *Odyssey* 1.405–11

Antinoös' remarks are especially intriguing if juxtaposed with Genesis 19. In claiming he was interested in getting to know the guest (*Od.* 1. 411),[46] his inquiry suggests, if in smaller degree, the mob's interest in Lot's guests. "To get to know" the guests is what the mob desires at Genesis 19:5.[47] Antinoös' word for "know," γιγνώσκω, can also mean "know carnally,"[48] though the only recorded uses are later than Homer (Menander, the Septuagint, Matthew, etc.).[49]

Responsible interpretation of Genesis 19 requires consideration of the mob's demand and Lot's response. Since the myth allows no possibility that the angels would consent to have sex with the mob, the narrative clearly presents an instance of attempted rape, not an act of sex. When

---

[46] On the translation see S. West (1988: 124): "for us to know him."
[47] See Speiser (1962: 139, 31–2), for discussion.   [48] LSJ sub III.
[49] It has been argued that the mob in Genesis 19 does not desire sexual relations with Lot's guests, but wishes to interrogate them to see if they are spies (discussion in Bolin 2004: 49–50). If so, parallels with Antinoös' request would be even closer.

the mob demands that he surrender his guests, Lot counters by offering his daughters, "Look, I have two daughters, virgins both of them; let me bring them out to you, and you can do what you like with them" (Gen. 19:8). Lot clearly assumes the mob will rape his daughters, as his emphasis on their virginity seems calculated to increase their appeal to the mob, while redirecting aggression away from his guests.[50] But why does Lot offer up his daughters to be raped? Of the three negative theoxenies we have, only in Genesis 19 do the guests attempt to spend the night, and only here does the host have daughters. By the implicit conduct illustrated in these myths, as well as the severe form of patriarchy upheld in OT myth (in which, for instance, neither Lot's wife nor daughters are given names), Lot is seen as acting correctly in valuing his guests, who are protected by the sacred tenets of hospitality, over his daughters.[51] It is thus hospitality, not sexuality, with which the myth is concerned. Since it presents the potential for both homosexual *and* heterosexual rape, the myth can hardly be seen as supporting a position on sexual preference.[52] Rather it presents a condemnation of violence attempted against guests.[53] But the angels intervene, in the manner we have already explored, disclosing their identities in the process (Gen. 19:10 and ff.), preventing the rape of the daughters, and violence against Lot.[54]

While the suitors do not attempt to have sex with Telemachos' guest, their sexual relations with the palace's serving women offer parallels with the mob's violations of hospitality in Genesis 19. Several passages depict some of the serving women, Melantho in particular, willingly having sex with the suitors (*Od.* 18.325, 19.87–8, 20.6–16, 22.445; cf. 17.319). The night before the suitors' destruction, the disguised Odysseus observes the maids as they leave to have sex (*Od.* 20.6–13). A few other passages, however, depict

---

[50] Cf. also the closely parallel episode at Judges 19:25 where a host offers up a woman to a similar mob, which had earlier sought his male guest, and they rape her.
[51] Cf. Speiser (1962: 143): "But true to the unwritten code, Lot will stop at nothing in his effort to protect his guests"; Irvin (1978: 22): "Lot twice shows hospitality to his visitors; first, in inviting them to spend the night at his house and in feeding them, and second in offering to sacrifice his daughters to the men of Sodom in order to protect his guests."
[52] Cf. Noort (2004: 4): "When Genesis 19 speaks of rape and the violation of the duty of hospitality, both homosexual and heterosexual relations are viewed as being perverted, the latter evident from Lot's offering of his two daughters to the mob."
[53] Cf. Irvin (1978: 22). Ovid's negative theoxeny of Baucis and Philemon (*Metamorphoses* 8. 611–724) offers indirect confirmation of such a view since sexuality plays no role whatsoever in this myth.
[54] A related, if less dramatic, moment occurs in the myth of Baucis and Philemon. When the latter prepares to sacrifice his gander, as the climax of the hospitality he can offer, Jupiter and Mercury stop him, revealing their divine identities in the process (*Metamorphoses* 8.684–8). In both contexts, when the host has demonstrated his hospitality, his divine guests prevent an act of violence and reveal their identities at the same time.

the serving women as harassed by the suitors (*Od.* 16.108–9 = 20.318–19).[55] The *Odyssey* thus presents a more complex, more variegated portrait of the suitors than the comparably monolithic depiction of the mob in Genesis 19. Even by the double standards of ancient patriarchy, however, the suitors who have sex with the serving women, whether willingly or not, are acting improperly. Since their principal reason for being in the palace is to seek marriage with Penelope, it does not follow that having sex with her female servants could be in any way seen as a proper part of that process. All mention of their doing so should be taken as critical commentary against them. Like the mob in Genesis 19, they have imposed their sexual intent upon the host's house.

VIOLENCE DIRECTED AGAINST THE HOST

Though Athena is not threatened, as are the angels, by other indices the situation in Ithaka is more critical, is at a fuller stage of development. The suitors will attempt violence not against the guest, but against the host in attempting to slay Telemachos (*Od.* 4.670–2, 16.364–406). Genesis 19 briefly implies that the mob would attack Lot as well. When he denies their demand for his guests, they threaten him, "'We will treat you worse than them.' They crowded in on Lot and pressed close to break down the door" (Gen. 19:9).[56] The suitors adopt a subtler route. When they learn that Telemachos has secretly gone, Antinoös proposes they lie in wait, and murder him on his return (*Od.* 4.670–2). His suggestion is not only adopted immediately (*Od.* 4.673), but soon the suitors, while in the palace, make cavalier comments about their plan:

> Truly now, our much-wooed queen prepares a
> marriage, not at all aware that the murder of her son is ready.
>
> *Odyssey* 4.770–1

Perhaps here the suitors most closely approach the wanton, dissolute atmosphere of the mob in Genesis 19.

In Books 17–21 Odysseus is not only the god in disguise in the virtual theoxeny, but he is also the actual host. Telemachos is now role-playing as host, just as he is in his relations with "the beggar." When Antinoös strikes Odysseus in Book 17, he not only parallels the mob's attempted violence against the disguised angels, but against the host, Lot. In this respect the *Odyssey* ratchets up the stakes by giving this disguised tester

---

[55] Cf. Fernández-Galliano's overstatement (1992: 275): "the women-slaves ... who as we know from xvi 108–9, xx 318–19 were ceaselessly molested by the other suitors."
[56] Guests also threaten violence against their host in Buñuel's *The Exterminating Angel*.

a less than pleasant appearance. Unlike the guise Athena assumes in the first part of the negative theoxeny, an aristocratic man of the world, who leaves a positive impression, Odysseus as a beggar presents a stranger less likely to be warmly accepted. The *Odyssey* emphasizes how unpleasant are his clothes (*Od.* 13.434–5, 14.342–3) and knapsack (*Od.* 13.437–8). That he is now bald further lessens his stature, in terms of visual impressions, and opens the door for additional abuse (*Od.* 18.354–5) of a sort that would not have been directed against the disguised Athena. In such ways the *Odyssey* anticipates some of the meaning and modality of Christian myth, as discussed in Chapter 12.

THE SUITORS/LOT'S SONS-IN LAW IGNORE WARNING OF THE APOCALYPSE

In both myths the host attempts to warn others that the gods are preparing destruction. But in each case they are ignored. Lot, after the angels have told him of the coming destruction of the city, warns his sons-in-law:

So Lot went out and urged his sons-in-law to get out of the place at once. "The Lord is about to destroy the city," he said. But they did not take him seriously. (Genesis 19:14)

Alter (2004) renders the end of 19:14 as "And he seemed to his sons-in-law to be joking." Little else is said about the sons-in-law.

In the *Odyssey* the disguised Odysseus approaches Amphinomos, earlier singled out as the least offensive member of the suitors (*Od.* 16.397–8), to warn him what awaits them if they continue their outrageous behavior (*Od.* 18.125–50). Odysseus elaborates at some length on the topic of how precarious is a mortal's existence, how dependent upon the gods' will. Claiming to have once been on his way to becoming a prosperous man, he implies that the gods reduced him to his present state of poverty because he committed reckless acts. As commentators have noted,[57] the term Odysseus uses for reckless acts, *atasthala* (πολλὰ δ' ἀτάσθαλ' ἔρεξα: *Od.* 18.139), serves in the *Odyssey* as a marked term, an index of characters who commit acts the gods find offensive. After implying that his own dire circumstances result from the gods having punished him for such acts, he describes the suitors with the same term, as having committed *atasthala* (*Od.* 18.143). But instead of continuing, as we might expect him, with the warning of divine punishment, the beggar instead asserts that Odysseus will return soon, and punish the suitors. His formulation thus continues the *Odyssey*'s

---

[57] See Jones (1954); Louden (1999: 16, 19, 23, 37, 46, 93, 97, 142nn. 73, 75).

presentation of virtual theoxeny, with Odysseus playing the role of the god in disguise. His trenchant remark near the beginning of the speech, "the earth breeds nothing worth less regard than man" (*Od.* 18.130), also suggests a divine perspective. In the *Iliad* Zeus makes a very similar remark when Hektor dons Patroklos' armor (*Il.* 17.446–7),[58] an act of reckless behavior offensive to the gods. Zeus and Odysseus both use their parallel observations to describe a mortal who, because he has committed an offence against the gods, is shortly to meet his doom.

Like Lot, Odysseus presents his addressee opportunity to heed his warning and escape the coming destruction. But the narrator describes Amphinomos as unable to leave, though aware of the coming destruction, because Athena bound him to be killed by Telemachos (*Od.* 18.154–6). Yahweh's treatment of Pharaoh in Exodus offers a relevant parallel to Athena's procedure. Moses performs miraculous act after miraculous act, each of which shows Pharaoh he is favored by god, as he claims. But each time Yahweh himself prevents Pharaoh from acquiescing, "But the Lord made Pharaoh obstinate" (Exod. 9:12). Both contexts should be understood as instances of Dodds' (1960) overdetermination, in which a mortal and an immortal share responsibility for causing an act. Since Lot has to leave his home to speak with his sons-in-law, some commentators conjecture that they may have been part of the mob in the earlier scene, which, if correct, strengthens their parallels with Amphinomos.

Negative theoxenies conclude in an apocalypse, in the *Odyssey*, Genesis 19, and in Ovid's myth of Baucis and Philemon. I postpone discussion of the destruction of the suitors and the mob outside Lot's house until the final chapter.

VIRTUAL THEOXENY IN OT MYTH

OT myth also has narratives that may be considered virtual theoxenies. The Elijah cycle of myths as a group offers the most parallels to Homeric epic of any one connected group of OT myths. He parallels the *Iliad*'s Kalkhas in his quarrel with a king (Louden 2006: 158–9); he shares a heroic motif with Akhilleus (*ibid.*, 168–70); he participates in a comic theomachy that offers parallels with the *Iliad* (*ibid.*, 221–2). In a general way, Elijah's status as a fugitive prophet (1 Kgs. 17) offers parallels with the *Odyssey*'s Theoklymenos (*Od.* 15.223–78). Because of the drought that serves as its general background, the Elijah cycle begins with a hospitality myth when Yahweh sends him to stay with a woman in the Sidonian (that is *Phoenician*)

---

[58] For discussion of the parallel, see Louden (2006: 200); cf. Clay (1983: 227–8).

village of Zarephath (1 Kgs. 17:8–24). Reaching her house, Elijah asks her for water and bread. When she replies that she has no food, except a handful of flour and a little oil, Elijah tells her to bake him a cake, for her oil and flour will not run out until Yahweh ends the drought.

Though the episode lacks some of the usual motifs (Yahweh has told the woman that he is coming), it features several details typically found in theoxenies. Yahweh specifically directs Elijah to the woman's house (1 Kgs. 17:8–9), as Athena instructs Odysseus to go first to Eumaios' hut (*Od.* 13.404–11), where he initiates his virtual theoxeny. The woman bakes a cake for Elijah (1 Kgs. 17:15), as Sara does for Abraham's divine guests (Gen. 18:6–7). Her stock of oil and flour becomes miraculously self-replenishing, just as the wine bowl in the myth of Baucis and Philemon (*Metamorphoses* 8.679–80). Elijah predicts the miracle of the self-replenishing stock of oil and flour (1 Kgs. 17:14) as the disguised angels predict the miracle of Sara's conception (Gen. 18:10). The basic underlying structure of a theoxeny remains clear: the host demonstrates hospitality and receives a miraculous reward.[59] Elijah, like Odysseus in *Odyssey* 14–22, functions both as a god's agent and as a mortal who performs the role theoxeny normally assigns to an immortal.[60] When the woman's son becomes ill, she blames Elijah, "You came here to bring my sins to light and cause my son's death" (1 Kgs. 17:18), ironically an accurate description of the function of the disguised immortal in a negative theoxeny. Taking him up to the roof-chamber where he has been staying, Elijah revives him, prompting the woman to declare she now knows him to be a man of God, much as the host in a theoxeny typically realizes the work of the immortal guest after the fact.

Elijah's successor, Elisha, whose myths often suggest thematic parallels with those of his predecessor, appears in a few virtually identical episodes. Again, the tradition places a hospitality episode near the beginning of his cycle of stories in the account of the well-to-do woman of Shunem who repeatedly gives Elisha extensive hospitality (2 Kgs. 4:8–17). Afterward Elisha prophesies that she will give birth to a son (2 Kgs. 4:16), as do divine guests in two theoxenies, the angel to Sara (Gen. 18:10), and in Ovid's myth of Hyrieus (*Fasti* 5.493–544). Immediately before this episode Elisha performs the miracle of the oil flask that keeps replenishing itself (2 Kgs. 4:1–6), just as Elijah (1 Kgs. 17:16),[61] again reminiscent of the self-replenishing wine bowl in Ovid's negative theoxeny (*Metamorphoses*

---

[59] Cf. Cogan (2001: 432): "The widow of Zarephath proved worthy of YHWH's care by complying with the prophet's request for drink and food, and she was duly rewarded."
[60] *Ibid.*, "the story proceeds, as do many biblical tales, on two levels, with YHWH and the human participant acting in tandem."
[61] See Cogan (2001: 432–3), on the many close parallels between the two myths.

8.679–80). Later the Shunammite woman's son dies, and Elisha revives him (2 Kgs. 4:18–35), as Elijah revives the widow's son.

To sum up, not only do both Homeric and OT myth employ theoxeny, but the parallels extend even to the three specific subtypes, positive, negative, and virtual. Both traditions employ theoxeny as moral indices illustrating positive characters' proximity to their deities, and negative characters' distance, and as illustrations of the miraculous powers of their gods for rewarding or punishing the behaviors depicted therein. In spite of significant differences between the two traditions (e.g., the monotheism or monolatry of OT myth, and its thematic polemics to support Yahwist religion), the constituent elements of theoxeny remain remarkably stable.[62]

THEOXENY IN NEW TESTAMENT MYTH

Theoxeny survives as a mythic type into Christian myth, though with less developed narratives than those in Genesis 18–19. Much as the *Odyssey*, NT myth uses hospitality episodes as indices of characters' morality. The admonition in Hebrews is a typical instance, "Do not neglect to show hospitality; by doing this, some have entertained angels unawares" (Heb. 13:2), which could serve as a tag line for Genesis 18 or 19. Most important, and most unexpected, however, is the central position theoxeny occupies in Jesus' prophecy of the Second Coming or Day of Judgment in the Gospel of Matthew.

When the Son of Man comes he will separate mortals into two groups, as a shepherd separates the goats from the sheep. A key criterion for his doing so is how they earlier treated him:

For when I was hungry, you gave me food; when thirsty, you gave me drink; when I was a stranger (ξένος), you took me into your home. (Matthew 25:35)

The mortals who will be judged favorably are those who extended hospitality to him. For those mortals who will not receive favorable judgment, the criteria are the same:

For when I was hungry, you gave me nothing to eat; when thirsty, nothing to drink; when I was a stranger (ξένος), you did not welcome me. (Matthew 25:42–3)

The passage functions as a shorthand version of theoxeny, positive and negative. Christ, a god, cast in the role of a guest (*xenos*) in need of hospitality here instantiates full theoxeny, simultaneously positive and negative.

---

[62] Cf. Bolin (2004: 47–8) on parallels between Gen. 18–19 and Ovid's two theoxenies: "The similarities between these tales and those in Genesis 18–9 reveal that, while the constituent elements in divine visitor tales can occur in a variety of combinations, the elements themselves remain fairly stable over time. Ovid's stories have three and two divine visitors respectively, as do Gen. 18:1–15 and 19:1–29."

A host's reception of his guest remains an index of his morality, but now the difference in outcomes, between moral and immoral behavior, is even greater than it is in the two opposite types of theoxeny in Genesis 18–19 and the *Odyssey*. In a considerable expansion of a traditional motif, as is characteristic of Christianity, the outcomes of both types of theoxeny are extended into eternity. Those who were hospitable, a positive theoxeny, will receive not merely a miraculous reward, but eternal life. While those who failed to be hospitable, a negative theoxeny, will not only be destroyed, in an apocalypse, but will receive eternal punishment (Matt. 25:46). In an additional expansion of the mythic genre, Christ declares that anyone who acted this way toward one of his followers will be so judged (Matt. 25:45). In so doing, he figures all of them in a virtual theoxeny, mortals playing the role of the disguised immortal to test a host's hospitality and morality.

Jesus' first miracle, or sign, in the Gospel of John also suggests connections with theoxeny. Since Jesus, his mother, and his disciples are guests at the wedding at Cana-in-Galilee, the episode is a hospitality myth. When Mary tells him that the wine has run out, Jesus has servants fill six huge stone jars with water. They then take the jars to the master, who, tasting, proclaims that the groom saved his best wine for the last (John 2:1–10). Only the servants know of the miraculous transformation of water into wine. The miracle, amid the hospitality setting, suggests the traditional motif of the self-replenishing vessel found in three theoxenies: the wine bowl in Ovid's negative theoxeny (*Metamorphoses* 8.679–80), and the oil jars in the virtual theoxenies with Elijah (1 Kgs. 17:16) and Elisha (2 Kgs. 4:1–6).[63] However, considerable differences between this narrative and those suggest that the Gospel of John is adapting the traditional motifs of theoxeny, putting them to a different purpose. The ties with hospitality are here less crucial: Jesus has no direct contact with either host or groom. Only the servants, and presumably the disciples and Mary, are in on the miracle, which remains secret from everyone else. The real focus is not, then, on the morality of the host, as in a theoxeny, but on Christ in performing the miracle and thereby earning the belief of his disciples (John 2:11).[64]

The intriguing tale in Acts 14:8–20 should also be considered an adaptation of theoxeny. In the Roman colony of Lystra, Paul, accompanied by

---

[63] Perhaps also cf. Ovid's positive theoxeny, *Fasti* 5.493–544, in which Jupiter drinks wine with the host. On the basic equation of Jesus' miracle here with those of Elijah and Elisha, see R. B. Brown (1966: 101): "the changing of water to wine to supply the wedding party may be compared with Elijah's miraculous furnishing of meal and oil in 1 Kings 8:1–16 and Elisha's supplying of oil in 2 Kings 4:1–7."

[64] R. B. Brown (1966) argues further that the wine serves as (p. 105) a sign of messianic times, and has (pp. 109, 110) possible connections with the eucharist.

Barnabas, heals a lame man while speaking to a public assembly. The crowd proclaims that they must be Zeus and Hermes in human form (Acts 14:11-12). But when the priest of Zeus is about to lead the crowd in a sacrifice of oxen to them as gods, Paul and Barnabas prevent them from doing so and proclaim their own faith. Though this myth lacks any overt connection with hospitality, with neither guest nor host, it is nonetheless suggestive of Ovid's theoxeny of Baucis and Philemon in a number of specifics. In Zeus and Hermes it features the same two gods assuming human form. In both narratives the two "gods" prevent the others from sacrificing an animal and offering it to them. But even more than John 2, Acts 14 employs these traditional motifs to further a very different agenda, serving as a polemical corrective to, perhaps even constituting a parody, of such myths.[65]

We conclude this chapter by adducing Jesus' allusions to Sodom and Gomorrah in Matthew and Luke. Both gospels present versions of the same basic episode, Jesus instructing his disciples how to approach a city to spread his gospel. They are to take no money with them, but to depend on the welcome the inhabitants offer (Matt. 10:9–13; Luke 10:4–9; cf. Mark 6:8–13). It is when he considers the towns that will not receive (μὴ δέξεται) his disciples that Jesus thinks of Sodom and Gomorrah, "on the day of judgment it will be more bearable for the land of Sodom and Gomorrah than for that town" (Matt. 10:15; cf. Luke 10:12). Making no reference to sexuality of any kind in his mention of Genesis 19, he focuses entirely on hospitality, whether a community receives his disciples or does not. The word he uses for receive, δέχομαι, *dekhomai*, is one of the standard Homeric verbs for "receive hospitably."[66] He thus not only affirms our reading of Genesis 19, but his own references to Sodom and Gomorrah (Matt. 10:9–15 and Luke 10:4–12) also function as virtual theoxenies, very like his shaping the Day of Judgment around the issue of hospitable reception in Matthew 25. Those cities that fail to receive his followers, who come in his name, will receive apocalyptic destruction, just as the inhabitants of Sodom and Gomorrah did. In a significant change, however, Jesus implies that hosts will be among those who fail to receive, and thereby demonstrate their failings, whereas in the earlier negative theoxenies the hosts pass the tests, but the surrounding communities (suitors, mob) are those who violate.

---

[65] The conclusion of the narrative of Paul's shipwreck and arrival at Malta (Acts 27:9–28:10) also employs motifs found in theoxenies.
[66] E.g., see Cunliffe (1963: s.v. 2).

CHAPTER 3

Romance
The Odyssey *and the myth of Joseph (Gen. 37, 39–47); Autolykos and Jacob*

Most of the different subgenres of myth the *Odyssey* employs are subordinated under the broader rubric of "the return of Odysseus." Odysseus' return, his voyages from Troy to Ithaka, and vanquishing the suitors constitutes the organizing framework of the entire epic (much as the *strife* between Akhilleus and Agamemnon provides the larger framework within which the *Iliad* incorporates other different types of myth),[1] from Book 1 to Book 24. Even theoxeny, in this respect, is subordinated under "the return of Odysseus" because the destruction of the suitors is presented as necessary to the hero regaining control of his home. The *Odyssey* has a specific term for a hero's return from Troy, *nostos*.[2] But the *Odyssey* does not use *nostos* to denote a type of myth, but merely to designate the act of a return. The *Odyssey* uses *nostos* not only of Odysseus' return, but also those of Nestor, Agamemnon, and Aias, narratives that employ radically different motifs, and which are, in fact, different genres of myth than that which the *Odyssey* uses for Odysseus' return. The other *nostoi* do not help construct a context for interpreting Odysseus' return, except by serving as foils (Menelaus' *nostos* is a partial exception, containing several motifs in common with Odysseus' own return). Instead, the *Odyssey* figures Odysseus' *nostos* within the well-defined conventions of another kind of traditional narrative, *romance*.

From the first mention of Odysseus trapped on a distant isle (*Od.* 1.14–15), to the recognition scene with his father, Laertes (*Od.* 24.216–355), romance is the other mythic type that, along with theoxeny, exerts the greatest influence on the structure and plot of the *Odyssey*. As noted in Chapter 2, the negative theoxeny that starts in Book 1 is not concluded until Odysseus slays the suitors in Book 22. Romance is started up in Book 1, and not concluded until Book 24. These two most important genres of myth

---
[1] On different subgenres of myth in the *Iliad*, see Louden (2006: chapters 5–7).
[2] On *nostos* as a possible "story pattern," see Foley (1999: 115–68).

provide the majority of the poem's episodes and motifs, and are the reason the epic gives the impression of having two endings. While the destruction of the suitors concludes the theoxeny, the emotional recognition scenes with Penelope (Book 23) and Laertes (Book 24) conclude the *Odyssey*'s use of romance. Not only do many episodes, and overarching movements of the poem, employ motifs and type-scenes frequent in romance, but several smaller, inset narratives, Eumaios' tale (*Od.* 15.403–84) and stories the disguised Odysseus tells (*Od.* 13.253–86; 14.192–359; 17.415–44; 19.165–202 + 221–48 + 268–99; 24.244–79 + 303–14) also utilize romance elements.

Why would the *Odyssey* employ romance? As with theoxeny, romance narratives feature a protagonist who is rewarded for acting virtuously.[3] In this respect the romance story type illustrates and supports Zeus' opening thesis about mortals' responsibility (*Od.* 1.32–4), and Athena's opening remarks, to which Zeus quickly agrees, about Odysseus as an antitype to Aigisthos (*Od.* 1.45–62). However, romance, like theoxeny, does not typically focus on heroic acts. But again, as with theoxeny, the *Odyssey* subordinates romance under the governing norms of heroic epic, imbuing it with a heroic modality by having a warrior hero as protagonist. Though romance is not usually thought of as a type of myth, it has a natural affinity with myth because a miraculous return from apparent death, and reunion with family, is at the core of romance. The theme of the miraculous return is central to ancient myth, whether in heroes, such as Herakles, Theseus, Odysseus, and Aeneas, who return from the land of the dead, or in a figure such as Orpheus, whose return depends on music, rather than heroism. A narrative with an apparent return from death thus resembles myth at a foundational level, regardless of other aspects of its plot.

I define romance as a narrative with the following characteristics (though a given romance may lack one or more features). The protagonist is regarded as a moral man[4] who has the favor of the supreme god. Through his own mistake, however, he becomes separated from his family for many years, usually the equivalent of a generation. He is trapped in a foreign land, a marvelous, exotic place, for all or much of this period. His imprisonment suggests thematic parallels with being in the underworld. Because of his piety the gods help reunite him with his family, who presume he is dead. He returns home with fabulous treasures. His return from such a long

---

[3] Cf. Lowe (2000: 140), "In the *Odyssey*, these rules are above all *moral* rules, and their sole and sufficient enforcer is Zeus ... the subjection of that entire universe to a set of *global rules of moral behaviour.*"

[4] Romances can have female protagonists, as in Euripides' *Iphigenia in Tauris* and Shakespeare's *Cymbeline*.

absence and reunion with family resembles a triumph over death. Romances climax in a recognition scene, in which the protagonist, in highly emotional circumstances, is reunited with a beloved family member. Romances depict a world in which the moral are rewarded and the immoral are punished in accord with the gods' dictates. In its larger sweep a romance depicts a cycle, the ending of which implies a return to the beginning, a reunion with a previous state. The reunion suggests a healing, a miraculous restoration of wholeness for the protagonist.

As with many types of myth, romance tends to have a patently unrealistic,[5] or perhaps it would be better to say, idealistic structure. A key instance of this is its tendency to have a clear stratification of characters as good or evil. Characters on Ithaka are either loyal to Odysseus or they are disloyal. The classic film, *It's a Wonderful Life*, which might be thought of as the Great American Romance, has a number of structural features reminiscent of the *Odyssey*, including a similar stratification of characters by their moral standing. The film opens with a divine council, in which the angels, Franklin, Joseph, and Clarence,[6] discuss the larger fate of the protagonist, George Bailey, much as do Zeus and Athena in the *Odyssey*'s opening divine council.[7] Clarence goes on to play a role more than a little like that of Athena in the *Odyssey*. When Clarence grants George's wish never to have been born the film even presents a modified descent to the underworld, with the town of Bedford Falls now turned into the demonic Pottersville. When all the selfless acts that George Bailey performed through his life, including saving several lives, never happened, the town instead receives its guiding impulse from the selfish Potter, the embodiment of greed. Now the suitors run the whole town, from the *Odyssey*'s perspective.

Greek literature has the single richest and most influential tradition of romance.[8] Though the *Odyssey* is the earliest representative, the classical period has Euripides' *Helen*, *Ion*, *Iphigenia in Tauris*, and the *Alcestis* (though it lacks the typical gap in time of a generation). The prose romances of Heliodorus, Achilles Tatius, and others prompted the tremendous vogue for romance in the sixteenth century. But Greece is not the only ancient culture to develop romance. Ancient Indian literature has several romances including the acknowledged masterpiece of classical Sanskrit drama, Kalidasa's *Shakuntala*, which, in its inclusion of a *Yavani*, a Greek woman, suggests unexpected ties with Greek culture. "Yavani" is the same word,

---

[5] Frye (1976: 46–52). [6] Basinger (1987: 111–13).
[7] See Louden (2009a) for fuller discussion of parallels between Frank Capra's film and the *Odyssey*.
[8] On some similar elements in Indo-European myth, see West's discussion (2007: 438–40) of "The Husband's Return," and the tale of Alpamysh.

mutatis mutandis, that Old Testament myth uses for Greeks, Javan (Gen. 10:2; Ezek. 27:13, et al.), both words reflecting the older form of "Ion," or "Ionic."[9] Throughout this chapter I will adduce parallels from romances that post-date both the *Odyssey* and Genesis, especially from Euripides (though he may not post-date Genesis as we have it) and Shakespeare. Romance remains a remarkably conservative or stable narrative organization over the millennia. Hence, an instance of a given motif in Euripides, Shakespeare, or other author, can help us understand how the same motif works in the *Odyssey* and Genesis.

EGYPT

Near Eastern narratives also offer a considerable context for romance. The ancient romance offering the most significant parallels for the *Odyssey* is the myth of Joseph (Gen. 37, 39–50). Before investigating the valuable context it provides, however, we first note that both Greek and Israelite romance have thematic connections with Egypt. Egypt provides not only the central setting for the myth of Joseph, but for the *Odyssey*'s tale of Menelaus' wanderings (*Od.* 4.83, 126–30, 351–586; 3.300), two of the tales the disguised Odysseus tells (*Od.* 14.246–86, 17.426–42), as well as the name of an elder Ithakan, Aiguptios (*Od.* 2.15). In subsequent Greek romance a connection with Egypt is even stronger, from Euripides' *Helen*, to Heliodorus' *An Ethiopian Story*, and the fragments of *Sesonchosis* (Reardon 1989: 819–21). Romance clearly has an affinity with things Egyptian. Or we might say that, since romance has a central concern to set part of its story in an exotic locale, Egypt has long served as the default exotic setting. But romance's association with Egypt may go deeper than that. A few Egyptian narratives that predate the Genesis account of Joseph suggest that some elements of romance may have originated in Egypt.[10]

The *Tale of Sinuhe* (Hallo 2003: 77–82, Pritchard 1969: 18–22)[11] features as its protagonist a royal attendant who flees from Egypt because he fears turmoil at the court. He makes his way to Byblos, settling in Asia, apparently among the Hyksos. He prospers, becomes a leader, defeats a champion warrior, but after many years, more than a generation (he now has grown children in his adopted homeland), is homesick and wants to return to Egypt. Receiving permission from the Pharaoh to do so, he

---

[9] Though Javan should probably be regarded as a later construct. Cf. Finkelberg (2005: 31) on Hellen, "a post-factum genealogical construct with no background."

[10] See Carr (1996: 279) on the uniqueness of the Egyptian setting in Joseph's myth.

[11] Pritchard (1969: 18) notes that some manuscripts of the tale are as early as 1800 BC.

returns, escorted by the Pharaoh's men, but leaving his children and family in Asia. The tale offers the earliest instance of such standard romance motifs as the protagonist's absence from home for a generation, the virtuous man prospering after a period of difficulty, and the emotional return home. At the same time, however, it lacks other hallmarks such as the reunion with family, and the use of complex, highly emotional recognition scenes to depict this. Sinuhe's desire for his homeland is stronger than his desire for his own family. Back in Egypt he has a recognition scene, but with the princesses of the court (his superiors), not with any family members. Consequently, the scene is devoid of the profound emotions normally found in a romance's climactic recognition scene.[12]

A second Egyptian narrative, *The Shipwrecked Sailor* (Hallo 2003: 83–5), employs even more of what will become key romance motifs. Here the protagonist is an attendant of a court official, who, to cheer up his despondent lord, tells the tale of what earlier happened to him. He is at sea with a crew of 120 sailors, when a storm suddenly wrecks his ship, killing everyone aboard except the protagonist. He washes up on an island, a virtual paradise, with food that grows there as if tended. He learns the island is ruled by a prophetic serpent, who tells him he shall stay on the island for four months, and not to worry (lines 133–5):

If you are brave and control your heart, you shall embrace your children, you shall kiss your wife, you shall see your home. It is better than everything else.

The attendant vows to make sacrifices to the serpent when he reaches home ("I shall slaughter oxen for you as burnt offering"), which the serpent says will be unnecessary. When the four months have passed, a ship comes for the attendant, as the serpent had prophesied. The serpent gives him all kinds of treasures when he leaves, and the ship takes him home.

Though the tone of the tale and the principal characters have little in common with Homeric epic, nonetheless, *The Shipwrecked Sailor* features a number of elements found in the *Odyssey* and central to romance conventions. There is not only the generic motif of the shipwreck, but the more specific subtype in which the protagonist is the only survivor of a large group of men, as the *Odyssey* presents with Odysseus at the end of Book 12, and, in slightly different form, in Book 13. After their shipwrecks both protagonists come ashore on paradise-like islands ruled by a god. The serpent god is beneficent, and broadly parallels several of Kalypso's

---

[12] There is always the possibility that this tale is already manipulating conventions, subordinating or changing some motifs in order to further other narrative agendas, here the overriding love of Egypt.

tendencies. But in his prophecies the serpent also serves functions very like those of Teiresias in the *Odyssey*, and, given the brevity of the myth, we should not be surprised if one character serves functions that in the *Odyssey* are performed by separate entities.

Perhaps most surprising of all the parallels, however, are the lines quoted above, set in one of the serpent god's prophecies. The lines sum up much of what is central to romance, the return home and reunion with family, but also strike notes particularly reminiscent of one of the *Odyssey*'s central themes, the importance of self-control,[13] "if you... control your heart... you shall see your home." This could almost serve as a shorthand version of Teiresias' prophecy of Odysseus' homecoming (*Od.* 11.100–37), which highlights the episode on Thrinakia, in which Odysseus' self-control will enable him to refrain from eating Helios' cattle. Teiresias concludes by mentioning sacrifice Odysseus must perform to Poseidon, but that his people will flourish around him, and he will die at a ripe old age. The serpent god rather similarly concludes, "You will embrace your children. You will flourish at home, you will be buried" (line 169). The protagonist returns home with considerable treasure given him by the serpent, who now suggests broad parallels with the island-dwelling Phaiakians, who similarly escort Odysseus home laden with their gifts. The attendant's role also broadly suggests some aspects of Eumaios' relationship with Odysseus, each telling a tale within a tale, with his master as audience.

A third Egyptian narrative, *The Tale of the Two Brothers* (Hallo 2003: 85–9, Pritchard 1969: 23–5) has an earlier version[14] of the motifs Genesis presents in the story of Joseph and Potiphar's wife (Gen. 39:6–20).[15] An older brother's wife propositions the younger brother, and, when he refuses her, falsely accuses him of rape. Much of the rest of the narrative develops into less relevant areas, and I would not necessarily classify it as a romance, as I do the *Tale of Sinuhe* and *The Shipwrecked Sailor*. But it has further common ground with the myth of Joseph, and thus, if indirectly, additional relevance to romance. There is conflict between the brothers, causing the younger brother to go away, which, as discussed below, suggests central parallels to the myth of Joseph.

The myth of Joseph and the *Tale of Sinuhe* both present instances of romance involving the intersection of Egyptian and West Semitic culture. The protagonist in *The Tale of Sinuhe* first sees himself as

---

[13] On self-control as a key theme in the *Odyssey*, see Athena's remark at 13.333–4, and Louden (1999: 5, 12–14, 30, 42, 46, 79, 98, 102, 128–9).
[14] Pritchard (1969: 23): "The manuscript can be closely dated to about 1225 BC."
[15] For brief discussion of the parallels, see Carr (1996: 289).

quite distinct from the peoples he encounters whom he refers to as "Asiatics." The Egyptians define themselves as distinct from "Asiatic" culture, by which they apparently mean West Semitic cultures that would include the later Israelites, and what the Greeks will call Phoenicians.[16] The tale has references to defensive installations designed to safeguard Egypt from "Asiatics" (line 17). Yet eventually Sinuhe assimilates with these peoples and, once he has returned to the Pharaoh's court, the princesses refer to him as an "Asiatic" (line 266). The *Odyssey* has similar references to West Semitic culture, the Phoenicians/Sidonians (*Od.* 4.84, 618; 13.285; 14.288; 15.118, 425, 473), against whom the Greeks define themselves in opposition, as do the Egyptians in the *Tale of Sinuhe*.

THE MYTH OF JOSEPH (GEN. 37, 39–47)

It has generally escaped notice that the most relevant ancient parallel to the *Odyssey*'s use of romance is the myth of Joseph (Gen. 37, 39–47). A few commentators have noted Joseph's myth's basic affinities with romance,[17] but as far as I know there is no substantive previous engagement of it and the *Odyssey*'s use of romance. Joseph's myth is essentially romance without the heroic modality that the *Odyssey* develops for its protagonist. Instead of a heroic modality, the myth of Joseph has imposed other concerns, providing etiologies for the Israelites' presence in Egypt, and offering interconnections with other OT myths of the patriarchs.[18] But beyond the absence of a heroic modality, the parallels are otherwise extensive and profound. Both narratives contain all of the motifs defined above as the constituent elements of romance.

The protagonist is regarded as a moral man who has the favor of the supreme god. The *Odyssey* articulates this key point when Zeus himself emphasizes the singular extent of Odysseus' sacrifices at Troy (*Od.* 1.65–7). Though the *Odyssey* has no scenes in which Zeus appears to or speaks with Odysseus, just as the *Iliad* has none with Akhilleus, it is clear that Odysseus has Zeus' full support in the present time of the poem, though the execution of his support is delegated to Athena.[19] Odysseus is aware of Zeus' support, as

---

[16] Cf. Pritchard (1969: 19, n. 12): "As it stands, the story gives a picture of Syria-Palestine in the patriarchal period."
[17] E.g., Hamilton (1997: 609): "The Joseph story in Genesis... his final reconciliation with his family– a plot of separation and reunion which resembles that of countless other romances."
[18] On how Joseph's myth was originally an independent narrative before being incorporated into Genesis, see Carr (1996: 271–85, 288–9).
[19] Athena, as mentor of the hero, expresses Zeus' will toward him; discussion at Louden (2005: 95–6).

when he asks Telemachos, with some irony, to consider whether the support of Athena and Zeus against the suitors will be enough (*Od.* 16.260). The *Odyssey*'s final divine council depicts Zeus still supporting and guiding Odysseus' fortunes (*Od.* 24.478–86). Genesis repeatedly emphasizes Yahweh's support for Joseph throughout his myth. Such favor is implicit in his first dreams (Gen. 37:7, 9), but more explicit once he is in Egypt, where it is expressed in a recurring formula, "Joseph prospered, for the Lord was with him" (Gen. 39:2), "the Lord was with him" (Gen. 39:3), "the Lord blessed the household through Joseph" (Gen. 39:5), "the Lord was with him and gave him success in all that he did" (Gen. 39:23).

Through his own mistake, he becomes separated from his family for many years, usually the equivalent of a generation. The *Odyssey* ignores Odysseus' time at Troy as irrelevant to the concerns of romance. Within the heroic ethos of epic he was correct to go, which the larger (extra-Homeric) tradition buttresses in the account of the oaths sworn by the suitors of Helen. At the beginning of his return home from Troy, however, the earliest episodes the *Odyssey* depicts (other than very brief retrospective narratives such as at *Od.* 19.393–466), Odysseus commits two errors, from which it takes him ten years to recover. His key mistake is his disrespect of Poseidon, whom he recklessly provokes when he asserts that not even the sea god will be able to heal a now blind Polyphêmos (*Od.* 9.525). The poem has carefully foregrounded references to this event so that the audience is aware of the broad outlines, but not the specific details, much earlier (*Od.* 1.20–1, 68–75). This one incident is the cause of Poseidon's wrath, which remains in effect from Book 1 to 13, and still has repercussions beyond the end of the *Odyssey*, as Teiresias' prophecy implies (*Od.* 11.121–35).

Shortly before the Polyphêmos episode, however, the violent storm that erupts after they sack Ismaros already signals some unspecified divine wrath:

> And now I would have come to the land of my fathers unharmed,
> but a wave and the current and the North wind beat me off course
> as I was rounding the Cape of Maleia, and <u>drove</u> me on past Kythera.
> *Odyssey* 9.79–81

The verb used here for "drive" is a compound of *plazo* (παρέπλαγξεν), used in the *Odyssey* to articulate a divine wrath against a mortal, particularly Poseidon's against Odysseus.[20] However, since this storm precedes the Polyphêmos incident, it should not be Poseidon, but some other deity who is angry here. I have argued elsewhere[21] that the *Odyssey* here implies

---

[20] See Louden (1999: 69–103).   [21] Discussion in Louden (1999: 77–80).

divine displeasure with the crew, not Odysseus, for their insubordination at Ismaros (*Od.* 9.44–5), a foreshadowing of their graver disobedience at Thrinakia, which will result in a Zeus-sent storm that kills all remaining crew members (*Od.* 12.405–19). But it is this earlier storm that drives Odysseus and crew off the map, without which they would not have encountered Polyphêmos, and provoked Poseidon's wrath. In this indirect manner, then, the two episodes are linked.

In Joseph's case there are two mistakes, or two sets of mistakes: those that drive his brothers against him, and those he commits in Potiphar's house after coming to Egypt. The intimations of negative traits in Joseph are well analyzed by Kugel. At the beginning of the myth the narrator suggests a pattern of behavior in Joseph that is the cause of his brothers' ill will toward him. While accompanying them as they shepherded flocks, "he told tales about them to their father," Genesis (37:2). Speiser (1962: 87) translates the passage more bluntly, "Joseph brought his father bad reports about them." As Kugel (1990: 276) interprets, "he was a tattle-tale." When the narrator later declares that he is Jacob's favorite, Joseph is quite tactless, even arrogant, when he recounts his dreams (in which they bow down to him) to his brothers (Gen. 37:6–9), and even to Jacob (Gen. 37:10–11). Their anger fueled by a series of incidents, the brothers conspire to kill him, but instead sell him into slavery, a common motif in the *Odyssey*'s inset narratives (*Od.* 14.296–7, 340; 15.483).

When in Egypt, working for Potiphar, the narrative emphasizes how physically attractive he is, "Now Joseph was handsome in both face and figure" (Gen. 39:6). In this comment by the narrator which precipitates the episode which causes Joseph to be imprisoned, Kugel sees a parallel with the earlier report that Joseph seemed to be tattling on his brothers (1990: 277), "since his days as a shepherd his besetting sin has been his vanity and open cultivation of his winning good looks." In the famous episode that follows, which gives its name to the motif (though as we noted *The Tale of the Two Brothers* has an earlier instance; cf. Speiser 1962: 304), Potiphar's wife desires Joseph, but, when rejected, falsely accuses him of rape, prompting Potiphar to imprison him.

Since Joseph is seventeen years old shortly before his brothers sell him into slavery (Gen. 37:2), thirty years old when he begins to serve Pharaoh (Gen. 42:46), and is reunited with his brothers in the second year of drought (Gen. 45:11) after seven years of bumper crops, his absence from his family thus amounts to twenty-one or twenty-two years, virtually identical to the *Odyssey*'s gap of twenty years. Romances often involve a gap of a generation so the protagonist's offspring (or in the case of the *Ion*, the protagonist himself) may grow to adulthood and play a role in the narrative, as is clearly the case in the *Odyssey*, and *The Winter's Tale*, to name only a couple. The myth of Joseph has altered this traditional motif and applied it to his youngest brother, Benjamin, though Speiser is certainly correct when he notes (1962: 335) what must be the central reason for Benjamin's prominence. As discussed below, Joseph tests his brothers by seeing if they would treat Benjamin, the brother most like him, the youngest, and Jacob's favorite, as they had treated him. Much as the *Odyssey* uses romance within a larger myth, an epic with at times a very different modality and set of goals than those of romance, so the myth of Joseph uses romance within the larger myth of the patriarchs, and is weighted with additional concerns at times counter to the usual goals of romance. The over-riding task of providing etiologies for the twelve tribes may thus exert influence on, and alter, this particular motif.

He is trapped in a foreign land, a marvelous or exotic place, for all or much of this period. The notion of wandering against one's will in foreign lands (which is often mistaken for traveling)[22] is central to romance, which frequently involves the protagonist in a state of unwilling exile from his homeland. For almost all of Books 5–12, Odysseus is in exotic lands, off the map, unable to return home. In the episode we identified as his key mistake, the encounter with Polyphêmos, he voluntarily goes ashore when he does not need to. But this is the exception. The opening and closing storms of the Apologue (*Od.* 9.67–81, 12.405–25) drive Odysseus against his will. This is not traveling. The majority of Odysseus' absence, seven of the ten years, is spent on Ogygia with Kalypso, as her prisoner. Though the goddess loves him, she keeps him against his will, as the poem repeatedly states (*Od.* 1.55–9, 4.557–8, 5.14–15, 17.143–4). In the myth of Joseph the captivity in Egypt, the country that has long embodied exotica, serves the same overall function. Joseph is not off the map, as Odysseus is, but for an even longer period of time, for all the years he is apart from his family, he is among an exotic alien people.

Both protagonists are desired by a sensuous female (Kalypso, Potiphar's wife) who has power over them and whose desire leads to their imprisonment. Kalypso may be grouped with a number of other goddesses who have sexual relations with mortals, which in Greek myth include Eos and Demeter, with whom Kalypso herself implies connections (*Od.* 5.121–8), and in Near

---

[22] E.g. Dougherty, who consistently treats travel and wander as equivalents, even translating ἀλάομαι as "travel" (2001: 63).

Eastern myth, Ishtar in particular.[23] Book 5 foregrounds these similarities with its initial focus on Eos leaving the bed of one of her mortal lovers, Tithonos (*Od.* 5.1–2). Hainsworth elaborates (1993: 254), "Tithonus is cited as a type of beauty by Tyrtaeus... he may bear a genuinely Asiatic name." Typically, a goddess who initiates this kind of episode is drawn by the mortal's beauty, as the *Odyssey* specifies of Eos with another lover:

> But Eos of the golden throne abducted (ἥρπασεν) Kleitos
> because of his beauty, that he might live among the immortals.
> *Odyssey* 15.250–1

The sexually aggressive Eos is linked with three different mortal lovers in the *Odyssey*, Tithonos, Kleitos, and Orion, whose story Kalypso relates:

> So, when rosy-fingered Eos took Orion for herself
> you gods, who live without effort, begrudged her this,
> until chaste Artemis of the golden throne coming upon him
> in Ortygia, slew him with her gentle arrows.
> *Odyssey* 5.121–4

In *Gilgamesh*, the goddess Ishtar is attracted to the hero when he bathes and dons fresh clothing after having slain Humbaba, "And Ishtar the princess raised her eyes to the beauty of Gilgamesh" (Vi.i. 6–7, Dalley [1991]; cf., "looked covetously on the beauty of Gilgamesh", George [2003]). Much as the *Odyssey* implies of Eos, the *Gilgamesh* epic contains a catalogue of Ishtar's mortal lovers which Gilgamesh himself recites to her when she propositions him (VI.ii.9–iii.9). Her previous lovers include Dumuzi, the allallu bird, a lion, a horse, a shepherd, and Ishullanu, her father's gardener. Aware that her previous lovers have suffered dire injuries or transformations Gilgamesh rightly rejects her proposition that he be her lover.[24] This episode has proven seminal for subsequent myth and seems to hover behind both Odysseus with Kalypso and Joseph with Potiphar's wife.

Though commentators more often compare Ishtar with Kirke because of the goddess' connection with animals, and ability to change men into them (e.g., Crane 1988: 63–70), the *Odyssey* simply does not depict Kirke as having sexual desire for a lover as do Kalypso, Eos, Demeter, and especially Ishtar. Opposite Kalypso, Kirke has no interest in keeping Odysseus with her when he wants to leave (*Od.* 10.483–9), and apparently only has sex

---

[23] This discussion builds on Louden (1999: 116–17). In Chapter 5 we return to a lengthier comparison of Kalypso and Ishtar.
[24] Though he is wrong to do so in such a disrespectful manner, as discussed in Chapter 5.

with him on his first day, in accord with Hermes' instructions. The *Odyssey* does not portray her as desiring Odysseus sexually, as does Kalypso.[25] So strong is Kalypso's sexual desire that it leads her to commit what our own culture would regard as rape, repeatedly compelling Odysseus to have sex with her against his will:

> ἀλλ' ἦ τοι νύκτας μὲν ἰαύεσκεν καὶ ἀνάγκῃ
> ἐν σπέσσι γλαφυροῖσι παρ' οὐκ ἐθέλων ἐθελούσῃ.
> But, by nights he was compelled to lie with her
> in the hollow caves, against his will, but she was willing it.
> *Odyssey* 5.154–5.

The oxymoronic juxtaposition of οὐκ ἐθέλων, "against his will," coupled with ἐθελούσῃ, "willing," encapsulates the problems in their relationship, and the chasms between Odysseus, Gilgamesh, and Joseph, and Kalypso, Ishtar and Potiphar's wife. Critical reception of both Kalypso and Kirke has tended to be highly romanticized, with commentators assigning them qualities the text does not actually indicate, seeing Odysseus as the willing lover of each goddess. Critics almost uniformly pass over the negative attributes the text assigns Kalypso.

Though Potiphar's unnamed wife may not at first glance appear much like Kalypso or Ishtar, her interactions with Joseph have a fair amount in common with both. Like Ishtar with Gilgamesh, and Eos with Kleitos, Potiphar's wife first desires Joseph because of his physical beauty:

Now Joseph was handsome in both face and figure, and after a time his master's wife became infatuated with him. (Genesis 39:6–7)

As Speiser (1962: 303) notes, the phrase used of Potiphar's wife's first attraction to Joseph, which he renders as "fixed her eye on" (Gen. 39:7), is the same as that used of Ishtar first noticing Gilgamesh, "The identical idiom is used in Akkadian to describe Ishtar's designs on Gilgamesh" (VI, 6). Potiphar's wife immediately goes on to ask Joseph to have sex with her (Gen. 39:7), much as Ishtar propositions Gilgamesh. Suggesting the sexual aggression of Eos and Kalypso, she propositions him, not once, but over and over, "Though she kept on at Joseph day after day, he refused to lie with her" (Gen. 39:10). Finally she grabs him by the loincloth, holding on so tightly that it remains in her hand as he runs off (Gen. 39:12). Her use of force against him, even if unsuccessful, approaches the *Odyssey*'s depiction of Kalypso acting out her desire for Odysseus.

---

[25] For further discussion of differences between Kirke and Kalypso, see Louden (1999: 110–15).

His imprisonment suggests thematic parallels with the underworld.[26] Though Kalypso's island, Ogygia, in some respects resembles a paradise (discussed in Chapter 5), at the same time it instantiates aspects of the underworld. A similar notion is already present in Ishtar's proposition to Gilgamesh. Abusch argues (1986: 152–3) that when Ishtar propositions Gilgamesh to be her husband she is also offering to make him lord of the Dead. Gilgamesh's rejection of Ishtar nonetheless still associates him with death, if less directly, as it leads both to Enkidu's death, and Gilgamesh's own concern with escaping mortality. Kalypso descends from similar conceptions and traditions. Many features of her island are common to depictions of the underworld (Crane 1988: 16–17, 24, n. 12). As Crane notes (1988: 16), Hermes' appearance on Ogygia suggests overlap with his usual association with the underworld as psychopomp, another way of implying Ogygia's thematic overlap with Hades. The detail of Odysseus not eating the special food Kalypso would serve him (*Od.* 5.196–9) suggests that he is participating in other underworld themes, and, as Crane puts it (1988: 20), "avoids a snare that entraps Persephone (and various other figures in folklore)." The repeated mention that she lives in a cave (*Od.* 1.15, 5.57, 63, 77, 155, 9.30), which in myth often serves as a displaced version of the underworld (e.g., as in Odysseus' escape from Polyphêmos' cave), is another such pointer. Eos' lover Orion and Demeter's lover Iasion, whom Kalypso mentions as parallels to her own involvement with Odysseus, as well as several of Ishtar's lovers, all meet with premature deaths. Odysseus held against his will on Ogygia thus invokes parallels with a stay in the underworld.[27]

Joseph's lengthy imprisonment, a result of being desired by Potiphar's wife, serves a similar function in his myth. Falsely accused of attempted rape, Joseph is imprisoned for years as a consequence of rejecting her. We noted that there are two sets of mistakes by Joseph, those with his brothers, and those in Potiphar's house. The friction with his brothers leads to his larger confinement in Egypt, while the friction with Potiphar's wife leads to his being cast in prison. The two episodes exhibit additional parallels. The brothers first strip him of his clothes (Gen. 37:23), then throw him into a pit, before selling him to slave traders. Potiphar's wife removes his loincloth (Gen. 39:12–13), before making the charges against him that result in his being cast in prison.

His being cast into a pit by his brothers thus prefigures his later imprisonment, as well as evoking, if only briefly, the sense of a descent to the

---

[26] We consider Odysseus' descent to the underworld in conjunction with his stay with Kirke in Chapter 9.
[27] See also Nakassis (2004: 221–2) on Kalypso's associations with the underworld.

underworld which internment often suggests in romance. Frye (1976) sets out the general tendency:

> At the beginning of a romance there is often a sharp descent in social status, from riches to poverty, from privilege to a struggle to survive, or even slavery. Families are separated. (p. 104)

> The general theme of descent, we saw, was that of a growing confusion of identity and of restrictions on action. There is a break in consciousness at the beginning, with analogies to falling asleep, followed by a descent to a lower world, which is sometimes a world of cruelty and imprisonment, sometimes an oracular cave... hero or heroine are trapped in labyrinths or prisons. (p. 129)

Shakespeare uses Hermione's imprisonment in similar ways in *The Winter's Tale*.[28] Like Joseph, she is imprisoned after a false charge of adultery (Act 2 Scene 1). Her time in prison is prelude and transition to her apparent death (Act 3 Scene 2), which lasts for sixteen years, a gap in time similar to the myths of Joseph and Odysseus. As in both of those myths, the sixteen-year gap provides sufficient time for her offspring, newborn daughter Perdita, to grow to young adulthood.

Because of his piety the gods help reunite him with his family. As noted, Zeus' comment about Odysseus' sacrifices at Troy (*Od.* 1.65–7) establishes him as a righteous man. In the second divine council Zeus declares that Hermes will go to Ogygia and command Kalypso to let him leave. With Athena as the other speaker at both divine councils, three gods are thus involved in freeing Odysseus from confinement with Kalypso. But in accord with an epic modality, though free to leave, Odysseus will have to cross the sea alone, on a raft he himself builds, and perform several heroic feats just to reach Scheria, an intermediate stage between Ogygia and Ithaka.

Like Odysseus, Joseph makes his way out of prison with help from god. His ability to interpret dreams, discussed below, brings him to the attention of Pharaoh, leading to a rapid reversal of his status, and startling rise in his fortunes. Joseph himself ascribes his ability to interpret dreams entirely to god (Gen. 40:8, 41:16), and it is through the medium of dreams that god most frequently acts in his myth. Making him his right-hand man, Pharaoh gives Joseph a bride, Asenath, daughter of a high priest. This is a stock romance motif. Apollonius, at roughly the same point in his romance, is given as bride the daughter of King Archistrates. Shakespeare's *Pericles*, modeled on the Apollonius romance, follows suit and has the title character marry Thaisa, daughter of King Simonides. Apollonius and Pericles marry their royal brides after they have lost everything in shipwrecks, a rough

---

[28] For recent discussion of the motif, see Louden (2007b).

parallel with Joseph's fortunes until he meets Pharaoh. The *Odyssey* offers up this same motif in Nausikaa, but Odysseus does not marry her. Joseph, Apollonius, and Pericles are the stock age for a romance protagonist, a young man, not yet married. Odysseus' greater age, at least forty when he meets Nausikaa, and greater maturity than Joseph, prevents the *Odyssey* from doing more than merely alluding to this standard motif.

He returns home with fabulous treasures. The Phaiakians, in accord with Zeus' earlier declaration (*Od.* 5.38–40), give Odysseus more treasure than the fabulous winnings he would have brought back from Troy (but are now lost). Three different passages attest how lavish are the Phaiakians' gifts (*Od.* 8.387–406; 13.10–15, 217–18). When he awakes, unaware that he is on Ithaka, he is concerned that the Phaiakians, who left while he was asleep, took some of the treasures. Joseph attains extraordinary prosperity when serving the Pharaoh. As we noted above, this is a formulaic theme in the myth, "the Lord blessed the household through Joseph" (Gen. 39:5), "the Lord was with him and gave him success in all that he did" (Gen. 39:23; cf. 39:2, 3). This tendency is codified in the name Joseph gives Ephraim, his second son by Asenath, "for God has made me fruitful in the land of my hardships" (Gen. 41:52). Joseph's unprecedented prosperity partly serves as his disguise when his brothers eventually come to meet with him during the famine.

In Joseph's myth his return has been adapted to serve another purpose, to provide an etiology for the Israelites dwelling in Egypt. Hence, the family, in the form of his brothers, comes to Joseph (discussed below) rather than the usual return of the protagonist to his homeland. But the traditional pattern reasserts itself when Joseph does go home to meet with his father. Both the *Odyssey* and the myth of Joseph find their conclusion in the protagonists' meetings with their father after recognition scenes between the protagonist and other family members have already taken place.

HIS RETURN AFTER SUCH A LONG ABSENCE IS AN APPARENT TRIUMPH OVER DEATH

Both protagonists are presumed dead during their lengthy absences, a stock motif throughout the romance tradition. In the *Odyssey*, even those loyal to Odysseus, declare that he must be dead (Telemachos: *Od.* 1.166, Eumaios: 14.130, 17.318–19), or refuse to believe that he could return (Telemachos: *Od.* 16.194–5, Eurykleia: 19.369; cf. Penelope: 18.271).[29] Those in the

---

[29] De Jong (2001: 25) refers to these passages as the "distrust" motif.

suitors' party often make such declarations (Melanthios: *Od.* 17.253, Agelaos: 20.333; cf. Eurymakhos: 18.392), on which tendency Odysseus himself comments (*Od.* 22.35). Infrequent is the opposite view, firm belief that Odysseus will return (Halitherses' prophecy: *Od.* 2.174–6).[30] Though Joseph's myth sounds the theme less frequently, when the brothers come to Egypt, and the unrecognized Joseph inquires about their family, they respond that one of their brothers remains with their father, "and one is lost" (Gen. 42:13; cf. 44:20). This is the same form of irony frequent in the *Odyssey*: when he stands before them in disguise, characters reminisce about the presumably absent Odysseus (Fenik 1974: 16, 22, 28–9, 42, 45; cf. de Jong 2001: 386). As Joseph presses his brothers about their family, demanding that they produce their youngest sibling, the brothers are prompted to further thoughts about the presumably deceased Joseph:

"No doubt we are being punished because of our brother. We saw his distress when he pleaded with us and we refused to listen. That is why this distress has come upon us." Reuben said, "Did I not warn you not to do wrong to the boy? But you would not listen, and now his blood is on our heads, and we must pay." (Genesis 42:21–2)

Speiser sums up their situation (1962: 323–4), "to the best of their knowledge, Joseph perished long ago in the wilderness near Dothan."

The narratives reach their climax in recognition scenes, in which the protagonist is reunited with family members under highly emotional circumstances. While such a climax is the standard way of romance, highly emotional recognition scenes between the protagonist and long-separated family members, the parallels between such scenes in the *Odyssey* and the myth of Joseph are closer than mere generic affinity. Both works feature preliminary encounters between the protagonist and family members in which his identity remains concealed while he subjects the other party to exacting tests. Both sets of scenes are not only highly emotional, prompting participants to break down and cry, but in both works the protagonist seems to act with unnecessary cruelty in doing so. The close parallels offer a context to analyze the more controversial aspects of Odysseus' interview and recognition scene with Laertes, which finds a surprisingly close parallel in Joseph's treatment of his brothers when they come to Egypt (Gen. 42–5).

---

[30] Below in Chapter 9, we consider the more heroic type of return from death seen in Book 11, and other episodes of the *Odyssey* which fall outside the romance rubric.

Romance

By recognition scenes[31] I mean the meetings between the protagonist and family members after his twenty-year absence. Since the protagonist is presumed dead, the vastly different circumstances in which both parties now find themselves after the twenty-year gap serve as a disguise for him. It is through recognition scenes that the protagonist re-establishes his identity with regard to his family, an identity he has not had since his separation from family.[32] Recognition scenes are thus the core and climax of the "happy ending," the central marker of the restoration of identity and cyclical movement that typifies romance. There are several different subtypes of recognition scenes, depending on a few key variables. Are both parties ignorant of each other's identities, or just one? How long does it take before the other member learns the protagonist's identity? Does the scene take place before the protagonist has regained his identity, or after? Which family member takes part in the recognition scene? We can construct a typology based on these variables, thereby ascertaining which particular scenes exhibit the closest parallels with each other, belong to the same subtype, and serve as the most reliable guides for understanding the dynamics of a given instance. Two of the variables situate the *Odyssey* and the myth of Joseph among other romances; two variables set the *Odyssey* and Joseph's myth apart from other romance; and one variable is operative only within the *Odyssey* itself.

When we consider romance in a broader perspective, adducing Euripides, Kalidasa's *Shakuntala*, the Greek novels, and Shakespeare, the most significant distinction is the knowledge the characters in a given recognition scene have about each other.[33] Either none of the participants is aware of the other's identity, or the protagonist is aware of the other family member's identity but temporarily conceals his own. This basic distinction divides recognition scenes into two broad subtypes. Most ancient romances, including Euripides' *Ion*, *Helen*, and *Iphigenia in Tauris*, and *The Story of Apollonius King of Tyre*, as well as Shakespeare's *The Winter's Tale* and *Pericles*, use the first type, in which neither party is aware of the other's identity. But both the *Odyssey* and Joseph's myth use the second type, in which the protagonist conceals his own identity in preliminary meetings with family members. To my knowledge, the only other ancient romances that feature

---

[31] See Gainsford (2003) for a recent analysis of recognition scenes in the *Odyssey*, though the most useful discussion remains Murnaghan (1987).

[32] Cf. Frye (1976: 54): "Most romances end happily, with a return to the state of identity, and begin with a departure from it."

[33] The two subtypes nonetheless can overlap in other ways: both employ the motif of other characters thinking about the protagonist while he is unknowingly before them.

this same subtype are Euripides' *Alcestis* and Kalidasa's *Shakuntala*, both of which use variants of the type. In the recognition scene between husband and wife that concludes the *Alcestis*, Admetos is unaware of the identity of the woman whom Herakles compels him to accept.[34] But it is not Alcestis who keeps her identity a secret. Awareness and subsequent manipulation of her identity is transferred to Herakles, a non-relative.[35] Kalidasa's *Shakuntala* also suggests a variation on this type. The protagonist is aware of her husband's identity, but does not disguise herself, or manipulate him. He is under a curse that prevents him from recognizing her.

A second distinction lies in the specific relationship between the protagonist and other family members who take part. Recognition scenes occur between parent and child (mother and son in Euripides' *Ion*, father and daughter in *Apollonius* and Shakespeare's *Pericles*), husband and wife (Odysseus and Penelope, Apollonius and his unnamed queen, Dushyanta and Shakuntala in the *Shakuntala*, Menelaus and Helen in Euripides' *Helen*, Leontes and Hermione in *The Winter's Tale*), or between siblings (Joseph and his brothers, Iphigenia and Orestes in Euripides' *Iphigenia in Tauris*). Of these variations arguably the most dramatic is that between husband and wife, which provides the main climax of the *Odyssey*, the *Shakuntala*, and *The Winter's Tale*. In the latter Shakespeare was criticized for not dramatizing the recognition scene between Leontes and his daughter Perdita.[36] But he correctly chose, in my view, to concentrate the audience's response on the recognition between husband and wife because of its deeper resonances.

A third variable is how much time elapses between the protagonist's first meeting with the family member, and actual disclosure of his identity. It is Athena who first signals the type of recognition scene that the *Odyssey* employs. Her first meeting with Odysseus on Ithaka serves as a blueprint for most of the subsequent recognition scenes. In this encounter Athena first approaches him disguised as a young man.[37] Since she knows his identity, while he is unaware of hers, she acts throughout the meeting as Odysseus will in later scenes with family members and trusted servants. She toys with him, implying she knows that he was at Troy (*Od.* 13.248), deliberately delaying mention of the name Ithaka (*Od.* 13.248). In playing with his emotions in matters important to him, she plays the same role Odysseus will in subsequent scenes, and which Joseph does with his family members. After she reveals her true identity, and demonstrates to him

---

[34] For a recent analysis of the scene, see Louden (2007).
[35] See Louden (2007) on parallels between the *Alcestis* and Shakespeare's *The Winter's Tale*.
[36] See discussion by Orgel (1996: 57).
[37] See Louden (1999: 4–6) on parallels between this episode and those at *Od.* 7.19–77, and 10.277–307.

that he is back on Ithaka, Athena declares that she is there to help him devise schemes (*Od.* 13.303), and defines Odysseus as a man who tests others (πειρήσεαι), even family members (*Od.* 13.335–6). Her assessment is programmatic for the entire second half of the epic.[38] Such testing defines the specific subtype of recognition scenes in the *Odyssey* and Joseph's myth. It is interesting to note that, while commentators often criticize Odysseus for this behavior, especially in the scenes with Laertes,[39] Joseph, acting in precisely the same manner, rarely provokes criticism.

All of the recognition scenes in the *Odyssey* are delayed, except Athena's and Argos' *immediate* recognitions of Odysseus in Books 13 and 17. There are also whole scenes in which Odysseus' identity is never disclosed while he tests a family member. I call such scenes (in which an unrecognized Odysseus interrogates a family member or servant, and receives proofs of loyalty) *postponed* recognition scenes.[40] The same type is found in the myth of Joseph. Each protagonist tests his relatives or servants, and only after they have passed the tests does he, in a later meeting, reveal his identity. This type of recognition scene is a hallmark of each character, as Athena declares of Odysseus (*Od.* 13.296–9), and a tacit form of self-identification for the audience.[41] There is a different context and different rhythm for each family member, a different sense of when is the right moment for the disclosure of identity. The *Odyssey* thus employs three cadences for disclosure of Odysseus' identity, *immediate*, *delayed*, and *postponed*. In an immediate recognition the other party recognizes Odysseus as soon as the encounter begins. In delayed recognition the other party learns Odysseus' identity by the end of the scene. In a postponed recognition the other party only learns Odysseus' identity in a later scene.

In a fourth variable, two recognition scenes feature Odysseus being tested by the other party, Athena in Book 13, and Penelope in Book 23. I call such episodes *reversed* recognitions.

A fifth and final distinction in the *Odyssey*'s recognition scenes is whether they occur before or after Odysseus slays the suitors. If they occur before, they are preparatory to defeating the suitors, and are, to some degree, involved in the conclusion of the *Odyssey*'s use of theoxeny. These scenes,

---

[38] Contra Hoekstra (1989: 185).
[39] E.g., Gainsford (2003: 48): "the cruelty of the testing of Laertes"; Murnaghan (1987: 32, n. 18): "gratuitously cruel"; see discussion in Wender (1978: 45) and on Penelope (Emlyn-Jones 1984: 7): "Notable is the apparent cruelty of the disguised husband."
[40] Cf. de Jong's (2001: 340, 386–7) "'delayed recognition' story-pattern." Gainsford (2003) separates the tests into tests and deceptions, with four subtypes of each.
[41] Cf. Block (1985: 1): "while his falsifications conceal him, they also affirm that he is Odysseus, the skillful deceiver."

except that with Argos, involve characters who can in some way assist Odysseus in defeating the suitors. Thus Athena, Telemachos, Philoitios, and Eumaios all take part in the suitors' destruction, while Eurykleia assists by locking the doors, keeping everyone within (*Od.* 21.380–7). But if the recognition scenes occur after the suitors' destruction, such as those with Penelope and Laertes, they conclude the *Odyssey*'s use of romance.

The *Odyssey* also employs recognition scenes in conjunction with larger structural concerns. Most recognition scenes have a specific counterpart, a complementary scene constructed in closely parallel fashion. Athena's scene in Book 13 is paired with Penelope's in Book 23 in being reversed recognitions, and in having Odysseus bestow a kiss. To a lesser degree Athena's scene is also paired with Argos' in being immediate recognitions. The episodes with Eumaios (Books 14–15) are closely connected with the recognition scene with Telemachos (Book 16),[42] just as in Book 19 the recognition with Eurykleia is related to the postponed recognition with Penelope. These two pairs of symbiotic recognition scenes frame the scenes of the suitors abusing Odysseus in the two books in between, Books 17 and 18. The final two recognition scenes, with Penelope in Book 23, and the Laertes scene in Book 24, also complement each other, forming a unit after the destruction of the suitors.

ATHENA: IMMEDIATE, BUT REVERSED, RECOGNITION (*OD.* 13.221–360)

Odysseus' meeting with Athena in Book 13 introduces and establishes the specific acts that define the subtypes of recognition scenes. In this reversed recognition, however, the various motifs appear in inverted or opposite form. Athena immediately recognizes Odysseus. This should be no surprise; she is a goddess, his mentor. But this is not how subsequent recognition scenes unfold. Here, unique in the poem's recognition scenes, Athena, not Odysseus, has an impenetrable disguise. She tests *him*, opposite all but one of the other recognitions. Lacking a physical disguise, Odysseus initiates the dialogue in verbal disguise, the first of a series of deceptive narratives in which he creates a temporary *alter ego*. But after teasing him by not naming his whereabouts for a while, then enduring his lengthy improvised tale, Athena sheds her disguise, assuming a more usual form,

---

[42] Cf. Murnaghan (1987: 39), and Woodhouse (1930: 151–2), though I do not agree with their hypotheses on how the scenes are linked.

"a woman beautiful and tall, skilled in goodly works" (*Od.* 13.289). The scene introduces all the motifs and patterns of behavior found in the other instances.

EUMAIOS: POSTPONED RECOGNITION (OD. 14.36–534)

The intricate scenes with Eumaios in Books 14 and 15 form the first instances of the more usual type of recognition scene Athena sets in motion. Appearing older, bald, dressed in shabby clothes, Odysseus cannot be recognized and is at leisure to test the loyalty of his retainer, and establish his new identity as a beggar. Here is Odysseus, the master of disguise, as is thematically central to his character, from his guise as an old beggar scouting out Troy (*Od.* 4.242–58), to his master stroke, the Trojan Horse that sacks the city. With his disguised king before him, Eumaios immediately thinks of and mentions the presumably absent Odysseus (*Od.* 14.40–1, 61–2, 67–71, 90, 96, 99–102). Odysseus compliments his host on his hospitality and hears confirmation of Eumaios' loyalty. As Dimock (1989: 190) notes of Eumaios in 14.139–44, "He would rather have him back than see his home and parents again, much as he longs for them."

Why not confide in Eumaios at this point? Odysseus may be concerned that he could inadvertently reveal his identity to Penelope. Blurting out Odysseus' identity at the wrong time is thematic in the *Odyssey*. Menelaus narrates how Antiklos, in the Trojan Horse episode (whose name, *Opposed to Fame*, embodies the risk of premature disclosure), would have cried out to answer Helen's bizarre mimicry of the voices of the Greeks' wives (*Od.* 4.285–8). Antiklos foreshadows Eurykleia's reaction when she blurts out Odysseus' identity in Penelope's presence (*Od.* 19.467–90). Only Athena's divine intervention prevents Penelope from learning the secret (*Od.* 19.478–9). Eumaios is close to Penelope, reports to her, and has her confidence (*Od.* 16.130–55; 17.507–71; cf. 14.373–6). Shortly after Odysseus reveals his identity to Telemachos, the goddess voices concern that if Eumaios were to see Odysseus without his beggar disguise he would reveal the secret to Penelope (*Od.* 16.457–9).

Eumaios' own life story (*Od.* 15.403–84) is a romance within a romance, with many motifs in common with Joseph's myth. Particularly central is the motif of the protagonist being sold into slavery. Eumaios, we are surprised to learn, is the son of a king, a rough parallel to Joseph's special status as a patriarch. It is Phoenician men who sell him into slavery, a Phoenician serving woman in his father's house who betrays him to the Phoenician men, giving his tale substantial ethnic overlap with Joseph's myth.[43] The Phoenician nurse in his father's house who has the complete trust of the young Eumaios betrays him, offering him to Phoenician traders as her fare back to her own family. She thus suggests a rough parallel with Joseph's brothers. Like them, it is the woman herself who suggests selling Eumaios into slavery (15.449–53). She in turn had earlier been kidnapped and sold into slavery by Taphians (*Od.* 15.427). As in Joseph's myth there are thus two sets of slave traders.[44] Though the Phoenicians go on to sell him to Laertes, Eumaios will shortly have his own happy ending, typical of romance. But at this point, his story is incomplete, as is his postponed recognition scene.

TELEMACHOS: DELAYED RECOGNITION (*OD.* 16.166–220)

When Telemachos returns from his encounters with Nestor and Menelaus, he too heads for Eumaios' hut, his recognition scene tied to Eumaios' postponed recognition by location, and by Eumaios' involvement in the scenes before and after, which frame this episode. Odysseus perceives that someone is approaching who is close to Eumaios when the dogs refrain from barking. Odysseus' deduction, a pre-recognition, signals the complexity of this episode, which features several different kinds of recognition. When Telemachos enters, Eumaios' emotional greeting (*Od.* 16.20–6), and the accompanying simile paralleling their reunion with that between a father and son (*Od.* 16.17–20), suggests the emotions usually found in the climax of a full recognition scene, an impression furthered by Telemachos' addressing him as father (ἄττα: *Od.* 16.31). After Eumaios offers him food, and brings him up to date about his guest, the disguised Odysseus, Telemachos sends him to the palace to inform Penelope of his return, affirming the swineherd's role as her informant and confidant. Eumaios having departed, Athena appears, described in the same formula as when she revealed herself to Odysseus in Book 13 (*Od.* 16.158 = 13.289), suggesting that the formulaic description is itself associated with recognition scenes. Restoring Odysseus to his normal form and appearance, she departs.

When Odysseus re-enters Eumaios' hut to reveal his identity to his son, a startled Telemachos is unprepared for his transformation, and fears he is a god. Wordplay[45] underscores Odysseus' difficulty in persuading Telemachos that he is his father:

---

[43] For a discussion of Phoenicians in the *Odyssey*, see Dougherty (2001: 46–7, 113).
[44] Midianites: Genesis 37:36, Ishmaelites 39: 1, though this is usually taken as evidence that Joseph's myth combines different sources; discussion in Speiser (1962: 329–30).
[45] Stanford (1962: 270); for further examples, see Louden (1995).

οὔ τίς τοι θεός εἰμι; (*theos eimi*) I am not some god…
ἀλλὰ πατὴρ τεός εἰμι; (*teos eimi*) but I am your father
Odyssey 16.187–8

The wordplay reiterates Telemachos' confusion and Odysseus' actual resemblance to a god. Telemachos' hesitation is typical of the middle degree of the recognition scenes. Normally at this point, a recognition token, or *sêma*, to use the *Odyssey*'s term, would come into play: the scar on Odysseus' thigh, the marriage bed, or the trees he planted with Laertes. But there is no such marker or proof between the two men, since Telemachos was an infant the last time he saw his father. In a further link with Eumaios' scenes, Telemachos' refusal to believe this is his father parallels the swineherd's refusal to believe the disguised Odysseus' claim that he would return. When Odysseus explains that his transformation is the work of Athena, Telemachos is persuaded. Telemachos' scene is linked with Penelope's in Book 23 and Laertes' in that only these three characters get to see Odysseus outside of his beggar guise in their recognitions.

Tears and crying, which figure prominently in several recognition scenes, first appear here.[46] When Odysseus discloses his identity to Telemachos, he cries (*Od.* 16.190–1). This unexpected show of emotion by Odysseus, the exemplar of self-control, is typical of the deep emotions recognition scenes arouse. What *is* unusual here, however, is that Odysseus' emotional reaction still leaves Telemachos unconvinced that this is his father. Telemachos' unexpected aloofness at this stage anticipates Penelope's more pronounced aloofness in Book 23. When Telemachos is persuaded that his father stands before him (after he mentions Athena's role), he embraces Odysseus, and cries (*Od.* 16.214–20). But their joint commiseration threatens to get out of control, going on for more time than they can spare. The narrator underscores the dilemma with a pivotal contrafactual (*Od.* 16.220–1) linked with two others following the recognition scenes with Philoitios and Eumaios, and Penelope:

> and now the light of the sun would have set while they were mourning, had not Telemachos at once addressed his father.
> *Odyssey* 16.220–1

> and now the light of the sun would have set while they were mourning, had not Odysseus himself restrained them and spoke.
> *Odyssey* 21.226–7

---

[46] Cf. Gainsford's final "move" in his schema (2003: 43), "R9: Joy and weeping at recognition."

> And now the rosy-fingered dawn would have appeared while they were mourning,
> had not Athena, the grey-eyed goddess, thought about other things.
>
> *Odyssey* 23.241–2

The three passages mark the potent emotional impact recognition scenes convey.[47]

ARGOS: IMMEDIATE RECOGNITION (OD. 17.290–327)

Unique among the mortal cast, Argos immediately recognizes Odysseus, linking this scene with Athena's in Book 13, as the only other instance of the same subtype.[48] Details in the preceding recognition scene prepare the way for this surprisingly moving encounter. Just before seeing Telemachos, Odysseus noted that Eumaios' dogs did not bark as someone approached, recognizing that someone known to Eumaios was approaching (*Od*. 16.4–10). When Eumaios goes off to inform Penelope of Telemachos' return, Athena approaches. Odysseus and the dogs perceive her as she approaches, but Telemachos does not (*Od*. 16.160–3). These two earlier passages contain most of the elements used in Argos' recognition scene, and begin a narrative focus on *dogs* as capable of discerning and recognizing.

Now as Odysseus and Eumaios approach, Argos raises his ears (*Od*. 17.291), much as Odysseus heard Telemachos draw near Eumaios' hut. But the action is suspended to give the audience background information about Argos and his present condition. As de Jong notes (2001: 421), the technique of creating suspense by stopping to insert information of this sort recurs in Eurykleia's recognition scene: details about Odysseus' scar and name. When the background information concludes, Argos immediately recognizes Odysseus, wagging his tail, and throwing back his ears in excitement (*Od*. 17.301–2), a canine version of the strong emotions prompted by recognitions. His doing so thus forms the cap for the preceding descriptions of Odysseus' interactions with Eumaios' dogs. As Odysseus then recognizes him, he sheds a tear, which he hides from Eumaios, the same form tears and crying will take in his first scene with Penelope. But as a result of advanced age and weak condition, when Argos recognizes Odysseus, he immediately

---

[47] On the three passages as parallel and as marking the end of the three recognition scenes, see Louden (1993: 193–4). On the tendency for pivotal contrafactuals to link separate sections for Homeric epic, see *ibid.*, 190–7.
[48] Cf. de Jong (2001: 421): "the dog Argus is the only one of Odysseus' *philoi* who immediately recognizes him, without a token of recognition (*sêma*)."

dies. Though the conjunction of his recognition with his own death may strike some as overly sentimental, it is a traditional form the emotional climax in ancient recognition scenes takes, also found in Joseph's myth, as discussed below.

PENELOPE: POSTPONED RECOGNITION (OD. 19.53–251, 508–99)

Odysseus' lengthy meeting with Penelope in Book 19 is the only other postponed recognition scene, forming a pair, in several respects, with Eumaios' earlier scene. Eumaios links with this scene as well by conveying to Odysseus Penelope's wish to meet with him, and relaying his response to her (*Od.* 17.544–88). Very like the scene with Eumaios, Penelope has a lengthy meeting with Odysseus, in which she gives evidence of her loyalty, but he refrains from disclosing his identity. Melantho's verbal assault on Odysseus (*Od.* 19.66–9) parallels the threatened attack by Eumaios' hounds (*Od.* 14.29–32). Both incidents occur immediately before Odysseus has his lengthy interviews with Penelope and Eumaios. Each host intervenes to prevent the assaults from occurring (*Od.* 19.89–95, 14.33–6). In each case the assailants are figured as dogs, actual dogs in the Eumaios episode (*Od.* 14.29: κύνες, 35: κύνας, 37: κύνες), metaphorically so in the case of Melantho, whom Penelope pointedly calls a bitch (*Od.* 19.91: κύον ἀδεές; cf. 19.154, 18.338). Both Penelope and Eumaios immediately think of the presumably absent Odysseus while he is before them in disguise. Both refer to Odysseus as having died (*Od.* 14.130, 19.141). Both episodes, unique among the recognition scenes, have a particular focus on clothing. In both episodes Odysseus encounters resistance and has to work to be able to persuade his listener. Eumaios remains somewhat aloof to some of his concerns, and does not appear to believe his claim that Odysseus will return. Similarly, Penelope requires proof that the stranger has really met her husband. The scenes differ, however, in emotional depth. Odysseus is not moved to tears with Eumaios, whereas with his wife he has to hide his tears (*Od.* 19.211–12), as with Argos (*Od.* 17.304–5).

There are many reasons why Odysseus does not disclose his identity here to Penelope.[49] The maidservant who betrays Eumaios does so in part because she has sexual relations with one of the Phoenician traders. A connection between sexual relations and betrayal is presumed to be a broader weakness of women in general:

---

[49] See de Jong (2001: 458–9) for a recent summary of reasons and arguments.

> When she had done the washing one (a Phoenician) first lay with her
> by the hollow ship, in lovely lovemaking, which leads the thoughts
> of women astray, even she who is moral (εὐεργός).
>
> Odyssey 15.420–2

The phrase "even she who is moral" figures two additional times in the *Odyssey* in comments on the virtues of women, both in Agamemnon's assessments of Klytaimnestra (*Od.* 11.434 = 24.202). The infidelity of both Klytaimnestra and Helen, whom the *Odyssey* puts forth as possible counterparts and/or foils for Penelope, reiterates this view. The three wives embody three different degrees of marital fidelity. Klytaimnestra, who takes a lover, and either helps him murder her husband, or does nothing to prevent his doing so, instantiates the most dangerous infidelity, from the husband's perspective. Helen, who leaves her husband for a lover, but eventually returns to him, occupies a middle degree of marital fidelity. Penelope, who remains faithful throughout, though surrounded by unmarried men, occupies the other extreme of marital fidelity. The *Odyssey* figures Penelope as potentially at each of the three different degrees of fidelity.

Throughout, the *Odyssey* suggests Agamemnon's family inhabits a parallel universe to that of the poem's central family (*Od.* 1.35–43, 298–302; 3.193–200, 248–312; 4.517–37). Odysseus may be murdered on his return, like Agamemnon; Penelope may betray her husband, like Klytaimnestra; Telemachos may have to act like Orestes and avenge the murder of his father. But after Odysseus' return, the *Odyssey* figures Penelope more as a potential Helen, especially the Helen of Menelaus' tale of the Trojan Horse (*Od.* 4.271–89). Intuiting the identities of the warriors within, she walks around the Horse, imitating the voices of their wives. Much as we noted of Eumaios, the *Odyssey* implies a concern that Penelope could jeopardize Odysseus' disguise. As with marital fidelity, Penelope would occupy the least likely degree of such jeopardy, opposite Klytaimnestra, with Helen in the middle. The motif of a woman blurting out Odysseus' name does occur, but given to Eurykleia (*Od.* 19.474), whose recognition is closely interwoven with Penelope's. Near the end of her second recognition scene, Penelope invokes Helen as a relevant parallel (*Od.* 23.218).

The Phoenician servant, Klytaimnestra, and Helen, all engage in sexual relations outside of marriage, while Penelope does not. But the *Odyssey* hints at such scenarios, by exploiting her and others' uncertainties about whether Odysseus is alive or dead. Though Penelope never expresses desire for any of the suitors, the poem raises this as an issue, if indirectly. The strongest such passage is when Athena stirs Telemachos into leaving Sparta, by suggesting Penelope may soon marry Eurymakhos:

> For you know the sort of heart there is in a woman's breast;
> she wishes to enlarge the household of the one she is marrying,
> no longer does she think of, or ask about,
> her previous children by her husband who has died.
> *Odyssey* 15.20–3

Even in this fabrication Penelope is portrayed as not desiring the marriage, but pressured by her father and brothers (*Od.* 15.16–17). Aimed at Telemachos, the emphasis here is more on inheritance, how Penelope remarrying could jeopardize his holdings. Both Eumaios and Penelope, then, whose scenes share a number of tendencies and parallels, are presented as loyal, but vulnerable, hence their postponed recognitions.

But more than anything else, the generic demands of romance preclude Odysseus' premature disclosure of his true identity to his wife. Recognition scenes function as a reward for the protagonist, after he has persevered, and not only survived considerable misfortune, but again attained a high level of prosperity (as at *Od.* 19.293–5). The governing dynamics of romance thus predetermine that Penelope's recognition scene comes near the end of the tale, and constitutes one of the epic's climaxes, but only after Odysseus has vanquished the suitors. Since the suitors mainly belong to the theoxenic layer of the *Odyssey*, recognition scenes with characters who play a part in their destruction take place earlier. When Penelope hears the wanderer's false claim about meeting her husband, she cries, "recognizing" the truth of his claim. Her crying is expanded by a five-line simile (*Od.* 19.205–9), which prompts tears in Odysseus, which he conceals. The episode builds on the scene with Argos in its development of this motif.

Though moved by his account, Penelope responds by demanding proof, testing Odysseus (*Od.* 19.215: πειρήσεσθαι). In this respect the episode has affinities with Athena's reversed recognition in Book 13, in which the goddess, not Odysseus, is in full control of the meeting, and knows his identity. I firmly disagree with commentators who argue that Penelope discerns her husband's true identity here (see Vlahos [2007], most recently). Such a view ignores the power of the impenetrable disguise Athena has given Odysseus, overlooks the profound parallels the scene shares with Eumaios' in Book 14, and retrojects a more modern sensibility on the text, against the tendencies of ancient myth, and in violation of the tendencies of romance. Why diminish and undercut the suspense of the complementary scene in Book 23? Rather, the *Odyssey*, in its virtuoso use of recognition scenes, here toys with the conventions it has established, slightly blurring, but not quite breaking, the line between delayed and postponed recognition scenes. Penelope comes teasingly close, as does Eurykleia in her apostrophe.[50] Penelope resembles Athena's toying with Odysseus in Book 13, but does not equal the goddess in knowledge. Penelope's test focuses on what Odysseus was wearing in his alleged encounter with the wanderer (*Od.* 19.218). In this respect the meeting is also influenced by another concern, Odysseus' interview with Arete on Scheria, in which he reaches an *initial* understanding with that queen on the basis of his account about clothing (*Od.* 7.237–97). That episode also features a later, complementary meeting: though apparently convinced by his account about the clothing, Arete does not recognize him as her guest until much later (*Od.* 11.336–41), just as Penelope will not recognize Odysseus as her husband until Book 23.[51] The thematic parallel with Arete also demonstrates that Penelope does not here recognize him, but will require the later meeting in Book 23 to do so.

Odysseus easily satisfies Penelope's test about clothing, since he remembers the brooch she gave him. His response, however, employs a surprising parallel with Eumaios' life story. He notes how all the women admired the brooch, very like the women in the house of Eumaios' father admiring the jewelry of the Phoenician traders (*Od.* 19.235, cf. 15.462). Commentators rarely note (except Russo 1992: 89) that it is the description of the herald Eurybates (*Od.* 19.244–8), not the clothing, which forms the cap of his proofs, prompting Penelope to even more tears (*Od.* 19.249–50). Why? In his description of Eurybates[52] Odysseus reveals a key feature of his personal relationships, as Russo well notes (1992: 90):

> another indication that "harmony of mind" ... is of prime importance to Odysseus in personal relationships ... It was also the similarity of mind between Odysseus and Athena that delighted the goddess and was the reason for her strong support.

Odysseus' comments about Eurybates also serve as a key indicator, not only of a parallel with Athena, but of how the recognition scenes themselves function: a full recognition occurs when the two characters reach a "harmony of mind" (ὁμοφρονέοντε).

---

[50] Russo (1992: 94): "a powerful dramatic device that startles us by its unexpectedness."
[51] Note that the distance between each complementary scene is very similar, from *Odyssey* 7.237–97 to 11.336–41 for Arete, from Book 19 to Book 23 for Penelope.
[52] For fuller discussion of Eurybates, and Odysseus' relationship with him, see Louden (2006: 121–34).

EURYKLEIA: DELAYED RECOGNITION (OD. 19.353–505)

Eurykleia's recognition scene is linked with both Telemachos' recognition, with which it forms a complement, and with Penelope's first scene, into the middle of which it is inserted. Eurykleia's scene has essentially the same relation to Penelope's postponed recognition as Telemachos' delayed recognition does to Eumaios' postponed recognition. The *Odyssey* signals Eurykleia's link with Telemachos in her first appearance in the poem (*Od.* 2.345–80). Telemachos has her swear an oath not to tell Penelope of his trip to meet with Nestor and Menelaus (*Od.* 2.373–8). This earlier act predicts the dynamics of the later recognition scenes: Penelope kept in the dark about Telemachos' trip points to her postponed recognition, while Eurykleia is let in on the secret both times.[53] Eurykleia's recognition (as with Eumaios') is grounded in hospitality. She will wash Odysseus' feet (*Od.* 19.317–18, 343–8, 356–60, 373–6), a standard motif in hospitality myth (cf. Gen. 18:4). But her washing of his feet, and her recognition, are delayed by an unprecedented series of special narrative techniques, the most unusual of which is her apostrophe to her presumably absent lord (*Od.* 19.363–9), a tour de force blurring of Odysseus' roles. As she then spots the scar on his thigh, the action halts while the narrative reveals how Odysseus received the scar, and what it means (*Od.* 19.393–466). This extraordinary sequence, anticipating the stream-of-consciousness technique of the late nineteenth and early twentieth centuries, lets the audience share Eurykleia's silent mental processes, as her memories of the scar flood her thoughts.

At this point, the recognition scenes of Eurykleia and Penelope briefly merge, as those of Telemachos and Eumaios almost do in Book 16. Eurykleia now blurts out his identity (*Od.* 19.474–5), exactly what Odysseus apparently feared he might suffer from Penelope. And now Penelope would have learned Odysseus' identity prematurely, if Athena had not acted. It seems odd that the *Odyssey* does not employ a pivotal contrafactual here (as I have in the previous sentence) to depict Athena's intervention. Athena also intervenes in Menelaus' tale by leading Helen away from the Horse (*Od.* 4.289) after Odysseus prevents Antiklos from crying out (*Od.* 4.287–8). Here Athena prevents Penelope from perceiving Eurykleia's outcry, while Odysseus grabs his servant by the throat (*Od.* 19.480). Eurykleia pledges her loyalty, as she swore an oath for Telemachos' cause (*Od.* 2.377–8). In doing so, Eurykleia utters her most ironic line, "My child, what sort of

---

[53] Cf. de Jong (2001: 64): "the narratorial motivation is to anticipate her exclusion from the much more important plot of Odysseus' return and revenge."

word has escaped the barrier of your teeth?" (*Od.* 19.492), sly irony at her expense.

Eurykleia's scene segues back to a second part of Penelope's postponed recognition scene. Addressing him as *xeine*, "guest" (*Od.* 19.509, 560), Penelope continues to engage in the lengthy exchanges that again link this scene with those between Odysseus and Eumaios in Books 14–15. An intimate bond has been established, as was formed between Eumaios and Odysseus, such that she recounts her dream to him (discussed below). She enjoys their conversations so much, says Penelope, that she could stay up all night talking (*Od.* 19.589–90),[54] very close to the sentiment Eumaios expressed (*Od.* 15.392–4).

EUMAIOS AND PHILOITIOS: DELAYED RECOGNITION (BUT FOR EUMAIOS = POSTPONED RECOGNITION; OD. 21.188–227)

The least complex of the recognition scenes,[55] this episode, and those of Telemachos, and Athena's, are the ones most closely involved with the destruction of the suitors. After hearing a pledge of loyalty from each man, Odysseus reveals his identity. But lacking the visual transformation Athena gives him before meeting Telemachos, Odysseus shows the men his scar, linking this recognition with Eurykleia's. As with Eurykleia, Odysseus issues a series of directives to the men, following a scene of weeping and commiseration, the second of three related pivotal contrafactuals (*Od.* 16.220–1, 21.226–7, 23.241–2), linking the recognitions of Telemachos, Eumaios and Philoitios, and Penelope.

PENELOPE: DELAYED, REVERSED, RECOGNITION (OD. 23.1–232)

Penelope's and Laertes' recognition scenes are distinct from the others in coming *after* the destruction of the suitors. Consequently they best typify the consummation of a romance, whereas the other scenes should perhaps be seen as partly hybrids, romance type-scenes with elements of a theoxenic story line mixed in. Penelope's scene is most closely linked with Athena's in Book 13 because she tests Odysseus, a reversal of the usual roles (though there is a trace of this element in Eumaios' unexpected

---

[54] De Jong (2001: 481–2) notes the desire becomes reality at *Odyssey* 23.308–9.
[55] Even Argos' scene is more complex by virtue of the background information (*Od.* 17.292–9), and Odysseus' hiding his tears from Eumaios.

resistance to Odysseus' designs). When Eurykleia bounds up the stairs to tell a less-than-enthusiastic Penelope that Odysseus has returned, Penelope's reluctance, extending a theme introduced in Telemachos (*Od.* 16.194–200), becomes the principal force in the scene. Eurykleia tells Penelope that she can see with her own eyes (*Od.* 23.6) that Odysseus has returned (cf. Joseph's myth: Gen. 46:30), and describes the scar (*Od.* 23.74–7), linking this recognition scene with her own earlier episode. Penelope's rejection of this visual evidence suggests her test will require an entirely different means of proving identity.

Odysseus' gruesome form here, bloodied from his slaughter of the suitors, hinders a recognition based on his appearance. Odysseus' appearance conforms exactly to Athena's earlier declaration of how she expected her protégé to proceed against the suitors. Eurykleia assumes Penelope will want to see Odysseus triumphant:

> like a lion, spattered with blood and gore.
> αἵματι καὶ λύθρῳ πεπαλαγμένον ὥς τε λέοντα.
> *Odyssey* 23.48 (= 22.402)

Athena had earlier hoped for a similar outcome:

> αἵματι τ' ἐγκεφάλῳ τε παλαξέμεν ἄσπετον
> your immense floor spattered with (the suitors') blood and brains.
> *Odyssey* 13.395

The violence resembles the iconography of the goddess Anat, whom I elsewhere argue may have influenced traditions behind the Homeric Athena (Louden 2006: 240–85).

In this reversed recognition scene, Penelope does the testing, not Odysseus (much as Athena in Book 13). When Telemachos criticizes her aloofness (*Od.* 23.96–103), without realizing it, he essentially criticizes her appropriation of the testing role. Odysseus, however, accepts Penelope's testing him (πειράζειν: *Od.* 23.114), but assumes she is concerned about his appearance, and, bathed, oiled and clothed by Eurykleia (*Od.* 23.153–64), then sits opposite Penelope. When she still remains aloof, it is Odysseus who first raises the topic of his sleeping in a bed other than in their bedroom (*Od.* 23.171), asking Eurykleia to make a bed for him. Building on Odysseus' own expression (στόρεσον... λέχος: *Od.* 23.177, 171), Penelope proceeds with her test, specifying that the bed is πυκινός, "well fitted," the one Odysseus fashioned himself, explicitly characterized by the narrator as a test (*Od.* 23.181: πειρωμένη). Though renowned for his self-control, as

Athena emphasizes in her recognition (*Od*. 13.333–4),[56] Odysseus, provoked by Penelope's testing, angrily blurts out the story of the bed.[57]

The bed is imbued with additional meanings beyond serving as recognition token, including an erotic element. The *Odyssey*'s three movements, centered around three islands, each feature a powerful female whom Odysseus must win over through delicate negotiations.[58] The two earlier females are Kirke, a goddess with whom Odysseus has sex as part of the process of coming to terms, and Arete. Odysseus' delicate maneuvers on Scheria to win over Arete prefigure his present negotiations with Penelope. Since Arete is a mother and a married woman, on Scheria the *Odyssey* instead presents the erotic element in her daughter Nausikaa, a nubile teenager, whom Odysseus must first win over in order to approach Arete. But on Aiaia Kirke's bed, mentioned several times (*Od*. 10.296–7, 334–5, 340, 342, 347, 480, 497), serves as the means by which Odysseus and the goddess come to an understanding. Once they have made love in it, she ceases to be a threat to him, and restores the crew to their human form. On Ithaka, Penelope's use of their marriage bed as recognition token parallels how Kirke comes to an understanding with Odysseus. On Aiaia Odysseus maneuvers Kirke into swearing an oath before they have sex. In her reversed recognition, Penelope maneuvers Odysseus into proving his identity before they have sex. Penelope's bed is literally tied to *eros* in its epithet, πολυήρατος (*Od*. 23.354).

As part of a tree, the bed is a living organism. An olive tree, untouched by the suitors, outside of and beyond their designs, embodies the core of Ithaka that remains unharmed, still alive, still strong. As an *olive* tree, this proof of Odysseus' identity is tied to Athena, and indirectly complements her description of how similar she and her protégé are (*Od*. 13.291–301). As something Odysseus himself made, the bed instantiates his skill as a carpenter, at fashioning objects from trees. To sack Troy Odysseus conceives of fashioning the wooden Horse (*Od*. 8.493–4; 11.523–32; cf. 4.271–89). To blind Polyphêmos Odysseus sharpens an olive beam to a point (*Od*. 9.319–28). To leave Kalypso Odysseus fashions his own raft (*Od*. 5.234–57). In the *Iliad* when he wrestles Aias a simile compares their interlocking arms to crossbeams which a κλυτὸς ἤραρε τέκτων, "renowned carpenter has fitted together" (*Il*. 23.712).

---

[56] On self-control in the *Odyssey*, see Louden (1999: 5, 12–14, 30, 42, 46, 79, 98, 102, 128–9).
[57] Cf. Russo's comment (1992: 333), "Odysseus is now very angry... This is of course the object of Penelope's carefully worked out plan to be absolutely sure of Odysseus' identity."
[58] See Louden (1999: 4–14; cf. 110–15).

But the climactic instance in Homeric epic of Odysseus' woodworking skills is his fashioning of Penelope's marriage bed. The *Odyssey* has deferred any mention of their bed, and its unique manner of construction, until now, postponing the account to serve in this climactic recognition. The episode first points to his connection with artisans when a simile compares Odysseus' head and shoulders, as he emerges from his bath, to the work of a skilled craftsman, endowed by Hephaistos or Athena (*Od.* 23.159–62). Penelope emphasizes he himself made (τόν ῥ᾽ αὐτὸς ἐποίει: *Od.* 23.178) the bed. His subsequent description (*Od.* 23.189: τὸ δ᾽ ἐγὼ κάμον οὐδέ τις ἄλλος) incorporates elements used when he fashions the raft (*Od.* 23.198: τέτρηνα δὲ πάντα τερέτρῳ, cf. 5.246–7: τέρετρα... τέτρηνεν δ᾽ ἄρα πάντα). In a finishing touch, he decorated the bed with gold, silver, and ivory (*Od.* 23.200: δαιδάλλων χρυσῷ τε καὶ ἀργύρῳ ἠδ᾽ ἐλέφαντι), reminiscent of the simile above comparing him to an artisan's work (*Od.* 23.159: ὡς δ᾽ ὅτε τις χρυσὸν περιχεύεται ἀργύρῳ ἀνήρ), and introducing the topic of Odysseus' craftsmanship into the scene.

Other than being "reversed," and using the bed as a proof, this recognition scene is composed of elements found in the other episodes. Before coming downstairs Penelope asserts to Eurykleia that Odysseus must have died far from home (*Od.* 23.68), as do Eumaios (*Od.* 14.68) and Penelope in her postponed recognition (*Od.* 19.141, cf. 315).[59] Eurykleia telling Penelope about the proof of the scar (*Od.* 23.74–7) indicates that the episode is using recognition tokens here self-consciously, almost in a meta-theatrical sense. The strong emotional element is present in several different registers. Tears and weeping are prominent (*Od.* 23.33, 207, 231–2), as in the other scenes (*Od.* 16.190–1, 17.304–5, 19.211–12, 21.213). Their kiss (*Od.* 23.208) complements Odysseus kissing Ithaka (*Od.* 13.354) in the recognition with Athena. This is the third and final of the three linked pivotal contrafactuals:

> And now the rosy-fingered dawn would have appeared while they were mourning,
> had not Athena, the grey-eyed goddess, thought about other things.
> *Odyssey* 23.241–2

But perhaps the strongest such detail occurs the moment Penelope recognizes him: her heart and knees are undone (*Od.* 23.205), which looks ahead to the intensity of Laertes' scene.

---

[59] Gainsford (2003: 43, 46–7) discusses this as his motif F4 (=R5); cf. Telemachos' remarks at 16.194–5.

LAERTES: DELAYED RECOGNITION (OD. 24.205–350)

Though criticized on various accounts (especially that Odysseus may here be unnecessarily cruel),[60] the *Odyssey*'s final recognition scene with Laertes is not only entirely traditional, but occupies a traditional position in the overall sequence of the recognition scenes, as comparison with Joseph's myth demonstrates. The behavior most often criticized, Odysseus' decision to test his father with mocking words (*Od.* 24.240), is closely paralleled in Joseph's treatment of his brothers in their recognition scene.

Laertes' scene is structurally linked to Penelope's recognition scene in Book 23 in several ways. These are the only recognition scenes to occur after the suitors' death. In Odysseus' account of how he fashioned the bed, he describes cutting the foliage and branches off the olive tree, and trimming the trunk (*Od.* 23.195–6). When Odysseus comes upon his father, Laertes is busy with a spade, digging around a plant (*Od.* 24.227, 242). The description of Odysseus trimming the trunk in Penelope's recognition thus points ahead, thematically, to Laertes' activity when Odysseus approaches him, father and son each depicted busily pruning a tree or plant. Both scenes depend upon the characters' connection with growing plants, the orchards, recognition tokens between father and son, and the olive tree, that between husband and wife.

In the story Odysseus spins for Laertes, he claims to be tied to Odysseus through hospitality (*Od.* 24.266–79, 312–14), linking this episode with Penelope's first recognition scene (*Od.* 19.185–202).[61] Partly invoking the presumed connection between the stranger and Odysseus, Laertes consequently addresses Odysseus as *xeinos* (*Od.* 24.281), as does Penelope (*Od.* 19.124, 215, 253, 309, 350, 509, 560, 589). Other details are more generic, occurring in several of the *Odyssey*'s recognition scenes. Laertes assumes that Odysseus has died (*Od.* 24.284, 291–6), giving an almost Priam-like perspective on his son's presumed death, shedding tears for his presumably absent son (*Od.* 24.280).

In his tale Odysseus uses a phrase that is part of the deeper structure of the *Odyssey*, that virtually serves as recognition token. Giving a false name, birthplace, and parentage, Odysseus tells Laertes that he came here, driven off course, "but a god/*drove* me away from Sikania, so that I came here against my will" (*Od.* 24.306–7). The *Odyssey* employs πλάζω, Odysseus'

---

[60] E.g., Gainsford (2003: 48); cf. Murnaghan (1987: 32, n. 18): "gratuitously cruel"; discussion in Wender (1978: 45).
[61] Cf. Gainsford's move D4 (2003: 43), "He recalls meeting Odysseus," though this omits reference to hospitality.

verb here for "drove," under specific circumstances. It is usually line initial, as here, usually refers to Odysseus, as here, usually depicts the working of a divine wrath, as here, and embodies Odysseus' difficulty returning home.[62] Odysseus' use of the verb here, even in a false tale, serves as a capsule version of his experiences over the last ten years. His description serves like a recognition token, proclaiming his identity, but more to the audience than to Laertes. The use of *plazo* demonstrates that the scene with Laertes is a traditional part of the *Odyssey*, that deftly manipulates key dynamics central to the working and meaning of the epic.[63]

At Odysseus' repeated claim to have encountered and entertained "Odysseus" Laertes mourns, pouring handfuls of dirt over his face (*Od.* 24.315–17). The *Odyssey* here depicts Laertes as a traditional figure, the deeply grieving father, as Priam, as Job.[64] Each makes extreme gestures in his extreme grief. Priam rolls around in dung, smearing it on his head and neck (*Il.* 24.163–5; cf. 22.33–78), very like Laertes' act. Job tears his clothes and shaves his head (Job 1:20), while his friends act very like Laertes, "they wept aloud, tore their cloaks, and tossed dust into the air over their heads" (Job 2:12). Laertes' scene resembles Penelope's in provoking a startling emotional response in Odysseus, who briefly loses control over the dynamics of the encounter, his shock caught in the unique description of sharp pain welling up in his nostrils (*Od.* 24.318–19). As with Penelope, the emotional reaction prompts disclosure of his identity, as Odysseus now declares to his father that he is the very man they were discussing (*Od.* 24.321). But where Penelope intentionally maneuvers Odysseus into disclosing his identity, Laertes is unaware that he does so. When Odysseus does disclose his identity, Laertes demands proof. Odysseus responds by showing his scar (*Od.* 24.331–5), proof of identity in Eurykleia's recognition, then recounts the day when Laertes had named and counted all the trees for Odysseus (*Od.* 24.336–44). Wood, woodworking, trees, it can be no accident that these topics link Laertes' and Penelope's recognitions.

Looking ahead to repercussions from his slaying of the suitors, Odysseus immediately tries to limit the weeping (*Od.* 24.323–4) their encounter has provoked. His reaction is quite traditional within the *Odyssey*'s recognitions. In his recognitions with Telemachos (*Od.* 16.220–1), Philoitios and Eumaios

---

[62] The verb occurs line initial thirteen out of sixteen times (Louden 1999: 155, n. 11). It refers to Odysseus ten out of sixteen occurrences (*ibid.*, 155, n. 13). It depicts difficulty in crossing the sea thirteen out of sixteen times (*ibid.*, 155, n. 14).

[63] Cf. Lowe (2000: 151, n. 18), " [I]t seems to me certain that the terrestrial events of XXIV, the Laertes scene and the involvement of the suitors' kin, are essential to the poem's total plot, being not only assumed but pointedly foreshadowed in the rest of the poem, and especially in the second book."

[64] Cf. Jacob/Israel in Joseph's myth, especially at Genesis 42:38 and 44:31.

(*Od.* 21.226–7), and the second scene with Penelope (*Od.* 23.241–2), unrestrained weeping and mourning which would last until dawn threatens to erupt. Respectively, Telemachos (Book 16), Odysseus (Book 21) and Athena (Book 23) all intervene, averting disaster through pivotal contrafactuals. The recognition concludes with another strong emotional reaction, as Laertes, now fully persuaded that this is Odysseus, embraces him, and almost faints (*Od.* 24.348–9, discussed below).

RECOGNITION SCENES IN THE MYTH OF JOSEPH (GEN. 42–5)

Like the *Odyssey*, and romance in general, the myth of Joseph reaches its climax in a series of highly emotional recognition scenes. With few exceptions, virtually every detail in these scenes also occurs in the *Odyssey*. The *Odyssey*'s recognition scenes play out against the backdrop of the suitors' oppression of the household. The drought and famine play a similar role, providing the background for the recognition scenes in Joseph's myth. The two sets of oppressive circumstances overlap in the *Odyssey*'s frequent descriptions of the suitors as eating up Telemachos' possessions (*Od.* 1.160, 2.55–8, etc.).

In terms of the larger typology of the two basic kinds of recognition scenes that exist throughout romance, Joseph's myth uses the same general type that occurs in the *Odyssey*: though they are unable to recognize him, the protagonist recognizes his relatives, but conceals his identity until they have passed various tests of loyalty or morality. This basic distinction aligns both works with each other, and separates them from almost all other ancient romances, such as Euripides' *Ion, Helen, Iphigenia in Tauris*, the Greek novels, Kalidasa's *Shakuntala*, the Apollonius romance, and later Shakespearean romance. It also means that Joseph's myth has all of the motifs used in this subtype, such as the protagonist having to conceal his tears, which Genesis employs as extensively as does the *Odyssey*. In terms of the typology of three subtypes *within* the *Odyssey*, Joseph's myth uses the specific form that the *Odyssey* reserves for Eumaios and Penelope, postponed recognition,[65] as his first encounter with his brothers demonstrates:

Joseph's brothers came and bowed to the ground before him, and when he saw his brothers he recognized them but, pretending not to know them, he greeted them harshly... Although Joseph had recognized his brothers they did not recognize him. (Genesis 42:6–8)

---

[65] Cf. Redford's comment on Joseph's recognition scenes (1970: 76), "the writer postpones the scene of revelation, and creates a tension among the principles which can scarcely be paralleled in literature."

But Genesis' use of postponed recognition is even more involved than in the *Odyssey*.

While withholding his identity and testing his brothers, Joseph goes to greater lengths in his deception than Odysseus does in the *Odyssey*. He keeps them in the dark longer than Odysseus does, making them suffer to considerably greater degrees. While Odysseus makes up false stories about himself, Joseph makes false charges against his brothers, accusing them of being spies (Gen. 42:9, 12, 14–16), and imprisoning them for three days (Gen. 42:16–24).[66] Then letting the rest go, he keeps Simeon in prison for an unspecified time (Gen. 43:23).[67] After they purchase grain with silver, he has their silver returned to their bags, which, when found, will make them fear they will be caught as thieves:

"My silver has been returned; here it is in my pack." Bewildered and trembling, they asked one another, "What is this that God has done to us?" (Genesis 42:28)

"We have been brought in here because of that affair of the silver... He means to makes some charge against us, to inflict punishment on us, seize our donkeys, and make us his slaves." (Genesis 43:18)

In a repetition of his deception, Joseph has his steward place his own silver goblet in Benjamin's pack. The deliberate anguish and torment he causes his brothers (Gen. 44:7–13) is far beyond anything Odysseus inflicts upon Penelope or Laertes, his deceptions more misleading and dishonest than anything Odysseus says or does in the *Odyssey*. But in a strange double standard in our culture, commentators criticize Odysseus for his acts, whereas more excessive behavior in Joseph is rarely noted, let alone criticized. Taken together, the parallels suggest that Odysseus' and Joseph's behavior is expected, even condoned in ancient romance.

The return of the brothers is set within a hospitality scene, as are many of the *Odyssey*'s recognition scenes. When Joseph sees that his brothers have brought Benjamin, as he commanded, he has his steward prepare a feast for them (Gen. 43:16). The steward provides them with water to wash their feet (Gen. 43:24), not only a standard motif in hospitality myth, but a pivotal motif in Odysseus' recognition scene with Eurykleia (*Od.* 19.343–470). Like Odysseus' relatives (and retainers) in the *Odyssey*, Joseph's brothers think about him while in his presence (Gen. 42:21, 44:28; cf. 42:32, 38), though unable to recognize him. Very much as in the *Odyssey*, his relatives assume that he is dead (Gen. 42:38, 44:20, 44:28). Joseph and Odysseus

---

[66] Cf. Leontes casting Hermione in prison, *The Winter's Tale* 2.3–3.2.
[67] Genesis 43:1, "The famine was still severe in the land," suggests that months have passed.

both have to make a supreme effort to control their emotions and hide their weeping during recognition scenes. Like Odysseus with Argos (*Od.* 17. 305), and before Penelope (*Od.* 19. 209–12), Joseph has to conceal his weeping from his brothers, as he faces them after twenty years (Gen. 42:24; 43:30; 45:1).

Joseph reveals his identity only after the brothers, and Judah in particular, satisfy him through a series of tests, suggestive not only of Odysseus' general tendency, but also of the tests Penelope imposes upon him. With Joseph presumed dead, Benjamin has become his replacement in Jacob's eyes, his youngest and only other son by the same wife (Gen. 44:20). Having compelled them to bring Benjamin before him, Joseph now has his silver cup placed in his younger brother's sack, so he will be found with it. He thus gives his brothers the opportunity to do to Benjamin what they did to him, sacrifice him for their own gain. As Speiser succinctly notes (1962: 335), "The brothers had indeed changed. They passed the ultimate test. And Joseph had his answer." His brothers having passed his tests, Joseph finally reveals his identity (Gen. 45:3). The brothers' reaction suggests Telemachos' response to seeing the undisguised Odysseus:

> They were so dumbfounded at finding themselves face to face with Joseph that they could not answer.
>
> (Genesis 45:3)
>
> And his own son was astonished, and out of fear averted his eyes lest he be a god.
>
> (*Odyssey* 16.178–9)

Also like Telemachos with Odysseus, as Carr notes (1996: 276), the brothers implicitly equate Joseph with god. Joseph's subsequent remark to them is close to Odysseus' address to Laertes when his father is reluctant to believe him, "I am he, about whom you were asking" (*Od.* 24.321); "I am your brother Joseph, whom you sold into Egypt" (Gen. 45:12).

In both narratives the protagonists' encounters with their fathers form the final recognition scene. Both elderly fathers are broadly painted in similar strokes as a sorrowful old man. Each particularly grieves over his presumably lost son, the protagonist (Gen. 42:36; *Od.* 24.288 ff.). Joseph repeatedly inflicts considerable anguish by making Jacob part with Benjamin as part of the testing of his brothers:

> "You have robbed me of my children. Joseph is lost; Simeon is lost; and now you
> would take Benjamin. Everything is against me."
>
> (Genesis 42:36)

> But Jacob said, "My son must not go with you, for his brother
>   is dead and he alone
> is left. Should he come to any harm on the journey, you will bring
>   down my grey
> hairs in sorrow to the grave."
>
> (Genesis 42:38)

> "If you take this one from me as well, and he comes to any harm,
>   then you will bring down my gray hairs in misery to the grave."
> (Genesis 44:31)[68]

In both myths the suffering the protagonist causes his father seems extreme or unnecessary. In Laertes' case commentators argue that, since the suitors have been slain, there is no need for deception (Heubeck 1992: 384, in Russo 1992). In Joseph's case he chooses a method of testing his brothers that causes more anguish to his father than to his brothers.

The emotions provoked in the father are so strong that both narratives hint at the possibility of his dying at the moment of recognition. Laertes breaks down and cries (*Od.* 24.280), castigating himself in his sorrow (*Od.* 24.315–17), and then faints (*Od.* 24.348–9).[69] Joseph's scene with Jacob employs a motif found in Argos' scene with Odysseus. Argos remains alive just long enough to take part in his recognition scene, dying as soon as he has recognized Odysseus (*Od.* 17.326–7). When Jacob recognizes Joseph, after all the brothers have, he articulates the same motif, "I have seen for myself that you are still alive. Now I am ready to die" (Gen. 46:30). In this respect Joseph's myth treats Jacob much as the *Odyssey* does Eumaios and Philoitios, who at the moment of their recognitions are incorporated into Odysseus' family:

> I will provide you both with wives and grant you possessions
> and houses, built next to mine, and in my eyes you will
> both be companions and brothers to Telemachos.
> *Odyssey* 21.214–16

Given that Eumaios was sold into slavery (*Od.* 15.450–83), and given a postponed recognition, his incorporation into Odysseus' family, much as Jacob is incorporated into Joseph's new family in Egypt, suggests a significant affinity with Joseph's myth.

---

[68] Cf. Genesis 43:6, 14; 44:29.
[69] Heubeck (1992: 399): "Laertes... briefly loses consciousness... A formulaic phrase which always denotes complete mental and physical effects induced by a deeply disturbing situation or piece of news, but which does not in other cases result in fainting."

Joseph's behavior throughout his recognition scenes conforms to Athena's description of Odysseus testing his relatives, if we switch Penelope to father and brothers (*Od.* 13.335–8). The disjunction between the audience's awareness of Penelope's fidelity, but Odysseus' desire to test her in a way that causes her to suffer, is reminiscent of how Joseph treats both Jacob and his brothers. Odysseus' interview with Penelope in Book 19 particularly resembles the dynamics in Joseph's first scene with his brothers in Egypt, Odysseus in making her cry, Joseph in his use of lies and deception.

Both myths innovate in where they place and how they employ their recognition scenes. The *Odyssey* organizes its recognition scenes around its negative theoxeny. All Odyssean recognition scenes, except that of Laertes and the second half of Penelope's, take place before Odysseus slays the suitors, and help provide him with aides for that act. Joseph's recognition scenes innovate in having the protagonist's family come to him rather than have him return home to them. Genesis alters this basic thrust of romance, subordinating it to its own larger agenda of providing an etiology for the Israelites' presence in Egypt. The separate recognition scenes Odysseus has with different family members are now separate arrivals in Egypt for Joseph's brothers and father.

DREAMS IN THE *ODYSSEY* AND JOSEPH'S MYTH

Dreams are a recurring motif in romance (*Iphigenia in Tauris* 42–55; *Rudens*: 593–5, 771; *An Ephesian Tale*: 1:12, 2:8, 5:8; *Apollonius*: 48; *Pericles* 21:226–37; *Cymbeline* 5.3.124–216; *The Winter's Tale* 3.3.17–38), also serving prominently in myth as early as *Gilgamesh*. In both Greek and OT myth, dreams are seen as embodying divine will, and gods appear to characters in their dreams (Gen. 20:3–7, 28:11–15, 31:19–24; *Od.* 6.13–41, 15.4–43), or send dreams to a given character (*Il.* 2.6–35; *Od.* 4.795–838, 20.87). Since dreams are understood as divine signs, a mortal who can correctly interpret dreams is loosely equated with a prophet, in both mythic traditions (Deut. 13:1; 1 Sam. 28:15). In Homeric epic the parallels between prophecy and dream interpretation are explicit, as Akhilleus notes when he searches for the cause of Apollo's plague as the *Iliad* begins:

> But come, let us inquire of some prophet, or priest,
> or a dream reader, since a dream also comes from Zeus.
> *Iliad* 1.62–3

While the *Odyssey* features dreams repeatedly (*Od.* 4.795–838, 6.13–41, 14.495, 15.4–43, 19.535–68, 20.87, 21.79, 24.12), dreams have an even greater importance in the myth of Joseph.[70] Speiser (1962: 315) sums up their general function in his myth, "It is God, the author assures us through Joseph, who causes dreams to serve as guideposts to the future."

But the *Odyssey* and Joseph's myth both make central use of dreams in ways that separate them from most other myths and romances. In a more specific parallel, in each myth the protagonist, Odysseus and Joseph, is asked to interpret dreams, and does so. It is thematic in Joseph's myth that he can interpret dreams (Gen. 40:12–13, 18–19; 41:25–32), though, as is characteristic of OT myth, Joseph sees himself as merely a conduit, or vessel in the larger process, "All interpretation belongs to God" (Gen. 40:8); "Not I, but God, can give an answer which will reassure Pharaoh" (Gen. 41:16). In the climactic instance of his dream interpretation Joseph is able to avert disaster from Egypt, and mitigate the impact of the seven-year drought.

The *Odyssey* delays depicting Odysseus' ability to interpret dreams until the night before the suitors' destruction, in Penelope's postponed recognition.[71] Penelope asks the disguised Odysseus to interpret her dream of the eagle that breaks the necks of the twenty geese (*Od.* 19.535–53). She concludes her account, noting that the eagle announces that what has happened in the dream will be accomplished, and that he is Odysseus (*Od.* 19.549). But Penelope wonders if the dream might not necessarily predict the future. Given myth's equation of dream interpretation and prophecy, when Odysseus interprets the dream as predicting the destruction of the suitors (*Od.* 19.555–8), he parallels Theoklymenos as a prophetic figure, though Theoklymenos does so in more apocalyptic fashion. Since the suitors' various depredations of Ithaka (devouring Odysseus' estates, being figured as blood-sucking ticks in Argos' recognition scene: *Od.* 17.300,[72] and the like) parallel the effects of the great drought in Egypt in Joseph's myth, Odysseus' ability to interpret the dream which signals the suitors' destruction broadly parallels how Joseph through his ability to interpret dreams contains the threat of the drought on Egypt.

ODYSSEUS AND JOSEPH: AUTOLYKOS AND JACOB

Odysseus and Joseph share additional key similarities beyond their parallel trajectories as protagonists in their respective romances. They have a parallel

---

[70] On dreams' centrality in Joseph's myth, see Redford (1970: 68–71, 89–91).
[71] *Apollonius* (line 48) and *Pericles* both employ dreams to set up their climactic recognition scenes.
[72] Cf., de Jong (2001: 421): "The dog's body is covered with vermin, just as the palace is infected by the parasitic Suitors."

family inheritance, and participate in another specific genre of myth, the sack of a city. Each is descended from a trickster figure, Autolykos and Jacob. Odysseus' grandfather Autolykos (*Od.* 19.395–8, 406–9) is described as surpassing all men in thievery and oaths, endowed by Hermes in these acts. The *Iliad*, in the *Doloneia*, has Odysseus wearing a helmet stolen by Autolykos (*Il.* 10.267). The *Iliad* also helps us understand what excelling in oaths means. In Agamemnon's narrative about Ate (*Il.* 19.91–133) Zeus announces in a divine council that his descendant, about to be born, will rule those around him (*Il.* 19.101–5). But Hera arranges for Eurystheus to be advanced, instead of Zeus' son Herakles. Insisting that he swear an oath that this will be so, Hera then descends to earth to retard the birth of Herakles, and accelerate the birth of Eurystheus, also descended from Zeus. She thus subverts Zeus' intent, his oath stated ambiguously so that it also applies to Eurystheus. While her own agent will make life miserable for Herakles (*Il.* 19.106–20), Hera initiates her wrath against him even before he is born. Autolykos' skill in oaths may resemble what Hera does to Zeus, exploiting ambiguity. Angered (*Il.* 19.127) at what Hera has done, Zeus hurls Ate from Olympos. When Autolykos names his grandson *Odusseus*, he does so because he says he himself has *odussamenos*, provoked wrath (*Il.* 19.407), implicitly, in those he has robbed or tricked in oaths. Odysseus is thus named for the strong emotions his grandfather's provocative skills prompt in others.[73]

Joseph's father Jacob is also a trickster. In a scene that is the same genre of myth as Hera's deception of Zeus, Jacob, at the instigation of his mother Rebecca, deceives his father Isaac, tricking his brother, Esau, out of his birthright (Gen. 27).[74] Isaac had intended to give Esau his blessing (Gen. 27:1–4), but as soon as Rebecca learns of this, she arranges for her favorite, Jacob, to receive the blessing. Deceiving her husband Isaac in a number of ways, she cooks the meal he had asked Esau to get him, by slaying some of their livestock. While Esau is hunting, she has Jacob wear Esau's clothing and places on him the skins of the animals she has just cooked so Isaac, if he touches him, will think he feels the hairy Esau. Jacob then serves the meal, lies that he is Esau, and asks his father's blessing. The blind Isaac thinks he hears Jacob's voice, but smells Esau's clothes and feels the animal skins and, deceived, blesses Jacob.

The episode offers a homology for each major character in Hera's deception of Zeus. Perhaps closest of all are Rebecca and Hera, the wife who

---

[73] Though this, like similar passages in OT myth is a folk etymology.
[74] I can find no earlier commentator who has noted this parallel.

deceives her husband, and prevents him from blessing his favorite son. Esau, the hunter (a rare profession in OT myth), with rough hairy skin, favorite of his father, clearly parallels Heracles, though he is here already a young man, not about to be born as in *Iliad* 19. Both myths see the blessing as a speech-act that cannot be withdrawn, or even corrected. Isaac is an infirm father compared to Zeus, an aged man, blind, victimized to a greater extent. While the parallels between Jacob and Eurystheus may seem less compelling, each emerges having power over his father's favorite son, as a leader with wealth and power over others, but in a none too positive light, reaping the rewards of a status he does not deserve. The Septuagint uses *dolos* of Jacob's deception (μετὰ δόλου ἔλαβεν τὴν εὐλογίαν σου: Gen. 27:35) as the *Iliad* uses δολοφροσύνη of Hera (*Il.* 19.97, 112, δολοφρονέουσα: 19.106). Semele's request to see Zeus in his natural form (*Metamorphoses* 3.281–309), where it is again Hera who instigates the oath, is another instance of the same genre.[75] In these related episodes, Jacob, Hera, and presumably Autolokyos, manipulate others into making oaths for their own benefit. Jacob, in doing so to his own father and brother, demonstrates a thematic tendency to deceive members of his own family, as noted below.

Though the *Odyssey* does not depict Autolykos stealing anything, the extra-Homeric accounts repeatedly associate him with rustling livestock. Fernández-Galiano notes the tradition that Autolykos stole mares from Eurytos (1992: 151), "apparently Autolycus... stole the mares from Eurytus and entrusted them to Heracles... Heracles later refused to give them up."[76] Russo (1992: 96) summarizes other testimony about Autolykos, "a thief of horses, cattle, and sheep, who was successful through his trick of changing the animals' brands so as to deceive their owners." The *Odyssey* has a brief reference to a young Odysseus sent to recover sheep that had been rustled from Ithaka by men from Messene (*Od.* 21.16–21), an episode that dovetails with Autolykos' theft of Eurytos' mares. In Messene Odysseus meets Eurytos' son Iphitos, who is himself searching for the mares Autolykos stole. As a result of meeting Odysseus, Iphitos gives him the bow with which he later slays the suitors. But shortly after his hospitable meeting with Odysseus, Iphitos will die when he tries to reclaim the mares from Heracles (*Od.* 21.22–38).

---

[75] See Gantz (1993: 474–7) on the myth. Cf. *Metamorphoses* 1.755–2.46, in which Clymene encourages Phaethon to go to Apollo for proof that he is his son, as yet another instance of the same mythic subgenre (see W. S. Anderson 1997: 366 on parallels between the two Ovidian episodes). In all four instances, the father's favorite, whether son or paramour, suffers a tragic reversal.

[76] Mentioned briefly in Apollodorus, II.6.2.

For its relevance to the myth of Jacob I quote Gantz's summary of the extra-Homeric tradition at length (1993: 110):

As early as the *Ehoiai*, Autolykos... has the capacity to make things "unseen," or change their skin color (*chroia*), or somehow alter their markings (*sphragides*); these talents bring him many of other men's herds and flocks. So too in Pherekydes he can change the nurslings of herds into whatever shapes he wishes, and in Ovid and Hyginus (*Fab.* 201) make white from black and black from white, or (Hyginus only) put horns on animals without them and take them away from those with them.

Gantz adduces additional late sources including paintings (1993: 176):

Later sources report that Autolykos, the father of Antikleia... had used his skills in thievery and metamorphosis to increase his own herds at the expense of Sisyphos', but was nevertheless caught when Sisyphos began carving a monogram of his name on the hooves of his animals... A Megarian bowl from the second century actually shows... scenes in which Autloykos... seems to be removing cattle from a protesting Sisyphos.

In the *Homeric Hymn to Hermes*, Hermes' theft of Apollo's cattle gives some idea of how Autolykos may have operated as a thief. At his birth Hermes is called both a robber (ληϊστῆρ') and a driver of cattle (ἐλατῆρα βοῶν), which, since they occur consecutively (line 14), may function as a hendiadys, a "robber of cattle." At Pieria, where the gods have their herds, Hermes separates fifty of Apollo's cattle from the rest, disguising his theft by having the cattle walk backwards (lines 76–8), leaving tracks suggesting they walked away from where he leads them. Hermes also makes sandals of green brushwood, twigs of tamarisk and myrtle (lines 79–84), to disguise his own footprints (Gaisser 1983: 8), which subsequently baffle Apollo (222–5, 342–9). Leading his stolen herd to the river Alpheios, Hermes cuts a bay branch, and invents the method of starting a fire by rubbing twigs together (lines 107–11). When Hermes takes Apollo to where the cattle are hidden, Apollo makes bonds for Hermes out of willow twigs, but instead of bonding Hermes the twigs grow around and conceal the cattle (lines 409–13). When Apollo is later reconciled to Hermes, accepting his gift of the tortoise-shell lyre for the cattle he sacrificed, Hermes proclaims that the bulls will mate with the cows and bear calves in plenty, as West points out (2003: 13), confirming Hermes as "god of the pastures."

While Jacob is not actually depicted stealing anything, he is thought a thief by his father-in-law, Laban (Gen. 31:26), and by Laban's sons (Gen. 31:1–2). The methods Jacob uses to acquire livestock from Laban resemble Gantz's descriptions of Autolykos and details in the *Homeric Hymn to Hermes*. Gantz (1993: 110) notes that Autolykos was able to "change the nurslings of herds into whatever shapes he wishes, and in Ovid and Hyginus (*Fab.* 201) make white from black and black from white." This is close to how Genesis depicts Jacob gaining livestock from Laban. Under Jacob's tendance, Laban's flocks prosper (Gen. 30:29, 43), roughly paralleling Hermes as the god of the pastures. When he attempts to collect wages from Laban, Jacob asks for new-born lambs that are black and brindled, and goats that are spotted (Gen. 30:32). If any are found among his flocks that are not so colored or marked they may be regarded as stolen (Gen. 30:33), associating Jacob with possible theft of livestock. Agreeing to the terms, Laban quickly removes all such livestock to prevent Jacob from being able to mate the appropriate animals. But taking fresh cuttings of poplar, almond, and plane trees, Jacob has regular lambs mate in the presence of these rods, and they bring forth appropriately colored offspring (Gen. 30:37–9). Working a similar strategy with the goats, he has only the stronger specimens mate, acquiring only the more vigorous offspring. (Gen. 30:41–2). Then keeping his departure secret, Jacob heads off with his now considerable flocks (Gen. 31:20–1).

Jacob, Hermes, and Autolykos all thus participate in the same genre of myth. Each uses what could be called magic to obtain herds of livestock by changing their form and appearance, and their coloring. Cut branches figure prominently in each to effect some of the magic or sleight of hand, and bring about the transfer of the livestock from Apollo to Hermes, Laban to Jacob, from Eurytos/Sisyphos to Autolykos. Jacob's myth sets his sneaky acquisition of livestock within the larger context of strife between the two brothers, Jacob and Esau, much as the *Homeric Hymn to Hermes* places Hermes' theft of Apollo's cattle within the context of a dispute between those divine brothers.

Apollodorus (II.4.9) relates that Autolykos taught Herakles how to wrestle, a talent that Odysseus also clearly inherits (*Il.* 23.700–37; *Od.* 4.343–4 = 17.134–5). Jacob's myth twice depicts him as a wrestler.[77] In the account of the brothers' birth, Jacob grasps Esau by the heel, while they are still in the womb (Gen. 25:26). In a later episode, Jacob wrestles with god (Gen. 32:23–32, explored in Chapter 4). Autolykos' only lines in all of Homer (*Od.* 19.406–12) contain his naming of Odysseus (*Od.* 19.406–9), which is also a blessing scene, like Jacob's with Isaac, but with the Jacob figure performing the blessing rather than receiving it.

---

[77] I thank Terry Bell for pointing out this parallel (oral communication 1994).

The characteristics inherited from their trickster progenitors, a willingness to use deception, a wiliness with words, to which the physical analogy is wrestling, are precisely the qualities that enable Odysseus and Joseph to manage the postponed recognition scenes to which they subject their relatives.[78]

JOSEPH IN GENESIS 34 AND ODYSSEUS IN THE TROJAN WAR

Before the romance portions of their myths begin, Joseph and Odysseus both take part in the sack of a city. Though there is a considerable difference in the scale of the Trojan War and the episodes involving Shechem (Gen. 34), the central motifs, the rape of Dinah and subsequent sack of Hamor's city by Jacob's sons, parallel those that form the core of the larger Trojan War saga.[79] Attracted to Jacob's daughter, Dinah, Shechem, a Hivite, rapes her, but then seeks to marry her. He persuades his father, Hamor, to meet with Jacob, and seek marriage with Dinah. But Jacob's sons are angry over Dinah's rape. Hamor offers to let the two peoples share the land, and let the sons of either people marry the daughters of the other (Gen. 34:8–10). Eager to make amends, Shechem offers to pay the highest bride-price (Gen. 34:11–12). But Jacob's sons deceitfully (Gen. 34:13: μετὰ δόλου in the Septuagint, as at Gen. 27:35 of Jacob deceiving Isaac) insist that Shechem, Hamor, and every male of their people be circumcised, or they cannot let their sister marry him. Shechem agrees. He and his father announce the condition to their city, persuading every able-bodied man to be circumcised (Gen. 34: 20–4). But while all the Hivite men are recovering, two of Jacob's sons, Simeon and Levi, enter the town and kill all the men, including Shechem and Hamor, and take Dinah back (Gen. 34:25–6). Jacob's other sons (including the unnamed Joseph) then go among the corpses and plunder the town, seizing flocks, wealth, women, and everything in the houses (Gen. 34:27–9).

The myth of Shechem offers parallels for many of the central motifs and characters of the Trojan War. Shechem is very much the sensualist that Paris is, though less irresponsible. He attempts to make amends, beyond what Paris offers in the *Iliad* (who offers only to return the goods he plundered from Menelaus' house: *Il.* 7.362–4). The fathers of Shechem/Paris,

---

[78] We reconsider much of Jacob's myth in Chapter 6 for its parallels with Odysseus, Nausikaa, and Kirke, and Jason and Medea.

[79] See Louden (2006: 152); Cf. Niditch (1993: 107) on Genesis 34: "As in the Greek Trojan War tradition or the biblical tale of Judges 19–21, the cause for war involves the misuse by men of a woman belonging to another man or men."

Hamor and Priam, are quite similar. Hamor's generosity, magnanimity, and gracious conduct, all parallel Priam's chief positive qualities. Hamor is perhaps too easily gulled into thinking all is well, as are the Trojans when they accept the Horse.

Dinah's brothers, Simeon and Levi, act much as the Greek brothers, Agamemnon and Menelaos (and those who had sworn oaths to aid Helen). When Menelaus considers sparing the Trojan Adrestos, Agamemnon persuades him not to:

> Did the Trojans really do best by you in your house?
> Let none of them escape sheer destruction at our hands,
> not even the babe whom a mother carries in her womb;
> let them all perish from Troy, unwept, without a trace!
> *Iliad* 6.56–60

Nestor urges the Greek troops to remember the rape of Helen:

> Therefore let no one be eager to return home
> until he lies next to a wife of the Trojans
> and avenges the mournful struggles of Helen.
> *Iliad* 2.354–6

Jacob's sons are quite close to such sentiments in their justification for sacking and looting the city: "Is our sister to be treated as a common whore?" (Gen. 34:31). Their use of deception, having the Hivites circumcised to incapacitate them, offers a rough parallel to the Greeks sacking Troy by deception and trickery with the Trojan Horse. Jacob's sons not only have the element of surprise, as do the Greeks, but the Hivites are already incapacitated, unlike the Trojan warriors. Dinah's beauty offers a smaller parallel to Helen's, though the myth gives no account of her own reactions, unlike Homeric epic's nuanced portrayal of Helen.

In perhaps the biggest difference, Shechem's myth depicts Jacob's sons in a dishonorable light, maximizing their dishonesty and deception, approaching a kind of Euripidean perspective, portraying the sack of the city through a more realistic, anti-heroic lens. Shechem is less reckless than Paris; his eagerness to undergo circumcision engages our sympathy more than do Jacob's sons. This roughly parallels the *Iliad*'s larger strategy of emphasizing sympathetic traits in Trojans such as Andromakhe, Hektor, and Priam, but ruthlessness in some of the Greeks (e.g., as at *Il.* 2.354–6, 6.56–60). Though not specified by name, Joseph is one of Jacob's sons who take part in the plundering of the city (Gen. 34:27–9). Jacob himself, now a peace-loving older man (Speiser 1962: 268), condemns what his sons have done, knowing they will now be hated throughout the area (Gen. 34:30).

Though Genesis leaves Joseph's role unspecified, as opposed to the Trojan War saga assigning Odysseus central responsibility, the unexpected parallel nonetheless remains. The larger myths of Odysseus and Joseph share parallel narrative trajectories, with each character coming from a trickster inheritance, to participation in the sack of a city, then becoming a romance protagonist. Since most of Genesis 36 offers unrelated background material, the romance part of Joseph's myth begins very quickly after he and his brothers plunder the city, just as happens with Odysseus.

CHAPTER 4

Odyssey 4
Helen and Rahab (Josh. 2); Menelaus and Jacob (Gen. 32:22–32)

Tales told by characters other than Odysseus comprise a significant part of the *Odyssey*. Unlike theoxeny, romance, Argonautic myth, or apocalypse, these tales do not inform the structure of the *Odyssey*, they reflect it, and have a more local impact and function. While he is Menelaus' guest, Telemachos hears two such tales, Helen's account of Odysseus entering Troy disguised as a beggar (*Od.* 4.242–58), and Menelaus' tale of how he wrestled the sea god Proteus (*Od.* 4.351–586). Both tales employ themes central to the *Odyssey*, disguise and espionage (*Od.* 4.242–58), wandering and prophecy (*Od.* 4.351–586), serving as miniatures of key parts of the epic's larger story. Helen's tale of Odysseus as a spy, disguised as a beggar to gain intelligence before Troy's destruction, prefigures his approach to the suitors, which will result in their apocalyptic destruction. The episode also serves as a miniature of one of the epic's favorite scenarios: Odysseus encounters a powerful female and comes to terms with her.[1] Menelaus' tale of being stranded on Pharos and wrestling Proteus prefigures Odysseus' wanderings, the prophecy he receives from Teiresias, and the climactic events on Thrinakia.

Both tales, however, have significant connections *outside* the *Odyssey* as well. Old Testament myth has a close counterpart for each narrative. When Joshua sends spies into Jericho, the narrative ignores intelligence gathering, focusing instead on their meeting with the prostitute Rahab, and her efforts to keep them safe and prevent their identities from being disclosed (Josh. 2). The tale is the same genre of myth as Helen's account of receiving the disguised Odysseus, and swearing an oath not to reveal his identity. Both narratives focus on the spies' interactions with the woman who is about to switch allegiance, deserting the people with whom she lives, going over to the side of the invaders plotting to sack the city. Jacob wrestling

---
[1] See Louden (1999: 4–14), on parallels between Odysseus' approaches to Kirke, Nausikaa, Arete, and Penelope, and 104–22 on how his relationship with Kalypso differs from that with Kirke.

with god and receiving a blessing (Gen. 32.22–32; cf. 28.10–22) is the same genre of myth as Menelaus wrestling with Proteus,[1] receiving answers to his question, and a prophecy of his own future blessed existence on the Elysian Isle. The parallels between the two sets of myths are extensive and instructive. The two OT narratives provide contexts for the two tales in Book 4, allowing us to gain a surer sense of what is traditional in these mythic genres, and what details may be more specific to the *Odyssey*'s own narrative agenda.

HELEN AND RAHAB: THE WOMAN WHO RECEIVES THE ENEMY SPY AND PRESERVES HIS IDENTITY (*OD.* 4.242–58, JOSH. 2)

While entertaining Telemachos in Sparta, Helen and Menelaus each narrates a tale, ostensibly, of Odysseus' exploits at Troy (*Od.* 4.240–1). The real focus of both tales, however, is Helen herself. Helen's own tale (*Od.* 4.244–64) relates how a disguised Odysseus entered Troy, shortly before it was to be sacked, for reconnaissance. For his disguise he whipped himself, and threw on some shabby clothes (σπεῖρα κάκ'), both acts intended to make him resemble a run-away slave, or beggar (*Od.* 4.244–8).[3] Once within the city no one recognizes him except Helen (*Od.* 4.250), who questions him, though unable to learn anything from him (*Od.* 4.251). She then bathes him, anoints him with olive oil (*Od.* 4.252: χρῖον), and clothes him, all acts of hospitality which mirror Telemachos' present circumstances (being hospitably received by Helen), and look ahead to how Odysseus will be received by Penelope and Eurykleia in Book 19.[4] When she swears an oath not to reveal his identity to the Trojans until he is back among the Greeks (*Od.* 4.253), he reveals to her the Greeks' plans for invading and sacking Troy, though the details are not given in this story. Odysseus returns to the Greek camp, slaying several Trojans on the way, and is said to bring back much information to the Greeks (*Od.* 4.258), though again the details are not given. While Trojan women cry out in horror when they find the men Odysseus has slain, Helen is happy, having switched her allegiance back to the Greeks (*Od.* 4.259–61).

Prior to attempting the sack of Jericho, Joshua sends two spies to scout the city. They go to the house of a prostitute, Rahab, to spend the night (Josh. 2:1). When the king of Jericho learns of their presence, he sends men

---

[2] Nagy (2005: 76) notes Lord's suggestion (1960: 197) that Jacob wrestling with the angel finds a parallel in Akhilleus' fight with Xanthos.
[3] See Gantz (1993: 643) for extra-Homeric references to Odysseus having himself whipped or beaten, to disguise his face.
[4] S. West (1988: 209).

asking Rahab to produce the spies. Rahab claims she does not know where the spies have gone, though she has hidden them on her roof (Josh. 2:2–6). Having misdirected the king's messengers, she meets with the spies (Josh. 2:7–8), declaring her belief that Yahweh will deliver Jericho to the invaders (Josh. 2.9–10). She then asks them to swear an oath that, as she kept them safe, so they will preserve her and her family when they sack the city (Josh. 2:11–14). Overseeing their escape, she advises them where to hide (Josh. 2:15–16). They arrange for her to leave a red cord as a sign for the invaders to spare her house when they sack the city (Josh. 2:17–21).

Though there are significant differences, some of which result from the different contexts and different purposes for which the *Odyssey* and OT employ the tales (e.g., the *Odyssey* places greater stress on the myth's use of hospitable reception and Odysseus' traditional traits as a master of cunning and disguise, while the OT myth employs Rahab for its favorite polemic, Yahweh as the one true god), a considerable number of parallels demonstrate that the two narratives are instances of the same genre of myth. Both tales are set immediately before the sack of their respective cities, Troy and Jericho. Both myths thus function as a subset of larger siege myths, in which each narrative identifies with the invading force planning to sack the city (as opposed to identifying with those about to be sacked).[5] Each larger myth, the sack of the respective cities, will conclude with a middle-degree apocalypse. Though the depiction of the god-directed sack of Troy falls outside of the *Odyssey*, the parallel episodes come shortly after Rahab's scene in Joshua. While Yahweh's wrath against Jericho is never specified, his anger against the Canaanites is mentioned. He and an unnamed angel (Josh. 5:13–15)[6] not only assist Joshua and the Israelites, but direct the entire sack of Jericho (Josh. 1:1–9, 2:9–11, 14, 24). The subsequent level of violence in the destruction of Jericho is, if anything, greater than that at Troy. All the inhabitants are put under the ban; all are slaughtered, men, women, and children, except Rahab and her household (Josh. 6:16–17, 20–4). Joshua wins fame (Josh. 6:27), from sacking Jericho, as Odysseus and other Greeks do from the sack of Troy.

In both narratives the spies' reconnaissance of the city is mere pretext to allow a focus on their interaction with the unique woman.[7] As the episode ends, we are told that Odysseus took back much intelligence

---

[5] On siege myth as a mythic genre, see Louden (2006: 149–54).
[6] See Louden (2006: 221) on this episode as broadly parallel to the aid Athena and Poseidon give to Akhilleus and other Greeks in the *Iliad*.
[7] Cf. Boling (1982: 144): "The narrator's interest does not center, really, in military reconnaissance"; and (145): "It remains true that the visit to her house was the sum total of the men's reconnaissance activity."

(*Od.* 4.258), but not told *what* the information is, just as we are not told what the Greek plans were that he communicated to Helen (*Od.* 4.256), reinforcing that the actual intelligence gathering is inconsequential, just a prompt for the plot (a Hitchcock Maguffin). Earlier, Odysseus dodges Helen's questions (*Od.* 4.251), but his ability to do so is thematic in the *Odyssey* (West 1988: 210), anticipating the scenes with Eurykleia and Penelope. This detail is not relevant to Rahab's myth, because the OT lacks any further depiction of the spies. They have no thematic traits to depict.

Helen and Rahab share a considerable number of thematic parallels. Both women are highly ambivalent characters, in their sexuality, and in switching allegiance during war. Both serve in their cultures as objects of sexual desire. Rahab is explicitly a prostitute (γυναικὸς ... πόρνης, in the Septuagint, Josh. 2:1).[8] Helen, most beautiful woman in the world (see *Il.* 3.154–60), Paris' prize, or bribe, for picking Aphrodite in the Judgment, suggests partial parallels to a prostitute as an unfaithful wife. Her sexual infidelity and marital ambiguity are highlighted in *Iliad* Book 3 when, knowing that Paris should be on the battlefield finishing his duel with Menelaus, she cannot resist having sex with him. In preserving Odysseus' safety, thereby ensuring Troy's destruction and Paris' death, Helen is now cheating on *him*, in a sense.[9]

Both women display similar ambivalence in their allegiance to the people among whom they currently live. Rahab and Helen each knowingly receives an enemy spy, and preserves his identity, suppressing information about their cities' impending destruction. Each woman, engaging in sex outside of marriage, forming temporary, impermanent unions, parallels her pivotal switch in allegiance in the war. In their allegiance to the advance spies and the invading forces that sent them, Rahab and Helen are duplicitous and treacherous to the people among whom they now live. The *Odyssey* addresses the moral dilemma in Helen's comment on her change of heart. In effect she apologizes for having temporarily gone over to the Trojans, assigning responsibility to Ate (*Od.* 4.260–4), much as Agamemnon does at *Iliad* 19.86–137, for his quarrel with Akhilleus. Rahab's myth subsumes her change of allegiance under a favorite OT polemic: since Rahab now recognizes Yahweh as "the one true god," the narrative ignores any moral ambiguity in her betraying her people, like Helen, switching her allegiance

---

[8] See Boling (1982: 144–5) on Rahab as a prostitute, her establishment as a brothel, and the debate about whether she is a secular or cultic prostitute.
[9] Cf. S. West's comment (1988: 209), "the lability of Helen's character."

right before her city is sacked. Both women will subsequently identify with the invaders.

Hospitality figures in both episodes, but in very different degrees. In Rahab's tale the spies intend to spend the night at her house (Josh. 2:1), which, though a brothel, makes her their hostess, in a sense. In her subsequent interaction with the king's men, she keeps the spies safe under her protection, somewhat as Lot and his angelic guests. Helen receives Odysseus into her house, bathes him, anoints him with olive oil, and clothes him, exemplary hospitality (*Od.* 4.252–3).[10] Since the *Odyssey* makes pronounced thematic use of hospitality myth, some details of Helen's reception, bathing, anointing, and clothing Odysseus (absent in Rahab's myth) are present for thematic reasons within the *Odyssey* and may not be part of the traditional mythic genre. Helen's hospitable reception of Odysseus looks ahead to Odysseus' scenes in Book 19 with Eurykleia and Penelope (de Jong 2001: 102) in addition to offering counterpoint to Helen's entertainment of Telemachos.

Both myths highlight the oaths sworn between the woman and the spy. Helen swears an oath that she will not reveal Odysseus' identity to the Trojans until he is back in the Greek camp (*Od.* 4.253–4). Rahab has Joshua's spies swear an oath that, because she has preserved their lives, they will spare her and her family when they sack the city (Josh. 2:12–14, 17–20). In both myths the spies reveal their plans to the woman who shelters them. Though the details are not given in either version to the external audience, Odysseus apparently reveals to her the plan of the Trojan Horse (*Od.* 4.256; de Jong 2001: 101). Rahab lies to the king's men to safeguard the spies (Josh. 2:2–7); Helen is delighted at the Trojan women's anguish when they discover the men Odysseus has slain (*Od.* 4.259–60).

Rahab and Helen know that the enemy army will be successful because both women have a special relationship with god, and are part of an illustrious line. Helen is the daughter of Zeus, and will not go to Hades when her mortal existence concludes, but will be rewarded with an existence on the Elysian Plain at the ends of the earth (*Od.* 4.564–9),[11] a topic we return to below. Rahab is not only depicted as fully aware of Yahweh's power, but given surprising prominence as Boling notes (1982: 146), "The pagan prostitute is the first one to recite saving history in the final edition of the book." It does not stop here. New Testament myth asserts Jesus is

---

[10] Cf. S. West (1988: 210): "Helen presents herself to Telemachus as his father's hostess."
[11] Discussion in S. West (1988: 227); cf. Apollodorus. *Epit.* 6.30.

descended from Rahab (Matt. 1:5),[12] giving her a status that in some ways parallels Helen's descent from Zeus in Greek myth.

Perhaps the biggest difference between the narratives, and an indication of how the two traditions put the same mythic type to different purposes through different emphases, is the identities of the spies. Rahab's two spies are anonymous figures with no existence outside of her tale. In the larger myth of the sack of Jericho they are subordinate to Joshua, who will sack the city. Quite opposite, in the larger myth of the sack of Troy, Odysseus is the advance spy *and* the city sacker. Much more than Joshua, let alone the nameless entities that are his spies, Odysseus is a complete, fully developed entity, center of an entire mythic tradition. That the *Odyssey* casts Odysseus in both roles is entirely appropriate given the thematic organization of Homeric epic. Since Odysseus is the spy in Helen's tale, certain Odyssean traits and skills are given his spy character, that Rahab's spies lack. In Helen's tale Odysseus is a master of disguise. None of the Trojans except Helen can recognize him (*Od.* 4.250). His disguise is the same he will have from the end of Book 13 to the middle of Book 23. Rahab's generic spies do not use or need disguise; Rahab hides them (Josh. 2:4, 2:6) among stalks of flax. Her concealing them functions thematically much as does Odysseus' disguise in Helen's tale. Only Rahab knows where she conceals them; only Helen recognizes Odysseus.

The presence of *two* spies in Rahab's myth suggests parallels with other Homeric episodes. In the *Iliad* diplomatic missions almost always involve *two* heralds (*Il.* 1.320–48, 9.170), recognized by those who receive them as serving a sacred function, under Zeus' protection. In a sense the spies in Helen's and Rahab's tales are engaged in covert diplomacy. They negotiate and agree upon terms, but with the mysterious woman, not the king of the besieged city. In the *Iliad* virtually all diplomatic missions are conducted by Odysseus,[13] who is also closely associated with heralds throughout Homeric epic, and has his own herald, Eurybates.[14] The *Iliad* recounts a diplomatic mission by Odysseus that preceded the Trojan War, when he and Menelaus came to Troy to seek the restoration of Helen by peaceful means (*Il.* 3.205–24). The present covert mission, also carried out by Odysseus, suggests something like ring composition with that earlier embassy. He now makes

---

[12] Boling (1982: 145).
[13] Cf. B. Hainsworth (1993: 81): "Diplomatic business in the *Iliad* is conducted by Odysseus alone ... or by Odysseus and an appropriate or interested party."
[14] On Odysseus' thematic association with heralds, and Eurybates, see our discussion in Chapter 3 of Penelope's postponed recognition scene in Book 19, and see Louden (2006: 121–34, 142–3).

arrangements that will result in the restoration of Helen to Menelaus, if by less than peaceful means.

THEANO AND THE PALLADIUM

Though not mentioned in the *Odyssey*, Theano, priestess of Athena and Antenor's wife, is a further instantiation of the same genre of myth in which Helen and Rahab here take part. Within the *Iliad* she serves as the example of a moral Trojan woman, as Antenor is the moral Trojan man (discussion in Louden 2006: 194). It is Theano who performs the sacrifice to Athena (*Il.* 6.297–311). In the larger extra-Homeric Trojan War saga, it is Theano, in several accounts (Gantz 1993: 643), who turns over the Palladium to Odysseus and Diomedes.[15] The Palladium, a sacred icon of Athena, functions in Greek myth much as the Ark does in OT myth (Louden 2006: 223; McCarter 1985: 109). The Ark itself figures in Rahab's myth, and is used in the sack of Jericho, though not in direct connection with Rahab. Like the Greeks' possession of the Palladium as necessary to sack Troy, the Israelites use the Ark as an offensive weapon while they sack Jericho (Josh. 3:3, 6; 4:11; 6:4, 6–9, 11–13). Elsewhere, the Ark is captured by an enemy, the Philistines (1 Sam. 4:11), that OT people most like the Greeks themselves, like Odysseus taking possession of the Palladium.

In the surviving elliptic accounts, Odysseus and Diomedes are involved in the theft of the Palladium. The duo, who serve as a pair thematically in the *Iliad* (10.349–469, 11.313, 19.47–49; discussion in Louden 2006: 132), suggest parallels with Rahab's *two* spies. Commentators have speculated that Helen's reception of the disguised Odysseus is connected with the theft of the Palladium (Gantz 1993: 642), the initial reconnaissance that makes the theft successful. Sophocles' lost play, the *Lakainai*, dealt with the capture of the Palladium, and apparently depicted Theano handing it over to Odysseus and Diomedes (Gantz 1993: 642–3, 645).[16] The title of the play, probably designating a chorus of Helen's servants (Lloyd-Jones 1996: 197), may suggest her involvement, or complicity, in the Palladium's theft. Other late sources depict Theano handing the Palladium over after

---

[15] Theano's turning over the Palladium may also be a thematic parallel to her husband Antenor's suggestion (*Il.* 7.347–53) that the Trojans return Helen to the Greeks. In some accounts (Gantz 1993: 643) it is Antenor who helps the Greeks obtain the Palladium, reinforcing the thematic parallels between husband and wife.

[16] Later accounts also depict Theano as present in the earlier diplomatic mission when Odysseus and Menelaus, another diplomatic duo, came to Troy to seek Helen's release before the war. Since the *Iliad* specifies that Antenor was their host on that occasion (*Il.* 3.205–24), Theano's involvement, and earlier acquaintance with Odysseus, also seems part of the Homeric tradition.

Odysseus and Diomedes apparently have come on an embassy to Priam (Gantz 1993: 643). Whether these details go back to Homeric epic or not, they suggest intriguing parallels with the prominence of the king of Jericho in Rahab's myth.

Theano and Rahab share further parallels that Helen lacks. Each is told to place a marker on the house so that it will be spared when the rest of the city is sacked. The spies tell Rahab to fasten a scarlet cord in her window so her household will be spared when Jericho is sacked (Josh. 2:18–21). Antenor is told to place a leopard-skin outside the door of his and Theano's house to indicate that it is to be spared.[17] A fragment from Sophocles' play, *Ajax the Locrian* (Lloyd-Jones 1996: 16–17) describes the leopard-skin. As priestess of Athena, Theano also offers more obvious parallels than Helen to Rahab's close relation with Yahweh. In handing over Athena's Palladium to the Greeks, implicitly, Theano puts loyalty to Athena above loyalty to her own people (the Trojans), making her unexpectedly parallel the specific trait OT myth most strongly emphasizes in Rahab. A fragment from Sophocles' *Lakainai*, thought to be spoken by Odysseus or Diomedes to Theano (Odysseus is more likely, given his thematic role of speaking for the Greek cause in the *Iliad*, e.g., 2.284–332, 19.155–83, and 19.216–37), articulates that, much as Yahweh is for the Israelites in Rahab's myth, the gods are on the Greeks' side:

> For the gods will never approve these things,
> if it is right at all for a mortal to reason,
> since the Phrygians began the outrage against the Argives.[18]

The motifs and key details in Rahab's myth are a composite of those in Helen's narrative and in the larger myth of Theano and Antenor.

Theano and Antenor serve as a frame, or bookends, around all of the fighting in the Trojan War, other than the actual sack of the city. Before fighting begins, they host the duo of Odysseus and Menelaus when they come on the embassy seeking Helen's return (*Il.* 3.205–24, Bacchylides 15, Gantz 1993: 594–6). After all fighting is complete, other than the sack of the city, Theano again "hosts" Odysseus (and Diomedes), much as Rahab hosts her spies. Though the *Iliad* makes no explicit reference to these events, the *Doloneia*, in which Diomedes and Odysseus, the same pair who gain possession of the Palladium, sneak into the Trojan camp at night, offers key parallels. Odysseus slays many Trojans on his way back to the

---

[17] "According to Sophocles during the capture of Troy a leopard-skin was placed in front of Antenor's house to indicate that his house was to be left unplundered" (Strabo, in Lloyd-Jones 1996: 54).
[18] Fragment 368, Lloyd-Jones (1996: 196–7).

Greek ships in Helen's narrative (*Od.* 4.257–8), just as in the *Doloneia* Diomedes and Odysseus slay thirteen Trojans on their way back to the Greek camp (*Il.* 10.482–97). Odysseus and Diomedes obtain the Palladium from Theano, as in the *Doloneia* Odysseus and Diomedes, having slain Rhesus, gain possession of his horses. The death of Rhesus and capture of his horses seem to serve within the *Iliad* as a thematic parallel for the items which, outside of the *Iliad*, the Greeks must obtain before Troy can be sacked, the Palladium, and Philoctetes' bow.[19]

Aeneid 2, in its portrayal of Helen from a Trojan perspective, depicts the flip side of the same genre of myth: the woman who helps the invading force shown from the perspective of the besieged people she now betrays. In his narration to Dido, Aeneas briefly mentions Odysseus and Diomedes' theft of the Palladium (*Aen.* 2.163–8) as a transition into the sack of Troy. The climax of his narration of Troy's fall is his own uncontrollable fury on seeing Helen. Only Venus' intervention prevents him from slaying her (*Aen.* 2.568–620). Aeneas' meeting with Deïphobos in the underworld (*Aen.* 6.509–34) brings out further parallels between Helen, Rahab, and Theano. Deïphobos narrates how after the Horse was drawn into the city, Helen led the women in a feigned ritual Bacchic dance in which her torch also served as a signal to the invading Greeks (*Aen.* 6.517–19). Helen not only replays her change of loyalty, as in her sheltering Odysseus, but instantiates the association with religious authority so central to Theano and Rahab.[20]

WRESTLING WITH GOD: MENELAUS (*OD.* 4. 351–586) AND JACOB (GEN. 32.22–32)

OT myth also offers a significant parallel for a second narrative Telemachos hears in Sparta, Menelaus' encounter with Proteus. Trapped in Egypt, Menelaus' struggle to return home offers a capsule version of several motifs used in Odysseus' wanderings. Like Odysseus, Menelaus has provoked a divine wrath, having offended a god (*Od.* 4.378: ἀλιτέσθαι),[21] and is now unable to cross the sea and return home from Troy. A lack of wind keeps him at Pharos (*Od.* 4.360–1), thematically parallel, if presented in its negative form, to events on Thrinakia, where adverse winds prevent

---

[19] Petegorsky (1982: 211, 222).
[20] Theano (10.703) and Antenor (*Aen.* 1.242, 6.483) are also mentioned in the *Aeneid*, but not in connection with the Palladium. Greek myth has a further instance of the same genre of myth, in the saga of the Seven Against Thebes, when Eriphyle betrays Amphiareus (Gantz 1993: 506–10).
[21] We discuss the nature of Odysseus' offence against Poseidon in Chapter 7.

departure (*Od.* 12.313–14, 325–6, discussed in Chapter 10). His men are reduced to fishing (*Od.* 4.368–9) as is Odysseus' crew on Thrinakia (*Od.* 12.331–2; S. West 1988: 216). A goddess comes to him out of pity, Eidothea, whose role suggests parallels with the similarly named Leukothea (*Od.* 5.336), but also with Kirke, and Nausikaa,[22] in their interactions with Odysseus. Once he has successfully managed his encounter with Proteus, because of Eidothea's advice, Menelaus receives divine information from him, including a prophecy about how his life will end (*Od.* 4.561–9), much as Odysseus does from Teiresias (*Od.* 11.134–7).[23] Menelaus also learns about the fate of various relatives and comrades, as Odysseus does in Hades immediately after his consultation with Teiresias (Plass 1969: 105). In this way Menelaus' tale of being stranded off Egypt offers in brief compass key motifs Odysseus experiences in several separate encounters in Books 9–12.

Though commentators usually compare the episode with others in Greek myth, Peleus wrestling Thetis, Zeus with Metis, or Herakles wrestling with the rivers Nereus and Achelous (e.g., Detienne and Vernant 1974: 111–14; cf. S. West 1988: 220), episodes that do contain relevant parallels, OT myth offers the closest ancient parallel. When Jacob takes his wives, slave girls, and children across the river Jabbok, he then wrestles a "man" (Gen. 32:22–4).[24] Like Menelaus with Proteus, key to his victory is maintaining his grip on his foe. His opponent turns out to be god, and the two eventually engage in dialogue. The Septuagint uses παλαίω twice to describe Jacob's encounter (Gen. 32:24, 25). Though the *Odyssey* does not use παλαίω of Menelaus' acts, the repeated emphasis on how he must hold Proteus aligns his encounter with wrestling.

Both encounters occupy parallel positions in the larger narrative trajectories of the protagonists. Menelaus and Jacob are both trying to return home after having been away for many years, a generation. For each, wrestling with god is the final obstacle in their attempts to return home. For each their encounter helps prepare them in some crucial way for their homecoming. Each awaits an anxious reunion with his brother, though both meetings will be distinctly anticlimactic. For both, their brothers are a key factor in their absence from home, though the reasons are quite different. Jacob fears Esau will want revenge for having been cheated out

---

[22] See Powell (1977: 56) on overall parallels between the two goddesses.
[23] Powell, *ibid.*; cf. de Jong (2001: 106) on the overall parallels. See also Beck (2005a: 218 ff.) on how Menelaus resembles Odysseus as a narrator.
[24] Lord (1960: 197) suggested Jacob wrestling with Yahweh as a parallel for Akhilleus' duel with Xanthos. But we will observe significantly closer correspondences with Menelaus wrestling Proteus.

of his father's blessing (Gen. 32:11–21); Menelaus does not yet know of Agamemnon's death, but will hear of it from Proteus himself.

For each protagonist the survival of his group is in jeopardy, immediately before his wrestling encounter. Menelaus has been unable to leave Pharos for twenty days, his food supplies exhausted and his men's strength failing (*Od.* 4.360–9). The goddess Eidothea comes to him out of pity (*Od.* 4.364) as he wanders by himself away from his companions. Jacob, "much afraid and distressed" (Gen. 32:7), divides his company into two, so that if Esau attacks him, at least half of his company will survive. He prays to god for help, invoking the previous time he crossed the Jordan (Gen. 32:9–12; discussed below).

Both then wrestle a god (*theopalaisty*, for those who would prefer a Greek designation), where the water meets the land. Proteus is a sea god, the Old Man of the Sea (γέρων ἅλιος). The episode unfolds on the shore of the island of Pharos, off Egypt. Jacob's narrative is more vague, even enigmatic, about the nature of his opponent, first referred to as a "man" (Gen. 32:24–8, ἄνθρωπος, in the Septuagint). But elsewhere OT myth refers to god or an angel in an encounter with mortals in this same way (cf., Josh. 5:13–14). As Menelaus wrestles Proteus in the breakers of the sea, Jacob wrestles Yahweh at the edge of the river Jabbok, or possibly in a ford in the river. Suggs (1992) (on Gen. 32:24–6) conjectures as to the nature of the god, "He may have been, in the earliest circulation of the story, either a border guardian or the 'spirit' of the river."[25] One of the forms Proteus assumes is that of "moist water"(*Od.* 4.458: γίγνετο δ' ὑγρὸν ὕδωρ), almost as if Menelaus were wrestling a river. Further, Menelaus is to perform his expiatory sacrifice, as required by Proteus, at the Nile (*Od.* 4.477–8).

Both encounters have an association with sleep or the border of consciousness, perhaps a thematic parallel to the border of water and land. Eidothea instructs Menelaus to approach Proteus while he is asleep (*Od.* 4.403–5, 413–14). Jacob arises during the night to lead his family across the river, then wrestles the "man" for the rest of the night. In another sense borders are traversed; disguise, important thematically throughout the *Odyssey*, is a prominent element in Menelaus' approach to Proteus. Eidothea prepares Menelaus for his encounter by having him don the skin of a seal. Proteus himself, during the encounter, takes on several different forms and guises.[26] Though not as prominent, disguise is relevant to Jacob's

---

[25] Cf. Mills (2003: 145): "There are indications that Jacob's antagonist had originally been a river spirit, whose defeat was necessary for his crossing of the river." Cf. Lord (1960: 197); M. L. West (1997: 483).
[26] See Lonsdale for analysis of this feature in particular. The shape changing on the part of the deity is common in other related Greek myths such as Peleus' wrestling of Thetis.

myth, in that Yahweh is initially "in disguise" in being indistinguishable from a man (Gen. 32:24–7). In locating itself at the edge of water, at the edge of sleep, between the recognizable and unrecognizable, the mythic genre highlights liminality.

Menelaus' myth particularly highlights liminality in the seals. Proteus acts as a shepherd over his seals (*Od.* 4.413). Detienne and Vernant, in their discussion of the seal's habitat, note (1974: 262), "the seal was a mediator between the dry and the wet, bringing together the elements of sea and land." They further explain (263):

> [T]he amphibian, whose position is profoundly ambiguous, is affected by a tension between two contrary influences; one connects it with the land and the human beings who live there, the other with the sea and the forces which are hostile to man.

As they further note (263–4), the seal has a certain resemblance to humans, also noted by Aristotle. The resemblance is implicit in the myth, in that Menelaus and his men are able to pass themselves off as seals before Proteus.

In having the protagonist wrestle with the god, both encounters center on a surprisingly physical confrontation between a mortal and a god. For both Menelaus and Jacob their key act is to keep holding on to their divine opponent. Eidothea advises Menelaus that he must grab hold of Proteus and not let go (ἔχειν… ἐχέμεν… πιέζειν: *Od.* 4.416–19). Forewarned, Menelaus successfully keeps Proteus within his grasp (*Od.* 4.454–9). Only here in Homeric epic does a hero successfully use such sustained physical contact against a god, as opposed to, say, Diomedes' successful, but instant, spear thrust against Ares (*Il.* 5.855–9). A similar emphasis is placed on Jacob not letting go of his opponent, who remains in his grip all night (Gen. 32:25–6). As with Menelaus, Jacob refuses to let go until his opponent will enter into a special form of discourse with him (Gen. 32:26).[27]

While Menelaus holds him, Proteus changes his form several times, a motif also present when Peleus wrestles Thetis, but not when Jacob wrestles Yahweh. Detienne and Vernant see Proteus' shape changing, and that of gods such as Thetis, and Nereus, as a sign that they are gods of cunning (1974: 20–1, 111–14). Except for the myth in which Zeus wrestles Metis, who clearly *is* a god of cunning, I am not persuaded by their analysis. It is a standard conception of deity that the gods can take on many forms. In the *Iliad* Poseidon takes on the form of Kalchas (*Il.* 13.45–61), and Hera that of Stentor (*Il.* 5.785–92), but few would argue that that makes them gods of

---

[27] Grabbing Esau by the heel while still in the womb, Jacob is also depicted as a wrestler at his birth (Gen. 25:24–6).

cunning. I take the divine transformations in these episodes as an aspect of wrestling, deity using its special powers to evade the grasp of an opponent. The motif cannot be present in Jacob's tale because OT myth usually avoids physical description of its deity (Ezekiel is a notable exception).

After the protagonists have successfully held the god for a long time, implicitly passing a test, both receive a privileged form of discourse with him. Menelaus' myth has earlier hinted at such an outcome in the epithet νημερτής (*nêmertês*), "unerring (in speech)," which Menelaus uses of Proteus the first time he mentions his name (*Od.* 4.349). Emphasis on the importance of divine speech continues in Menelaus' final prefatory remark, a gnome often criticized as spurious, "for the gods always desire that their behests be kept in mind." Against the critics (e.g., S. West 1988: 215), the remark prepares for the climactic role served by Proteus' lengthy divine discourse. Menelaus' privileged dialogue serves a number of purposes,[28] including offering a parallel for Odysseus' later dialogue with Teiresias. Like Odysseus, Menelaus learns key details about how to complete his homecoming (*Od.* 4.466–85), and about the fates of several of his comrades at Troy, including Agamemnon and Odysseus. For Menelaus' audience, Telemachos, this divine declaration constitutes the first evidence that Odysseus is alive (though the poem's audience has long known this). The conclusion of Proteus' divine discourse is his declaration that Menelaus is not to die, but is destined to go to Elysium and maintain a paradise-like existence (*Od.* 4.561–9). Proteus' prophecy of a blessed afterlife for Menelaus serves as the climax of the tale.[29]

A very similar outcome holds for Jacob's myth, but with the complication that some aspects of the privileged form of discourse with god, which takes the form of a blessing, are suppleted by an earlier episode, linked to his wrestling with god. Jacob earlier left home as a result of the tension he provoked when tricking Esau out of Isaac's blessing (Gen. 27). At that time, on his way to Bethel to find a wife, he had a night-time vision in which he saw angels going up and down a ladder reaching to heaven (Gen. 28:11–15).[30] Commentators have seen that night-time vision and the nocturnal wrestling with god as linked, complementary episodes underscoring parallels between his departure from and return to his family.[31] Further

---

[28] For a possible Indo-European parallel, see West's account (2007: 364) of Yudhisthira tested by a supernatural being who guards a lake, and asks him a series of questions (*Mahabhârata* 3.297).
[29] See West (2007: 349) on a blessed afterlife in Indo-European myth.
[30] On this episode as a late part of Jacob's myth, see Sparks (2005: 303).
[31] E.g., Speiser (1962: 256); Mills (2003: 147), "the night-time crossing is designed to balance the vision at Bethel."

cementing the parallels is Jacob's friction with his brother Esau. Having gone to Bethel largely because of the anger he provoked in tricking Esau out of his father's blessing, on his return, years later, Jacob still lives in fear of retaliation from Esau (Gen. 32:11–21).

Having wrestled him until daybreak, Jacob refuses to let go of his opponent, "I will not let go unless you bless me"(Gen. 32:26). His opponent complies, revealing his identity, "Your name shall no longer be Jacob but Israel, because you have striven with god and with mortals, and have prevailed"(Gen. 32:28). In the earlier episode, after Jacob's vision of the ladder, god declares:

This land on which you are lying I shall give to you and your descendants. They will be countless as the specks of dust on the ground, and you will spread far and wide... All the families of the earth will wish to be blessed as you and your descendants are blessed. I shall be with you to protect you wherever you go, and I shall bring you back to this land. (Genesis 22:13–15)

If the divine discourses Jacob receives in the two suppletive episodes[32] are combined, Jacob's prophecy and blessing resemble Proteus' climactic utterance to Menelaus. Both divine discourses underscore the protagonist's privileged relation with god. Both guarantee a special life for him and his family, though reflecting key differences in the characters. Menelaus' prophesied future is more that of a hero, Jacob's that of a patriarch.

MENELAUS WRESTLING PROTEUS AND THE *ODYSSEY*

While several thematic parallels between Menelaus' encounter with Proteus and Odysseus' adventures in Books 5–12 have long been noted (discussed above), ties with the larger plot of the *Odyssey*, and the character of Odysseus, remain unexplored. I argue that Menelaus' wrestling with the sea god Proteus serves as a metaphor for Odysseus' relationship with Poseidon. Odysseus is himself a wrestler, thematically in Homeric epic. In the funeral games for Patroklos he wrestles Telamonian Aias to a draw (*Il.* 23.700–39). Just before his tale of Proteus, Menelaus recalls how Odysseus wrestled king Philomeleïdes of Lesbos (*Od.* 4.342–4). The encounter is an instance of a common genre of heroic myth, in which the hero, in a foreign land, meets an oppressive figure who compels guests to compete in an athletic event, usually slaying them (discussion in Louden

---

[32] Again, cf. Mills (2003: 148): "The two events are related. In the first, Jacob is told, 'Your name shall no more be called Jacob, but Israel'. In the second, Jacob asks his adversary's name, but instead of an answer, he receives a blessing."

1999: 17). Numerous examples exist in the myths of Herakles and Theseus, and in the Argonauts' encounter with Amykos, king of the Bebrykians, who forces guests to box with him (*Argo.* 2.1–97; cf. Herakles wrestling Thanatos on behalf of his host in the *Alcestis*). Eustathius and Hellanicus supplement Menelaus' account, noting that Philomeleïdes challenged every passerby to wrestle until Odysseus and Diomedes killed him, establishing an inn for ξεῖνοι at his tomb.[33] As Lonsdale notes (1988: 168), Menelaus' reference to Odysseus wrestling Philomeleïdes (*Od.* 4.343) serves as segue into the Proteus story, offering yet another parallel between Menelaus and Odysseus. Telemachos repeats the tale to Penelope shortly after his return to Ithaka (*Od.* 17.133–5), just before Odysseus sets foot in the palace.

Though the *Odyssey* never depicts Odysseus wrestling in present-time narratives, his run-in on Scheria with Euryalos is the same genre of myth as the Philomeleïdes anecdote. Like that incident, the Euryalos episode also falls under the larger rubric of hospitality. Alkinoös arranges the athletic events as a diversion after his mysterious guest has been driven to tears hearing Demodokos' song about a quarrel (*neikos*) at Troy between Odysseus and Akhilleus (*Od.* 8.73–82). Nagy (1979: 22) takes this mention of a quarrel as support for his theory that *echthros* in Akhilleus' famous remark on the hateful man (*Il.* 9.312) designates Odysseus. But the *Iliad* uses *eris* (*Il.* 1.8, 1.177, 1.210, 1.277, 1.319, etc.), for the quarrel between Agamemnon and Akhilleus, *not neikos*, as the *Odyssey* does of this quarrel. Furthermore, a *neikos* between Odysseus and Akhilleus has an immediate relevance at this point in the *Odyssey*. Demodokos' quarrel involving Odysseus thematically introduces the tension that erupts only eighty lines later between Odysseus and the rude Euryalos, which both the narrator (*Od.* 8.158) and Alkinoös (*Od.* 8.239) subsequently characterize as *neikos*, the same term the poem just used of the strife between Odysseus and Akhilleus, rather than the more Iliadic *eris*. There is no evidence that this *neikos* alludes to events within the *Iliad*. Demodokos' second song, which he performs where the athletic games are held, also offers oblique comment on the friction between Odysseus and Euryalos, as is generally agreed.

To divert his guest, then, Alkinoös has his people compete in athletic games. In the catalogue of Phaiakian youths who will compete, Euryalos receives the lengthiest description (*Od.* 8.115–17), just before his strife flares up with Odysseus. Defeating all contestants in wrestling (*Od.* 8.126–7),

---

[33] See S. West (1988) on *Od.* 4.342–44 and Russo (1992) on *Od.* 17.134.

Euryalos then insults Odysseus (*Od.* 8.158–64), a clear violation of hospitality, when he declines Laodamas' challenge to compete in the games. The details suggest a slightly displaced version of the same genre of myth as the Philomeleïdes episode. Odysseus, on an island (Scheria/Lesbos), is rudely urged to compete in an athletic event. If he took part in one of the enumerated contests (boxing, wrestling, leaping, and running: *Od.* 8.103), Odysseus would respond to Euryalos' challenge by wrestling him (as with Philomeleïdes), the sport in which Homeric epic elsewhere demonstrates Odysseus' superiority. Instead, Odysseus competes in the discus, a less confrontational form of competition. In besting any possible Phaiakian attempts at the discus (*Od.* 8.186–98), Odysseus indirectly defeats the violator of hospitality (Euryalos/Philomeleïdes).

His attempt at cheering his guest through athletic games foiled, Alkinoös has Demodokos sing again, to defuse the tension Euryalos has provoked. The singer's second song, about Hephaistos, Aphrodite, and Ares, serves not only as a miniature of the *Odyssey*, but as commentary on Odysseus' "triumph" over Euryalos. In using cunning to foil an adulterer, and in having less-than-perfect legs (*Od.* 8.230–3), Odysseus parallels Hephaistos, whose triumph over the adulterous Ares predicts Odysseus' eventual defeat of those would-be adulterers, the suitors. But since the catalogue of Phaiakian athletes likens Euryalos explicitly to Ares (*Od.* 8.115–16), the song also replays the central dynamic from the athletic games, with the physically slower Odysseus defeating the brash youth.

As a Phaiakian, Euryalos is also linked to Poseidon. The Phaiakians, who enjoy close relations with the gods in general (*Od.* 7.201–5), are Poseidon's chosen people.[34] As the disguised Athena informs Odysseus, their wondrous ability with ships is Poseidon's special gift to them (*Od.* 7.34–6). She notes how they are descended directly from him: Alkinoös' father, Nausithoös, is Poseidon's own son (*Od.* 7.55–63). His blood connection, that the Phaiakians are family, prompts Poseidon's wrath when he later learns they have ferried Odysseus home (*Od.* 13.130).[35]

Euryalos' name also links him with Poseidon. Though a consensus has not been reached on an etymology, the meaning "wide sea" is clearly

---

[34] If it seems odd that Poseidon would subsequently wish to destroy his chosen people, as will be discussed in Chapter 9, in Exodus 32 Yahweh acts out precisely the same dynamic, but like Poseidon with Zeus, is talked down to a lower level of destruction and only causes the deaths of those who have committed offence against him.

[35] Cf. de Jong (2001: 319), "Poseidon complains to Zeus that the Phaeacians, his own progeny, no longer honour him."

tenable.³⁶ As is often noted, many Phaiakian names have connection with the sea. Among the athletes named when Euryalos first appears are the similarly named Amphialos, Anchialos, Okyalos, and Halios (*Od.* 8.111–19), which last has confirmed marine associations since it serves as an epithet of Proteus (*Od.* 4.384, 401, 542, 349, 365, 17.140) and Nereus.³⁷ Since such compounds are often possessives, "having wide seas," or "rich in seas," are possible meanings, and appropriate for a Phaiakian, chosen people of the sea god Poseidon, whose sole two appearances in the *Odyssey* mark Odysseus' approach to and departure from Scheria. Though Odysseus does not come into physical contact with Poseidon, as Menelaus does with Proteus, in his friction with the wrestler Euryalos, the *Odyssey* figures a displaced version of Odysseus as antagonist with Poseidon, drawing it into the same genre of myth as Menelaus wrestling with another sea god, Proteus, and Jacob with Yahweh at the riverbank.

Though my default position on parallels between the *Odyssey* and OT myth remains that the Greeks and Israelites each acquired or learned the genre from another Near Eastern culture (Phoenician or other), a few details in this case may make a Greek origin more likely, whatever form the resultant dispersion may have taken. Wrestling is simply not as common or prominent in Near Eastern myth as it is in Greek, though *Gilgamesh* has wrestling between the protagonist and Enkidu in the OBV (Dalley [1991] has "As wrestlers they grappled/And crouched").³⁸ Not only Odysseus against mortals, not only Menelaus with Proteus, but Herakles and Peleus both wrestle gods, the former even wrestling river gods, closely aligning the encounter with those of Menelaus and Jacob. To me this suggests the possibility that a genre more at home in Greek myth traveled eastward from Greek culture to West Semitic.

The prominence and the function of seals in Menelaus' myth are also suggestive of much that is central to the *Odyssey*. The seals' domain, the amphibious space between the land and the sea, is largely the domain of the *Odyssey* itself from Books 5–13, the area Odysseus inhabits until he reaches Ithaka.³⁹ As Menelaus temporarily "becomes" a seal (*Od.* 4.436–53) to wrestle Proteus, Odysseus spends much of Book 5, just after his first

---

³⁶ Chantraine (sub ἅλος), while not mentioning the name Euryalos, regards Amphialos, which is clearly a parallel formation, as deriving from "sea." See also discussion in Louden (1999: 20). Von Kamptz (1982) takes the second component of Euryalos as either "sea" (p. 28) or "leap" (p. 180).
³⁷ Dee (2001: 94, 102). For other relevant formations, cf. Homeric ἁλόθεν and ἁλοσύδνη.
³⁸ Cf. George (2003 Vol.I: 456): "Enkidu bars Gilgamesh from entering the house where the wedding ceremony is to take place and two heroes wrestle."
³⁹ Cf. Detienne and Vernant (1974: 263): "The analogy between the floating island and the seal ... For mythical thought the position of both was half-way between the earth and the water. They do not

encounter with Poseidon, swimming along the shore of Scheria until he enters the river-mouth (*Od.* 5.374–462). The next day, the sight of a naked, brine-encrusted Odysseus (*Od.* 6.137: κεκακωμένος ἄλμῃ, cf. 6.224–6) makes Nausikaa's handmaids scatter across the seashore (*Od.* 6.138).

Teiresias' mysterious phrase to describe Odysseus' death ties all these elements together. Though commentators[40] typically insist that *ex halos* (ἐξ ἁλὸς: *Od.* 11.134), Teiresias' phrase for how a "gentle death" will eventually overtake Odysseus in old age, must mean *away* from the sea, all other occurrences of the formula in the *Odyssey* and the *Iliad* suggest otherwise. The *Odyssey* uses the formula three times in Menelaus' encounter with Proteus, two of Proteus emerging from the ocean in his daily routine (*Od.* 4.401), and as he emerges when Menelaus wrestles him (*Od.* 4.450). But Menelaus' narrative also uses *ex halos* to describe the seals as they emerge from the sea to lie down under Proteus' direction (*Od.* 4.448). As he approaches Scheria in the aftermath of the storms Poseidon has provoked, Odysseus fears the sea god (*daimon*) will cause a sea monster (κῆτος) to come out of the sea (*ex halos*: *Od.* 5.422) and harass him. In Book 24, when Agamemnon describes Akhilleus' funeral, he twice mentions Thetis' arrival as she emerges from the sea, *ex halos* (*Od.* 24.47=55). The *Iliad* uses the formula *ex halos* exclusively of Poseidon himself emerging from the sea (*Il.* 13.15, 13.44, 20.14). The only other occurrences of the phrase in Homeric epic are the two instances in Teiresias' prophecy of Odysseus' death *ex halos* (*Od.* 11.134, 23.281).

Since all other occurrences of the formula depict either a sea deity (Poseidon, Proteus, Thetis) or sea creature (seals, sea monster) emerging from the sea, the usual interpretation that *ex halos* in Teiresias' prophecy means "away from," or "far from" the sea is not tenable. Since all three occurrences in the *Iliad* refer to Poseidon, three in the *Odyssey* refer to Menelaus wrestling with Proteus (which encounter is a metaphor for Odysseus' relationship with Poseidon), and another depicts Odysseus tormented at sea (*Od.* 5.422), it is far likelier that *ex halos* points to Poseidon's involvement in Odysseus' death. When Odysseus leaves the sea behind and returns to Ithaka Poseidon has not fully relinquished his wrath against him. Consistently in myth, the gods' sense of time differs from that of mortals. They often act after years or decades to administer punishment,[41] whether causing Troy to fall

---

belong totally either to the one or to the other and because they combine elements of the sea and the earth equally, both act as mediators between the two."

[40] Heubeck (1989: 86): "We may, however, be sure that Tiresias foresees for Odysseus a death 'away from the sea'"; cf. Stanford (1961: 387).

[41] See Louden (2006: 10, 185, 230); Lefkowitz: (2003: 151).

ten years after Paris has violated the tenets of Zeus Xenios, or effecting an inherited curse through three generations of a family. Nestor still honors Poseidon by offering a hecatomb ten years after safely crossing the sea (*Od.* 3.5–66). When Jacob wrestles Yahweh, his thigh is dislocated, his name changed, underscoring the danger and transformations involved in such encounters. Poseidon will eventually claim Odysseus' life as the final act of his wrath, emerging from the sea.

CHAPTER 5

Odyssey 5
Ogygia and creation myth; Kalypso and Ishtar

When the *Odyssey* brings Odysseus onstage after a four-book focus on Telemachos, he has no connection to the circumstances with which the poem has so far been concerned (the crisis the suitors cause in Ithaka for Telemachos and Penelope). He is *off the map*, as far as normal human existence is concerned. To insert Odysseus into its plot the *Odyssey* draws on three overlapping genres of myth. In placing Odysseus in a paradise[1] where he could remain forever and be immortal, the *Odyssey* employs key motifs from creation myth. In his relationship with Kalypso, the *Odyssey* draws upon the mythic genre of the hero's involvement with a goddess who offers to make him her consort,[2] as *Gilgamesh* depicts in his encounter with Ishtar. But Book 5 combines these two types with a third genre of myth, a hero's blessed afterlife in a paradise set at the ends of earth, to which the *Odyssey* briefly alludes in Menelaus' encounter with Proteus (*Od.* 4.561–9). All three genres focus on the possibility of the hero becoming immortal. The first and third types overlap in their paradise setting, which by definition is cut off from usual mortal existence.

KALYPSO AND OGYGIA, PARADISE AND CREATION MYTH

Since epic can incorporate any kind of myth, it is not surprising that the *Odyssey* draws on creation myth[3] for several elements of Book 5. In the Deception of Zeus, Book 14 of the *Iliad* also incorporates elements of creation myth, as several commentators have shown. The background story involving Okeanos and Tethys that Hera tells Zeus draws on cosmogonic and theogonic creation myths.[4] *Gilgamesh* incorporates extensive motifs

[1] See Bremmer (1999) on the ancient Iranian origin of the word, and early use in Greek.
[2] On Yahweh's original consort, Asherah, see Sparks (2005: 451).
[3] See Sparks (2005: 305–34) for a recent overview of Near Eastern creation myths, and 339–40 for a summary of the parallels Genesis exhibits with the Atrahasis and Eridu myth.
[4] See especially Janko (1992: 180–2, 193, 247).

from creation myth in its account of the creation of Enkidu. The goddess Aruru fashions Enkidu from clay, creating him in the form of an adult male (*Gilg.* I. ii), just as Yahweh does Adam. Also rather like Adam, Enkidu lives a pastoral existence, associating and able to communicate with animals. While Tigay (2002: 194–7) discusses the theory that *Gilgamesh* here draws upon the *Atrahasis*, the correspondences are strictly generic resemblance, and therefore it may be that *Gilgamesh* draws on the *idea* of creation myth, rather than on the specific instance that is the *Atrahasis* (but see Carr 1996: 215–16, 242–5 on how the *Atrahasis* probably influenced the Genesis creation myth). The examples already noted illustrate that elements of creation myth can occur in myths set in later times.

The depiction of Odysseus in the first half of Book 5 employs standard features of creation myth also found in the myths of Enkidu and Adam. Ogygia is commonly held to be paradise (Crane 1988: 15: "An island paradise on the edge of the world"), with a careful sense of design (Austin 1975: 150: "her landscape has idyllic perfection").[5] Even Hermes (whose role is discussed below) stops to admire the beauties of Ogygia when he first arrives (*Od.* 5.73–6). Austin has perhaps best summarized Ogygia's paradise features (149):

[T]here is an encircling forest, flourishing with alders, black poplars, and fragrant cypresses... not simply a grove but a grove of three kinds of trees, not simply birds but three kinds of birds, a meadow of two kinds of plants, the smell of two kinds of burning wood.

His emphasis on the trees accords well with the description of Eden, "The Lord God planted a garden in Eden... made trees grow up from the ground, every kind of tree pleasing to the eye and good for food" (Gen. 2:8–9).[6] The four fountains on Ogygia (*Od.* 5.70–1) offer an unexpected parallel to Eden's four rivers (Gen. 2:10–14).[7] Eden's four rivers are probably to be thought of as supplying water to all parts of the garden ("There was a river flowing from Eden to water the garden" Gen. 2:10), much as S. West conjectures of Kalypso's four fountains (1988: 263), "The four springs presumably water every quarter of the island." Though Odysseus has parents, and grew up in the world of mortals, the *Odyssey* first presents him as an adult male in paradise, much as with Adam, and Enkidu. By first depicting Odysseus in such an environment, Book 5 in a sense "creates" Odysseus within the *Odyssey*. In the *Odyssey*'s opening divine

---

[5] Cf., S. West (1988: 262): "The poet describes the Greek notion of an idyllic spot."
[6] On trees as central to ancient Iranian concepts of paradise, see Bremmer (1999: 4–5).
[7] I am unable to find a previous commentator who has noted this parallel.

council Athena calls Ogygia the "navel (*omphalos*) of the sea" (*Od.* 1.50). Though commentators usually argue *omphalos* here has some figurative meaning (e.g., Chantraine [1990] regards it as meaning "center"), it is cognate with Latin *umbilicus* and English "navel," and, if taken more literally, reinforces a paradise and creation modality.

The absence of any other humans, other than the lone adult male (Odysseus, Adam, Enkidu), typifies creation myth (as distinct from a *locus amoenus*, which is fit for dialogue among several people). But the adult male soon has a female companion who is his sexual partner (Kalypso, Eve, Shamhat). His sexual relationship with this female leads, one way or the other, to his departure from paradise. As in Genesis, the pivot of the narrative of Enkidu's creation is his making love to a woman, Shamhat. His doing so brings about a stark change in his status. The animals will no longer associate with him, nor can he run as fast as they do, as he used to. The narrator says that he has acquired judgment, and Shamhat goes further, "You have become [profound] Enkidu, you have become like a god"(*Gilg.* I.iv). Persuading him that he should no longer live among the animals, Shamhat advises Enkidu to go to Uruk to confront Gilgamesh. As with Adam, Enkidu's narrative associates his having sex for the first time with a fundamental change in his status, expulsion from his original idyllic environment, and movement to a city.

When Book 5 first depicts Odysseus, he is alone, crying on the shore of Ogygia (*Od.* 5.151–8). Such loneliness, even alienation, is typical of the lone male adult in creation myth. Though Adam's account does not give his perspective, Yahweh announces, shortly after placing Adam in Eden, that "it is not good for the man to be alone; I shall make a partner suited to him"(Gen. 2:18). But after making all the animals, again from earth, Yahweh still leaves Adam as the lone human, "but for the man himself no suitable partner was found"(Gen. 2:20). The *Odyssey*, in first showing Odysseus weeping on the shore, modifies this motif, showing his sadness, missing his wife of twenty years, though he has companionship in the form of Kalypso.

In perhaps the most intriguing parallel, in all three narratives the sky father arranges for the protagonist's departure from paradise at a divine council. In the first divine council in *Gilgamesh*, Anu, prompted by complaints from the people of Uruk about Gilgamesh's intrusions into their lives, tells the goddess Aruru to create Enkidu as a rival for Gilgamesh so Uruk will have peace (*Gilg.* I.ii). Anu's plan requires Enkidu, after his creation, to leave his pastoral environs and proceed to Uruk to challenge Gilgamesh, as he does after his encounter with Shamhat. In the *Odyssey*,

Zeus dispatches Hermes to Ogygia, in Book 5's divine council, to tell Kalypso to let Odysseus leave (*Od.* 5.28–43). In Genesis, Yahweh prefaces Adam's creation by saying, "Let *us* make human beings in *our* image, after *our* likeness"(the plurals are quite clear in the Septuagint: Gen. 1:26: ποιήσωμεν... ἡμετέραν). The vestigial divine council generically parallels that in *Gilgamesh* when Anu instructs Aruru on the creation of Enkidu. After Adam and Eve break the divine interdiction, eating from the tree of knowledge, in another vestigial divine council, Yahweh declares, "The man has become like one of *us*" (Gen. 3:22: ἡμῶν in the Septuagint). On this second brief reference to a divine council, Speiser notes (1962: 24), "*one of us*. A reference to the heavenly company of beings which remains obscure."[8] Banishing Adam from Eden, Yahweh stations cherubim with a sword, guarding the way to the tree of life (Gen. 3:24). Hermes serves a function similar to the cherubim: after a divine council (*Od.* 5.3–43), lesser immortals dispatched by the sky father oversee the protagonist's departure from paradise. Leaving the *omphalos*, Odysseus cuts the umbilical cord that ties him to paradise and to a divine, non-aging life centered around Kalypso. Ogygia, under Kalypso, has womb-like associations; Odysseus' departure from it draws on metaphors for birth.

After departure from his paradise-like setting, Enkidu immediately confronts and challenges Gilgamesh, contact that is figured as a wrestling match. Once in the Phaiakians' city, Odysseus is compelled to compete in an athletic event (*Od.* 8.131–234). Though he competes in the discus, wrestling is thematically significant in the *Odyssey*, as noted in Chapter 4, with Odysseus victorious in those matches in which he competes. After Adam and Eve leave Eden, the narrative focus quickly shifts to the strife between Cain and Abel (Gen. 4:1–16), and the existence of the first cities (Gen. 4:14).

KALYPSO AND ISHTAR: THE HERO REJECTS THE GODDESS'S OFFER TO BE HER CONSORT

Myths in which immortals couple with mortals can function almost as a subset of creation myth, or serve as a subsequent development to it, as at Gen. 6:2–4. The first four verses of Genesis 6 function as a transition out of the preceding creation myth, and segue to the apocalyptic flood myth that immediately follows (Gen. 6:5 ff.). As the creation myth retains

---

[8] Cf. Carr (1996: 238) on Gen. 3:22 as a divine council, and Suggs (1992: 12), "The plural *us*... may be a majestic plural, or else refer to the minor divine beings thought to surround god."

vestiges of a polytheistic background in its implied divine council, so does this transitional passage.

> The human race began to increase and to spread over the earth and daughters were born to them. The sons of the gods saw how beautiful these women were, so they took for themselves such women as they chose... In those days as well as later, when the sons of the gods had intercourse with the daughters of mortals. (Genesis 6:1–4)

The formula "sons of the gods" (rendered as "divine beings" by Speiser [1962]) designates lesser immortals, as Suggs (1992) clarifies in his note on Gen. 6:2, "*Sons of the gods*: a term of Canaanite origin for members of the pantheon ('assembly of the gods')."[9] Though the Old Testament passage only refers to male gods coupling with female mortals, within heroic and epic myth a mortal male having sex with an immortal goddess is a well-attested genre of myth.

While commentators often suggest parallels between Kalypso and Siduri (see Bakker 2001: 344), when considered through the lens of this subgenre of myth (*The hero rejects the goddess' offer to be her consort*), Kalypso shares more parallels with Ishtar than with Siduri. For instance, *Odyssey* 5 and Gilgamesh's rejection of Ishtar both refer to other related narratives of mortal men who suffer because of their relationships with goddesses. The *Odyssey* employs this mythic genre in connection with the hero's departure from paradise whereas *Gilgamesh* employs it in connection with the hero's defeat of Humbaba (discussed in Chapter 7). Noting certain elements that are more explicit in *Gilgamesh* VI helps clarify how they function in *Odyssey* 5.

After defeating Humbaba, Gilgamesh bathes, changes his clothes,[10] and immediately attracts the attention of the goddess Ishtar, who offers to make him her husband:

> Come to me, Gilgamesh, and be my lover!
> Bestow on me the gift of your fruit!
> You can be my husband, and I can be your wife.
> *Gilgamesh* VI.i

The goddess describes the chariot and house he would assume, the respect he would receive. But as Gilgamesh well knows, such couplings between an immortal and mortal are dangerous for the mortal, often leading to

---

[9] See further discussion by Speiser (1962: 45–6).
[10] Cf. *Odyssey* 6.224–3, Odysseus' bath and Nausikaa's reaction, and 23.153–64 where Odysseus, bloodied from his defeat of the suitors, bathes and dons new clothes to meet with Penelope.

disfigurement, possible castration, or death. In his response he enumerates a catalogue, itemizing several of her former lovers, and their subsequent fates, which range from physical suffering to harsh metamorphoses (men turned into frogs or wolves).

While Kalypso's offer is essentially the same as Ishtar's, that Odysseus stay with her as her consort, the *Odyssey* presents it in a different manner. We only learn of Kalypso's offer through a retrospective account she gives to Hermes (*Od.* 5.129–36, but cf. *Od.* 5.208–9), though in present time the *Odyssey* gives something of a replay of that episode at 5.202–18, whereas *Gilgamesh* depicts Ishtar's proposal in present time. The *Odyssey* paints Kalypso in more intimate colors, since, unlike Ishtar with Gilgamesh, she shares Odysseus' company for seven years, demonstrating other sides of her character, even a maternal aspect, "I loved him and I nurtured him" (*Od.* 5.135: τὸν μὲν ἐγὼ φίλεόν τε καὶ ἔτρεφον). She gives Hermes a brief account of former lovers (*Od.* 5.121–8), not of her own previous consorts, as *Gilgamesh* gives of Ishtar, but of other goddesses, Eos and Demeter. In both epics the catalogues serve as a complaint, but where Gilgamesh complained about the fates of Ishtar's previous lovers, Kalypso complains about how the Olympians interfere with mortal/immortal relationships. In the *Odyssey* Eos is a closer parallel to Ishtar than Kalypso in being linked to several mortal lovers (Tithonos: *Od.* 5.1, Orion: *Od.* 5.121–4, and Kleiton: *Od.* 15.250–1).[11] But it is highly ironic that Kalypso herself details a catalogue which, since both mortals involved die, underscores the incompatibility of such relationships just as Gilgamesh's catalogue of Ishtar's lovers does. In this respect Gilgamesh would seem to present the more traditional form of the motif while the *Odyssey* probably innovates in having Kalypso provide such a catalogue.

Her catalogue notwithstanding, Kalypso seems more aware of the inherent complexities of such a relationship than Ishtar. She offers to make Odysseus both immortal and ageless (θήσειν ἀθάνατον καὶ ἀγήραον ἤματα πάντα: *Od.* 5.136 = 7.257, 23.336), whereas Ishtar makes no such offer or claim. Making him immortal *and* ageless would make their relationship less imbalanced. In beginning Book 5 with a reference to Tithonos (*Od.* 5.1–2), the *Odyssey* seems to employ that myth as a negative parallel, Eos asking Zeus to make him immortal, but neglecting to ask him to make Tithonos ageless (cf. *Homeric Hymn to Aphrodite*, 218–38).[12] A fuller

---

[11] On Eos herself as descending from an Indo-European tradition, see West (2007: 217–32).
[12] Tithonos' subsequent predicament seems a likely source for Swift's Struldbruggs (*Gulliver's Travel's* part III, Chapter X).

version of the myth suggests a very dangerous possible outcome for Odysseus, should he stay with Kalypso.

Kalypso would accomplish this, make him immortal and ageless, by feeding him nectar and ambrosia (*Od.* 5.135–6, 199, 209). A substance which, ingested, makes a mortal immortal thus occurs in all three parallel traditions, *Odyssey* 5, *Gilgamesh*, and Genesis 1–3. *Gilgamesh* and the Genesis creation myth both have the same traditional motif, a plant of eternal life, but Genesis uses it as part of creation myth, while *Gilgamesh* has it as the object of a hero's quest. The tree of eternal life in Eden is initially *not* forbidden, implying that Adam and Eve would have been free to eat it had they not violated the divine interdiction against eating from the tree of knowledge. Gilgamesh's pursuit of a plant with the same properties also involves a serpent, whereas Greek myth uses that same combination in Heracles' quest for the Golden Apples of the Hesperides. The *Odyssey*, then, employs this motif very differently. Odysseus is offered immortality of a sort better analyzed in the following section (Kalypso and Ishtar: marrying Death).

While both Odysseus and Gilgamesh reject the goddesses' offers, Odysseus serves as a positive example of how to do so, Gilgamesh a negative. Each scene features a lengthy speech by the protagonist. Both make the correct answer in declining to be the goddess' consort (the dangers of accepting are discussed below), but in his tactless response Gilgamesh offends Ishtar, provoking her divine wrath. He arrogantly enumerates her lovers and details their suffering (*Gilg.* VI.i–iii), addressing the goddess in the manner that only another god should. When he concludes by declaring she will treat him in the same way as her other lovers, he provokes her divine wrath, "When Ishtar heard this,/Ishtar was furious, and [went up] to heaven." The contrast in how Odysseus handles essentially the same situation could hardly be stronger. In a tactfully restrained speech (*Od.* 5.173–9, 215–24) that manipulates her into swearing an oath (*Od.* 5.173–91), Odysseus prevents Kalypso from developing a divine wrath at him.

Odysseus' first speech in the poem establishes his foremost characteristic of self-control, as he displays neither joy nor surprise when Kalypso informs him that he may leave Ogygia. Instead, suspecting a trick (*Od.* 5.173–4), noting how dangerous it is to cross the sea on a raft, he declares that he will not proceed unless she swears an oath that she intends no evil against him (*Od.* 5.177–9). When Kalypso tries one last time to persuade him to stay with her, he cautions her not to be angry with him (πότνα θεά, μή μοι τόδε χώεο: *Od.* 5.215). He then flatters her, noting that she is more beautiful than Penelope (*Od.* 5.215–18), more beautiful than any mortal woman. But in his key move he declares that he most yearns to go home, to see his homecoming (*Od.* 5.219–20), rather than say how much he desires Penelope, which might provoke Kalypso's jealousy. By so doing Odysseus instantiates his role as the consummate persuasive speaker in Homeric epic and Greek myth. Gilgamesh, on the other hand, is more like Akhilleus, so blunt in his frankness as to unintentionally damage his own prospects (as does Akhilleus in Book 1 of the *Iliad*).[13] He gives no thought to the consequences of his remarks to Ishtar, no anticipation that he provokes a divine wrath that will result in Enkidu's death.

Though OT myth does not develop this specific mythic genre, it may draw upon such a tradition in its account of the queen of Sheba and Solomon. Like Ishtar with Gilgamesh, the queen of Sheba enters the story because of Solomon's fame, "The queen of Sheba heard of Solomon's fame and came to test him" (1 Kgs. 10:1; cf. 2 Chr. 9:1). Where Ishtar responds to Gilgamesh's prowess against Humbaba and his physical beauty, the queen of Sheba is prompted by accounts of Solomon's wisdom. Ishtar offers Gilgamesh a chariot made of gold and lapis lazuli, produce from the mountain and country, a palace made of scented pine (*Gilg.* VI.i). The queen of Sheba offers very similar gifts to Solomon. She comes bringing "camels laden with spices, gold in vast quantity, and precious stones" (1 Kgs. 10:2). While Gilgamesh and Odysseus implicitly pass a test in rejecting the goddesses, Solomon explicitly passes the test, giving the right answers to the queen's questions, though none of these are reported. In making her visit more explicitly a test of Solomon, OT myth seems to have brought the episode under the same rubric as when an immortal offers a mortal a choice between riches, immortality and the like, which 1 Kings earlier presents in the narrative of Solomon's dream (1 Kgs. 3:5–15).[14] Though the account in 1 Kings contains no trace of the sexual tone so central to the episodes with Gilgamesh and Ishtar, and Odysseus and Kalypso, extra-biblical accounts do link Solomon sexually with the queen (Cogan 2001: 315).

KALYPSO AND ISHTAR: MARRYING DEATH

Gilgamesh and Odysseus are correct in declining the goddesses' offers to become their consorts since, were they to accept, their subsequent position would be as some kind of functionary in the underworld. Each

---

[13] But see Abusch (1986: 148) on the unusual length of Gilgamesh's speech.
[14] For discussion of the mythic type, which includes the Judgment of Paris, the Temptation of Christ, and Anat offering an exchange for Aqhat's bow, see Louden (2006: 263–6).

goddess has ties to the underworld, and can be thought of, from the Greek perspective, as chthonic goddesses. Abusch classifies them in a similar way (1986: 161), "Like Calypso, Circe, and Ereshkigal, Ishtar is a death goddess." To marry such a goddess means that the hero becomes a masculine version of Persephone, and like her, marries "Death." One such outcome is hinted at in the myth of Admetos (cf. Leontes in *The Winter's Tale*), whose home becomes a tomb through his marriage to a Persephone/Demeter figure (*Alcestis* 336–44, 863–9, 939–40, 960–1).

Hermes, *psychopomp*, conductor of souls, conducts the narrative to Ogygia, as he leads it to Hades in Book 24. The boundary-crossing god, most sociable of the Olympians, according to Zeus (*Il.* 24.334–5), is the only one who enters Hades. In Book 5, as Hermes makes for Ogygia, he takes his magic staff, his ῥάβδος, as Crane (1988: 16) explains: "Hermes takes his ῥάβδος... because the ῥάβδος marks him here, as it does in *Odyssey* 24, as the psychopomp, the mediator between this world and the next."[15] This is one of many connections Kalypso's island has with the underworld. In Hesiod the adjective "Ogygian" is used as an epithet of the river Styx (*Theogony* 805–6). As several commentators have noted, Ogygia's groves (*Od.* 5.63–4) have features in common with groves in the underworld. Poplars grow both on Ogygia and in Hades (*Od.* 5.64, 10.510). Ogygia's meadows suggest further parallels with typical features of the underworld.[16] Kalypso's cave (*Od.* 1.15, 5.57–74, 5.194) also has broad thematic associations with the underworld, as do other caves in Greek myth such as Polyphêmos', or even Plato's (*Rep.*, Book 7; cf. Cacus' cave, *Aen.* 8.193–265). It is Hermes who is the agent to arrange for Persephone's freedom from Hades (Crane 1988: 18–20), much as he does for Odysseus' departure from Ogygia.

Were Gilgamesh or Odysseus to marry Ishtar and Kalypso, they would essentially be like masculine versions of Persephone, and marry Death. Abusch (1986) has made the strongest argument along these lines in Gilgamesh's case. He sees Ishtar in this episode as a goddess who behaves in much the same way as do the chthonic Kalypso and Kirke (159):

Her nature and behavior in our text are characteristic of a type of early earth goddess who is both the source of fertility and life as well as the cause of death and the receiver of the dead.

---

[15] See Cook (1995: 41) on further links between Hermes' role on Ogygia and in *Iliad* 24.
[16] E.g., Crane (1988: 16): "Second, consider the conclusion of the ekphrasis (5.72–3)... These are the meadows which persistently appear in descriptions of the Beyond." Crane (1988: 24n. 12): "compare the asphodel meadows in the Hades of the *Odyssey* (11.539, 573; 24.13)."

Because such is Ishtar's nature and status, her offer to Gilgamesh, Abusch argues, is really a coded proposition for something quite different (149):

[T]he proposal has its setting in the infernal regions, that Ishtar is inviting Gilgamesh to become her husband and thereby formally to join the denizens of the netherworld.

Each detail of her offer, Abusch argues, while seeming to refer to a mode of existence attractive to Gilgamesh, in reality refers to life in the underworld (152):

Of course, Ishtar intended Gilgamesh to think that the power and status she was offering him were to be his in this world; in reality she was offering him the obeisance of dead rulers in the netherworld.

Abusch thus explains Gilgamesh's arrogance to Ishtar when he rejects her offer as evidence that he understands the true nature of her proposition (158, 175).

Similar tendencies govern the Homeric conception of Kalypso. The *Odyssey* does not depict how matters would stand should Odysseus become Kalypso's consort. But from the point of view of the Homeric Odysseus, Ogygia has little to offer him in providing a setting in which his usual character may function as a warrior, a hero, deviser of the Trojan Horse. In its lush fertility Ogygia seems like an extension of Kalypso herself. Even if she makes Odysseus immortal and ageless, Ogygia will always be *her* island. In this sense, Odysseus would always be in a subordinate position in their relationship. In my view, commentators typically see Kalypso in too positive a light.[17] Though she may genuinely love Odysseus, at the same time she is depicted as compelling him to have sex with her (*Od.* 5.154–5), keeping him on her island against his will (*Od.* 1.14–15, 55–6, 4.557–8, etc.). While this fundamental ambivalence may be an expected expression of her chthonic nature, it is also a sign that what she wants for herself is in conflict with what is best for Odysseus. Her love has a smothering, oppressive quality that negates and even consumes his identity, as her name (*The Concealer*) suggests. Were Odysseus to become her consort, it would be much as Abusch argues about Ishtar (1986: 173), "To love her is to surrender one's identity"; (p. 174), "In proposing marriage, Ishtar offers to enhance Gilgamesh's identity while at the same time depriving him of it."

---

[17] E.g., Austin (1975: 150–1): "The portrait of Kalypso...is one of the most sympathetic in the *Odyssey*...Kalypso's character has a restraint that suggests a depth and poignancy scarcely matched in the poem except by Penelope."

Book 5 signals just such dangers for Odysseus in its opening reference to Eos and Tithonos. The goddess to whom Kalypso will shortly compare herself (*Od.* 5.121), who repeatedly enters into intimate relationships with mortal men, regularly marks the beginning of a new day (*Od.* 2.1; 3.404, 491; 4.306, 431, 576; etc.). But in a key instance of Homeric epic's selectivity, only here (*Od.* 5.1–2) in the *Odyssey* does she do so in connection with Tithonos, and his "unfortunate immortality," as S. West describes it (1988: 254). The unique, if understated, reference establishes the central thrust of the entire depiction of Kalypso and Ogygia, that such pairings of mortals with immortals are inherently problematic, usually tragic. Having introduced the theme at the outset, Book 5 expands its examples of this theme in Kalypso's mention of the deaths of Orion and Iasion after their relations with Eos and Demeter (*Od.* 5.124, 128). For Odysseus and Kalypso even their diet is incompatible. Kalypso dines on nectar and ambrosia (*Od.* 5.199), foods that in some way help sustain the immortals' metabolism, but call attention to death in their triumph over it, while Odysseus eats strictly mortal fare.[18] The separate foods for mortal and immortal form yet another link to the myth of Persephone, as Crane (1988: 20) notes:

The distinction between the mortal and immortal food is... critical: even as Calypso graciously serves Odysseus, we see how he does not eat the food of the other world, and thus avoids a snare that entraps Persephone.

Though less well known to us than Persephone, Greek myth had a similar notion of a man marrying death, as Crane notes (1988: 16–17), "Calypso is a nymph... To be among the nymphs was a synonym for death... Death itself can be viewed as a marriage with Hades or Persephone." I quote Abusch once more (1986: 152), "Ishtar's marriage proposal constitutes an offer to Gilgamesh to become a functionary of the netherworld."

---

[18] On the gods' food in Indo-European myth, see West (2007: 157–60).

CHAPTER 6

Odyssey 6–8, 10–12, 13.1–187; Genesis 28–33; Argonautic myth
Odysseus and Nausikaa/Kirke; Jason and Medea; Jacob and Rachel

Argonautic myth is the third most dominant genre of myth in the *Odyssey*, providing the framework or larger organizing structure for much of Books 6–12. Odysseus' encounters with Nausikaa, Alkinoös, and the Phaiakians, Kirke and Helios, and Antiphates and his daughter (*Od.* 10.81–133), are three variations on the same group of underlying motifs. The *Odyssey* unmistakably demonstrates awareness of Argonautic myth when Kirke gives Odysseus instructions on how to continue his voyage home:

> For only one sea-faring ship has ever sailed by there,
> Argo, known to all, sailing back from Aietes,
> and then she would have swiftly struck the great rocks
> but Hera sent her through, since she was so fond of Jason.
> *Odyssey* 12.69–72

The prominence of her remarks has led many to conclude that not only is the *Odyssey* aware of Argonautic myth, but uses some form of that myth to inform its own structure.[1]

Page, building on observations of earlier commentators, noted some broad connections between the *Odyssey* and Argonautic myth (1955: 2):

Circe is sister of Aietes, the guardian of the Golden Fleece... *The Wandering Rocks* belong only to the story of the Argonauts... The *Laestrygones* have a fountain called Artakia... On the island of *Thrinakia* the companions of Odysseus kill the sacred cattle – of what god? Of Helios, the Sun, so important in the story of the Golden Fleece... The *Sirens* too were at home in the story of Jason long before they transferred their affections to Odysseus.

---

[1] West (2005: 39): "One of the most certain results of Homeric scholarship, in many scholars' view, is that some of Odysseus' adventures owe something to a pre-existing narrative about Jason and the Argonauts." Cf. Heubeck (1989a: 121): "The passage is the most important evidence for a pre-Homeric Argonautica as a source and model for Odysseus' adventures in ix–xii." Cf. two references in the *Iliad* to Euneos, Jason's son (*Il.* 7.467–82; 23.746).

There are additional episodes that he omits. The *Catalogue of Women* (*Od.* 11.235–332) and even the brief Leukothea/Ino episode evidence additional links to Argonautic myth.

Though we are handicapped in lacking an early account of the myth, it is clear that Medea played a significant role from early on.[2] But since Odysseus is a married man, as opposed to the more youthful Jason, and romance constitutes a dominant part of the forces that govern the plot, the *Odyssey* cannot present Medea in the same role that she plays in the *Argonautica*, from whatever period. Essentially the *Odyssey* takes the already traditional figure of Medea and splits her into two separate characters, the young princess Nausikaa and the more mature witch Kirke, each retaining various motifs from Argonautic myth. Kirke's island, Aiaia, and her father Helios, are thematically linked to Argonautic myth in a number of ways. Books 10–12 thus give us a version of Medea's more potent side in Kirke, her aunt, while Books 6–8 feature her more girlish aspect in Nausikaa, the princess swept off her feet by a foreign hero. Old Testament myth offers a relevant parallel in its account of Jacob leaving home to win Rachel as his bride, the difficulties he encounters from her father Laban, the magic he uses to increase his flocks, and Rachel's theft of Laban's household gods.[3]

ODYSSEUS AND NAUSIKAA, AND THE OT BETROTHAL TYPE-SCENE

After Odysseus makes the passage from Ogygia to Scheria, Nausikaa is the first mortal he encounters. His first meeting with her in Book 6, and with Athena in the form of a girl fetching water shortly thereafter (*Od.* 7.19–78),[4] have close parallels in OT myth. Abraham's servant meets Rebecca at a well (Gen. 24:10–61), as does Jacob, Rachel (Gen. 29:1–20), and Moses, Zipporah (Exod. 2:15b–21). Alter, who has analyzed the three OT episodes as instances of a recurring "betrothal type-scene," argues for the following underlying rubric (1981: 52):

The betrothal type-scene, then, must take place with the future bridegroom, or his surrogate, having journeyed to a foreign land. There he encounters a girl . . . or

---

[2] Cf. Gantz (1993: 358): "One can scarcely doubt in any case that she is an early part of the story, assisting Iason in an otherwise impossible task as Ariadne does for Theseus."

[3] Genesis source criticism of Jacob's myth is very complicated. Much is priestly material, much of it is other sources. There are both pre-priestly and priestly accounts of Jacob's departure and return, for instance. The more trickster kinds of motifs – Jacob stealing Esau's blessing, Rachel stealing Laban's household gods – are usually assigned to the pre-priestly account. For a thorough overview, see Carr (1996: 96, 106, 126–7, 168–9, 178, 181, 212–14, 248, 257–72, 298).

[4] In spite of some differences, this should be regarded as a doublet of the Nausikaa episode, as Reece (1993: 12) notes. Note that Nausikaa herself also links the two scenes: *Odyssey* 6.300–1.

girls at a well; afterward, the girl or girls rush to bring home the news of the stranger's arrival... finally, a betrothal is concluded between the stranger and the girl, in the majority of instances, only after he has been invited to a meal.

Placing Odysseus' encounter with Nausikaa, as well as some of his subsequent interactions with Alkinoös and other Phaiakians, in such a context helps demonstrate the logic of certain details sometimes thought incongruous. Crane notes the underlying clash of opposing narrative trajectories (1988: 138):

> Book 8... the narrative moves simultaneously in two different directions. Odysseus is, on the one hand, an honored guest of the Phaeacians, waiting to return home and, in the meantime, enjoying their hospitality... On the other hand, the narrative provides the backdrop for a very different story: that of the stranger who must prove himself and will win the daughter of the king in marriage.[5]

Though Odysseus has no interest in marrying Nausikaa, his interactions with her, with the Phaiakian athletes, and with her father Alkinoös, contain all the elements of Alter's betrothal type-scene. We first review the three main OT instances of the type-scene, then explore Odysseus' involvement with Nausikaa.

Abraham dispatches a trusted servant to find a wife for his son Isaac (Gen. 24:2–9). Reaching Nahor, the servant halts his camels at a well, outside the city, knowing that women come there to draw water (Gen. 24:10–11). Praying to Yahweh for a sign, he asks that the girl who lets him drink from her jug will draw water for his camels (Gen. 24:12–14). Rebecca appears, a beautiful virgin with a jug on her shoulder, draws water, lets him drink when he asks, and draws water for all his camels (Gen. 24:15–21). The servant then gives her gold jewelry, asks who her family is, and if they can shelter him. She gives her parentage (informing the servant that he has met a relative of Abraham), declaring they will receive him (Gen. 24:22–5). As the servant bows, expressing thanks to Yahweh, Rebecca runs ahead to her mother's house (Gen. 24:26–8). Rebecca's brother, Laban, goes out and ushers the servant in (Gen. 24:29–31). Received with full hospitality, a footbath, and offered food, he declines to eat until he has said why he has come (Gen. 24:32–3). Recounting his errand from Abraham, repeating his prayer to Yahweh, the servant asks if Rebecca will become Isaac's wife. Laban and her father say Yahweh has already indicated that this is so (Gen. 24: 49–52). Bringing out costly presents for Rebecca, for her mother and brother, he and his men eat, and spend the night there (Gen. 24:53–4). The

---

[5] Cf. also G. P. Rose (1969) on tensions in the *Odyssey*'s depiction of the Phaiakians.

next morning when the servant asks if Rebecca may now leave with him, her mother and brother ask that she stay with them for ten days, and then follow. But the servant urges them not to restrain him, to let him leave now with Rebecca. When they ask her what she wishes, she says she will go with Abraham's servant (Gen. 24:55–9). Her mother and brother then bless her, and she and her maids mount the camels and follow the servant (Gen. 24:60–1).

A generation later Jacob, fleeing the wrath of his brother Esau (discussed below), also heads to Nahor to find a wife. He comes to a well in the countryside, with three flocks of sheep beside it, and a huge stone over its mouth (Gen. 29:1–3). When Jacob asks the shepherds if they know Laban, they so affirm and point out his daughter Rachel, approaching with a flock (Gen. 29:4–6). Then rolling the well stone off by himself (below as parallel to Jason's labors for Aietes), Jacob waters Laban's flock for Rachel (Gen. 29: 7–10). Kissing her, he tearfully tells her he is Rebecca's son, her father's kinsman, whereupon she runs home to tell Laban (Gen. 29:11–12). Laban now meets Jacob, welcoming and acknowledging him as family (Gen. 29:13–14).

When Moses flees Egypt after having killed a man, he comes to Midian and sits by a well (Exod. 2:12–15). Seven daughters of the priest Reuel come to water their father's sheep and fill the troughs, only to have shepherds drive them away (Exod. 2:16–17a). Moses, however, comes to their aid, watering their sheep. When they recount what happened to their father, he tells them to go and invite Moses to dinner (Exod. 2:17b–20). Moses, now agreeing to stay with Reuel, is given his daughter Zipporah in marriage (Exod. 2:21).[6]

Odysseus' encounter with Nausikaa at the river closely parallels the OT scenes at the wells. In a dream Athena appears to Nausikaa, prompting her to do the family laundry at the river, and thus encounter Odysseus (*Od.* 6.21–40). Nausikaa's own concern, however, is her marriage (*Od.* 6.27), to look nice as it approaches. In its greater interest in female characters than is usual in OT myth, the *Odyssey* begins the encounter from Nausikaa's perspective (unlike any of the OT betrothal scenes), maintaining her point of view until Odysseus awakes. As in Gen. 24:12–14, a god brings about the encounter, though Athena works in a more direct manner than Yahweh. For Nausikaa the central theme becomes her presumed imminent courtship (*Od.* 6.33–5, 66–7, 109, 158–9, 181–5, 244–5, 276–88).[7] Two handmaidens

---

[6] See Alter (1981: 52–62) for additional discussion of the OT episodes.
[7] Cf. Crane (1988: 137–8).

also sleep in her room (*Od.* 6.18–19), which, de Jong notes (2001: 153), signal her chastity, much as Rebecca's virginity is stressed (Gen. 24:16). Nausikaa's beauty is described repeatedly (*Od.* 6.16, 101–9, 149–52; 7.291; 8.457), as are Rebecca's (Gen. 24:16) and Rachel's (Gen. 29:17).

Prompted by Athena, Nausikaa will go to the washing places (*Od.* 6.40), the river where Odysseus came ashore the previous night. In the desert-set OT myths, the well is the body of water where such encounters unfold. Though Alter may be right in seeing the well as a natural feminine symbol (1981: 52), Homeric and OT myths employ the body of water, whether river or well, as locations where a foreign man may encounter local women performing chores (Gen. 24:11), fetching water, or washing clothes for a household (cf. *Od.* 15.420–2). Genesis 24, first referring to a well (Gen. 24:11), later speaks of a spring (Gen. 24:13, 30), suggesting a middle ground between well and river, underscoring that the particular form the water source takes in these myths is not crucial. The young woman demonstrates her suitability as a wife by carrying out such household tasks. The Phaiakians' washing places are far from the city (*Od.* 6.40), as Rebecca's (Gen. 24:11) and Rachel's well is outside the city.

The morning after her dream Nausikaa asks her father for a wagon to wash her brothers' clothes. Deducing his daughter's real intent (*Od.* 6.67), that her *own* clothes will be fresh, in assenting he implicitly consents to her plans for an approaching marriage, rather like Rebecca's father letting her decide when to leave (Gen. 24:55–9).[8] Accompanied by her maids (as Rachel), Nausikaa drives the wagon to the washing places (*Od.* 6.85–7). As Nausikaa drives her father's cart bringing the laundry to the river, Rachel drives Laban's flock to the well (Gen. 29:10), as Zipporah and her sisters drive their father's sheep (Exod. 2:16). Waiting for the wash to dry, having anointed themselves with olive oil, Nausikaa and her maids remove their veils to play ball. The anointing with oil, removing the veil, and the vigor with which they play, all heighten Nausikaa's physical appeal, increasing the erotic potential of the subsequent encounter.[9] At Athena's urging, Nausikaa makes an errant toss, the ball landing in the river where Odysseus sleeps, waking him. In the OT episodes the man who will encounter the girl is already at the well when she arrives, as Odysseus is already at the river.

The narrative's focus now turns to the naked Odysseus, not knowing where he is, awakened by the girls' excited cries as they play. Hiding his

---

[8] Cf. de Jong (2001: 155): "His all-encompassing formulation 'I do not begrudge you the mules *nor anything else*' can be seen as an implicit, positive answer to her unexpressed desire to marry."

[9] Cf. J. B. Hainsworth on their having removed their veils (1988: 299), "note the erotic undertone."

genitals with a branch, he goes forward. The maids scatter, but Nausikaa remains as he approaches. Unlike men in the OT betrothal type-scenes, Odysseus is completely without resources, or clothes. The girl is the first local inhabitant addressed by the foreign man at Genesis 24:17, where he makes a specific request of her in his first speech, there for water, here for clothes. Both Genesis 24:17 and Odysseus's speech here serve as supplications. Equipped only with his masterful speaking ability, Odysseus addresses Nausikaa at length. Given his immediate need to persuade her that he presents no threat, his speech lacks any counterpart in the OT myths, which are less likely to contain the kind of extended speeches common in Homeric epic. Nonetheless, his speech touches on most of the same topics found, or implicit, when the foreign man addresses the girl in the OT betrothal type-scenes. He praises her beauty (*Od.* 6.149–52, 157, 160–1; cf. Gen. 24:16 and 29:17), implicitly asks about her parents (*Od.* 6.154–6), and twice raises the issue of her future marriage (*Od.* 6.158–9, 181–5). Though without a counterpart in the OT myths, Odysseus' nudity here finds a parallel in at least one other related scene, Jason as he performs Aietes' labors. Jason is explicitly naked in his *agon* in Apollonius (3.1282), and implicitly in Pindar (*Pythia* 4 232). The branches Odysseus holds also find parallels in the wood sprigs and shoots in Jacob's myth, while Hermes offering a herb to Odysseus as he approaches Kirke may also be relevant (*Od.* 10.276–306, discussed below).

Nausikaa grants his supplication, as does Rebecca (Gen. 24:18–22). She offers him a bath (*Od.* 6.210), as Rebecca offers water from her jug, both activities being subsets of the women's work, the reason they are present at the river/well. The maids, by coming back to bathe him, as Nausikaa instructs, find a parallel in Reuel urging his daughters to go back and invite Moses to dine with them (Exod. 2:20). Now he is bathed, dressed in clothes provided by Nausikaa (the reason Athena prompts her to do laundry), and anointed with grace by Athena, Nausikaa sees Odysseus as her potential husband:

> If only a man of this sort were to be called my husband
> and was living here; if only it pleased him to stay here.
> *Odyssey* 6.244–5

After having her maids offer Odysseus food and drink, Nausikaa prepares to lead him to the city, and her parents' home. Her lengthy speech (*Od.* 6.255–315) employs topics standard in OT betrothal type-scenes: her father's name, his position among the Phaiakians, and directions to his household. Alter notes (1981: 52–7) in all instances of the OT type-scene the girl hurriedly runs to her parents' house, arriving there ahead of the foreign man (Rebecca: Gen. 24:2, Rachel: 29:12, Zipporah: Exod. 2:18), as does Nausikaa here, though stating a different reason for doing so.

She (*Od.* 6.273–84) raises the possibility that there will be friction between Odysseus and the Phaiakian men, in rivalry over her. Already picturing Odysseus as her husband, Nausikaa imagines she will provoke animosity by choosing a man outside her own people.[10] Friction between the foreign man and local men, or athletic competition between them, develops around the girl in two of the OT betrothal scenes. In Exodus, when some shepherds come and drive Zipporah and her sisters away from the well, Moses intervenes, coming to the girls' help and watering their sheep for them (Exod. 2:17). As soon as Jacob sees Rachel at the well, by himself he rolls away the well stone that all the shepherds together are needed to roll away (Gen. 29:2–3), and waters her flocks for her (Gen. 29:10), besting the other shepherds in a show of strength. Speiser notes (1962: 223), "True to the ageless pattern, the prospective suitor is inspired to a display of superhuman prowess at the very first sight of Rachel."

But after suggesting such friction between Odysseus and Phaiakian men here in Book 6, the *Odyssey* postpones any until Book 8, in the athletic games. Insulted and challenged to compete in the games, Odysseus is victorious in the discus throw (*Od.* 8.100–98). Demodokos' first song (*Od.* 8.75) introduces Odysseus involved in competition as a theme in its mention of a quarrel, strife (*neikos*) between Odysseus and Akhilleus at Troy. Demodokos' topic is a first sounding of a traditional theme also common to OT betrothal type-scenes and Argonautic myth, as discussed below. Friction develops between Odysseus and the rude Phaiakian athlete Euryalos. In his victory in the games Odysseus thus parallels Jacob in the OT betrothal scene, implicitly besting all the other shepherds in rolling the stone away from the well (Gen. 29:10). But unlike the OT betrothal scenes, the *Odyssey* develops this friction without Nausikaa's actual involvement. She is neither present when Odysseus accomplishes his feat, nor does he compete for her attention when he does so. Similar motifs occur near the end of the poem on Ithaka when the mysterious wanderer, who appears to come from abroad, by winning the contest of the bow, defeating rude men in an athletic competition, wins the bride, who had earlier begun to show him favor which she denied the local men.

---

[10] Cf. Crane (1988: 139): "Nausikaa anticipates that her countrymen would resent a marriage to an outlander."

As Nausikaa drives ahead with the wagon, and Odysseus and the servants walk behind, he stops to pray to Athena (*Od.* 6.321–8; 7.1), very like Abraham's servant first praying to Yahweh in his betrothal scene (Gen. 24:12–14, 26–7, 52). In answer to his prayer, Athena appears in the form of a virgin girl carrying a water pitcher (*Od.* 7.20), just as in the OT betrothal scenes. When he asks her if she knows where Alkinoös' house is, she leads him, telling of Alkinoös' nobility and advising him about Arete. With no hints of marriage between Odysseus and *this* girl, however, the scene is distinct from the betrothal type-scenes, but similar to an episode in 1 Samuel. Saul and his attendants, looking for some donkeys, meet girls drawing water who give them directions and information about how to find a seer (1 Sam. 9:11–14). The two episodes suggest the existence of a subtype of this genre, with most of the same basic motifs as the betrothal type-scene, but without *eros*, with no suggestion of romantic or marital involvement, or athletic contests. The basic motif may reflect a certain realism: a foreign man would know that if he waited at a well or fountain, he could obtain information from girls drawing water.

Odysseus' subsequent interactions with the Phaiakians suggest further parallels with Jacob's interactions with Laban and his people, beyond the betrothal type-scene. With unexpected suddenness, for most readers, Alkinoös proposes that Odysseus marry Nausikaa (*Od.* 7.311–15), after only a brief exchange of remarks at their first meeting. This is just what happens, as noted, in the OT betrothal type-scenes (Gen. 24:50–5; Exod. 2:21). It is interesting that Alkinoös attracts criticism[11] for acting in exactly the same way as the OT characters, who escape similar criticisms.[12] Only Jacob's offer is exceptional in coming after he has been there for a month (Gen. 29:18–19), but this is thematic for his interactions with Laban, as discussed below. Alkinoös' offer uses very similar terms as Nausikaa's remark at *Odyssey* 6.244–5, affirming its status as a usual part of such a narrative:

αἲ γὰρ (1) ἐμοὶ τοιόσδε (2) πόσις κεκλημένος (3) εἴη
ἐνθάδε ναιετάων, καί οἱ ἅδοι αὐτόθι μίμνειν (4).
Odyssey 6.244–5

αἲ γὰρ, (1) Ζεῦ τε πάτερ καὶ Ἀθηναίη καὶ Ἄπολλον,
τοῖος (2) ἐὼν οἷός ἐσσι, τά τε φρονέων ἅ τ' ἐγώ περ,
παῖδά τ' ἐμὴν ἐχέμεν καὶ ἐμὸς γαμβρὸς καλέεσθαι (3)
αὖθι μένων (4).
Odyssey 7.311–14

---

[11] E.g., Woodhouse (1930: 59): "For it is clear that Alkinoös is conceived to be somewhat of a buffoon."
[12] Though see Propp (1999: 175) on Exod. 2:15–23, "We may wonder why Reuel is so quick to bestow his daughter on a violent if well-intentioned stranger."

The offer of marriage comes after Odysseus recounts how he arrived on Scheria, what happened between him and Nausikaa (*Od.* 7.290–7, 303–7), very like in the first OT betrothal type-scene when Abraham's servant recounts how he came, and how he met Rebecca (Gen. 24:37–48).

ODYSSEUS AND NAUSIKAA, JASON AND MEDEA

But before considering further parallels with the myth of Jacob, Laban, and Rebecca, we engage the myth of Jason and Medea for its significant parallels with Odysseus' encounter with Nausikaa, which many commentators have noted.[13] Crane remarks further on the tendency of Books 6–8 to offer a conflicting portrait of the Phaiakians, as simultaneously hospitable and inhospitable to Odysseus (1988: 138):

> On the other hand, the narrative provides the backdrop for a very different story: that of the stranger who must prove himself and win the daughter of the king in marriage... Athena makes Odysseus physically more impressive so that he can perform the many ἄεθλοι that the Phaeacians will impose upon him.

He observes that Athena prepares Odysseus for *tests* (*Od.* 8.22), though only a single incident, Euryalos' provocation and Odysseus' subsequent participation in the athletic games, is depicted. Adducing additional evidence, Crane, and others, argue that the *Odyssey* here incorporates a myth much like that of Jason and Medea.[14] Nausikaa, like Medea, is the princess daughter of the local king, for whose hand the wandering hero competes in a series of tests imposed by her father, as Crane summarizes (1988: 140):

> The overall similarity between Medea and Nausicaa – two young princesses in a distant, mysterious land and ready for marriage – is clear enough. In particular, we might compare the "many" ἄεθλοι with which the Phaeacians will supposedly test Odysseus, with the ἄεθλοι that Aietes actually does impose upon Jason.

This is not to deny profound differences in the characters of Nausikaa and Medea. The latter is a curious mixture of the naive innocent girl, which we recognize in the Phaiakian princess, but also a potent sorceress, capable of acting outside the mortal sphere. Apollonius' depiction of Medea's dream, the night she first meets Jason, presents such a mixture within the space of a few lines:

---

[13] See Woodhouse (1930: 54–65), and Crane (1988: 135) for a summary of previous work, especially Meuli.

[14] Cf. Woodhouse (1930: 60): "Is it not perfectly clear that we have before us an adaptation of a story in which a stranger is brought to a test of athletic feats, in which he proves himself to be the superior of all competitors?"

> She thought that the stranger undertook the contest (ἄεθλον)
> not being eager to carry off the fleece of the ram,
> not for this had he come to Aietes' city,
> but so he could lead her to his own home
> as his wedded wife. She thought that she herself contended (ἀεθλεύουσα)
> with the oxen, accomplished the toils easily
> and that her parents made light of their promise, for they
> did not order the maiden to yoke the oxen but the
> stranger himself.
>
> Argonautica 3.619–27

The dream begins by suggesting a Medea very like the self-absorbed Nausikaa (3.619–22), but then alludes to her real powers, that she, through her magic, will be able to perform the difficult labors.

GENESIS 27–31: JASON: JACOB; MEDEA: RACHEL; HERA: REBECCA; AIETES: LABAN

Jason's labors for Aietes and his marrying Medea give us a context not only for parts of the *Odyssey*, but for the myth of Jacob, Laban, and Rachel. Jacob's interactions with Laban to win Rachel are the same genre of myth as Jason's with Aietes for Medea, though differing in a few respects. In Apollonius' account, Jason and Medea first meet in the temple of Hecate, though the Argonauts first come ashore in the river Phasis, where they moor their ship (*Argo.* 2.1262–81), which may indirectly instantiate the expected first meeting at the river or well.[15] In a key difference, Jason's encounter with Aietes and Medea is initially subordinated to his quest for the Golden Fleece, while Jacob's myth is not heroic (except for his wrestling with god, noted in Chapter 4), and thus has a different modality throughout, compared to Jason's quest. Consequently, though Laban's myth has a counterpart to the Golden Fleece (his household gods, as discussed below), it plays a smaller role, and is not the reason for Jacob's meeting with Rachel, as for Jason and Medea. Jacob's labors for Laban are less heroic but involve significant passage of time, two terms of seven years, rather than a series of daunting tasks that might be completed in a day, as for Jason. Though on a much smaller scale, a tendency for events to be postponed also defines Odysseus' stay on Scheria (Fenik 1974: 7, 11, 22, etc.).

---

[15] When Medea first sees Jason, and, spurred by Cupid's arrow, desires him, she is compared to a toiling woman stoking a fire (*Argo.* 3.291–7), which maintains the usual focus on women's work when the girl first sees the hero.

Jacob and Jason both go abroad because of a crisis at home that originally has no connection with obtaining a wife. Later, their cause for being abroad becomes intertwined with finding wives. As noted in Chapter 4, Jacob's deception to cheat his brother out of his father's blessing enrages Esau, who vows to kill him (Gen. 27:41–2). When Rebecca learns of Esau's anger, she orders Jacob to go stay with her brother, Laban (Gen. 27:43–5). When she explains to Isaac, Rebecca adds, as a pretext for his going abroad, her insistence that Jacob not marry any of the local women, but one of her own kin. But the root cause and original motivation for Jacob's leaving is to avoid Esau's wrath (Gen. 27:42–5). Carr (1996: 86) argues that the myth combines two separate versions, "one where marriage is not at all an issue (Gen. 27:1–45), and one where it is the only issue (Gen. 27:46–28:5)." Jason is being denied his right to the throne by Pelias, a usurper (Pindar, *Pythia* 4 109–16), who, in a motif common in Greek heroic myth, sends Jason off to perform a presumably impossible task, from which he will never return.[16]

Jacob and Jason both receive crucial advice and support from an influential female who intervenes on their behalf, a mentor. For Jacob, this is his mother Rebecca, who more than counterbalances Isaac's own preference for Esau (Gen. 25:28). She contrives Jacob's deception of Isaac and Esau, and oversees his departure when Esau threatens to kill him. When Jacob hesitates to follow her advice, she reassures him, "only obey my voice" (Gen. 27:13). In so doing she parallels Hera's repeated interventions on Jason's behalf. After helping him when disguised as an old woman, Hera is thereafter Jason's mentor deity (Hera herself mentions the incident later, *Argo.* 3.66–73). When Isaac is startled by how quickly Jacob has brought the venison he desired, Jacob claims that Yahweh brought it to him (Gen. 27:20), assigning divine agency to acts that Rebecca herself accomplishes. By so doing, the narrative implicitly suggests a divine parallel in Rebecca's actions.

Rebecca parallels Hera in additional ways, both playing a central role in a further genre of myth. In tricking her husband into blessing the son she favors, Rebecca closely parallels Hera's role in the myth of Herakles (briefly noted in Chapter 3), as depicted in Book 19 of the *Iliad*. When Zeus announces his plans for his special son Herakles, Hera subverts his wish, manipulating him into swearing an oath that will, unknown to Zeus, apply to Eurystheus, not Herakles (*Il.* 19.96–133). A close homology exists between all the main characters. Each father (Isaac and Zeus) carelessly

---

[16] Pelias thus resembles Eurystheus in Herakles' myths, an illegitimate king who acquires power over the hero.

misuses the power he intends to bestow upon his favored son (Esau and Herakles). Deceived by his wife (Rebecca and Hera), he is tricked into blessing her favorite (Jacob and Eurystheus, Gen. 27:30, 33; *Il.* 19.112–13), her reason for having intervened. While Rebecca is Jacob's mother, Hera suggests a maternal relationship to Eurystheus, acting almost as a midwife to encourage his birth and delay Herakles' (*Il.* 19.118–19).

The father's favorite son, Esau and Herakles, is the more heroic of the two, a hunter (Gen. 25: 27–8; 27:5, 39–40), who uses the bow (Gen. 27:3), known for his appetite (Gen. 25:29–34),[17] and who is so hairy that Jacob must wear animal skins to resemble him (Gen. 25:25, 27:11–24; on Herakles as hirsute see Hard 1998: 212). Like Esau to Jacob, Herakles is the first born of twin brothers, born the night before Iphicles (Apollodorus II.4.8). These defining characteristics, uncommon in OT myth,[18] establish Esau as a typological equivalent of Herakles. But in spite of his father's favor, and his own physical endowment, he is made subservient to the mother/stepmother's favorite (Gen. 27:37; *Il.* 19.122–33). So close are the two traditions that Alter's note (2004: 145) on how Esau is disadvantaged by Isaac's blessing could apply to Herakles' subsequent laborious life, "Deprived by paternal pronouncement of political mastery, he must make his way through violent struggle."

Laban has more than a little in common with Aietes as devious fathers of the young woman the protagonists will marry after accomplishing a series of difficult tests. Rebecca originally intended that Jacob stay with Laban for only a few days (Gen. 27:44–5). But when avoiding Esau's anger combines with finding a wife, for whom he must then perform a series of labors, Jacob's stay grows to years, due to Laban's deviousness. Striking a bargain that will require Jacob to work for seven years to win Rachel, Laban apparently pays Jacob nothing for the previous month (Gen. 29:15). When the seven years are finished, Laban breaks the bargain, giving Jacob not Rachel, but her older sister, Leah (Gen. 29:20–6), behavior aligning him with Laomedon, the king of Troy who cheated Poseidon and Apollo out of their wages (*Il.* 21.441–57; cf. 7.452–3). Aietes also breaks the contract for which he himself proposes the terms (*Argo.* 3.400–21; 4.7–10, 228–35). In his first remarks to Aietes Jason characterizes Pelias as *atasthalos*, "reckless" (*Argo.* 3.390).[19] The narrator first characterizes Aietes as *huperphialos*, "arrogant" (*Argo.* 3.17). Jason has thus traded one negative

---

[17] See Alter's note (2004: 131) on Esau's "coarsely appetitive character."
[18] The only other OT character so emphatically hairy is Elijah (2 Kgs. 1:8).
[19] *Atasthalos* serves as a moral term in Homeric epic, "denoting behavior . . . that goes against the gods' designs, much like 'sin'" (Louden 2006: 228).

father figure for another, with Aietes imposing labors on top of those Pelias earlier imposed.[20] Both Jacob and Jason trade friction at home for similar friction from the fathers of the women they will marry. Unexpectedly applicable to Laban, and Aietes, is Jason's description of Pelias from Pindar's *Pythia* 4:

> For I give over to you the sheep,
> the tawny herds of cattle, and all the fields which you stole
> from my parents and administer to fatten your wealth –
> I do not mind if these overly enrich your house.
>
> *Pythia* 4, 148–51[21]

Though Rachel is not a witch, as is Medea, magic is present, even prominent, in her myth. Unable to bear children, when she learns that Leah's first son, Reuben, has found some mandrakes (Gen. 30:14, μῆλα... μανδραγορῶν in the Septuagint), Rachel asks if she may use them, presumably as an aphrodisiac (Speiser 1962: 231, Alter 2004: 160). In Apollonius' account, a love-charm, in the form of Eros' agency, is the central means of assuring Medea will unite with Jason. In Jacob's myth Rachel, already married to Jacob, seizes upon a similar agent to obtain offspring from him. Apollonius' key depiction of Medea's magic (*Argo.* 3.845–66) describes her use of the "Prometheion" drug. Particular emphasis is placed on the plant's root, said to resemble "newly-cut flesh" (*Argo.* 3.857), which, when cut, causes an earthquake, prompting Prometheus himself to groan (*Argo.* 3.864–6). Hunter notes the plant's likely identity (1989: 188),

Greek myth knew of many plants which grew from blood... and scholars have sought a real plant lying behind Apollonius' description... The most likely candidate is mandrake, around which there was extensive folklore.

Each myth thus depicts both young wives with the same plant, aware of its magical properties, though putting it to different uses in their differing contexts. In Euripides Medea knows how to use drugs to produce children as she so advises Aegeus (*Medea* 717–18).

Central to Medea's magic is *cutting roots*, as in the episode just mentioned, which twice juxtaposes the two terms (ῥίζης τεμνομένης: *Argonautica* 3.865; cf. νεοτμήτῳ... ῥίζα: 3.857; δυσπαλέας ῥίζας: 4.52; ἀρκεύθοιο νέον τετμηότι θαλλῷ: 4.156). Sophocles' play, the *Rhizotomoi*, *The Root*

---

[20] Cf. Hunter (1989: 143): "both Aietes and Pelias set Jason tasks which they have no expectation he will survive"; and (145): "Aietes conceals his desire to destroy Jason behind the mask of a high 'heroic code.'"
[21] Translation by Race (1997).

Cutters, focused on Medea tricking Pelias' daughters into slaying him (Gantz 1993: 366). A surviving fragment again juxtaposes the two terms, κίσται ῥιζῶν κρύπτουσι τομάς, "boxes conceal the cuttings of the roots" (Lloyd-Jones 1996: frag. 534). The same belief in magic lying in cut roots underlies the episode of Hermes and the black root of the moly drug (*Od.* 10.276–306). "Moly" itself may be cognate with Sanskrit *mûlam*, "root" (Heubeck 1989: 60). There is no mention of its root having been cut, but Odysseus' emphasis on how difficult it is to dig it up may imply this (*Od.* 10.305–6). While Kirke is not mentioned cutting roots, implicitly Hermes enables Odysseus to beat her at her own game, so to speak, with the moly. Adding parallels to Medea, the episode opens with the *Odyssey*'s only use of the epithet *polypharmakos* (*Od.* 10.276), "having many drugs," here uniquely used of Kirke.

Euripides' treatment of the same characters later in their saga, a Jason who no longer desires Medea, complements suggestions in Apollonius that he is exploiting her, eager to benefit from her powers, but not originally intending to marry her, until she maneuvers him into an oath to do so (*Argo.* 4.95–8). Though Jacob is not depicted so callously in his relations with Rachel, he spreads his sexual attentions far more broadly than Jason, having sex with at least three other women (Leah, and the two slaves, Bilhah and Zilpah) while married to Rachel. Rachel's use of the mandrake as a love philter, though set within the polygamy of the patriarchs' myths, suggests parallels with Medea's larger relationship with Jason.

When Rachel gives birth to Joseph (a consequence of the mandrake?), Jacob, after fourteen years with Laban to win Rachel, now wants to take his wives and children and leave. He suggests that he be allowed to keep, as his wages, "every black lamb, and all the brindled and the spotted goats" (Gen. 30:32). Saying he agrees to these terms, Laban has his sons remove all livestock meeting the specifications. But Jacob then takes rods of poplar, almond, and plane trees, and strips of bark, and has animals mate before them, causing them to give birth "to young that were striped and spotted and brindled" (Gen. 30:39). Jacob vastly increases his holdings, drastically decreasing Laban's future holdings, using a form of magic using freshly cut plants which the narrative first associates with Rachel, but that also resembles Medea's craft.[22]

Jacob's use of magic to obtain offspring from the livestock, the precise varieties to which Laban had agreed, suggests parallels with the labors

---

[22] On Jacob's method as magic, see Carr (1996: 270): "Jacob's use of magical means to cause Laban's flocks to produce more speckled and spotted goats...for himself."

Jason performs for Aietes, aided by Medea's magic. As Aietes specifies (*Argo.* 3. 400–21), Jason yokes the bulls, sows the fields with the dragon's teeth, and then fights the sown men, through Medea's magic from the cut root of the "Prometheion." Rachel intends to use the mandrake to obtain offspring, children; Jacob uses the tree shoots and bark strips to obtain offspring from Laban's livestock. Both activities depend upon the character's ability to exert control over a form of procreation. The same is true of Jason's labors for Aietes: yoking the bulls, sowing the fields, and fighting the sown men, all, as Gantz notes, suggest Jason can be seen as harvesting a crop (1993: 361), "rushing among them and mowing them down while they are still in the ground, as if he were a harvester." Jacob's earlier rolling away of the stone on first seeing Rachel, Laban's daughter (Gen. 29:10), while a miniature of his later successful accomplishment of the other labors, is also a thematic equivalent of Jason's more vigorous labors for Aietes.

Laban's treatment of Jacob, after his son-in-law accomplishes what had been agreed upon, is very like how Aietes acts after Jason accomplishes the labors Aietes specified for winning the Golden Fleece. His trick method of "harvesting" blemished livestock a great success, Jacob finds himself out of favor with Laban and his sons:

> He noticed also that Laban was not so well disposed to him, as he had once been.
> (Genesis 31:2)

> Jacob learnt that Laban's sons were saying,
> "Jacob has taken everything that our father had, and all his wealth has come from our father's property."
> (Genesis 31:1)

Aietes is outraged when, contrary to his expectation, Jason accomplishes his labors (*Argo.* 3.1404–6; 4.6–11, 4.212–35). Deciding to leave in secret, Jacob persuades Rachel and Leah to leave their father, citing Laban's history of shortchanging him (Gen. 31:7), "yet he has cheated me and changed my wages ten times over." Lacking the heroic dynamic and royal intrigue of Jason's myth, Jacob's dispute with Laban seems more mercantile than heroic, until Rachel steals Laban's household gods, which thrusts the ensuing portions of the narrative into some unexpected areas.

Rachel stealing her father's household gods (Gen. 31:19–35) is a close thematic parallel to Medea helping Jason make off with Aietes' Golden Fleece. Her motivation for doing so is how her father has treated her (Gen. 31:14–16). It is Rachel's idea to steal Laban's household gods (τὰ εἴδωλα:

31:19 and τοὺς θεούς: 31:30 in the Septuagint), and Rachel who actually steals them, an aggressive act worthy of Medea. While the myth never demonstrates the function of the household gods, Alter notes the parallel in Aeneas taking the Trojan Penates in *Aeneid* 2 (2004: 169). Suggs offers further explanation (1992: 40), "Possession of the household gods insured safety and prosperity and possibly the right of inheritance." In stealing her father's gods, Rachel replicates the central role Medea plays in Jason obtaining the Golden Fleece from her father.[23] Both acts are done in stealth, outraging the fathers when they learn of it.

Material remains demonstrate that such acts occurred between different cultures, as the myths of Jason and Medea and Jacob and Rachel suggest. Morris notes how the phrase "Potnia Aswiya" on a Mycenaean tablet at Pylos (2001: Fr 1206) apparently designates a goddess imported into Greece from Asia. Yasur-Landau notes the opposite, evidence that the cult of an Aegean goddess was apparently introduced into Canaan. Providing a context for interpretation, he observes instances of priestesses introducing cults of female deities into newly established colonies, described by Strabo and Pausanias (2001: 336–7),

The foundation of cult is done by transfer of an *Aphidrum*; a statue or another sacred object ... The participation of a priestess is in this, as perhaps in other cases of transfer of cult of female deities, an essential one: only women could wash and adorn a female cult image.

Though the gender of Laban's household gods is not specified, nor an issue in the myth, nor is the Golden Fleece gendered, we should, nonetheless, be struck by the parallel roles of the women. Medea, priestess of Hecate, helping Jason take the sacred Golden Fleece corresponds closely to the priestesses in Strabo and Pausanias, and to Rachel, though she is not depicted as a priestess. All of which again recalls Theano, and her role in handing over the Palladium to Odysseus and Diomedes, as noted in Chapter 4.

Jacob and Jason both subsequently sneak off with their wives, and their entourages, to begin the journey home. In the face of such malicious fathers-in-law, Jacob and Jason have little choice than to act as they do, as Alter notes of Jacob (2004: 169):

In heading for Canaan with his wives, children, and flocks, Jacob is actually taking what is rightly his ... but he has good reason to fear that the grasping Laban will renege on their agreement, and so he feels compelled to flee in stealth.

---

[23] The Golden Fleece and Laban's household gods also suggest a basic equivalence, or similar thematic function, with the Palladium of the Trojan War and the Ark of OT myth, sacred items which, for those who possess them, keep them safe from defeat, but, when taken, lead to their loss of power.

The dynamics of their flight, the pursuit by the livid fathers and their sons, are quite close. Each father is enraged over the taking of the sacred article (Golden Fleece, household gods) and his daughter's flight. Each father launches a lengthy pursuit in which his son(s) also take part. In the more heroic style typical of epic, Aietes reacts to Jason's triumph and formulates his response in an assembly:

> Aietes with the men of his people, as many as were the bravest,
> all night within his halls was contriving utter cunning against
> the Argonauts, for he was enraged in his heart at the dreadful
> contest, unceasingly, nor did he suppose at all
> that these things were accomplished without his *daughters*.
> *Argonautica* 4.6–10

In a further parallel both Medea and Rachel have older sisters, Chalciope and Leah, who have extensive interaction with the respective protagonists, Jacob and Jason, and support them over their own fathers. In the *Argonautica* Chalciope's four grown sons (Argus, Cytissorus, Phrontis, and Melas) have earlier become part of Jason's group of heroes (*Argo.* 2.1155–6), while Leah's sons are also part of Jacob's entourage. Aietes subsequently demands Medea be brought back to him, threatening to kill his people if they fail to do so (*Argo.* 4.228–35). When Laban learns that Jacob has departed in secret, he and his unnamed sons pursue them for seven days (Gen. 31:20–3).

Apsyrtos, Aietes' son, and Laban and his sons, both pursue and overtake the two protagonists as they flee with Aietes' Fleece and Laban's household gods. Apsyrtos' ability to pursue is hinted at in earlier scenes where he holds the reins of Helios' chariot (*Argo.* 3.245, 1236).[24] Leading a group of Colchians in pursuit (*Argo.* 4.305–28), he outmaneuvers Jason, hemming him in, where the river Ister separates around a group of islands. In a thematic, if land-locked, parallel, Laban overtakes Jacob, camping opposite him in the hill-country in Gilead (Gen. 31:25). Though Laban takes the lead in the pursuit (whereas Aietes remains at his palace), his sons accompany him, and are depicted expressing an aggressive, even threatening attitude toward Jacob (Gen. 31:1).[25] In a speech which could easily be delivered by Apsyrtos on Aietes' behalf, if Fleece is substituted for household gods

---

[24] Hunter (1989: 125): "Apsyrtus acts as his father's charioteer in contexts where Aietes' links with Helios are important."

[25] Cf. Alter's comment on Laban's sons (2004: 166), "Here they are used to dramatize in a single quick stroke the atmosphere of suspicion and jealousy in Laban's household: they make the extravagant claim that the visibly prospering Jacob 'has taken everything of our father's,' thus leaving them nothing. The anonymous sons would presumably be members of the pursuit party Laban forms to go after the fleeing Jacob."

(Gen. 31:26–30), Laban accuses Jacob of having deceived him, kidnapping his daughters, fleeing in secret, and stealing his household gods.

In both myths subsequent negotiations result in Jason and Jacob keeping the sacred article and Aietes'/Laban's daughter, though the nature of the negotiations differs considerably. Since Jason satisfied Aietes' own terms for obtaining the Fleece, Apsyrtos, negotiating on Aietes' behalf, determines that he may keep it (*Argo.* 4.338–49). More incensed by Medea's role (*Argo.* 4.228–35), Aietes has Apsyrtos attempt to negotiate her return. Laban likewise criticizes Jacob at greater length for taking his daughters than for stealing his household gods, which is entirely attributed to Rachel (Gen. 31:19). At this juncture each myth compares the daughter to a woman captured as a slave in war (*Argo.* 4.400; Gen. 31:26). Absent from the OT myth, however, is any violence against Laban's sons that would parallel the slaying of Apsyrtos in the *Argonautica* (though, as discussed below, Jacob fears a violent confrontation with his own brother Esau).

When Jason proposes tricking Apsyrtos in order to ruin him (*Argo.* 4.404–5), he veers into behavior rather like Jacob's earlier conduct toward his family members. Immediately before, when Medea fears that Jason will turn her over to Apsyrtos to be taken back to Aietes, she accuses him of breaking his oaths to her (*Argo.* 4.358–9, 388), also suggestive of Jacob's deceitful dealings with both Esau and Isaac. But it is Medea who converts Jason's broad suggestion into a plot to murder her brother, feigning hospitality in order to slay him at Artemis' temple (*Argo.* 4.15–22, 468–81) and dispatch the other pursuing Colchians in similar fashion (*Argo.* 4.482–9). Though Rachel makes no such proposal, she suggests a similarly aggressive nature in executing the theft of Laban's household gods. When the remaining Colchians in pursuit learn of Apsyrtos' death, they are afraid to return to Aietes, and settle instead in the islands nearby (*Argo.* 4.507–21).

As a result of what they gained on their journeys, Jacob and Jason are better prepared to deal with the crisis each left at home. But both first perform one additional labor during their journey home. Jason must overcome Talos, the bronze giant who guards Crete. Jacob, in his most overtly heroic act, wrestles Yahweh, as discussed in Chapter 4. But after Talos' defeat Apollonius' *Argonautica* ends abruptly, breaking off more than concluding, without depicting Jason's return to Iolkos or subsequent encounter with Pelias. In most accounts Jason and/or Medea slay(s) Pelias (*Argo.* 4.249–50; Gantz 1993: 365–7), or cause(s) him to be slain by others (Euripides, *Medea* 9–10, 486–7). Jacob, expecting a violent confrontation with Esau, like Jason's friction with Pelias, or even his confrontation with Apsyrtos, instead achieves reconciliation with his previously hostile brother.

When he learns that Esau is on his way to meet him with a company of 400 men (Gen. 32:6),[26] much as Aietes sends his men after Jason, fearing destruction of his entire group, he divides his company into two halves (Gen. 32:7–8), so at least some will survive. His act offers yet another parallel with Odysseus, who divides his crew in half on Aiaia between two relevant encounters, just before meeting with Kirke, Medea's aunt (*Od.* 10.203–7), right after the devastating confrontation with the Laistrygones (*Od.* 10.81–134), discussed below.

ARGONAUTIC MYTH AS A THEMATIC FRAMEWORK IN *ODYSSEY* 6–8, 10–13

Having established that the tale of Jacob and Rachel is the same genre of myth as that of Jason and Medea, we reconsider Odysseus' encounter with Nausikaa, and other thematically relevant episodes in the *Odyssey*. Following Crane (1988), I argue that the *Odyssey* has taken a Medea figure and distributed her chief qualities among two characters, Nausikaa and Kirke, an instance of bifurcation, "a Homeric technique by which the functions of one key character are split into two separate characters who both parallel the key character."[27] In another instance, Nausikaa and Arete together serve the composite functions that Penelope does by herself (Louden 1999: 7). In the *Iliad*, Diomedes and Aias in Books 5–7 serve as a composite Akhilleus, as do Agamemnon and Patroklos in Books 11–16 (discussion in Louden 2006: 3, 80–1). Jacob's myth suggests a similar bifurcation: when meeting Jacob at the well, and directing him to her father's house, Rachel is Nausikaa, but fourteen years later, using magic, and stealing her father's household gods, she is Medea.

Through her advice and prophecy, Kirke serves as a link connecting episodes throughout Books 10–12, causing some features of Argonautic myth to run the length of this part of the *Odyssey*. Aiaia, the name of her island, and her own epithet (*Od.* 9.32; 12.268, 273), reflects her intrinsic connection with Argonautic myth. As Odysseus narrates (*Od.* 10.137), she is sister of the malevolent (*oloophrôn*) Aietes himself, foregrounding their connection before his ship lands on her isle. She and Aietes are both children of Helios, a god with considerable impact on the *Odyssey*'s plot. Kirke and Helios replicate for Odysseus the same dynamic that Medea

---

[26] Alter (2004: 177) notes that the size of the company "is a standard number for a regiment or raiding party, as several episodes in 1 and 2 Samuel indicate."
[27] Louden (2006: 3); cf. Louden (2006: 18, 80–1, 103, 103, 120–1, 129, 259).

and Aietes present for Jason, but divine versions, a goddess in place of the maiden, a soon-to-be-wrathful god in place of a malevolent father-in-law. Repeated emphasis on her serving potions (*Od.* 10.234–7, 316) may be a divine equivalent of drawing water from the well (Rachel), or Rebecca serving a drink of water to Isaac's attendant (Gen. 24:17–18), and Athena as a girl carrying an urn of water (*Od.* 7.19–20). As the nubile daughter of the father figure, she has sex with Odysseus, but with considerably less emphasis on *eros* than for Jason and Medea, or even than is hinted at in Nausikaa. Nor is there any discussion of marriage between Kirke and Odysseus,[28] other than the formula, "desiring him as husband," applied to her only outside of the actual episodes (*Od.* 9.32).[29] Central to her character, as for Medea, and, in a more peripheral way, for Rachel, Kirke is a witch.

Though Kirke and Helios are not onstage together, and she never refers to him as her father, the epic links the two figures in several ways. When first landing on Aiaia, Odysseus notes that Helios is her father (*Od.* 10.138). When Odysseus returns from Hades, he says that Aiaia is where Helios has his *antolai*, his risings (*Od.* 12.1–4). Kirke gives the hero careful instructions on how to approach her father (*Od.* 12.127–41), as do Nausikaa (*Od.* 6.291–310) and each of the young women in the OT betrothal type-scenes. Though remote, compared to Aietes, Pelias, or Laban, never interacting personally with Odysseus or Kirke, Helios is a divine version of the deadly father-in-law figure. Like Laban, Aietes, and Pelias (*Pythia* 4, 148–51), Helios is known for his flocks. The crew's violation of his cattle is the climax of Odysseus' wanderings (*Od.* 12.340–419). Odysseus' self-control on Thrinakia, *not* succumbing to the desire to eat and profane Helios' cattle, as both Kirke herself and Teiresias warn against, clearly constitutes an *agon* of sorts, what Friedrich (1987: 394) has called "the *aristeia* of Odysseus' *tlemosyne*." Odysseus is thus revealed as "victor" over the crew, set apart by his unique accomplishment, a thematic parallel with Jason successfully accomplishing the labors Aietes demands, and those Jacob performs for Laban to win Rachel.

Figuring prominently in Kirke's advice about how to approach Thrinakia is her mention of the *Planktai* (*Od.* 12.59–72), the Clashing Rocks, which contains an overt reference to Jason and the Argonautic myth (*Od.* 12.69–72),[30] the one passage in which the *Odyssey* explicitly connects Odysseus'

---

[28] Cf. de Jong (2001: 228): "Circe never wanted to make Odysseus her husband."
[29] See Louden (1999: 119–20) on a possible narrative strategy Odysseus employs in using a formula that is accurate for Kalypso, but not for Kirke.
[30] On how the *Planktai* became confused with the *Symplegades*, see Crane (1988: 153–4).

voyage with Jason's. As Heubeck notes (1989: 121), Kirke's formulation casts the *Planktai* as an alternate route to the one Odysseus will actually take, that past Skylla and Charybdis. Kirke, and the *Odyssey*, thus mention the *Planktai* more as a foil than anything else. Dimock expands on this view (1989: 167):

This is the way Homer presents the hero of what was evidently a contemporary poem which rivaled his own, intending to show his own hero to be the greater man. Kirke sets up a choice, and the choice is between Jason's exploit and something peculiarly Odysseus's own.

In the one passage where the *Odyssey* most forcefully acknowledges its awareness of Argonautic myth, it does so to show how it alters components of that myth. Crane (1988: 153–4) demonstrates that the *Odyssey* has innovated, moving the *Planktai* from their original position as part of Jason's outward voyage (in some earlier form of the myth), to their present position as part of Odysseus' return voyage.[31]

While Alkinoös, Nausikaa's father, exhibits little of the expected animosity typical of the figure, as evident in Aietes and Laban, and thus suggests a toned down version in that respect, like Pelias, he is descended from Poseidon (Alkinoös: *Od.* 7.56–63, Pelias: *Od.* 11.241–54, discussed below). If milder in temperament, he nonetheless parallels key functions the father-in-law figure typically performs. He sets in motion, if indirectly, events which cause Odysseus to compete in athletic contests with the Phaiakian youths. Attempting to cheer up his guest, Alkinoös has the Phaiakians demonstrate their skill in boxing, wrestling, gymnastics, and track (*Od.* 8.100–3). But after the Phaiakian youths take part in several events, his son, Laodamas, challenges Odysseus to compete (*Od.* 8.132–51). Both father and son repeat the same formula, "to make trial through tests" (ἀέθλων πειρηθέωμεν: *Od.* 8.100; πείρησαι ἀέθλων: *Od.* 8.145). Alkinoös and his son thus combined act as an Aietes to Odysseus' Jason, or Laban to Jacob, the potential father-in-law who demands the hero perform labors to win his daughter, or his sacred possession (Golden Fleece). In besting all the Phaiakians at the discus throw (*Od.* 8.186–98), Odysseus is the foreign hero accomplishing the labors imposed by the father-in-law. Though Nausikaa is neither present at the games nor mentioned in connection with them, she makes her final appearance in the poem shortly after Odysseus' triumph. She and Odysseus exchange farewells (*Od.* 8.457–68) in the *Odyssey*'s deft way of terminating her plot line, but not without another parallel with

---

[31] But cf. West (2005: 39–43), who thinks the *Planktai* are the same as the Wandering Rocks.

Medea. The *Argonautica* credits Medea as crucial to Jason's accomplishment (*Argo.* 3.1247 ff., 4.143–61, 4.364–65; cf. Euripides, *Medea* 478–82). In her farewell, Nausikaa asks the stranger to remember her after he returns home, because he owes her for saving his life (ζωάγρι': *Od.* 8.462; cf. *Medea* 482). Odysseus clearly exploits Nausikaa, having encouraged her to see him as potential husband (*Od.* 6.181–5), a lesser degree of Jason with Medea.

Though Nausikaa exits, her other family members continue to behave in ways typical of Argonautic myth. Alkinoös twice speaks to Odysseus similarly to how Aietes addresses Jason. Having seen his attempts at providing hospitality backfire, the Phaiakian king urges his guest to reveal himself:

> Therefore, now, do not conceal with cunning intent (νοήμασι κερδαλέοισιν)
> what I am asking, for it is better that you say.
>
> *Odyssey* 8.548–9

J. B. Hainsworth puts it bluntly (1988: 382), "νοήμασι κερδαλέοισιν means a lie." In speaking to his guest in such a brusque manner, after his triumph in the athletic contests, Alkinoös resembles the conclusion of Aietes' first address to the Argonauts, "the sorts of lies you have uttered against the blessed gods" (*Argo.* 3.381). Even closer is Pelias' charge to Jason in Pindar's account, "Tell me your lineage/and do not stain it with most hateful lies" (*Pythia* 4.99–100, Race trans. (1997)). During the *Intermezzo* Alkinoös again associates Odysseus with falsehoods:

> Odysseus, as we look at you we do not at all liken you
> to a deceiver or a cheat, the very type of man whom
> the black earth breeds in multitudes, spread among the peoples,
> contrivers of falsehoods, from whom one might not learn a thing.
>
> *Odyssey* 11.363–6

Though asserting that Odysseus is *not* this sort of man, Alkinoös describes the type at such length and in such detail that Odysseus' association with it remains, as does Alkinoös' own thematic parallel with Aietes, and the type of discourse the hostile father-in-law uses with the foreign hero.

As the *Odyssey* presents a milder version of the hostile father-in-law in Alkinoös, so it does with the violence that erupts between Jason and Apsyrtos. The *Odyssey* first alludes to this motif when Nausikaa characterizes Phaiakian men as *huperphialos*, "reckless" (*Od.* 6.274), that they may resent her marrying a man from elsewhere (*Od.* 6.273–85). When Odysseus is given a seat by Alkinoös, the king displaces his favorite son, Laodamas

(*Od.* 7.167–71), to seat him. Though Laodamas' reaction to being displaced is not given, it is he who challenges Odysseus to compete in the games the next day (*Od.* 8.132–51). Is there a connection between his having been displaced the previous day by a guest whom he now challenges to compete? Friction between the foreign hero and the eldest son suggests a displaced form of sibling rivalry. By accomplishing the father-in-law's task, the hero displays his excellence, and, perhaps symbolically, replaces the favorite son. The hero is then subject to the son's resentment, as in Laban's sons' attitude toward Jacob ("Jacob has taken everything that our father had, and all his wealth has come from our father's property," Gen. 31:1), or as in the actual sibling rivalry of Joseph's brothers ("when his brothers saw that their father loved him best," Gen. 37:4), or Jacob's machinations to wrest the blessing Isaac had intended to bestow upon Esau. Jason's interactions with Apsyrtos are an extreme form of such friction.

Shortly after Odysseus wins Arete's favor (*Od.* 11.335–41), the Phaiakians ferry him home to Ithaka. The unnamed crew, selected earlier (*Od.* 8.36, 48), and, having finished preparations for the trip, enter Alkinoös' palace for a feast (*Od.* 8.55–6). When he proposes holding the games, he leads those assembled in the palace, including the crew, out to the competition. It seems clear that the crew is composed of the athletes who compete in the games (Louden 1999: 17–18), including Laodamas and Euryalos, the rude athlete who insults Odysseus (*Od.* 8.158–64).[32] In a specific parallel with the *Argonautica*, the king's son does not return, but dies, his body buried at sea, as a result of interaction with the foreign hero. The entire crew perishing when Poseidon petrifies their ship (*Od.* 13.161–4) also parallels the Colchians' failure to return after their encounter with Jason.

The *Odyssey* hints at such a scenario in the other two bands of young men who parallel the Phaiakian athletes in provoking friction with Odysseus, his crew, and the suitors.[33] The crew's unsubstantiated complaint (*Od.* 10.34–45) that Odysseus always receives more booty than they, their pretext for opening Aiolos' bag of winds, is similar resentment to that between Laban's sons and Jacob. On Thrinakia, Helios' island, the crew all fail the *agôn* except Odysseus, Helios, a father-in-law figure, causing the deaths of the crew. On Ithaka the suitors attempt to catch and slay Telemachos (*Od.* 4.670–1, 16.394–405), acts containing elements also found in the Colchians' initially successful strategy for catching Jason (cf. Laban's pursuit of Jacob).

---

[32] Cf. Louden (1999: 17–18), which also notes additional parallels between Euryalos, Eurylochos, and Eurymachos, which support his likely death in Book 13.

[33] On the larger parallels of Euryalos and the Phaiakian athletes, Eurylochos and the crew, and Eurymachos and the suitors, see Louden (1999: 14–23).

Like Apsyrtos, the suitors lie in wait, to trap the hero on an island they know he must pass by.

Though Nausikaa lacks the older sister that both Medea and Rachel have, Arete suggests parallels with Chalciope and Leah. These older female relatives are cast in a non-erotic role (as opposed to Nausikaa, Kirke, Medea, and Rachel), an emphasis on their maternal qualities. As Arete to Nausikaa, Chalciope is considerably older than Medea, married, with grown sons. As Chalciope to Jason, Arete sides with the foreign Odysseus, which will end up costing the Phaiakian people, and being contrary to Alkinoös' interests (though this is not her reason for supporting the hero). At least three of her grown sons, Laodamas, Halios, and Klytoneus, apparently end up being part of the crew that ferry Odysseus home (*Od.* 8.118–19). Chalciope's sons serve in Jason's crew, much as Leah's sons become part of Jacob's large entourage (Gen. 30:14 ff.). Though Apollonius could be influenced by the Homeric Arete in his Chalciope, the presence of Leah in Jacob's myth is independent confirmation that an older sister for Medea may antedate Apollonius' version of the myth.

If the Phaiakians seem to lack the divine possession – the Golden Fleece, the household gods – their magical sea-crossing ability, a gift from Poseidon, is a partly displaced version of the motif. Though Odysseus does not run off with it, as Medea and Jason, and Rachel and Jacob do with theirs, the divine ability sets the Phaiakians apart from all people, and gives them their specific identity, as the Golden Fleece does Aietes. Because of Poseidon's petrifaction of the returning ship, they will never again exercise their god-given ability – a result of their encounter with Odysseus. Poseidon's petrifaction of the Phaiakian ship and crew should also be seen as a reworking of the Clashing Rocks, a further potent tie-in with Argonautic myth. Never again will a ship pass this way. Access to the Phaiakians is now removed, their almost-paradise existence cut off, marking the ending of a heroic era.[34]

ANTIPHATES, HIS DAUGHTER, THE LAISTRYGONES (*OD.* 10.81–134), AND ARGONAUTIC MYTH

As commentators have noted (Crane 1988: 140, Reece 1993: 12), the Laistrygones episode is an inverted version of the same mythic type as Odysseus' encounter with Nausikaa. This means it may also be seen as a refraction of the characters and relationships that constitute Argonautic myth. As with Nausikaa and the three OT betrothal type-scenes, the daughter is first

---

[34] Cf. West (2005: 42).

to meet the hero's group (*Od.* 10.105). In drawing water outside the city when she meets them (*Od.* 10.105–8), the Laistrygonian episode is even closer to the OT episodes (Rachel, Rebecca, and Zipporah) than is that of Nausikaa.[35] The spring from which the Laistrygonian princess draws her water is called Artakie, also used of a spring in the *Argonautica* (*Argo.* 1.957), prompting Heubeck's assertion (1989: 49), "The name of the spring Artakie (10.108) is almost certainly drawn from an older Argonautica."[36] She informs the foreign men where her father's house is (*Od.* 10.110–11), as do Nausikaa, Rebecca, and Rachel. The daughter has no direct contact with Odysseus, but his representatives, as Rebecca meets not with Isaac, but with his proxy (Gen. 24). The romantic element, substantial in Jason and Medea, present in Jacob and Rachel, present in Nausikaa only on her part and in Odysseus' awareness of her potential to play such a role, is absent in Laistrygones' daughter (as with Athena carrying the water urn at *Od.* 7.19–78, and 1 Sam. 9:11–14). Directing them to her father's house, she leads most of the crew to their deaths, as Kirke does indirectly by pointing the crew to Thrinakia, her father's isle, where all but Odysseus perish.

Antiphates, the Laistrygonian king, is the most deadly of the hostile father-in-law figures. A giant, a cannibal, but with highly developed civilization, unlike the Cyclopes, he easily surpasses in his destructive potential such unpleasant fathers-in-law as Aietes and Laban. While Helios kills a considerable number of Odysseus' crew, Antiphates is the most aggressive of all such figures, personally leading his people in the slaughter that inflicts the heaviest casualties of all the episodes in Books 9–12. At the assembly when he learns of the crew's presence (*Od.* 10.114), he instantly rouses his people, as Aietes plots his most aggressive moves against Jason from the assembly (*Argo.* 4.212–14, 228–36; cf. 4.6–10). Antiphates' every move is suggested by his name, "killing in return."[37] Paralleling the destructive Antiphates, the mother, absent in the myths of Rachel and Medea (because of the prominence of their older sisters), benign in Nausikaa's case, is only here a monstrous figure (*Od.* 10.113–14).

The Laistrygones collectively catch, slay, and presumably eat Odysseus' men (*Od.* 10.115–32). Spearing his crew, as if they were fish (*Od.* 10.124), the Laistrygones offer a thematic parallel for the mortal labors and contests that Aietes imposes upon Jason, and Laban upon Jacob. The labors often have athletic associations: Jason rolling the well stone off by himself, Odysseus

---

[35] Page (1972: 30) briefly notes the resemblance between Antiphates' daughter and Rebecca.
[36] Cf. Page (1972: 38–9).
[37] Cf. von Kamptz (1982: 56): "in Erwiderung, zur Vergeltung"; and (78): "aus Rache, zur Vergeltung tötend... θείνω..."

besting the Phaiakian athletes in the discus, Jason as a warrior against the sown men. Against the Laistrygones, however, instead of competing in sport, the wandering heroes are themselves the prey of "sportsmen." In all other episodes the foreign hero is victorious in the contests, proving himself in an *agôn*. Here Odysseus' men are completely vanquished, slain in activities that seem almost parodies of athletic competitions. Pelting the men with stones (*Od*. 10.121–3), the Laistrygones improve upon Polyphêmos' relative failure at striking Odysseus and his crew.

The Laistrygonian shepherds herding sheep and cattle and earning a double wage (*Od*. 10.82–6) find thematic parallels in the myths of Jacob, Jason, and the *Odyssey*'s episode on Thrinakia. The mythic type tends to be set in the East, with an overt connection with the solar.[38] Jacob is specifically headed east right before he sees Rachel at the well, "And Jacob lifted his feet and went on to the land of the Easterners" (Gen. 29:1, Alter [2004]; εἰς γῆν ἀνατολῶν, in the Septuagint). The land of the Laistrygones is set where "the paths of night and day are close" (*Od*. 10.86), as Heubeck (1989: 48) interprets, "The lines convey a sense of the topographical strangeness of the legendary country in the far east." A land of perpetual daylight,[39] in which work can be performed around the clock; a shepherd who does not need to sleep could earn double wages, herding two different flocks (*Od*. 10.82–5).[40] Jacob literally earns double wages as a shepherd, having to work separate terms for each of his two wives, Leah and Rachel. Doubling is common throughout Jacob's myth: he is a twin; marries two sisters; has two concubines.[41] In his labors for Laban, essentially a magical method of managing livestock and produce, Jacob suggests a thematic parallel to the Laistrygonian shepherd earning double wages in his herding. Kirke briefly turns Odysseus' crew into livestock. On Thrinakia, the isle of Kirke's father, Helios, the crew violates the sacred cattle of Helios.

The Laistrygones and Kirke episodes are consecutive, the former leading directly to the latter. The crew associate their initial circumstances on Aiaia with the Laistrygones episode (*Od*. 10.198–202). Larger parallels between the two episodes play out over much of Books 10–12. Both locations are clearly set in the East (Nakassis 2004: 222–5), Kirke's island a short sail from the Laistrygones (Nakassis 2004: 225). Like the daughter of

---

[38] On Kirke as possibly descended from the Indo-European dawn goddess, see West (2007: 230).
[39] Page (1972: 39–40): "Herdsmen go out at daybreak and come in at nightfall. So when you say that the herdsman going to work meets the herdsman returning from work, and that the man who could go without sleep could do a double shift and earn a double wage, you imply that daylight prevails for almost the whole twenty-four hours." Cf. Nakassis (2004: 224).
[40] Cf. Page (1972: 122, n. 26).
[41] Cf. Alter (2004: 183) on Genesis 33:1, "Again the principle of binary division running through the whole story comes into play."

Antiphates, Kirke, if indirectly, leads Odysseus' crew (but not Odysseus) to their deaths at the hands of her father, Helios. After Odysseus' successful return from Hades, Kirke gives an extensive prophecy of the next phase of his journey (*Od.* 12.37–141), which likely draws on an Argonautic episode of Phineus prophesying for Jason. Like the daughter of Antiphates, Kirke gives directions on how to reach her father's "residence," and how Odysseus and his crew must behave if they are to survive his ordeal. Antiphates and Helios are linked as the two most deadly and destructive Aietes figures. But the Laistrygones episode, in its parallels with the *Cyclopeia* (Odysseus encountering a race of giant cannibals), looks forward and back, playing a variation on some elements of Book 9, while also anticipating motifs central to Kirke and events on Thrinakia. The Laistrygones and Kirke/Helios episode are further linked in that both are narrated to the internal audience of Alkinoös, Arete, and the athletes/crew, all of whom serve as partly parallel figures to the characters in those two versions of Argonautic myth.

The *Odyssey* has another Antiphates, the son of Melampous (*Od.* 15.242–4), who also suggests connections with Argonautic myth. Mentioned in the back-story for Theoklymenos, Melampous' myth is, in fact, composed almost entirely of the same elements as the myths of Jason and Medea and Jacob and Rachel, except that Melampous undergoes his ordeal for his brother, not for himself; and he is a prophet not a hero. I quote at length the account Book 15 gives of Melampous:

> who before used to live in Pylos, mother of flocks,
> dwelling in a fine mansion among the Pylians, a wealthy man,
> but then he went away to the land of another people, fleeing his homeland
> and great-hearted Neleus, most illustrious of men then living,
> who kept many of his possessions by force until a year
> was fulfilled. But meanwhile he (Melampous) was restrained
> in painful bonds in the palace of Phylakos, suffering pains,
> on behalf of Neleus' daughter, and grievous infatuation,
> which the goddess who strikes houses, the Fury, had placed in his mind.
> But he escaped death and drove the loud-bellowing cattle
> from Phylake to Pylos and satisfied the hard labor
> for godlike Neleus, and led the woman to the home
> of his brother.
>
> *Odyssey* 15.226–38

Additional details given at *Od.* 11.287–97 supplete Book 15's elliptic account.[42] Hoekstra (1989: 246–7) fills in the gaps from other sources. Melampous' brother, Bias, wooed Pero, Neleus' daughter. But the Pylian

---

[42] See de Jong (2001: 282–3) on how the two separate accounts add up to a whole; cf. Apollodorus I.9.12.

king demanded as bride-price the cattle of Phylakos.[43] Melampous attempted to win the bride-price on behalf of his brother, but was imprisoned in the process, languishing in Phylakos' prison for a year until, with his prophetic powers, he learned from a termite that the building's collapse was imminent. He sent word to Phylakos, who, grateful for the warning, freed him, and gave him the cattle.

The recurring central elements, travel to a foreign land to accomplish a labor which will win a bride, tricky dealings with a foreign father figure, imprisoned by him for a year, but eventually satisfying his demands and returning home with the young foreign bride and the father's flocks are especially close to the myth of Jacob and Rachel. In place of magic, a key to success for Jason and Jacob, Melampous has prophetic powers that enable him to escape imprisonment by Phylakos. Like Jason, Melampous must meet the demands for *two* hostile father-in-law figures, Neleus and Phylakos. Neleus parallels Pelias in demanding the initial difficult task, whereas Phylakos parallels Aietes in possessing the required item, and adding to the difficulties the protagonist must surmount to obtain it. Like Jacob, Melampous returns not only with a foreign bride but with a prized herd of livestock. In performing the labors for his brother, Melampous parallels the first of Alter's (1981) OT betrothal type-scenes in which a surrogate, Abraham's servant, wins the bride on behalf of Isaac.[44] Like Jason with Pelias, Melampous cannot stay in his homeland but has to move on (to Argos) after apparently revenging himself upon Neleus (de Jong 2001: 283).

ARGONAUTIC MYTH AND THE *CATALOGUE OF WOMEN* (*OD.* 11.235–332)

We have seen that the *Catalogue of Women* is indirectly associated with Argonautic myth in the account of Melampous winning Pero for his brother (*Od.* 11.287–97). This is not the only such connection. Other entries in the *Catalogue*, especially Tyro (*Od.* 11.235–59; cf. 2.120), Pelias (*Od.* 11.254–7), Aison (*Od.* 11.259), Periklymenos (*Od.* 11.286), feature characters with connections to Argonautic myth, or, as in the mention of Iolkos (*Od.* 11.256–7), a place prominent in it. By Poseidon, Tyro is the mother of both Pelias and Neleus. These two sons serve parallel roles to each other in the myths of Jason, in which Pelias demands that he go east and obtain the

---

[43] In the variant version, the role of Phylakos is played by his son, Iphiklos (Hoekstra 1989: 246).
[44] Cf. Bhishma winning a bride for his brother Vicitravirya in the *Mahabhârata*.

Fleece, and of Melampous, in which Neleus demands that he win the cattle of Phylakos/Iphiklos. By her husband Kretheus, Tyro is mother to Aison, Jason's father, and grandmother to Jason. In a sense Tyro is herself thus the foundation story for much of those portions of Argonautic myth set in Greece. Neleus' son Periklymenos is an Argonaut (*Argo.* 1.156–60).

Why would the *Odyssey* make allusions to Argonautic myth in the *Catalogue of Women*? Poseidon serves to interconnect the two myths. Poseidon's son, Nausithoös, is Alkinoös' father. Arete is daughter of Rhexenor (Alkinoös' brother), and therefore granddaughter of Poseidon. Pelias as a son of Poseidon (*Od.* 11.254) thus suggests parallels with the Phaiakians themselves. As with all of Books 9–12, other than the *Intermezzo* (*Od.* 11.330–84), Odysseus is the narrator, his principal audience, Alkinoös and Arete. Since Tyro and Arete are both connected to Poseidon (Tsagarakis 2000: 87), Odysseus' implicit praise of Tyro also serves, by implication, as praise of Arete, part of Odysseus' means of winning her over, his main objective until, in the *Intermezzo*, she promises to send him home. Odysseus' references to Argonautic myth also serve to clarify his own intentions.

Odysseus as narrator alludes to Argonautic myth to emphasize how he *differs* from Jason. He wants to return to his wife. He is not seeking to marry the local princess.

CHAPTER 7

Odysseus and Jonah
Sea-monsters and the fantastic voyage

At the core of the *Odyssey*, especially in the popular imagination, is what we might call the fantastic voyage, the incredible adventures at sea. Though most of the epic does not actually involve such phenomena, the few instances of the fantastic voyage and its attendant monsters have intriguing ties with other ancient myths. When, in Book 5, Odysseus sees Scheria's jagged, rocky coast after swimming for two days, his raft destroyed by Poseidon, he is afraid to turn back to the open sea for two reasons:

> I fear lest a great gust having snatched me away again
> would bear me, groaning deeply, back to the sea, teeming with fish,
> or lest a god would send a great monster (*kêtos*) against me
> from the sea.
>
> *Odyssey* 5.419–22

If only in passing, the *Odyssey* here briefly points to a mythic type that involves a lone protagonist, separated from his crew, threatened by a fantastic sea-monster. The same genre of myth is extant in the Book of Jonah, a few other episodes in the *Odyssey*, and a brief passage in the *Iliad*. The Egyptian tale, *The Shipwrecked Sailor*, also offers partial parallels. Since the great fish in Jonah combines what are in the *Odyssey* the separate functions of the sea-monster and Poseidon, we also reconsider elements of Odysseus' interactions with Poseidon under this rubric.

Some features of this mythic type overlap with two genres of myth already covered. In romance shipwrecks and fantastic voyages figure as a means for delaying the protagonist's return home. Within the *Odyssey* the fantastic sea journey, and/or shipwreck, accounts for why *He is trapped in a foreign land, a marvelous or exotic place, for all or much of this period.* Furthering the association, the mythic genre of the fantastic voyage is attested in the same three cultures in which we located romance, Greek, the Old Testament, and Egyptian myth. The fantastic voyage also tends to culminate in an apocalypse, a wrathful god's destruction of a whole group of mortals. Odysseus' final sea crossing, the return to Ithaka from Scheria, complements his approach to the Phaiakians' island in Book 5. The two scenes together comprise the entirety of Poseidon's present-time appearances in the *Odyssey*. His threatened but averted destruction of the Phaiakians' city (*Od.* 13.78–164) finds an exact parallel in Yahweh's threatened but averted destruction of Nineveh in Jonah's myth (Jonah 3). Because of Poseidon's divine wrath against him, and because gods and monsters tend to be linked in myth (discussed below), all passages in the *Odyssey* which depict Odysseus by himself on the open seas, 5.269–462 (which includes the passage quoted above), 12.403–48 (Odysseus going by Skylla and Charybdis alone), and to a lesser extent, 13.78–164, belong to this mythic genre.

AND I ALONE SURVIVED

A signature motif in this genre of myth is the depiction of the protagonist as the sole survivor of an incredible event at sea. Melville, to close his mythic *Moby Dick*, incorporates the motif in his protagonist's encounter with the title character, "And I only am escaped alone to tell thee."[1] The Egyptian myth, *The Shipwrecked Sailor*, provides the earliest instance of this key motif. When a massive wave strikes his ship, the protagonist alone survives, while all of the crew perish (as at *Od.* 12.408–19 and 13.161–4),

> Then the ship died. Of those in it not one remained.
> (Hallo 2003: 83)

> Then the boat died. And of those who were in it not a single one survived.
> (Simpson 1972: 52)

Shipwrecked, the protagonist washes up on the shore of an island paradise, much as Odysseus on Ogygia at *Odyssey* 12.447–8. He later meets not a goddess, but a giant benevolent serpent. When Zeus strikes the crew's ship with lightning, punishment for their having violated Helios' cattle, all hands perish except for Odysseus, who is able to survive by riding the keel and mast (*Od.* 12.415–25). In what should be considered an adapted form of the motif, Poseidon destroys the Phaiakian crew after they have ferried Odysseus home (*Od.* 13.161–4), leaving the hero as the only one who survives a fantastic sea crossing.

---

[1] Though Melville in fact is quoting the refrain used four times in Job 1:14–19 (Bryant 2007: 570, n1).

THE SEA-MONSTER

Odysseus' word for a sea-monster is *kêtos* (*Od.* 5.421), which J. B. Hainsworth (1988: 285) glosses as "any sort of sea-monster... This is the sole allusion in the *Odyssey* to such a danger." Though we will have cause to question his assertion that this is the *Odyssey*'s sole allusion to sea-monsters, his explanation of the use of *kêtos* is correct. The *Iliad* also uses *kêtos* of a sea-monster in its brief account of Herakles battling the monster that earlier threatened Troy (*Il.* 20.147). Part of the elliptic tale of Laomedon cheating Poseidon after he had built the walls of Troy, in the fullest version, perhaps that alluded to in the *Iliad*, the sea god responds by sending a sea-monster against Troy, which Laomedon then attempts to appease by offering up his daughter Hesione.[2]

The *Odyssey* has three broad types of beings, mortals, immortals, and monsters, who can combine features of mortals and immortals. What is a monster? Typically they are more powerful than mortals, but less powerful than gods, and usually liable to death. Hansen classifies the monsters of Greek myth according to three principles (2004: 228), "increase the size of a naturally occurring creature, multiply a body part, and/or combine body parts from two or more creatures." The *kêtos* Odysseus fears is indistinct, but presumably of a large enough size to fall under Hansen's first category. In a further tendency in which the *Odyssey* expresses repeated interest, monsters usually lack civilization, and function as a law unto themselves, as Odysseus says of the Cyclopes (*Od.* 9.112–15, 187–9). This lack of civilization is concretized in the monster's isolated dwelling, often far removed from any other being. Though laws unto themselves, monsters are usually subordinate to the gods, aligned with or empowered by them in some specified way. Odysseus assigns divine agency to the sea-monster he fears, assuming that a god (*daimon*), by whom he clearly means Poseidon, as he goes on to say (*Od.* 5.423), would send it against him because of his wrath.

THE SIRENS (OD. 12.39–55, 167–200)

Though less *monstrous* in some ways, and more like goddesses in their omniscience and power of speech, the Sirens are deadly, and their encounter employs more than one of the motifs common to other sea-monster

---

[2] See N. Richardson (1993: 91, in note on *Il.* 21.441–57) on Poseidon as having sent the sea-monster against Laomedon.

episodes. Emblematic of both the fantastic voyage and the sea-monster, the Sirens' isolated location firmly aligns them with most of the *Odyssey*'s monsters. Like Skylla and Charybdis, they are apparently set on a small jut of land surrounded by the sea (*Od.* 12.45–6), which Odysseus calls an island (*nêsos*: *Od.* 12.167, 201). This is consistent with depictions in later vase painting, as Heubeck (1989: 120) notes, "the Sirens are portrayed on vases as sitting on a rock." They sit in a meadow, but before them are heaps of the skeletons of men who have encountered them, a juxtaposition of elements suggestive of the underworld. Unlike the *Odyssey*'s other monsters, their threat depends upon indirection. They themselves will not kill Odysseus or his crew, nor personally offer any actual threat. They will lure them, unsuspecting, onto rocks, essentially the same form of death Odysseus fears as he approaches Scheria (*Od.* 5.415–16). In the *Odyssey*'s terms they take away the homecoming of any man who approaches them by enchanting him through their song. While their power of enchantment aligns them with Kirke, their plurality aligns them with groups of goddesses such as the Muses or Fates. But this same plurality prohibits a man from encountering them one on one, and thereby reaching an understanding with them, as Odysseus is able to do with Kirke and Kalypso.

In spite of their plurality, Odysseus *alone* encounters them, another key link with more typical sea-monster episodes. Though his crew is present, the experience is primarily auditory, and, with their ears plugged with wax, only Odysseus hears the Sirens' song. While death at the Sirens' hands remains a threat throughout the scene, no one actually dies. Nonetheless, the episode should be seen as a modified instance of the motif "And I alone survived," in Odysseus' isolation from the crew. Odysseus alone hears their song, which no other mortal has previously heard and lived (*Od.* 12.186–8; cf. de Jong 2001: 303). He survives the encounter tied to his ship's mast (*Od.* 12.50–1, 178–200), which links the episode with his second encounter with Skylla and Charybdis at the end of Book 12 (discussed below). Since the crew does not encounter the Sirens, they cannot survive them either, in the way that Odysseus does. The encounter thus looks ahead thematically to the climactic events on Thrinakia, Odysseus' survival and the crew's destruction.

SKYLLA AND CHARYBDIS (*OD.* 12.85–126, 235–60, 428–47)

Though both are gods, Skylla and Charybdis nonetheless simultaneously function as sea-monsters within the *Odyssey*'s thematic construction of the fantastic voyage. Kirke labels Skylla a god (*Od.* 12.117–19), while Charybdis seems one in her capacity as a personification of natural forces. In a thematic link with the Sirens, each inhabits a rocky crag (*skopelos, Od.* 12.73–5, 101). Skylla inhabits a cave set in a steep rock (*Od.* 12.75–100, 430), underscored by her unique epithet, *petraiê*, "dwelling in a rock" (*Od.* 12.231). Her monstrous nature is emphasized by another epithet, *pelôr*, "monstrous, prodigious" (*Od.* 12.87), also used of Polyphêmos (*Od.* 9.428). Charybdis' epithet, *oloê*,[3] "destructive, deadly" (*Od.* 12.113, 428) also suggests her monstrous, rather than divine, nature.

Both Skylla and Charybdis are capable of devouring mortals, the central threat they embody whenever Odysseus and his crew are in their vicinity, the central motif of Jonah's myth, and what Odysseus fears at *Odyssey* 5.421–2. Skylla embodies this threat in a highly graphic manner, compounded not only by her having six heads, but three rows of teeth in each, "full of black death," as Kirke warns (*Od.* 12.90–2). So great a voracious threat is she that she even devours other sea-monsters (*kêtos, Od.* 12.97). The description is closely linked to Odysseus' earlier fear in Book 5, both being variants of a similar formula depicting the great number of such sea-monsters:

κῆτος... οἷά τε πολλὰ τρέφει κλυτὸς Ἀμφιτρίτη
Odyssey 5.421–22

(a sea-monster, of the sort famed Amphitrite nourishes a multitude)

κῆτος, ἃ μυρία βόσκει ἀγάστονος Ἀμφιτρίτη
Odyssey 12.97

(a sea-monster, which roaring Amphitrite breeds in the thousands)

Living up to this advance billing, Skylla devours six of Odysseus' crew when they have no choice but to sail within her grasp, avoiding complete destruction by steering clear of Charybdis (*Od.* 12.244–57). Odysseus regards Skylla devouring his crew as the most pitiable sight he ever saw in all his voyages (*Od.* 12.258–9).

After the events at Thrinakia (explored in Chapter 10), Zeus destroys the crew and Odysseus' ship, turning the episode's conclusion into another instance of the motif, "and I alone survived." Odysseus must now pass by Skylla and Charybdis again, alone, without ship or crew, which episode thematically suppletes his earlier passage by the two sea-monsters. This time he has no contact with Skylla (responsible for all the destruction in the first episode), for which he credits Zeus (*Od.* 12.445–6). Instead the great ordeal comes from Charybdis. Now living up to *her* advance billing,

---

[3] Used of no other god in Homer, except *oloophrôn* once of the Titan Atlas (Dee 2001: 132).

she gulps down all the surrounding sea water, including the ship mast and timber on which Odysseus has thus far survived, as the storm winds from Thrinakia carried him against his will back to her (cf. his fear at *Od.* 5.419–20). Odysseus survives, perhaps his greatest feat of endurance, by grasping the roots of the fig tree on her rocky crag, hanging from them until she spews the water back, carrying with it his mast and keel. Charybdis' swallowing of these parts of the ship points to the unstated fear of his being swallowed by the sea-monster, Jonah's temporary fate, what happened to the six men earlier with Skylla, and probably what Odysseus fears at *Odyssey* 5.421–2.

Sea-monsters are typically under the control of the gods. Odysseus' fear of a sea-monster at *Odyssey* 5.421–2 is predicated on his assumption that Poseidon would send it against him. In the myth of Jonah, Yahweh sends the great fish against the protagonist (discussed below). Herakles' battle with the sea-monster, mentioned in the *Iliad*, employs the same conception (N. Richardson 1993: 91, on *Iliad* 20.147). But Charybdis proves the exception. According to Kirke (*Od.* 12.107), not even Poseidon could save Odysseus from Charybdis should he fall within her reach.[4] In this respect Charybdis, a being beyond even the control of Poseidon, represents the culmination of the horror sea-monsters embody, the uncontrollable panic that can strike at sea, along the lines of H. P. Lovecraft's depiction of unspeakable marine terrors that reduce men to madness in "The Call of Cthulhu." Three times Odysseus refers to the terror that grips his men as they approach Charybdis (*Od.* 12.203, 224–5, 243–4).

The encounter with Skylla and Charybdis offers two further links with the Sirens episode. In her preliminary description, Kirke notes that it is impossible to sail by Skylla without losing men:

> for not ever do sailors boast that they pass by her in their ship
> unharmed, but rather, she, with each head having snatched
> a man, carries him away from the black-prowed ship.
>
> *Odyssey* 12.98–100

The Sirens themselves address Odysseus with a similar description, emphatic in the negative:

> for not ever has anyone driven by here in his black ship
> before hearing the honey-toned voice from our mouths.
>
> *Odyssey* 12.186–7

---

[4] See de Jong (2001: 299) on her classification of the assertion as "description by negation," and the "'(not)even + hyperbole' motif."

The two passages, both instances of de Jong's "description by negation" (de Jong 2001: 299, 303), would be even closer if not for the Sirens' use of misdirection, as earlier noted. Kirke essentially says *no crew* sails by Skylla without loss of life, whereas the Sirens, tailoring their comment to Odysseus, say *no one* sails by without hearing them. But, implicitly, to hear their song is to die, as they intend, increasing the parallels between the two passages. Both monsters are assigned unique vocal qualities. While the Sirens' use of misdirection is centered in their misleading remarks, and their song's enchanting properties, Skylla's voice, only as loud as a puppy's (*Od.* 12.86), also seems to mask her greater threat, until it is too late to escape her, as with the Sirens.

THE MYTH OF JONAH

The Book of Jonah is a narrative with considerable relevance, largely untapped, for classical literature, not only for the *Odyssey* but perhaps even more so for Apuleius' *Golden Ass*. Unique in its maritime setting in Old Testament myth, which is usually landlocked compared to Homeric epic, the myth of Jonah is built largely from the motifs the *Odyssey* uses for the fantastic voyage, the sea-monster, the god-sent storm, and apocalypse. Since OT myth imposes other agendas upon the traditional motifs it inherits, the usual polemics validating Yahweh are also here. But there are other key differences. As often in OT myth, the protagonist is a prophet rather than a hero, but a prophet may still be a heroic character, as is Elijah, for instance. Jonah is not only resolutely non-heroic, but repeatedly exercises poor judgment, antithetical to Odysseus. In Aristotle's terms, Jonah is less moral (χείρονας: *Poetics* 1448, a4) than the audience, conferring on the narrative an emphatically non-epic, parodic modality.[5] Though composed of many of the same motifs found in the *Odyssey*, in its inverted modality, the myth of Jonah resembles Odysseus' epic in much the same way that Euripides' *Helen* or *Iphigeneia in Taurus* do, or, even more, as does Apuleius' *Golden Ass*.

JONAH AND THEOKLYMENOS

But before turning to the traditional motifs of the fantastic voyage and the sea-monster in Jonah's myth, we first briefly note how Jonah's function as

---

[5] Cf. Crenshaw (1993: 380), "The antihero of the book of Jonah ... the target of didactic satire ... The author wrote a short parable characterized by fantastic events to poke fun indirectly at a man whose inner thoughts remain virtually hidden"; and Ackerman (1987: 234, in Alter and Kermode [1987]), "elements in the narrative that bring it close to classical satire."

a prophet also resembles other sections of the *Odyssey*. Jonah's myth begins with him in flight, unwilling to carry out Yahweh's command that he go to Nineveh, and denounce the wickedness of the city (Jonah 1:1–3). Jonah books a fare on a ship as a passenger (Jonah 1:3), shifting the remainder of this myth to its marine setting, "But to escape from the Lord . . . [he] went on board to travel . . . to Tarshish out of the reach of the Lord" (Jonah 1:3). As a fugitive prophet, received onto a ship in his flight, Jonah suggests broad parallels with Theoklymenos, the prophet Telemachos receives aboard his ship (*Od.* 15.223–94). Each prophet goes on to prophesy a coming apocalypse, speaking directly to the wrongdoers whom the apocalypse would strike. Jonah's myth threatens a middle-degree apocalypse, the destruction of all the inhabitants of Nineveh (Jonah 3:4), while Theoklymenos, in the *Odyssey*'s thrice-repeated pattern (explored in Chapter 13), invokes a contained apocalypse, the suitors and their retainers (*Od.* 20.351–7, 364–70). The so-called "wickedness" (Jonah 1:2) of the people of Nineveh is generic,[6] never specified in any way, whereas the audience witnesses the suitors' repeated misbehavior. In a key difference, Nineveh's apocalypse is ultimately averted, which is probably meant to reflect upon Jonah, undermining his supposed abilities as a prophet. Theoklymenos, by contrast, is the real thing, a prophet who correctly prophesies the suitors' approaching doom.

THE GOD-SENT STORM

Once he is at sea, Jonah's myth is composed almost entirely of motifs also present in the *Odyssey*. Yahweh immediately provokes a storm against Jonah and the ship that carries him, "The Lord let loose a hurricane on the sea, which rose so high that the ship threatened to break up in the storm" (Jonah 1:4). Such god-sent storms are thematic in the *Odyssey*. The earliest such storm, chronologically, concludes the *Apologue*'s first episode, after Odysseus and crew sack Ismaros (*Od.* 9.67–83). In the mythical conceptions that inform both Homeric and OT myth, storms at sea result from divine wraths. Odysseus assigns Zeus credit for provoking the storm, though the *Odyssey* leaves unexplained why he would do so.[7] The *Odyssey* particularly uses forms and compounds of the verb *plazô*, "beat, drive," to express the divine agency behind such storms.[8] Thus Odysseus in his narration of this first storm uses *paraplazô* (*Od.* 9.81) to describe how the

---

[6] Cf. Crenshaw's comment on common ground with the destruction of Sodom and Gomorrah (1993: 381), "Linguistic features link Nineveh and the cities of Sodom and Gomorrah."
[7] For fuller discussion of this storm, see Louden (1999: 76–80).
[8] See Louden (1999: 69–94) for thorough analysis of how πλάζω functions in the *Odyssey*.

resultant wind and waves drove him off course, and similarly *apoplazô*, when he later refers back to the same storm (*Od.* 9.259).

Most of the *Odyssey*'s storms fall into two distinct subtypes: they result from a divine wrath against Odysseus, or from one against his crew. Clearly the two storms Poseidon directs at Odysseus, while he heads for Scheria alone on his raft, result from the sea god's wrath against the protagonist. Conforming to the practice noted, the principal narrator uses *plazô* to depict how these storms *drive* Odysseus (*Od.* 5.389). In the poem's first divine council, Zeus uses *plazô* to describe how Poseidon generally prevents Odysseus from crossing the sea, driving him away from Ithaka (*Od.* 1.74–5). On the other hand, the storm that Zeus raises to destroy the crew after they violate Helios' cattle on Thrinakia clearly results from a divine wrath against the crew, not Odysseus. The *Odyssey* uses *plêssô*, a verb etymologically related to *plazô*, to depict the force of this storm (*Od.* 12.412, 416).

In Jonah's myth, Yahweh clearly directs the storm at him, much as Poseidon in Book 5 against Odysseus, "The Lord let loose a hurricane on the sea" (Jonah 1:4). When the storm first strikes, Jonah is fast asleep below deck (Jonah 1:4), offering parallels with Odysseus' situation in the aftermath of the Aiolos episode (*Od.* 10.31–55) and on Thrinakia (*Od.* 12.338). When Odysseus and crew are close enough to Ithaka to see people tending fires, sleep overcomes him, tired from constantly managing a line on one of the sails. As he falls asleep, an unnamed member of the crew persuades the others to open the bag Aiolos had given Odysseus. But as soon as they do so furious winds rush out, which blow them across the sea, all the way back to Aiolos' isle. In effect the opened bag lets loose a storm (*thuella*, *Od.* 10.48) which should be understood as an expression of Poseidon's divine wrath. *Thuella* is also used of storms explicitly prompted by Poseidon (*Od.* 5.317, 419). The formula *thuella* + *anarpazô* used several times to depict a storm carrying people off (*Od.* 4.515, 20.63; cf. 8.409) is also used here (*Od.* 10.48). Upon their unexpected return to his isle, Aiolos declares that they are under a divine wrath, which the audience knows results from Polyphêmos' curse in Poseidon's name (*Od.* 9.527–35).

THE PROTAGONIST IN OPPOSITION WITH THE CREW

In both myths, an opposition develops between the protagonist and the rest of the crew; he becomes separate, isolated from them. In the *Odyssey* such frictions arise in the second part of the Aiolos episode, but they are part of a larger pattern of tensions between Odysseus and the crew.[9] The unnamed crew member that instigates the disastrous opening of the bag of winds is probably Eurylochos, who plays the mutineer thematically in the *Apologue* (Louden 1999: 19–21; his role on Thrinakia is discussed in Chapter 10). His opening of the bag is a typical form of his insubordination. With no basis, the crew here assumes Odysseus does not dispense rewards fairly among them, and therefore covets the gift Aiolos gave him. Eurylochos' reckless opening of the bag not only prevents their relatively easy return to Ithaka but points ahead to their failure ever to return home. As Odysseus sees the storm winds driving him away from Ithaka, he briefly considers throwing himself into the sea to die (*Od.* 10.50–1). Only here in the *Odyssey* does Odysseus briefly succumb to the defeatism so characteristic of Jonah, as he momentarily considers suicide, much as Jonah will ask his crew to end his life (Jonah 1:12).[10]

Jonah's myth features a similar opposition between the protagonist and crew, but, typical of its inverted modality, in this myth the crew acts responsibly, even piously, while the protagonist acts irresponsibly. Though they are strangers, with no previous acquaintance with each other, unlike Odysseus' crew who served under him at Troy, the crew treats Jonah fairly and respectfully. Their previous lack of acquaintance is signaled in a verbal exchange close to many hospitality scenes in the *Odyssey*, "'What is your business? Where do you come from? Which is your country? What is your nationality?'" (Jonah 1:8). Their multi-part question is very like the *Odyssey*'s standard formula when two strangers meet, τίς πόθεν εἰς ἀνδρῶν; (*Od.* 1.170, 10.325, 14.187, 15.264, 19.105, 24.298; cf.7.238). When the storm Yahweh directs at Jonah suddenly threatens, the sailors are alarmed (Jonah 1:5, 10), much as Odysseus' crew grows anxious on their approach to Skylla and Charybdis (*Od.* 12.203, 224–5, 243–4).

EURYLOCHOS AND JONAH

In both mythic traditions mortals cast lots to determine responsibility in unexpected situations.[11] Intuiting that Jonah's storm is directed at one of them, the sailors decide to determine the culprit by drawing lots, "The sailors said among themselves, 'Let us cast lots to find who is to blame for our misfortune'" (Jonah 1:7). As part of the mounting tensions between

---

[9] Heubeck (1989: 45), "His companions appear throughout the *nostos* in opposition to Odysseus."
[10] Cf. Heubeck (1989: 45), "the delineation of Odysseus' options serves... to illustrate his desperate plight, and his mood." Apuleius' protagonist Lucius thematically considers suicide.
[11] Cf. *Iliad* 7.171–83. See Sasson (1990: 107–27) for numerous OT instances.

Odysseus and the crew, lots are drawn to see who will scout out Aiaia, with Eurylochos chosen to do so (*Od.* 10.206–7). In the *Odyssey* Eurylochos most closely resembles Jonah in temperament and thematic irresponsibility.[12] Each is the only individual character in his myth to be designated by lot. Each may be characterized as having a defeatist attitude. After drawing the lot to scout out Aiaia, Eurylochos fails to execute his task successfully. Returning to the ship without the other members of the crew, all of whom have been turned into swine by Kirke, he refuses Odysseus' request to lead him to Kirke's palace:

> Don't take me there against my will, Zeus-nourished, but leave me here;
> for I know that neither will you yourself return, nor will you bring back
> any of your crew. But let us flee from here with these,
> immediately, for we might still escape the evil day.
>
> *Odyssey* 10.266–9

In trying to measure Odysseus by his own capabilities, Eurylochos is wrong on all counts. Like Jonah he is a non-heroic, even cowardly character,[13] a failure by epic standards. His remarks look ahead thematically to the defeatism that will prove ruinous on Thrinakia.[14] When the lot designates him as responsible for the great storm, Jonah admits his culpability ("I know it is my fault that this great storm has struck you": Jonah 1:12), and asks the sailors to throw him into the sea, a thematic equivalent with Eurylochos' view of the crew's chance of surviving Kirke.

Closest to Jonah's storm in outcome is the storm Zeus sends against the crew for their violation of Helios' cattle. Both storms result in the respective protagonists, Odysseus and Jonah, separated once and for all from their crews, about to undergo the fantastic voyage, meet with a sea-monster, and serve as an instance of "And I alone survived." Consistent with the inverted modality of Jonah's myth, the sailors act respectfully and piously, "Seized by a great fear of the Lord, the men offered a sacrifice and made vows to him" (Jonah 1:16), the precise opposite of how Odysseus' crew acts on Thrinakia, in their perverse sacrifice to Helios. The sailors' piety here predicts how the inhabitants of Nineveh will also act to avert the apocalypse threatening their city later in the myth.

---

[12] In Chapter 10 we also observe that Eurylochos, in the events on Thrinakia, resembles the same traditional character type as Aaron, Moses' brother.
[13] See de Jong (2001: 255) on Eurylochos as a coward.
[14] Cf. de Jong (2001: 255–6) on thematic links between the two episodes.

THE SEA-MONSTER

Though Jonah's sea-monster serves functions familiar from related episodes in the *Odyssey*, it also fulfills additional roles resulting from the myth's comic modality and larger OT concern with validating the monotheistic Yahweh. The monster itself is generic, never described or individuated. The Septuagint also uses *kêtos* for the sea-monster (Jonah 2:1, 2, 11), the *Odyssey*'s default term, as at 5.421 (cf. *Il.* 20.147). As we have noted, in Homeric epic's usual conception sea-monsters are thought of as under the direction of Poseidon, as at *Odyssey* 5.421–2. A similar conception holds for Jonah's sea-monster, which is depicted as acting under Yahweh's command (Jonah 2:1, 11). From the *Odyssey*'s perspective, Jonah's sea-monster combines functions found separately in Poseidon and in sea-monsters. It briefly threatens the protagonist when he is alone at sea, separated from other sailors, and does so as an expression and agent of divine wrath. In these respects Jonah's sea-monster resembles the *Odyssey*'s use of the verb *plazô* (πλάζω) to articulate Odysseus' difficulty crossing the sea while Poseidon's wrath remains in effect. But in the inverted modality that characterizes Jonah's myth, the sea-monster is a *positive* entity. Ultimately it drives Jonah to *safety*, spitting him out on the shore, roughly paralleling Odysseus' landfall on Scheria, which removes him from the immediate danger Poseidon embodies. The monotheism of Jonah's myth requires the sea-monster to be completely under Yahweh's control, whereas in Homeric polytheism Poseidon has much greater independence, and therefore harries Odysseus to a greater degree, more as Satan does Job.

Though Jonah is actually swallowed by his sea-monster, the unspoken fear behind several of the *Odyssey*'s sea-monster episodes, his three-day imprisonment in its belly causes him no harm. The Egyptian *The Shipwrecked Sailor* offers an earlier version of this motif when the giant serpent on the island carries the protagonist in its mouth, later setting him down unharmed (lines 77–9). Jonah's being confined in the monster's belly also draws upon another very different genre of myth, the descent to the underworld. The myth itself equates being in the monster's belly with being in Sheol, the OT equivalent of Hades, "From the fish's belly Jonah offered this prayer to the Lord his God... 'from deep within Sheol I cried out for help'" (Jonah 2:1).[15] In New Testament myth Jonah's safe return is used to predict Christ's resurrection, both after three days in the "underworld"

---

[15] The Septuagint has Hades here for Sheol (Jonah 2:3).

(Jonah 1:17; Matt. 12:40; cf. Luke 11:29–32). It should not be forgotten, after all, that the *Odyssey* has Odysseus *sail* rather than descend to Hades. Consequently, even Odysseus' "descent" to Hades is subsumed under the organizational device of the fantastic voyage (analyzed in Chapter 9). In this respect Jonah's myth resembles a miniature of several mythic types the *Odyssey* employs in Books 9–12.

Another, less fantastic, but equally dire threat each protagonist faces as a consequence of divine design is the possibility of drowning. The prospect of being swallowed by the sea itself is one way of understanding what Charybdis represents in the *Odyssey*. As he approaches Scheria, Odysseus several times comes close to drowning (*Od.* 5.313–26, 360–91, 425–35), much as he does the second time he passes by Charybdis (*Od.* 12.424–6). After the sailors throw Jonah into the stormy seas, the myth jumps ahead to the description of the great fish swallowing him. But his prayer to Yahweh from the fish's belly refers to his time in the turbulent seas, "You cast me into the depths, into the heart of the ocean, and the flood closed around me; all your surging waves swept over me" (Jonah 2:3). While the lines are traditional, perhaps adapted from Psalm 30:2–3, Jonah's predicament is fairly unique within OT myth, but rather close to Odysseus' in the passages mentioned above.

Jonah's myth also instantiates the "And I alone survived" motif, but with significant adaptation. He survives his ordeal, the encounter with the sea-monster, which no other man can claim to, but not because of positive qualities or abilities, or his heroic endurance, as in Odysseus' case. His myth presents his survival as entirely predicated upon Yahweh's favor. In a further inversion, none of the sailors perishes, which thematically parallels how the apocalypse threatening Nineveh will be averted. None of this crew has offended god, only the protagonist. The monster is merely a tool Yahweh uses to return Jonah to land to carry out his commission, which he earlier refused, to go to Nineveh and warn of the coming apocalypse. Hence the motif survives in the form "I alone experienced the fantastic voyage."

APOCALYPSE AVERTED

Each of the *Odyssey*'s three sequences concludes with a contained apocalypse (explored in Chapter 13),[16] two of which, those in Books 12 and 13, offer significant parallels with what Jonah expects to happen to Nineveh. The

---

[16] See discussion in Louden (1999: 20–5, 98–103).

apocalypses in Books 12 and 13 take place at sea, conclude a fantastic voyage, and culminate in the "And I alone survived" motif. In Book 12 Zeus brings about the destruction of all remaining members of the crew for their disobedience on Thrinakia, destroying them at sea, the fate Jonah's sailors fear near the beginning of his myth, "The Lord let loose a hurricane on the sea, which rose so high that the ship threatened to break up in the storm" (Jonah 1:4). In Book 13 Poseidon, incensed at the Phaiakian crew, initially wants to destroy the entire city of the Phaiakians, the same middle-degree apocalypse that threatens Nineveh at the end of Jonah's myth. In both episodes, as discussed in Chapter 1, Zeus mediates the wrathful deities, Helios and Poseidon, urging them away from the high levels of destruction that they originally seek. Jonah's myth offers parallels for all of these motifs, but alters them, as throughout, to fit its parodic modality.

Jonah's whole myth is framed by the threatened apocalyptic destruction of Nineveh, cast before the audience in the rough mold of the destruction of Sodom and Gomorrah in Genesis 19.[17] But such a trajectory is immediately interrupted when Jonah refuses to go to Nineveh and denounce its wickedness as Yahweh commands ("Go to the great city of Nineveh; go and denounce it, for I am confronted by its wickedness," Jonah 1:2). The abrupt change in the myth's expected trajectory right at the start introduces the inversions that characterize most of the narrative and the averted apocalypse that concludes it. While the averted apocalypse at Nineveh combines elements visible in both of the *Odyssey*'s marine-based apocalypses, it is particularly close to subsequent events in the city of the Phaiakians.

Odysseus' sojourn among the Phaiakians has several motifs in common with Jonah's interactions with the inhabitants of Nineveh. When Jonah comes ashore he goes straight to the city of Nineveh, as Yahweh commands, as Odysseus, after reaching Scheria, goes to the Phaiakians' city. Jonah prophesies the coming destruction of Nineveh, as Yahweh has told him to do (Jonah 1:2, 3:3–4), somewhat as, elsewhere in the *Odyssey*, Theoklymenos does to the suitors (*Od.* 20.351–7, 364–70). Odysseus does not play the role of a prophet, but, as the audience is aware, he comes in fulfillment of a prophecy similar to the one that Jonah delivers among the Ninevites.[18] Phaiakians have earlier had warning of threatened apocalyptic destruction, as Alkinoös relates that his father Nausithoös once said that Poseidon would pile a great mountain on their city some day, when one of their

---

[17] Again, cf. Crenshaw (1993: 381): "Linguistic features link Nineveh and the cities of Sodom and Gomorrah."

[18] Cf. de Jong (2001: 219, on *Od.* 8.564–71): "At this point the narratees may already have a premonition that the fatal escort will be that of Odysseus."

ships returned from conveying someone home (*Od.* 8.564–71). This is typical Odyssean irony in which characters talk about Odysseus without realizing he is present (Fenik 1974: 16, 22, 28–9, 42, 45; cf. de Jong 2001: 386). During the course of the *Apologue*, it becomes clear, as the external audience has earlier known (*Od.* 1.20–1, 68–79), that Poseidon has a divine wrath against Odysseus (*Od.* 9.527–35; 10.64–78), and that the Phaiakians' ferrying him home fulfills the prophecy Alkinoös relates at *Odyssey* 8.564–71. When the Phaiakians convey Odysseus home, a man hated by Poseidon, they provoke his wrath against them (cf. de Jong 2001: 219).

In his wrath Poseidon wishes to destroy the entire Phaiakian city (*Od.* 13.152), the most common form of apocalypse in ancient myth, as noted in Chapter 1. In Jonah's myth Yahweh also purportedly plans to destroy all of Nineveh, angry over unspecified wrongdoing by its inhabitants. Both narratives set their apocalypses after a myth of fantastic voyage: Odysseus' final crossing of the sea in the present-time of the *Odyssey*, courtesy of a crew with fabulous marine abilities; Jonah's fabulous adventure with the seamonster. In both myths the apocalyptic destruction of the respective cities has been earlier prophesied, but in each case such destruction is averted. The scene in which Zeus persuades Poseidon to punish only the sailors and not destroy the city of the Phaiakians (*Od.* 13.125–58) is part of a recurring pattern earlier established when Zeus talks Helios out of destroying the world, and instead punishing only that other group of sailors, Odysseus' crew (*Od.* 12.377–88). Different here, however, is the reaction of the other Phaiakians. Since he does not know Zeus has already talked Poseidon out of pursuing further destruction, Alkinoös urges the Phaiakians to propitiate the god through prayer and sacrifice (*Od.* 13.179–87).

The king of Nineveh acts in much the same way as Alkinoös when he learns of Jonah's warning of coming destruction, with much of Jonah 3:4–10 closely paralleling the Phaiakians' actions at *Odyssey* 13.179–87. The Ninevite king commands his people to cease their "wicked ways and the injustice they practice" (Jonah 3:8), which practices, never specified, are what had angered Yahweh. Alkinoös commands his people to cease conveying strangers across the sea (*Od.* 13.180–1), the specific act that has angered Poseidon (*Od.* 13.173–4). The Ninevite king commands his people to fast, livestock as well, don sackcloth, and all pray to god (Jonah 3:7–9). Alkinoös commands the Phaiakians to sacrifice twelve bulls to Poseidon, as the leading men pray to him, standing around his altar (*Od.* 13.181–7). As Poseidon, Yahweh does relent, as the myth's comic modality has indirectly suggested he will all along. But when he does, Jonah is angry, and prays for death. As we have observed, OT myth contains at least two apparent variations on the traditional divine mediation the *Odyssey* depicts between Zeus and Poseidon: Abraham's attempted mediation with Yahweh before the destruction at Sodom and Gomorrah (Gen. 18:22–32); and Moses' more successful instance of the same in Exodus 32 (explored again in Chapter 10). Jonah's complaints to Yahweh, *disappointment* that he does not destroy Nineveh (Jonah 4:1–3), are a parody of the kind of mediation Abraham and Moses attempt with Yahweh, both of whom try to talk him out of executing high levels of destruction in his wrath.

The author of Jonah carefully manipulates the traditional motifs, imposing a comic sensibility that inverts the usual serious modality, and significantly reverses how Yahweh is perceived. In place of the usual divine wrath, he promotes a conception of deity that allows greater forgiveness, not only for Jonah himself, but for the inhabitants of Nineveh. The myth dates to or is redacted in the time when animal sacrifice is no longer the norm, as do many passages in the prophetic books. But the comic sensibility and treatment of Jonah are the biggest innovation. Like Lucius throughout the first ten books of Apuleius' *The Golden Ass*, Jonah seems incapable of learning, of avoiding making the same mistakes again. His disappointment that Yahweh spares Nineveh from apocalypse is a thematic parallel to Lucius' failing to understand the Judgment of Paris acted out before him (*Golden Ass* 10.30–4). The scene is essentially a non-epiphany, paralleling and parodying the true epiphany by Isis that follows shortly (*Golden Ass* 11.3–6). In the Judgment of Paris, Lucius sees acted out before him in detail a reading of his own life, as one way or another is each smaller narrative set within the *Golden Ass*. Paris famously selects the goddess of sexual pleasure, rejecting the heroic Athena, and the regal Hera. This is Lucius' own life choice as well, but just as Jonah does not get it at the end of his myth, Lucius' chief reaction is to lament the importance of bribery as a factor in Paris' choice, and the problem of bribery as a general vice.

CHAPTER 8

The combat myth
Polyphêmos and Humbaba

The *Odyssey* marks Odysseus as an epic hero in a number of different ways in several different episodes. But perhaps the most important, and traditional, such episode is his defeat of the giant, one-eyed, monster, Polyphêmos, the Cyclops.[1] As de Jong notes (2001: 231),

> It shows us Odysseus at his worst... and at his best... It deals with three central issues of the *Odyssey*: cunning versus force... hospitality... and delayed recognition.

In myth a hero's victory over a powerful monster typically embodies a triumph of good over evil, order over chaos, civilization over nature. To analyze the episode, commentators have tended to overlook ancient Near Eastern parallels, preferring to find a context for it in folktales, in the *Iliad*, or recently, within the discourse of colonialism. But there are significant drawbacks to all three approaches.

Folktales offer a considerable number of parallels with the Polyphêmos episode,[2] (see Glenn [1971] and Mondi [1983], for instance) to be sure, and often help us understand how the *Odyssey* may alter a specific motif occurring elsewhere. But almost invariably the folktales used as *comparanda* differ fundamentally from Homeric epic in their tone or modality, featuring non-heroic characters, lacking gods, or such pivotal motifs as divine wraths.[3] They also date from such later periods that the possibility clearly exists, though it is rarely acknowledged, that the folktales themselves indirectly descend from the *Odyssey*'s account.

A second approach has been to see much of the episode through the lens of the *Iliad*, as a reaction to episodes in that poem. In my view, this

---

[1] I take the term "combat myth" from Fontenrose (1959), though he uses it of encounters with dragons, and consequently, does not analyze the Polyphêmos episode.
[2] On a possible Indo-European parallel for the Polyphêmos episode, see West (2007: 297).
[3] Cf. Heubeck (1989: 30): "The epic elements in the episode are of course unparalleled in the folklore material, and serve to characterize Odysseus as a true hero of the Trojan War."

has been a widespread problem with secondary literature on the *Odyssey* over the years – commentators' assumption that it has the *Iliad* as its only possible conceptual model. In this view any divine council in the *Odyssey*, for instance, must be based upon those in the *Iliad*; Odysseus' defeat of Polyphêmos must be based upon, or serve as an intertextual comment upon *aristeiai* in the *Iliad*, and so on. While the *Iliad* remains an invaluable hermeneutic for understanding the *Odyssey*, I do not share commentators' assumptions that any generic similarity between it and the *Odyssey* means the latter poem imitates the former,[4] or that resemblances between the poems are evidence of inter-textuality, or the like. Rather, as this study seeks to demonstrate, the *Odyssey* has been widely influenced by Near Eastern works with which it has many motifs and genres of myth in common. Each genre of myth in the *Odyssey* has counterparts in various Near Eastern mythologies.

Springing primarily from the description of Goat Island (*Od.* 9.116–41) and its mention of how perfect the island would be for human habitation, how its rich natural resources, unused, are going to waste, several recent commentators would view the Polyphêmos episode through the lens of colonialism (see especially Dougherty 2001: 127–42; cf. Byre [1994]). But the passage (*Od.* 9.116–41) may just as easily be explained by other motives, unrelated to colonialism: implicit praise of Odysseus' Phaiakian audience, the orderliness of their society (Byre 1994: 362). As noted below, the passage has a counterpart in *Gilgamesh* (5.1–9), which would seem to have little, if any, potential for a colonialist reading. Odysseus is himself a carpenter, thematic in Homeric epic, maker of his marriage bed and his raft (cf. *Il.* 23.710–13), and sees potential applications of his own craftsmanship. Odysseus' skill as carpenter will prove crucial to the episode in his fashioning of the olive tree to blind Polyphêmos. But it is necessary to impose considerable changes on the myth to see him as a colonist, making him a traveler, rather than a wanderer, a trader, rather than warrior and guest, and so on.

On the other hand, the *Gilgamesh* epic, widely acknowledged to offer multiple correspondences with Homeric epic (see recently Bachvarova 2005, Bakker 2001, Abusch 2001), offers a very similar episode, potent in its parallels, in that hero's defeat of the monster Humbaba. There are differences between the two myths. Humbaba is not one-eyed, though

---

[4] Cf. Louden (1999: 6), "I suggest, therefore, that Hermes' youthful form on Aiaia is not modelled on *Iliad* 24.347, but is better understood as an element in the *Odyssey*'s own repeated pattern"; cf., *ibid.*: 138n.14.

he is a giant monster. There is no cannibalism in the Humbaba encounter. Gilgamesh is accompanied and closely aided by Enkidu, whereas Odysseus' crew, none of whom is individuated in the episode, play a less central role.[5] But the larger parallels outweigh these more specific divergences between the two tales. George's recent two-volume edition of the Standard Babylonian Version of *Gilgamesh* significantly updates our understanding of the epic, bringing together recent research and arguments. It seems strange that the parallels between the Polyphêmos and Humbaba episodes have been so infrequently analyzed.

Our most frequent *comparanda* in this study, Old Testament myths, have little in the way of monsters, instead preferring the divine version of the combat myth, Yahweh's defeat of the primordial dragon, Leviathan/Rahab. Mentioned frequently (Isa. 27: 1; Psa. 74:13–15, 87:4, 89:10; Job 26: 12), and put to many different purposes, these tantalizing references parallel Zeus' victory over Typhoeus,[6] and Marduk's defeat of Tiamat. Such combats between a god and a cosmic monster are typically set before mortals yet exist, and tend to be cosmogonic, the defeated dragon's body used to form the earth or the heavens (Cross 1973: 111; Louden 2006: 219). In myths set in later eras when mortals exist, the hero's defeat of a monster suggests a similar dynamic, the creation of order or civilization, the liberation of crucial resources hoarded by the monster.

At an earlier stage, in some earlier form, OT myth clearly had narratives about mortals and monsters, for it does retain a few brief allusions. Perhaps most important is Genesis' brief, rather Hesiodic, mention of the Nephilim, an obscure race of giants:

The human race began to increase and to spread over the earth and daughters were born to them. The sons of the gods saw how beautiful these daughters were, so they took for themselves such women as they chose... In those days as well as later, when the sons of the gods had intercourse with the daughters of mortals and children were born to them, the Nephilim were on the earth; they were the heroes of old, people of renown. (Genesis 6:1–4)

The passage startles in a number of ways, perhaps none more than the polytheistic "the sons of the gods," glossed by Suggs (1992) as "a term of Canaanite origin for members of the pantheon ['assembly of the gods']." Alter (2004: 38–9) offers a general perspective:

This whole passage is obviously archaic and mythological. The idea of male gods coupling with mortal women whose beauty ignites their desire is a commonplace

---

[5] The crew nonetheless do offer some specific parallels with Enkidu's role, as discussed below.
[6] For brief discussion of the parallels, see Louden (2006: 219–21).

of Greek myth... One suspects that these words are either a citation of an old heroic poem or a stylistic allusion to the epic genre.[7]

OT myth retains a trace of the combat with the giant monster in its depiction of Goliath the Philistine (1 Sam. 17: 4), "A champion came out from the Philistine camp, a man named Goliath, from Gath; he was over nine feet in height." The Philistines, the OT people with the most in common with Homeric Greek culture, and who many assume are connected with or related in some way to Mycenaean culture (Bierling 1992: 71, Stager 1998: 152–79, Hindson 1971), are said to be descended from the Nephilim. When the Israelites mull over their invasion of Canaan, OT myth draws on a similar, once more complete, tradition:

All the people we saw there are men of gigantic stature. When we set eyes on the Nephilim (the sons of Anak belong to the Nephilim) we felt no bigger than grasshoppers; and that is how we must have been in their eyes. (Numbers 13: 32–3)

Closely related are references to the Rephaim (e.g., Josh. 12:4, 13:12; 2 Sam. 21:16, 18), another race of giants, whose descendants also figure in stories of heroic duels set in the larger David saga, very like Goliath. Bierling, reasoning, like others, that the Sea Peoples, as attested in Ramesside Egypt, included some component of Mycenaean Greek culture, ascribes the parallels to some form of dispersion between them and the West Semitic milieu in which Israelite myth developed (1992: 71),

It is logical to assume that the Sea Peoples, when they migrated from the Aegean and from western Anatolia and the plains of Ilium to Egypt and Palestine, carried with them the stories and ritual of their culture.

In an earlier stage of OT myth the Nephilim and Rephaim may have occupied a position closer to that of Humbaba and Polyphêmos in their mythologies.

In spite of the different uses to which their respective epics put them (the Polyphêmos episode, for instance is subordinated under the *Odyssey*'s thematic concern with hospitality), Odysseus' victory over Polyphêmos and Gilgamesh's defeat of Humbaba share a considerable number of common motifs, occurring in roughly the same sequence. There are homologies not only between the two heroes, the two monsters, and their subsequent curses on the heroes, but between the crew and Enkidu, between the gods Poseidon and Enlil, and their eventual wraths against the heroes, all of

---

[7] Cf. Finkelberg 2005: 162–3: "[T]he Genesis passage makes perfectly good sense when taken against the background of Greek heroic traditions... versions of the myth of the destruction of the Race of Heroes, probably a reflection of the historical cataclysm that accompanied the end of the Bronze Age, circulated not only in Greece but also in wider regions of the Eastern Mediterranean."

which supports the view that the two narratives are separate instances of the same genre of myth.

The parallel motifs may be schematized as follows:
1. The hero has a pivotal encounter with a giant monster.
    a. The encounters take place at roughly the same point in each epic.
    b. Each epic gives considerable advance notice of the coming encounter.
    c. The encounter shapes the hero's progress through much of the rest of his epic.
2. Both monsters have similar ties to the natural world.
    a. Each lives in the mountains,
    b. where marvelous trees grow.
3. The monster's face is distinguished by some unusual physical feature.
4. Learning of the hero's presence, Polyphêmos and Humbaba address him scornfully, calling him a fool, asking why he has come.
    a. The monster's bellowing can be heard from a distance.
5. Central to the monster's defeat, the hero fells a tree, or fashions one already cut down.
6. The monster is defeated as a result of having been blinded.
7. The hero wounds or slays the monster by stabbing it.
8. The hero despoils the monster of the item with which he is most closely identified (flocks, cedars).
9. The hero's defeat of the monster brings him fame.
10. The hero commits an act of hubris against the gods.
    a. His crew/Enkidu attempt(s) to prevent him from doing so.
11. The monster, though wounded or dying, curses the hero, inflicting tremendous suffering on him.
12. The god specifically linked to the monster develops a divine wrath against the hero.
13. The episode concluded, the hero sails away.
    1. The hero has a pivotal encounter with a giant monster.
        a. The encounters occur at roughly the same point in each epic.
        b. Each epic gives considerable advance notice of the coming encounter.
        c. The encounter shapes the hero's progress through much of the rest of his epic.

The most famous, most definitive encounter, for each hero, within his epic,[8] is his defeat of a giant monster. For each hero the encounter is

---

[8] Odysseus' definitive exploit may be the Trojan Horse, but it only figures peripherally within the *Odyssey*.

his most pivotal, cementing his fame (below as no. 9), but also causing him considerable grief (no. 11). In *Gilgamesh*, Tablet 5, whether out of a total of 11 or 12, is similarly placed as the *Odyssey*'s Book 9 out of 24, essentially in the third sixth. In each epic the episode's location allows for considerable anticipation and buildup, and a lengthy aftermath to develop the remarkably negative consequences of the great exploit. Both epics point to the problematic outcomes of the episodes before they unfold.

In *Gilgamesh* concern with battling Humbaba starts early, 2.217–29 (B), after Gilgamesh meets and defeats Enkidu, and the latter then meets Ninsun, Gilgamesh's mother. Preparation for the upcoming encounter dominates Tablet Three, the lengthy trek to reach the Cedar Forest fills Tablet 4, before the entire Tablet 5 is dedicated to the encounter. The *Odyssey* mentions Polyphêmos even earlier, in its first episode (*Od.* 1.68–75), intermittently thereafter (*Od.* 2.219–20, 6.206),[9] before devoting most of Book 9 to the encounter. The *Odyssey*'s first mention of Polyphêmos is coupled with a lengthier mention of Poseidon's divine wrath (*Od.* 1.68–75, motif no. 12), in which Zeus links him with his thematic verb of *plazô*, which depicts him acting on his wrath, *driving* Odysseus away from Ithaka (πλάζει δ' ἀπὸ πατρίδος αἴης: *Od.* 1.75). This central dynamic of the *Odyssey* is stated in the poem's first two lines (ὃς μάλα πολλὰ / πλάγχθη), but without naming Poseidon. In *Gilgamesh* Enkidu is concerned they will provoke divine wraths before they actually slay Humbaba, because he is aware that Enlil had appointed him guardian of the forest (*Gilg.* 2.217–219a SBV).

The two epics have differing motives, different emphases in how they employ these common motifs. Gilgamesh knowingly seeks out Humbaba, determined to combat him and win fame (no. 9). Odysseus does not know of Polyphêmos in advance, but voluntarily initiates the episode in his desire for a guest-gift, and for finding out what sort of people live there. To pursue these debatable aims, he willingly enters Polyphêmos' cave, his single greatest error in the poem (coupled with his disrespect to Poseidon at the episode's conclusion, discussed below).[10]

2. Both monsters have similar ties to the natural world.

  a. Each lives in the mountains,

  b. where marvelous trees grow.

Monsters are typically figured as representing, or integrally connected with, a natural, uncivilized state of existence. Humbaba and Polyphêmos both

---

[9] Below we will argue that Book 3's visit with Nestor also makes extended allusion to the Polyphêmos episode.

[10] Cf. Heubeck (1989: 7): "Only once does curiosity impel him into a situation of danger which could have been easily foreseen and avoided, when, quite unnecessarily, he ventures from the Island of Goats to the Land of the Cyclopes."

embody such a connection to nature through where they live, and the particular object with which they are most closely identified. Both live in the mountains, suggesting not only their remoteness from the world of mortals but their vertical proximity to the gods, a figurative expression of their power. Polyphêmos and the other Cyclopes are specifically said to dwell in the peaks of lofty mountains (*Od.* 9.113). Each monster, or his abode, is particularly associated with mountains and special trees. Polyphêmos, in a passage that combines both traits, is likened to the wooded peak of a mountain (*Od.* 9.191–2). Near the episode's conclusion, he breaks off the top of a mountain to hurl at Odysseus (*Od.* 9.481). His cave is overgrown with laurel trees (*Od.* 9.183); when he first enters he is carrying a load of dried-out wood (*Od.* 9.233–4); and at the back of his cave is the mammoth olive tree (*Od.* 9.319–35), which he uses as a walking stick. Polyphêmos is a shepherd, closely identified with his flocks throughout the episode (see especially *Od.* 9.446–61). Humbaba also combines both associations, mountain and tree, by living on Cedar Mountain (*Gilg.* 5.6–7). George (2003, Vol. 1: 144) notes his essential arboreality:

> He is essentially anthropomorphic in the Sumerian and Babylonian texts that relate his encounter with Gilgamesh, but at the same time represents the terrifying numinous power of the remote and ancient forest and has tree-like characteristics.

Gilgamesh underscores Humbaba's vital identification with trees at the beginning of Tablet 5 of the SBV, which opens with Gilgamesh and Enkidu marveling at the fabulous trees growing in Humbaba's forest:

> They marveling at the forest,
> Observing the height of the cedars,
> Observing the way into the forest ...
> [on the] very face of the mountain the cedar was proffering its abundance,
> sweet was its shade, full of delight.
> [All] tangled was the thorny undergrowth, the forest was a thick canopy.
> *Gilgamesh* 5.1–9 (George 2003)

The brief episode has more than a little in common with Odysseus' lengthy description of Goat Island (*Od.* 9.116–41), which, like the lines above, serves to introduce his encounter with the monster. Odysseus' description is full of admiration for the island's flora and fauna, unhampered by human contact. The parallels suggest that the Goat Island description may have its origin not in a contemporary Greek attitude toward a colonialist impulse, but as an inherited part of the genre, reflecting the monster's location in a part of the world free from contact with mortals, and looking ahead to both myth's focus on fashioned wood and carpentry.

3. The monster's face is distinguished by some unusual physical feature.

While a modern audience immediately associates the word Cyclops with a one-eyed giant monster, the Homeric account gives little actual description of his face, or the number of eyes he may have. As Mondi demonstrates (1983: 19–21, 31–5; cf. Glenn 1971: 154–6), Polyphêmos' monocularity is more problematic within the episode and within the larger context of archaic Greek myth, than is generally realized. As is often noted, Hesiod's Cyclopes are specifically one-eyed (*Theogony* 142–4), but since they are otherwise very different from those in the *Odyssey*, this is not taken as persuasive evidence that Polyphêmos is one-eyed. Nonetheless, though the *Odyssey* never specifies his single eye in the way a modern audience might expect, the episode's repeated emphasis on the word "eye" (*ophthalmos*: *Od.* 9.333, 383, 394, 397, 453, 503, 516, 525) in the singular would seem to suggest the audience's acquaintance with a tradition at least partly in line with Hesiod's account. The name Cyclops (explained at *Theogony* 144–5) also focuses attention on his eye, throughout the episode.

Though details are also lacking for Humbaba's face, the tradition makes it quite clear that his features, particularly his eyes and nose, are of unusual size, as George (2003, Vol. 1: 145) notes, "Humbaba was famous for his unusual physiognomy... Commentaries explain that a bulbous nose and big eyes are the characteristic features." In both myths the monsters' unusually prominent eye(s), whether exceptionally large, or single, constitute a vulnerability, a means for their defeat, that the hero will exploit, discussed below in no. 6.

4. Learning of the hero's presence, Polyphêmos and Humbaba address him scornfully, calling him a fool, asking why he has come.
   a. The monster's bellowing can be heard from a distance.

Polyphêmos and Humbaba are both extremely talkative for inhuman monsters, which surprising loquaciousness prompts several other events in each myth. Each is adept at taunting his opponents, epic flyting. Enkidu earlier warns Gilgamesh of Humbaba's powerful voice, "his voice is the Deluge, his speech is fire" (*Gilg.* 2.221–2). As they draw near the forest, they apparently hear Humbaba from a distance, exercising his ability to scare with his voice:

> Like a fierce wild bull, horns locked [...,]
> he bellowed once, and it was (a bellow) full of terror.
> The guardian of the forests was bellowing.
> *Gilgamesh* 4.201–3

The monster's first words in the epic are mocking and insulting:

> Let fools, Gilgamesh, take the advice of an idiot fellow!
> Why have you come here into my presence?
> Come, Enkidu, (you) spawn of a fish, who knew not his father.
> *Gilgamesh* 5.86–7

Polyphêmos' loquaciousness is even evident in his name, literally, "Having many utterances."[11] Like Humbaba to Gilgamesh, he addresses Odysseus as "fool" (*nepios*: *Od.* 9.273), and offers further insults (*Od.* 9.460). As Shamash ascribes to Humbaba, Polyphêmos' voice is terrifying (*Od.* 9.257). Polyphêmos even whistles loudly (*Od.* 9.315), as he leads his flocks out for the day, a harsh, monstrous juxtaposition, after having eaten two of Odysseus' crew. When blinded by Odysseus, he bellows in pain so loudly that other Cyclopes hear him even in his closed cave (*Od.* 9.395–401). The monsters' potent powers of speech lead to one of the two negative outcomes for each hero, the monster's curse, discussed below at no. 11.

5. Central to the monster's defeat, the hero fells a tree, or fashions one already cut down.

As George notes (2003, Vol. 1: 467), in the Sumerian *Gilgamesh* poems and the Hittite paraphrase, Humbaba first learns of the presence of Gilgamesh and Enkidu when he hears them felling his trees. Given Humbaba's tree-like nature and close identification with his forest and trees throughout, it is clear that the felled tree points ahead to his own death at Gilgamesh's hands (discussion below at no. 8). After Humbaba's death, Gilgamesh and Enkidu fell additional trees (SBV: 5.289–91), which cement the association and underscore their triumph over him. Central to Odysseus' defeat of Polyphêmos is his fashioning of a pike from the length of the mammoth olive tree, the "marvelous tree" in this myth, which Polyphêmos had earlier felled for use as a walking stick (*Od.* 9.320–8). The episode is part of the *Odyssey*'s thematic concern with depicting Odysseus as a carpenter, skilled at woodworking (*Od.* 5.234–61, 23.189–201; cf. *Il.* 23.712–13).[12] Gilgamesh is also depicted as a builder in his epic, fashioning, like Odysseus, a raft (discussed below at no. 13), credited as well with constructing the city walls of Uruk.

6. The monster is defeated as a result of having been blinded.

Both myths draw attention to the monsters' eyes, in Polyphêmos' case, even whenever the word Cyclops occurs. Key to their defeat at the hands of a smaller, weaker being is their loss of sight at the pivotal moment in their

---

[11] On this as the meaning of the name, see Louden (1995: 41–2).
[12] See Louden (1996) for further discussion of these passages, as well as references to Odysseus' role in the construction of the Trojan Horse.

narratives. In *Gilgamesh* Shamash, mentor god for the hero, as Athena is for Odysseus,[13] sends the winds against Humbaba:

> Shamash roused against Humbaba the mighty stormwinds:
> South Wind, North Wind, East Wind, West Wind, Blast,
> Counterblast, Gale, Tempest, Typhoon,
> Hell-Wind, Icy Blast, Hurricane, Tornado.
> Thirteen winds rose up and the face of Humbaba darkened.
> *Gilgamesh* 5.137–41

George interprets (2003, Vol. 1: 468), "The thirteen winds he [Shamash] sends against Humbaba duly blind the ogre with dust and immobilize him, thereby giving Gilgamesh the chance of striking the telling blow." The *Odyssey*'s use of blinding the monster is more decisive and climactic, accomplished by the hero himself. Odysseus tells the audience in advance of his plan; we observe him fashioning the implement to do so; we hear Polyphêmos' eye sizzle as the red-hot olive wood pierces it (*Od.* 9.387–94); and, since he remains alive after the blinding, we see him grope about, blinded, after the incident. The *Odyssey* may innovate in presenting Odysseus on his own unaided by Athena in this episode, to increase the thematic importance of Poseidon's divine wrath, and to offer additional support for why Odysseus takes ten years to return home. The primacy of the olive tree here, sacred to the goddess, may suggest her actual involvement in some earlier version of the myth, as Shamash with Gilgamesh. Support for such a view is evident when Odysseus links his idea of fashioning the olive tree to Athena (*Od.* 9.316–28).

7. The hero wounds or slays the monster by stabbing it.

Once Humbaba is temporarily blinded by Shamash, Gilgamesh stabs him in the neck, the specific locus of many climactic mortal woundings in myth. George (2003) translates the SBV as follows, "he drew forth [the dirk at] his side. / Gilgamesh [smote him] in the neck" (*Gilg.* 5.263–4). Humbaba expires immediately. In the *Odyssey* motifs nos. 6 and 7 are simultaneous: Polyphêmos is blinded when Odysseus stabs him in the eye. Odysseus and four crew members, chosen by lot, stab Polyphêmos in the eye with the sharpened, fired olive pike (*Od.* 9.387–96). After David defeats the giant Goliath by means of a small stone in a sling, he decapitates him (1 Sam. 17: 51), which may thus continue the implicit association of the Philistine giant with a monster myth tradition. Somewhat relevant is the *Iliad*'s careful pattern of victorious Greeks wounding or slaying their Trojan

---

[13] On parallels between the functions of Shamash in *Gilgamesh* and Athena in the *Odyssey*, see Louden (2005: 90–6).

enemies in the neck (Aias against Hektor: *Il.* 7.261–2, Athena against Ares: *Il.* 21.406, Akhilleus against Hektor: *Il.* 22.326–8).[14]

Unexpectedly, both *Gilgamesh* and the *Odyssey* make a reference to metalworking shortly before the hero strikes the climactic blow against the monster.[15] The simile at *Odyssey* 9.391–3, comparing Polyphêmos' eye as it sizzles from the red-hot olive pike to the hiss of an iron blade a blacksmith tempers in water, is well known. De Jong (2001: 43) offers a representative assessment:

> As technical similes, describing the activities of a carpenter and a smith, they contribute to the depiction of Odysseus' skill, and to the general theme of the victory of culture over nature.

Gilgamesh offers a partial parallel at a similar point in the encounter with Humbaba. When Gilgamesh briefly loses his nerve before the combat, Enkidu seeks to reassure him with the following remarks, which seem to suggest something along the lines of, we should strike while we are ready:[16]

> To gather up the copper (ingots) from the channel-moulds of the copper founder?
> To blow on the coals for a double hour, to ... what is alight for a double hour?
>
> SBV: 5.103–4

Though the *Odyssey*'s simile anachronistically mentions iron (*sideros*), which would have been unavailable to Homer's Bronze Age Greeks (Heubeck 1989: 34), Odysseus' tale seems to retain a traditional, inherited sequence which fuses imagery from metal-working to the climactic moment when the monster is wounded. Hesiod's *Theogony* confirms such a traditional association, the hero as an embodiment of civilization, when Zeus decisively wounds Typhoeus, and the heat of his thunder-blasts is compared to a craftsman melting tin (*Theogony* 861–7).

8. The hero despoils the monster of the item with which he is most closely identified (flocks, cedars).

The crew had earlier, on first entering the cave, urged Odysseus to drive the flocks off before they encountered Polyphêmos, but Odysseus overruled them (*Od.* 9.224–9). Later, after six crewmen have died, Odysseus concocts a plan to escape the now blind Polyphêmos by hiding under his

---

[14] For additional instances, and discussion, see Louden (2006: 43–4, 71–3, 75, 215).
[15] I am unable to find a previous commentator who notes this parallel.
[16] Cf. George's interpretation (Volume II) 2003: 826, "'A task of mythical proportions calls for swift and sudden action!'" See *ibid.*, 823–6 for detailed discussion of these lines.

rams (*Od.* 9.425–34). When dawn comes he and his crew escape, driving off Polyphêmos' cherished flocks (*Od.* 9.464–5). The episode places unusual emphasis on the loss Polyphêmos feels. As a now blind Polyphêmos questions his favorite ram, wondering why it is taking him so long to leave, the audience finds itself pitying the cannibal monster, now victimized, displaying somewhat human emotions.

After slaying Humbaba, Gilgamesh cuts many of his timbers for several undertakings, a memorial, a door for Shamash's temple, and a raft. Above in no. 5 we noted that George describes (2003, Vol.1: 467) how in the Sumerian and Hittite versions, Humbaba first learns of the presence of Gilgamesh and Enkidu when he hears them felling his trees. When the text resumes after the lacuna that follows Humbaba's death, both Gilgamesh and Enkidu are busy felling trees and fashioning them into mementoes:

> As Gilgamesh cut down the trees, Enkidu was seeking out the best timber.
> Enkidu opened his mouth to speak, saying to Gilgamesh:
> "My friend, we have cut down a lofty cedar,
> whose top abutted the heavens.
> I made a door – six rods is its height, two rods its breadth, one cubit its thickness,
> its pole, its top pivot and its bottom pivot are all of a piece."
>
> *Gilgamesh* 5.291–6

The audience may also begin to pity Humbaba when he pleads for his life, offering his fabulous trees if Gilgamesh will not slay him:

> "Trees as many as you command from me [. . . . . . ,]
> I will guard for you the myrtle, the [. . . . . . ,]
> timber that is the pride of a palace [. . .]"
>
> *Gilgamesh* 5.153–5

9. *The hero's defeat of the monster brings him fame.*
Epic tends to depict a hero achieving a form of eternal fame as a means by which he transcends mortality. Though Homerists often assume such epic fame is an inherited Indo-European tradition, Near Eastern cultures had a very similar view, as *Gilgamesh* repeatedly demonstrates. Earning fame is Gilgamesh's principal motive throughout the encounter, from the episode's earliest mention to its conclusion. Having resolved early on to face Humbaba, at the end of Tablet 4, as he reassures Enkidu, and notes the power of friends to help one another, he links their pursuit with achieving fame, "It is they who have established a name [for] future [*time*!]." The connection between encountering Humbaba and earning fame is most

explicit in the Old Babylonian Version (OBV). In Tablet 3, as he discusses with Enkidu his plan to combat Humbaba, Gilgamesh notes how he will win fame even if he dies in the attempt:

> Mankind can number his days.
> Whatever he may achieve, it is only wind.
> Do you fear death on this occasion?
> Where is the strength of your heroic nature?
> Let me go in front of you,
> And your voice call out: "Go close, don't be afraid!"
> If I should fall, I shall have won fame.
> People will say, "Gilgamesh grappled in combat
> With ferocious Huwawa."[17]

During the combat Enkidu repeatedly reiterates the link with fame, as he encourages Gilgamesh to finish Humbaba off, so they can proceed to celebrate their accomplishment:

> Establish an eternal [...,]
> how Gilgamesh *slew* Humbaba [...]
> *Gilgamesh* 5.244–5

A hero erecting a memorial for his accomplishments finds parallels with Hektor in *Iliad* 7.82–91, and with Saul in 1 Sam. 15:12. The Genesis passage given above, with its connection between a race of giants and heroes, concludes with the phrase "men of renown" (Gen. 6:4), of which Speiser notes (1962: 45), "literally 'men with a name'," and adduces as parallel the *Gilgamesh* passage given above that concludes Tablet 4.

The very first lines of the *Odyssey* show that Odysseus already has epic fame from his role in bringing about the sack of Troy (*Od.* 1.1–4). Within the subsequent poem, however, his defeat of Polyphêmos is clearly the episode, of those the *Odyssey* depicts, most concerned with earning him additional heroic fame.[18] The poem demonstrates this on a number of levels, from the link to Poseidon's wrath, to Zeus himself discussing the incident (*Od.* 1.69), to Odysseus singling the episode out when he needs to reassure himself the night before slaying the suitors (*Od.* 20.18–21). As with no. 4, this motif is also inherent in Polyphêmos' name, which can also be rendered as "having much fame," a property that the poem transfers to Odysseus.[19]

---

[17] Dalley (1991: 144).
[18] Cf. Cook (1995: 94), "Polyphêmos more than any other character in the enchanted realm provides Odysseus with *kleos*."
[19] See West (2007: 403) on Karna choosing to win fame in the *Mahabhârata* (3.284.31).

10. The hero commits an act of hubris against the gods.
   a. His crew/Enkidu attempt(s) to prevent him from doing so.
Commentators lack a clear consensus on what it is specifically that Odysseus does that offends Poseidon, or perhaps even more important, why Zeus validates Poseidon's subsequent wrath (since, by contrast, he does not fully validate Poseidon's wrath against the Phaiakians). I follow Friedrich (1991) in finding Odysseus justified in blinding Polyphêmos, who has, after all, slain and eaten six of his men. The traditional heroic act of defeating the monster is not problematic. Vaunting after such an accomplishment is also not problematic, contrary to frequent claims by commentators. But when, in his vaunt he specifies, "not even the Shaker of the Earth will ever heal your eye for you" (*Od.* 9.525), he shows disrespect to Poseidon by placing limits on his power, which he has no business doing. This is his offence. This makes a heroic vaunt, an acceptable act under the circumstances, an act of hubris, a succumbing to his pride, his *thumos*.

Thematically the *Odyssey* depicts the crew as acting irresponsibly,[20] from the opening mention in the proem, to their climactic mutiny on Thrinakia (discussed in Chapter 10). But the encounter with Polyphêmos proves the exception to this otherwise consistent thematic.[21] Here the crew acts more responsibly at the beginning, urging Odysseus to drive off Polyphêmos' flocks but leave before encountering him. When Odysseus shouts his vaunt, a blind Polyphêmos, better able to gauge where their ship is because of the shouts, breaks off the top of a mountain and hurls it at them, narrowly missing, driving them closer to him (*Od.* 9.480–6). When the crew row to twice the previous distance, and Odysseus prepares to vaunt again, they try to dissuade him (*Od.* 9.494–9), though unable, as he narrates, to persuade his "great-hearted spirit" (*thumos*: *Od.* 9.500). Revealing his name, patronymic, and homeland (*Od.* 9.502–5), placing limits on Poseidon (9.523–5), acts the crew tried to prevent, Odysseus alone is responsible for the subsequent curse and divine wrath.

In Gilgamesh's case, an act of hubris is implicit in his slaying of Humbaba, because the god Enlil had appointed him guardian of the forest (2.217–19a SBV). Enkidu, offering a rough parallel to the crew, is concerned that their slaying of Humbaba may provoke a divine wrath from Enlil or from the other gods:

---

[20] Their thematic irresponsibility is part of a larger pattern the *Odyssey* deploys, which aligns them with Aigisthos, the suitors, and the rude Phaiakian athletes, all sharing similar traits. See Louden (1999: 14, 23) for discussion.
[21] Within the episode, then, the crew provides a surprising parallel to the crew in Jonah.

> Finish him, slay him, do away with his power,
> before Enlil the foremost has learned (about it)!
> The [great] gods could be angry with us.
> *Gilgamesh* 5.184–6 (cf. 5.243–4)

But after they slay and despoil the monster, they return to Uruk without incident (unlike Odysseus, whose wanderings are just beginning, prompted by Poseidon's wrath). Instead of Enlil, whom we expect to be wrathful, Ishtar enters the narrative, propositioning Gilgamesh, as discussed in Chapter 5. The epic prefers to emphasize this more blatant act of hubris by Gilgamesh. When he rudely rejects her offer, a wrathful Ishtar sends the Bull of Heaven against Uruk. When they battle the Bull of Heaven, Enkidu connects the episode with the encounter with Humbaba:

> My friend, we were too arrogant [when we killed Humbaba].
> How can we give recompense [for our action]?
> VI.iv (Dalley 1991: 81)

Though earlier depicted as having more concern with possible offence in their acts, here Enkidu acts out of hubris. Hurling a haunch of the slain Bull of Heaven before her, Enkidu rudely taunts the goddess:

> You too, had I caught you, I would have treated you like it!
> I would have draped its guts on your arms.
> SBV 6.156–7

Because of Enkidu's arrogance, the goddess' wrath is now turned more against him than Gilgamesh.

11. The monster, though wounded or dying, curses the hero, inflicting tremendous suffering on him.

In a second (in addition to the divine wrath), more ironic, negative outcome from the encounter, Odysseus and Gilgamesh are both cursed by the monster they defeated. Polyphêmos' curse (*Od.* 9.528–35), the cap of the speeches exchanged between monster and hero noted above, is quite specific, consisting largely of details the audience knows have already come to pass at the beginning of the poem (*Od.* 9.534–5):

> May he come home late, wretchedly, his companions destroyed,
> on a ship belonging to another, and may he find pains in his house.

In having Polyphêmos pronounce his curse as the son of Poseidon, the *Odyssey* employs very specific circumstances. *Gilgamesh* uses the motif in a more general way. As he dies, Humbaba curses both Gilgamesh and Enkidu (Dalley 1991: 76):

Neither one of them shall outlive
His friend! Gilgamesh and Enkidu shall never become (?) old men (?).

In this form the curse, as given, applies equally to either man. The SBV is more specific:

May they not [.........]
May the pair of them not grow old,
apart from his friend Gilgamesh, may Enkidu have nobody to bury him!
Gilgamesh 5.255–7

Here the curse clearly specifies Enkidu, as logic dictates in an epic titled *Gilgamesh*. In both epics, then, though the hero triumphs over and despoils him, the surprisingly articulate monster gets the final word, causing him considerable suffering, transforming the heroic achievement into a Pyrrhic victory.

12. The god linked to the monster develops a divine wrath against the hero.

The *Odyssey* alerts its audience from the beginning to Poseidon's role as the god with a wrath against Odysseus and his link to the hero's encounter with the monster. The following episode with Aiolos (*Od.* 10.64–75) quickly demonstrates that Poseidon's curse is in effect. *Gilgamesh* is less direct in how it depicts the gods' reactions to Gilgamesh's defeat of Humbaba. Having placed Humbaba in charge of the forest (*Gilg.* 2.217–19a, 298–9; SBV), Enlil parallels Poseidon as the god most involved with the defeated monster. But *Gilgamesh* does not depict him with the kind of visceral reaction as in the divine wraths of Poseidon against Odysseus, Athena against Hektor in the *Iliad*, or Anat against Aqhat. Though Enkidu twice expresses concern that Enlil will be wrathful if they slay Humbaba (*Gilg.* 5.185, 242), Enlil's reaction survives only in the Hittite insertion at the beginning of Tablet 7, after the intervening episode with Ishtar and the Bull of Heaven that fills Tablet 6. Here Enkidu is depicted dreaming of a divine council attended by Anu, Enlil, Ea, and Shamash. But it is Anu, not Enlil, who suggests that, since Gilgamesh and Enkidu have slain the Bull of Heaven and Humbaba, one of them must die. Enlil chimes in, "Let Enkidu die, but let Gilgamesh not die." When Shamash protests, Enlil confronts him (Dalley 1991: 84):

But Enlil turned in anger to heavenly Shamash, saying,
"(The fact is), you accompanied them daily, like one of their comrades."

Though he is depicted as wrathful (his support for Enkidu's death finds parallels with Hera supporting Sarpedon's death in the divine council at

Iliad 16.431–58), the episode does not quite live up to expectations in presenting Enlil as angry at Gilgamesh.

As noted in Chapter 1, in most divine councils the speakers belong to a central configuration of three deities, the epic triangle. The roles in the Hittite insertion to Tablet 7 conform to those expected in an epic triangle, with Anu, who clearly presides over the council, as the sky father figure, Shamash as the hero's mentor, and Enlil as the wrathful god. As mentor god, Shamash comes to Gilgamesh's aid (whereas the *Odyssey* may innovate in keeping Athena offstage in Odysseus' encounter with Polyphêmos). Three times *Gilgamesh* links the two gods Shamash and Enlil, the lower two gods of the triangle (SBV: 5.187, 244; VII.i: Dalley 1991: 84). All of this suggests that if we, for the moment, ignore Tablet 6, *Gilgamesh* has at its core an epic triangle corresponding to that in the *Odyssey*, Zeus, Athena, and Poseidon (cf. the *Aeneid*, Jupiter, Venus, and Juno, or the *Aqhat*, El, Baal, and Anat), and the events at the beginning of Tablet 7, Enlil supporting Enkidu's death, could proceed right from the end of Tablet 5. Is Ishtar's prominence in Tablet 6 as the wrathful god a later development?

13. The episode concluded, the hero sails away.

While it is hardly unusual for Odysseus to conclude an episode by sailing away,[22] it is less expected when Gilgamesh and Enkidu conclude their encounter by building a raft (SBV 5.300–1). They need one to transport the timbers they have plundered from Humbaba's forest, including a door Gilgamesh has fashioned, as well as Humbaba's head and tusks (*Gilg.* 5.293–302). The *Odyssey* vastly complicates Odysseus' sailing away by including within it the lengthy bandying back and forth between hero and monster, his vaunts and Polyphêmos' climactic curse.

---

[22] See Glenn (1971: 146) on his assumption that the *Odyssey* adapted the Polyphêmos episode from an original non-marine setting. This final parallel with *Gilgamesh*, though slight, may undercut such an assumption.

CHAPTER 9

Catabasis, *consultation, and* the vision
Odyssey *11, 1 Samuel 28,* Gilgamesh *12,* Aeneid *6,* Plato's Allegory of the Cave, *and the Book of Revelation*

Book 11 of the *Odyssey* combines three distinct genres of myth, *catabasis* (or the descent to the underworld), consultation with the shade of a deceased prophet, and *the vision*.[1] *Catabasis*, a particularly common mythic genre in Greek myth, survives in several other examples. Both the *Iliad* (8.363–9) and the *Odyssey* (11.623–6) refer to Herakles' descent (cf., Bacchylides *Ode* 5.56–175), performed as his final labor for Eurystheus. Orpheus and Theseus also made descents to the underworld, though not mentioned in Homeric epic. But in having Odysseus *sail* to Hades, the *Odyssey* subordinates *catabasis* under the framework of the fantastic voyage, explored in Chapter 7. In having *Kirke* require Odysseus' voyage to the underworld, the *Odyssey* simultaneously subordinates its consultation under the framework of Argonautic myth which not only shapes much of Books 6–12, but surfaces again in Book 11 in the *Catalogue of Women* (*Od.* 11.225–329).

Perhaps because of these two factors, the *Odyssey* largely dispenses with any real depiction of the *catabasis*, as it would later appear in Book 6 of the *Aeneid*.[2] Instead, with typically Homeric economy, the episode (after the surprising appearance of Elpenor) quickly focuses on Odysseus' meeting with Teiresias (*Od.* 11.90–151), the reason Kirke ordered the trip to Hades (*Od.* 10.490–5). The hero's consultation, as directed by Kirke, with a legendary deceased prophet finds a close parallel in Old Testament myth's account of Saul consulting Samuel (1 Sam. 28) with the help of the unnamed female necromancer. Thereafter, Odysseus talks at length (longer than his consultation with Teiresias) with his mother Antikleia. After which, and, as if under her guidance, he witnesses the parade of famous women. Long criticized as an addition or intrusion, the catalogue has recently gained acceptance as key to Arete's sudden declaration of

---
[1] See Crane (1988: 87–134) and Tsagarakis (2000) for summaries of previous scholarship on the *Odyssey*'s use of *catabasis* and consultation (*nekuomanteion*).
[2] Crane (1988: 88) argues that Book 11 becomes a *catabasis* after the *Intermezzo*.

support for Odysseus as soon as he finishes recounting it (*Od.* 11.335–41).³ The *Catalogue of Women* also serves additional functions, as an instance of another traditional, though less well known, mythic type, *the vision*.

I define *the vision* as a genre of myth in which the protagonist is removed from the mortal plane, accompanied by an otherworldly guide, who reveals to him a large truth, the "big picture," previously hidden from his view. This basic structure, also familiar from texts such as Cicero's "Scipio's Dream," Dickens' *A Christmas Carol*, and the film *It's a Wonderful Life* (in which the angel Clarence shows George Bailey what Bedford Falls would have been like if he had never been born), is also the central organizing device in the Book of Revelation, which is largely an extended instance of the vision.⁴ In Odysseus' interview with his mother, the *Odyssey* presents a germinal, not fully developed instance of this narrative form that will become common in myth, as in the *Aeneid* and the Book of Revelation, in philosophical texts, popular literature, and movies. *Catabasis* and *the vision* are often linked in other texts, as they are in the *Odyssey*. Book 6 of the *Aeneid*, *It's a Wonderful Life* (with Bedford Falls transformed into Potterville as a descent to Hell), and implicitly Plato's *Allegory of the Cave* in Book 7 of *The Republic* all link them, whereas "Scipio's Dream" and Revelation link the vision to the thematic opposite, *anabasis*, setting *the vision* in heaven.⁵

CONSULTATION WITH THE DECEASED PROPHET
(OD. 11.90–151 AND 1 SAM. 28)

1 Samuel 28 depicts Saul deep in a crisis of his own making, like Odysseus, having provoked a divine wrath. When Yahweh commanded him to make war upon the Amalekites, and put them under the ban (1 Sam. 15: 1–3), Saul achieved a significant military victory, but spared Agag, the Amalekite king, and the best of the sheep and cattle, violating the ban. The prophet Samuel tells him that an angry Yahweh has turned away from him, rejecting him as king (1 Sam. 15: 22–3). Saul is largely the same character type as Agamemnon, and shares several larger thematic parallels with the Greek commander, including contentious relations with prophets.⁶ Saul goes on

---

³ Louden (1999: 12–13).
⁴ All of Dante's *Inferno*, after the first Canto, is an extended instance of *the vision*.
⁵ Cf. Sparks (2005: 240): "the otherworldly journey... narrates the prophet's visionary experience in the heavens or in the underworld," though this is part of his definition of apocalypse. I address overlap between my use of the vision and the mythic type apocalypse in Chapter 13.
⁶ Discussion in Louden (2006: 161–3).

to develop considerable friction with David (much as Agamemnon with Akhilleus), who, after having defeated Goliath in a duel, later allies himself with the Philistines. With Yahweh against him, the prophet Samuel now dead, the Philistines ready to attack, and David apparently allied with Achish,[7] the Philistine king of Gath, Saul, desperate to discern god's will, enlists a female necromancer, which activity he had recently forbidden (1 Sam. 28:3). Notwithstanding parallels with Agamemnon, in his consultation scene Saul shares motifs with Odysseus consulting Teiresias. Both, beset by insurmountable difficulties (see Saul's summary at 1 Sam. 28:15), consult with a deceased prophet (Samuel, Teiresias) guided by a female with magical powers (the necromancer, Kirke).

While Saul's consultation with Samuel is a straightforward necromancy, the *Odyssey* makes the consultation of a prophet into a heroic act, more suitable for an epic, by combining it with a *catabasis*. Odysseus has to endure the terrors of Hades to consult with the legendary prophet. But, as noted above, the *Odyssey* subordinates the *catabasis* to the consultation.[8] Saul's consultation with the woman from En-dor, while "orthodox" necromancy, and lacking any heroic modality, reflects a tension between the religious views of the redactor and those practices the inherited myth depicts. OT myth believes necromancy to be real, but a practice Yahweh forbids. Alter, noting common ground with *Odyssey* 11, offers a brief sketch (1999: 172):

> Biblical views about post-mortem existence tend to fluctuate. Often, the dead are thought to be swallowed up in "the Pit" (*she'ol*) where they are simply silenced, extinguished forever. Sometimes, the dead are imagined as continuing a kind of shadowy afterlife in the underworld, rather like the spirits of the dead in Book 11 of the *Odyssey*. Following on this latter view, necromancy in the ancient Hebrew world is conceived not as mere hocus pocus but as a potentially efficacious technology of the realm of spirits which, however, has been prohibited by God, Who wants no human experts interfering in this realm.[9]

Halpern (2001: 22) deduces from the conflicting attitudes toward necromancy that the story originates in a period when Jerusalem accepts or tolerates necromancy, and that the original intent is to criticize Saul's hypocrisy for first outlawing the practice, then resorting to it in his moment of need.

In the *Odyssey*, and Greek myth in general, necromancy involves digging a pit (*bothros*), and making "libations and blood offerings to the dead"

---

[7] Several commentators have connected the name Achish with Anchises.
[8] See Crane (1988: 93) for evidence of Etruscan and Persian *nekuomanteia*, and Herodotus' mention of the same in Thesprotia.
[9] McCarter (1985: 420) notes additional OT references to necromancy (Lev. 19:31, 20:6, 27; 2 Kgs. 21:6, 23:24), which also reflect similar ambiguity toward the practice.

(Tsagarakis 2000: 37). 1 Sam. 28, by contrast, offers no details about how the woman from En dor initiates the necromancy, as Alter (1999: 174) points out:

> It is noteworthy that the narrator is discreetly silent about the actual mechanics of the conjuration procedure, perhaps out of a kind of monotheistic reticence.

The Septuagint refers to her as *eggastrimuthos* (1 Sam. 28: 3, 7, 8, 9), implying that she conducts a séance, in which the voice of the deceased speaks through her (cf. McCarter 1985: 417, who refers to the episode as "The Seance at En-Dor"). Alter offers another view (1999: 174):

> As other biblical references to conjuration of the dead suggest, the usual method would be for the necromancer to listen and interpret the supposed "chirping" (*tsiftsuf*) or murmuring sounds made by shadows or wispy wraiths believed to be the presences of the dead. (There is scant biblical evidence for the claim that the necromancer was a medium from whose throat the ghost spoke.) In this case, however, the spirit appears not as a murmuring wisp or shadow but as the distinctly defined image of Samuel, in his prophet's cloak (see verses 13–14), and the woman of En-dor immediately realizes that it is only for the king that the prophet Samuel would have thus risen from the underworld in full-body image.

Alter's observation on the shades' chirping resembles the *Odyssey*'s description of the sounds of the suitors' souls, as Hermes conducts them to Hades (*Od.* 24.5–9).

The woman who conducts Saul's necromancy shares several thematic parallels with Kirke. First there is the gender parallel: both Odysseus and Saul undergo necromancies under the direction of a female invested with supernatural powers. While goddesses and authoritative women such as Arete are central to the *Odyssey*, OT myth rarely depicts females with similar powers. Halpern refers to her as a witch (2001: 22, 368),[10] a common frame of reference for Kirke, who, as a chthonic goddess, has a natural association with the underworld and the dead, the woman of En-dor's own area of expertise. Each female's potency partly resides in a supernatural power of speech. One of Kirke's epithets, *audeessa* (αὐδήεσσα: *Od.* 10.136, 11.8, 12.150), stresses her divine articulation (though there is no consensus as to the epithet's application), and the epic consistently highlights her prophetic powers. The woman of En-dor serves as Saul's verbal intermediary for the beginning of the episode, describing to him what she sees, and consoling him afterward, when he is shaken by Samuel's prophecy. The Septuagint's

---

[10] McCarter (1985) calls her a "ghostwife," explaining (418), "In both occurrences MT conflates two terms referring to a (female) necromancer."

term for her, ἐγγαστρίμυθος, literally something like ventriloquist, indexes her unique power of articulation.

Odysseus and Saul already know of her powers when they seek out the female with supernatural ability. Odysseus, after a year on Aiaia, asks Kirke to help him return home. Saul seeks a necromancer because he is in dire straits:

I am in great trouble; the Philistines are waging war against me, and God has turned away; he no longer answers me through prophets or through dreams.[11] (1 Samuel 28: 15)

Though initially unable to recognize them, the woman from En-dor and Kirke both deduce the identity of the protagonists shortly after first encountering them (*Od.* 10.330; 1 Sam. 28: 12). The woman from En-dor cannot first recognize Saul because he is in disguise, having made necromancy illegal. Alter (1999: 173) notes a combination of factors at work:

The narrative motivation is obvious: as the very ruler who has made necromancy a capital crime (see verse 9), Saul can scarcely come to engage the services of a necromancer unless he is disguised as a commoner. But his disguise also is the penultimate instance of the motif of royal divestment... Now, in an unwitting symbolic gesture, he divests himself of his royal garments before going to learn of his own impending death.

Failing to recognize him when she first has him enter, seats him, serves him a drugged potion, and strikes him with her wand, Kirke recognizes Odysseus only when he remains untransformed and draws his sword against her.

The deceased prophets, Teiresias and Samuel, share several thematic parallels. Both are distinguished as exceptional prophets, having a special relation with god. Kirke describes Teiresias as the only man in Hades with intelligence, or consciousness:

> Teiresias, the blind
> Theban prophet, whose thoughts are clear,
> to him alone, though dead, dread Persephone
> has granted a thinking mind, but the shadows flit about.
> *Odyssey* 10.492–5

Samuel's close relation with Yahweh is thematic (1 Sam. 2:26; 3:1–14, 19; 7:1–9; etc.).

Both prophets also have an article that makes them easy to recognize. Teiresias has a distinctive staff (*Od.* 11.91), Samuel a cloak (1 Sam. 28: 14).

---

[11] On myth's frequent equation of prophetic utterances and dreams, cf. Akhilleus' comment at *Il.* 1.62–4.

The Witch of En-dor further distinguishes Samuel when she describes his approach, "I saw a ghostly form coming up from the earth" (1 Sam. 28:13), for which the Septuagint has θεοὺς ἑόρακα ἀναβαίνοντας ἐκ τῆς γῆς, "I saw *gods* coming up from the earth," a literal rendering of the Masoretic Text's *elohim*. Alter suggests possible interpretations of the plural (1999: 175):

When she says she sees "*elohim* rising up," she probably means an imposing figure like unto a god, or an angel, or perhaps she is using it as a term for "spirit."

If functioning as an actual plural, it parallels the first and last entities Odysseus sees in Hades, hordes of shades gathering around him (*Od.* 11.36–7, 632–3).

Each prophet, having recognized the respective protagonist, in his first remarks asks why he has consulted him. Addressing Odysseus by name, Teiresias asks why he has come (*Od.* 11.92–4). Samuel, on first coming up, immediately turns to Saul and, though not addressing him by name, clearly recognizes the king (1 Sam. 28:15). Teiresias, after drinking the sacrificial blood, answers his own question, which prompts Heubeck (1989: 82) to conclude, "Teiresias' opening question is rhetorical (cf. x 281), as the prophet knows full well the reason for Odysseus' coming." Samuel's first words are "Why have you disturbed me and raised me" (1 Sam. 28:16).

Both prophets assign the protagonists' difficulties to a divine wrath. Teiresias declares that Poseidon will make Odysseus' homecoming difficult, because he has a divine wrath against him (*Od.* 11.101–3). Teiresias' word for Poseidon's anger is *kotos*, which, with its related forms, such as the verb *koteo*, Walsh argues (2004: 23–39, 50, 52–4, 79–80, 97, 101) is Homeric epic's term for the long-term anger typical of a divine wrath. Samuel describes the reasons for Yahweh's wrath at Saul in some detail:

Why do you ask me, now that the Lord has turned from you and become your adversary? He has done what he foretold through me... You have not obeyed the Lord, or executed the judgment of his fierce anger against the Amalekites; that is why he has done this to you today. (1 Samuel 28:16–18)

Having identified the divine wraths behind the protagonists' difficulties, the deceased prophets predict further suffering for them, and the specific circumstances of their deaths. Teiresias spells out the choices that await Odysseus, centered around the events on Thrinakia (*Od.* 11.104–13). He goes on to prophesy the difficulties the suitors will cause (*Od.* 11.114–18), but then shifts to two topics that extend beyond the *Odyssey*, the expiatory labor and sacrifice Odysseus must perform for Poseidon

(*Od.* 11.121–34), and a prophecy of Odysseus' own death, years later, in old age, his people comfortable around him (*Od.* 11.134–7).[12] Samuel, after declaring how Saul brought Yahweh's wrath on himself, prophesies his imminent death:

For the same reason the Lord will let your people Israel fall along with you into the hands of the Philistines. What is more, tomorrow you and your sons will be with me. (1 Sam. 28:19)

Saul is terrified by Samuel's prophecy (1 Sam. 28:20), falling to the ground in a faint. At the beginning and ending of his consultation, fear seizes Odysseus as hordes of shades gather around him (*Od.* 11.43, 633). Saul's necromancy is also marked by an attack of fear at its beginning and end. The witch shrieks from fear as she sees Samuel appear (1 Sam. 28:12).

Contrasts between the two episodes suggest that consultation scenes come in two types, positive and negative, as is often the case in myth.[13] Odysseus' encounter with Teiresias is a positive instance, while Saul's encounter with Samuel is negative. Odysseus and Saul exhibit thematically opposite relations with prophets in general, and in their consultation scenes. Odysseus has no friction with Teiresias, and, as de Jong argues (2001: 276), the deceased prophet shows pity for Odysseus. Though the prophecy Teiresias gives him entails suffering for the immediate future, it suggests that Odysseus can partially propitiate Poseidon. And though the god's potential reaction to the sacrifice is not mentioned, the fact that Odysseus will live to a comfortable old age implies some degree of reconciliation with the now wrathful god. Saul, on the other hand, has earlier been at odds with Samuel, and the two still bear considerable friction toward each other in the consultation. According to the prophet, Saul has no chance of propitiating Yahweh, and Samuel clearly has no pity for Saul as he informs him of this. Saul's death will be imminent, tomorrow. In all these particulars, Odysseus is successful in negotiating his consultation with the deceased prophet, Saul a failure. By the norms of these myths, Odysseus is a man who largely lives his life correctly, in accord with divine will, whereas Saul, like Agamemnon, puts personal wants ahead of divine dictates, bringing suffering upon himself and his army.

---

[12] Teiresias' prophecy that Odysseus' people will be prosperous when he dies in old age (*Od.* 11.135–7) finds a close parallel in Genesis in descriptions of the patriarchs' deaths, "Death in good old age and gathered to his people" (Gen. 25:8); "Death and gathered to his people old and full in years" (Gen. 35:29a); "Death and gathered to his people" (Gen. 49: 33b; translations by Carr [1996]). The three passages are all assigned to the later priestly account. See discussion in Carr (1996: 94, 126–7).

[13] E.g., theoxenies are positive or negative, as noted in Chapter 2; cf. archer myths, Louden (2006: 272–4).

THE VISION: ODYSSEY 11.152–327, GILGAMESH 12, AENEID 6, PLATO'S ALLEGORY OF THE CAVE, "SCIPIO'S DREAM," AND THE BOOK OF REVELATION

At the end of his consultation, Odysseus tells Teiresias that he sees (*Od.* 11.141: ὁρόω) his mother, Antikleia, and wants her to be able to perceive his presence. Having earlier seen (*Od.* 11.87: ἰδών) her shade, he did not let her approach the blood, until first having consulted Teiresias. Following his dialogue with his mother, Odysseus sees the parade of legendary women, each introduced by him saying, "and then I saw" (εἶδον). By contrast his later dialogues with comrades from the Trojan War, are introduced merely by his noting that so-and-so "came" to him (e.g., *Od.* 11.387: ἦλθε).[14] A visual dimension to Odysseus' experience of Hades is first highlighted in his meeting with his mother, developed more fully in the subsequent *Catalogue of Women*.

His meeting with Antikleia furthers an emphasis on the visual when Odysseus three times tries unsuccessfully to embrace her, insubstantial, a shadow or a dream (*Od.* 11.206–8). Whether or not the gesture is modeled on Akhilleus' equally vain attempt to embrace Patroklos' ghost (so Heubeck 1989: 89), the *Odyssey* uses the incident to reinforce how Hades is a *visual* experience for Odysseus. When Odysseus wonders if she is an *eidôlon* (*Od.* 11.213), a phantom sent by Persephone, Antikleia replies that the soul flies from the body like a dream, another primarily visual experience. The *Odyssey* uses this same word, *eidôlon*, cognate with the verb of vision noted above (εἴδω), of a character in a dream (*Od.* 4.796, 824, 835), Penelope's sister Iphthime. *Eidôlon* is used of Elpenor a line before Odysseus first sees his mother (*Od.* 11.83). When Theoklymenos later prophesies the destruction of the suitors, he says that he sees them as *eidôla, phantoms*, on their way to Erebos (*Od.* 20.355), cementing the word's connection with the dead and the visual. The last thing Antikleia says to Odysseus is that he should "learn/know all these things," that he sees in Hades, so he can tell his wife afterward (*Od.* 11.223–4). Antikleia's verb for "learn about/know" is the same root, εἴδω (ἴσθ'), cognate with Latin *video*.

By introducing an emphasis on the visual in Odysseus' dialogue with his mother, the *Odyssey* transitions into the specific genre of myth *the vision*, in which the protagonist, removed from the mortal plane, has an otherworldly guide, who *shows* him a truth, otherwise hidden from his view.

---

[14] Though Agamemnon, perhaps because he is the first of the series, is also given the same line as Antikleia and Elpenor, with ἰδών (*Od.* 11.395 = 87, 55).

"Removed from the mortal plane" means that the protagonist is either set in the underworld, as is Odysseus, or in a heavenly setting, as Scipio the Younger in Cicero's "Scipio's Dream," or John in the Book of Revelation. "An otherworldly guide" means a being belonging to a non-mortal plane of existence, as are both Teiresias and Antikleia, now shades, denizens of Hades. Scipio the Elder inhabits the Milky Way, and Christ and the unnamed angel are inhabitants of heaven in the Book of Revelation. There is often a dream-like quality to *the vision*, evident not only in the *Odyssey*'s common use of the same term, *eidôlon*, for a shade in the underworld (*Od.* 11.83, 213, 602) and a figure in a dream (*Od.* 4.796, 824, 835), but the epithet *amenenos*, describing the lack of physical efficacy of the dead (*Od.* 10.521, 536; 11.29, 49), also gives a dream quality (*Od.* 19.562). While all of Odysseus' visit to the underworld can be regarded as an instance of *the vision*, the *Odyssey* and the *Aeneid* share a more distinct structural variant: they each present a second vision within a vision.

THE VISION IN *GILGAMESH*

Tablet 12 of the Standard Babylonian Version of *Gilgamesh* contains a scene quite close to what we have defined as *the vision*. The relation between Tablet 12 and the rest of *Gilgamesh* is problematic.[15] The same basic narrative exists independently as a free-standing Sumerian work, "Bilgamesh and the Netherworld." Tablet 12's presentation of Enkidu narrating what he sees in the underworld to Gilgamesh also overlaps with Tablet 7, where Enkidu dreams of his death and *catabasis*, but lacunae prevent us from having a complete account of the episode. George notes that one surviving line from a heavily damaged section implies that Enkidu relates to Gilgamesh various persons that he saw in the underworld in his dream (2003, Vol. 1: 483),

An isolated phrase... "[I] saw his person" (221), clearly suggests that the missing passage included a report by Enkidu of individuals that he saw in the Netherworld, perhaps known to him such as famous figures of legend (as in the *Odyssey* XI and the *Aeneid* VI).

This suggests something along the lines of *the vision* in *Odyssey* 11, particularly in how Odysseus introduces each new heroine with the phrase "and then I saw" (εἴδον).

Tablet 12 offers much greater common ground with *Odyssey* 11. Though it is often asserted that it has no link with the narrative of the first eleven

---

[15] See George (2003: Vol.1: 47–54) for a recent summary of the key issues.

tablets,[16] Tablet 12 *does* have a specific, and potent, link with an earlier part of the epic. When Humbaba has been seriously wounded, he curses Enkidu in a specific way, in what will become a central theme of Tablet 12, "apart from his friend Gilgamesh, may Enkidu have nobody to bury him!" (*Gilg.* 5.257).[17] Tablet 12 opens with Gilgamesh lamenting that a toy he made has fallen into the underworld. Enkidu volunteers to bring it up to him. The text as we have it does not provide details about how they are conversing. Since this does not appear to be a dream, their dialogue could be regarded as a form of necromancy.[18] Gilgamesh gives Enkidu detailed instructions on how best to retrieve his toy without drawing attention to himself, which Enkidu promptly ignores, and is subsequently seized and held in the underworld (*Gilg.* 12.11–78). The god Ea, in a brief divine council (*Gilg.* 12.79–84), now asks Shamash, the sun god, to retrieve Enkidu, and he acts accordingly (*Gilg.* 12.87), "(Shamash) brought the shade of Enkidu up from the Netherworld like a phantom." Reunited with Gilgamesh, Enkidu now reports on what he saw in the underworld.[19]

Gilgamesh asks him questions about what the underworld is like, and more specifically, about individuals Enkidu saw there (*Gilg.* 12.90–153). For the numerous latter cases, Enkidu each time replies, "I saw him" (*Gilg.* 12.102, 104, 106, 108, 110, 113, 115, 117, 132, 134, 144, 146, 148, 150, 152). The arrangement and structure of the episode, visible in spite of the damaged text, seem close enough to what *Odyssey* 11, and, as discussed below, *Aeneid* 6, and the Book of Revelation present, that it can be regarded as an instance of *the vision*, with a few different functions by some of the characters. The resultant episode, in our terms, does not involve a *catabasis* by the protagonist, Gilgamesh, but an *anabasis* by Enkidu through the agency of Shamash. The sun god can be seen as like the otherworldly guide, in that his agency makes it possible for Gilgamesh to learn what Enkidu has seen. Gilgamesh performs a very active role in questioning Enkidu, something like Odysseus' strong interest in speaking with other individuals in Hades, once he has completed his dialogue with Teiresias, as Kirke had instructed.

---

[16] E.g., George (2003, Vol.1: 48): "These three factors, then – language, plot, and structure – clearly mark Tablet XII out as a separate text with no original connection to the eleven-tablet epic."

[17] All translations of *Gilgamesh* in this section are by George.

[18] Cf. George (2003, Vol.1: 483–4): "As a necromancy, the famous dialogue that terminates the Sumerian tale of Bilgames and the Netherworld and the prose Tablet XII, in which Gilgames asks Enkidu about the conditions encountered in the Netherworld by the shades of various classes of person, takes the form of question and answer."

[19] The *Iliad* offers a related scene when Akhilleus converses with Patroklos' ghost in a dream (*Il.* 23.65–108). As with the episode in *Gilgamesh*, the issue of unperformed burial rites is also key (*Il.* 23.71–4).

Gilgamesh's questions revolve particularly around the threat Humbaba raised when he cursed Enkidu: who will provide funerary offerings for Enkidu? Gilgamesh implicitly raises this as an issue in his question, repeated in seven variants, "Did you see the man with one /two/three/four/five/six/seven sons?" (*Gilg.* 12.102–15). Enkidu's responses underscore the increasingly better status of the man who has more sons, and therefore, the greater number of relatives who will see to his funerary rituals. Worst off is he who has neither a son, nor anyone else to perform such rituals (*Gilg.* 12.152–3). Enkidu's own circumstances, since he has no sons, are clearly alluded to, if indirectly. If I am correct in seeing these portions of Tablet 12 as prepared for by Humbaba's curse, it is worth noting that other aspects of the manuscript tradition of *Gilgamesh* suggest that Tablet 12 has been part of the epic for longer than is generally realized.[20]

Several particulars of this exchange also suggest common ground with Elpenor's circumstances in the *Odyssey*. After one of Tablet 12's lacunae, Gilgamesh asks and Enkidu responds as follows (*Gilg.* 12.144–5):

> "Did you see the one who was struck by a mooring-pole?" "I [saw (him).] Alas for his mother [and father!] When pegs are pulled out [he] wanders about."

A sailor who dies an accidental, non-heroic death, and consequently finds no rest in the underworld comes very close to the plight of Elpenor, the crew member who begs Odysseus to erect a burial mound for him, planting his oar on top (*Od.* 11.71–8). Subsequent comments, though less specifically suggestive of Elpenor, evoke circumstances similar to his (*Gilg.* 12.150–3):

> "Did you see the one whose corpse was left lying in the open countryside?"
> "His ghost does not lie at rest in the Netherworld."
> "Did you see the one whose ghost has no provider of funerary offerings?"
> "He eats the scrapings from the pot (and) crusts of bread that are thrown away in the street."

From the *Odyssey*'s perspective, Elpenor combines the various situations depicted here (*Gilg.* 12.144, 150–3). These passages not only suggest that *Gilgamesh* has something along the lines of *the vision*, if in a slightly altered form, but that it provides a context for how *the vision* functions in *Odyssey* 11.

---

[20] George (2003, Vol.1: 49): "two Late Babylonian manuscripts... speak for the inclusion of Tablet XII in the traditional text of the Series of Gilgames as handed down over the centuries in the Babylonian capital."

THE VISION IN *AENEID* 6

The elements of *the vision* are clearer in *Aeneid* 6, where Vergil employs a more developed instance of the form. Earlier, in Book 2, Vergil presents an abbreviated instance of *the vision* when Venus, briefly endowing Aeneas with a divine power of sight, shows him that it is really Neptune, Juno, and Minerva who are sacking Troy (*Aen.* 2.604–20). Repeatedly she tells him to look (*aspice*: *Aen.* 2.604, *vides*: 2.609, *respice*: 2.615). Here Venus is the otherworldly guide, revealing a larger reality unknown to the protagonist, which scene also has a Homeric precedent, *Iliad* 5.127, as R. D. Williams (1977: 255) notes. It lacks only the transfer of the protagonist off the mortal plane of existence, by *catabasis* to the underworld or *anabasis* to heaven. However, a connection with the underworld is suggested in the apocalyptic nature of the destruction, somewhat as the *Odyssey* juxtaposes the imminent destruction of the suitors with Theoklymenos' vision of them as already in Hades (*Od.* 20.350–7).

Vergil's more developed version of *the vision*, in Book 6 of the *Aeneid*, builds directly on the instance in *Odyssey* 11. Aeneas consults first with a prophet, the Sibyl, who enables him to see the underworld, and to meet with a deceased parent, as Teiresias enables Odysseus to meet with Antikleia. Vergil employs the traditional *catabasis*, as Aeneas, having obtained the Golden Bough, physically descends to the underworld (*Aen.* 6.262 ff.), guided by the Sibyl. While all of Aeneas' visit to the underworld is an instance of *the vision*, it is his meeting with Anchises, *the vision* within *the vision*, which most closely replicates the particulars of Odysseus' meeting with Antikleia. The Sibyl escorts him on his descent explicitly for this purpose (*Aen* 6.403–4), and, as in *Odyssey* 11, it is when Aeneas approaches the shade of his parent that the episode repeatedly stresses a visual element. As he enters the Groves of the Blessed (*Aen.* 6.651: *miratur*; 6.656: *conspicit*), and especially when he catches sight of Anchises, the *Aeneid* repeatedly draws attention to his *seeing* his father, and the *visions* to which Anchises directs him (*Aen.* 6.695: *imago*, 6.703: *videt Aeneas*, 6.710: *visu*, 6.716: *ostendere*, 6.760: *vides*, 6.779: *viden*, 6.788: *aspice*, 6.818: *videre*, 6.825: *aspice*, 6.826: *cernis*, 6.855: *aspice*, 6.860: *videbat*).

The vision through which Anchises guides Aeneas is the climactic instance of many such prophecies,[21] the zenith of the first half of the *Aeneid*. After an introductory section explaining reincarnation (*Aen.* 6.724–51), Anchises proceeds to show Aeneas, as in a parade before him, his

---

[21] Cf. R. D. Williams (1977: 505): "752 f. The pageant of Roman heroes is the most sustained of all the patriotic passages in the *Aeneid*."

future descendants (*Aen*. 6.756–853), culminating in a definition of who the Romans will be (*Aen*. 6.847–53). Before seeing *the vision*, Aeneas is not mentally or emotionally prepared for going on with his task. But once he has witnessed the future greatness of Rome, his earlier anxieties about his larger mission are assuaged, removing the last obstacles as he approaches the future site of Rome.

Since *Odyssey* 11 is Vergil's central structural model, some components of which he has expanded and put to different purposes, Book 6 of the *Aeneid* helps clarify elements also present, if less obvious, in Odysseus' vision. Vergil employs his instance of *the vision* to remove the final obstacles that prevent Aeneas from carrying out his mission, reaching the site of Rome, bringing the other Trojans with him. Though lacking the monumental scale of *Aeneid* 6, the *Odyssey*'s Book 11 serves a similar function: it provides the means for Odysseus to return to Ithaka, the thematic parallel with Aeneas' reaching Rome.

Like Aeneas, Odysseus has two figures who serve as his guide, Teiresias and Antikleia, precursors of Vergil's Sibyl and Anchises, respectively. Like the Sibyl, Teiresias is not only a prophet, who gives Odysseus a prophecy that marks the end of his wanderings, he also has a larger knowledge of the workings of the underworld. It is Teiresias who instructs Odysseus how to meet with Antikleia and the other souls (*Od*. 11.139–51), a smaller version of the more detailed guidance Sibyl gives Aeneas about how to navigate the different regions of Hades, how to negotiate with various entities they encounter. Most important for the present-time episodes of the *Odyssey*, Teiresias gives Odysseus the information that will allow him to survive the ordeal at Thrinakia, the final event in the wanderings depicted in Books 9–12. In this respect Teiresias informs Odysseus of a larger reality, a version of "the big picture," which *the vision* typically conveys to the protagonist. Because of Teiresias' prophecy Odysseus will be the only member of his crew to remain alive after setting foot on Thrinakia.

Antikleia also gives Odysseus a "big picture," though quite different than that Teiresias presents. Where the Theban prophet deals with the heroic side of Odysseus, Antikleia imparts information of a more personal, familial nature, Odysseus as son, father, and, especially, husband. In a most personal exchange she informs him of Penelope's fidelity and sorrow, of Laertes' sad existence, mourning his absent son, and of her own death, prompted by grief for her son. But it is after Odysseus tries in vain to embrace her that Antikleia functions as the second guide in *the vision*, corresponding to, if smaller in scope, Anchises in *Aeneid* 6.

When Odysseus, unable to embrace her, asks if she is merely an *eidôlon*, sent by Persephone (*Od.* 11.210–14), she replies with an account of the nature of the soul after death (*Od.* 11.216–22), the brief germ, I suggest, of Anchises' considerably lengthier account of the nature of the soul and reincarnation (*Aen.* 6.724–51). She concludes with the admonition that he should learn/understand/remember (ἴσθ') all these things so that afterwards he can tell them to his wife (*Od.* 11.223–4). Her admonition points ahead to Odysseus' recitation of his wanderings to Penelope, as Heubeck (1989) notes.[22] But more important for our purposes, her sudden final focus on Penelope also serves as the narrative trigger for the *Catalogue of Women*.[23] In so doing, Antikleia becomes Odysseus' second otherworldly guide. As Anchises in *Aeneid* 6, the deceased parent of the hero directs him to witness a vision within a vision (with the prophets, Teiresias, Sibyl, serving as guides for the outer vision). As soon as Antikleia concludes, the women begin to gather. Odysseus directs their access to the blood, as Teiresias instructed.

When he has finished recounting the women he saw, Odysseus unexpectedly stops his lengthy recital (*Od.* 11.328–32), a unique moment in the *Odyssey*.[24] His audience, apparently startled by his surprising break, remains silent, the same reaction as when Odysseus first entered the palace, and supplicated Arete, the same formulaic line used both times, "but then they all stayed quiet, in silence" (*Od.* 7.154=11.333). Why does Odysseus halt his narration immediately after relating the *Catalogue of Women, the vision within a vision*? Or to put the question a bit differently, what effect does his narration of the *Catalogue of Women*, his vision, have on his Phaiakian audience?

Odysseus' main objective since reaching Scheria has been to secure passage from there to Ithaka. Twice, Arete has been singled out as the key to his return (*Od.* 6.313–15 = 7.75–7); for unstated reasons, she alone will make the decision to grant him conveyance to Ithaka. When Odysseus first broached the subject, firmly supplicating the queen in *Od.* 7.142–52, she made no answer, remaining silent with the rest of the Phaiakians (*Od.* 7.153–4). But now, when Odysseus has finished narrating *the vision* of the legendary women, Arete breaks the silence, as she might have been expected to after his supplication in Book 7. She praises Odysseus for his beauty and balanced thoughts, declaring that he is her guest (*Od.* 11.335–41). In proclaiming him her guest (*xeinos*), she must mean that his earlier

---

[22] Heubeck (1989: 90): "The line [11.224] prepares for xxiii 310–41, esp. 325."
[23] Cf. Heubeck (1989: 91): "The encounter with Anticleia prepares for the catalogue."
[24] Though de Jong (2001: 283) sees a parallel at 4.240–3, both as her *recusatio* motif.

supplication will now be granted, as her asking the other Phaiakians to bestow gifts suggests.

Why does she make her decision at this particular point? Why, as we asked above (but have not yet answered), does Odysseus halt his narration at the end of the vision of the legendary women? A consensus seems to be emerging (Stanford 1961: 64; de Jong 2001: 284) that the pause is intentional strategy on Odysseus' part. In breaking off where he does, he confers additional emphasis on his last topic, the vision of the women. Odysseus' narration of the *Catalogue of Women* and the preceding encounter with his mother both depict him as sensitive to women's needs.[25] A devoted son, he is moved to do the impossible, to try to embrace the ghost of his deceased mother. He dutifully carries out her advice, which pertains not only to the parade of women, listening carefully as each tells her story, but ultimately centers on his carrying out her admonition that he tell Penelope all he sees in the underworld. In all these particulars, his determined focus on his wife (Arete herself has earlier witnessed that the offer of her own daughter in marriage does not sway him), Odysseus presents a version of himself that seems carefully calculated to impress Arete.

Odysseus' objective in relating *the vision* is to win over Arete, his most important audience. Antikleia, his guide for *the vision*, thus gives him the wherewithal to win over Arete, securing the penultimate stage in his homecoming, the sea crossing from Scheria to Ithaka. Since the components of *the vision* are probably traditional, the *Odyssey* may thus already modify its more expected tendencies by placing it within Odysseus' *narration* of the event (as opposed to *Aeneid* 6), and by further having *the vision* shaped by its being directed to a specific internal audience, Arete, queen of the Phaiakians. *Aeneid* 6, on quite the other hand, directs its vision to the epic's external audience.

EXCURSUS: PLATO'S *ALLEGORY OF THE CAVE* AND *THE VISION*

Nightingale, noting that no earlier philosophic texts anticipate Plato's *Allegory* (2004: 32–3), associates it, and its notion of the contemplative philosopher, with the institution of the *theoria*, in which an individual serves as a spectator at a religious ceremony:

> In the traditional practice of *theoria*, an individual (called the *theoros*) made a journey or pilgrimage abroad for the purpose of witnessing certain events and spectacles.

---

[25] Cf. Louden (1999: 11–12).

Her study establishes the relevance of *theoria* to the *Allegory of the Cave*, and, by placing it in such a context, helps account for its form in new ways. But there is an earlier narrative that anticipates much of the *Allegory*, *the vision* in Book 11 of the *Odyssey*.

Plato's *Allegory* employs components of *the vision* we have observed in *Odyssey* 11 (and *Aeneid* 6). The *Republic* makes sustained engagement with *Odyssey* 11 outside of the *Allegory*, stressing Akhilleus' declaration to Odysseus that he would rather be alive, even as slave to a poor man, than be honored in Hades (*Rep.* 386c). Book 3 continues a dialogue with the *Odyssey*'s underworld episodes, noting how Teiresias uniquely retains the power of reason in Hades, and the suitors' descent in Book 24 (*Rep.* 386d and 387a, respectively) among other references to Hades. Much of Book 10 of the *Republic* uses Book 11 of the *Odyssey* as a backdrop or frame.[26] Plato also alludes to elements of Odysseus' homecoming (discussed below). Deliberation on the connections increases our understanding of how *the vision* works in *Odyssey* 11, and lays the groundwork for matters we will consider in Chapter 12.

In several ways Plato sets his *Allegory* against the background of a traditional *catabasis* to Hades. The cave itself is repeatedly associated with the underworld, its setting explicitly underground (κατάγειος: *Rep.* 514a3). Each time Socrates describes returning to it, he uses forms of the verb *katabaino* (*Rep.* 516e3: *katabas*, 519d5: *katabainein*, 520c1: *katabateon*), all related to the noun *catabasis*, used of a descent to the underworld.[27] Among these generic underworld associations, one passage points specifically to Book 11 of the *Odyssey*. When Socrates discusses how someone who has left the cave will be reluctant to return to existence inside it, he again quotes Akhilleus' declaration to Odysseus about preferring a menial existence on the earth's surface rather than honor in the underworld (*Rep.* 516d5–6; *Od.* 11.489–90).[28]

Socrates begins the *Allegory* declaring its purpose is to illustrate to what degree our nature is educated or uneducated (*Rep.* 514a1–2). Throughout the *Allegory*, seeing is associated with understanding and education; not seeing is equated with ignorance, lack of education. Plato's chief conceptual model is *the vision* in *Odyssey* 11. We have seen that the *Allegory* has links with the larger framework in which the *Odyssey* sets its vision, a mythic *catabasis*, as Nightingale also notes (2004: 102). Plato points specifically to

---

[26] Cf. Bloom (1968: 427): "The text for *Republic*, Book X, is *Odyssey*, Book XI, the account of Odysseus' visit to the dead."
[27] Cf. Nightingale (2004: 102) on the passage in 516e.
[28] Cf. *Od.* 11.484: ἐτίομεν; *Republic* 516d2: τιμωμένους.

Odyssey 11 when Socrates quotes from Akhilleus' underworld dialogue with Odysseus. Akhilleus' lines are relevant to the *Allegory* in additional ways we have not yet considered, suggesting Plato has in mind a broader thematic engagement.

In response to Odysseus, Akhilleus asserts that he would rather maintain a menial existence on the earth's surface than be greatly honored in the underworld (*Rep.* 516d5–6; *Od.* 11.489–90). He rejects as without substance the honors awarded him in the underworld. The inhabitants in the shadowy cave compete for, and are awarded, honors the protagonist finds completely without substance once he becomes aware of existence outside the cave. Akhilleus' declaration, that what is important in the underworld does not compensate for even meager existence in the world above, thus anticipates the reaction of Plato's protagonist in the *Allegory*.[29] His rejection of what *seems* important in the underworld and his stark contrast between life in the world above with existence in the underworld predict two of the central thrusts of Plato's *Allegory*.

But *Odyssey* 11 also provides an antecedent for the "sacred spectating" which constitutes the pivotal act or event in the *Allegory*. *The vision* serves a similar, if less dramatic, function in Odysseus' *catabasis*. In Plato and in the *Odyssey* what the protagonist sees in *the vision* has a direct bearing on how he returns to his previous plane of existence. As we argued above, it is Odysseus' narration of the *Catalogue of Women* that moves Arete to secure his return to Ithaka (*Od.* 11.223–341). Odysseus himself does not undergo a dramatic change vis-à-vis his views on life and death as a result of seeing *the vision*, as does Plato's protagonist. Instead, *Odyssey* 11 articulates such a transformation through another character, Akhilleus. Odysseus' witnessing *the vision* results in a dramatic change of his circumstances. His having seen it becomes the means by which he persuades Arete. He may now accomplish what has otherwise been unattainable for ten years – his homecoming.

However, Plato makes several radical innovations, altering or rearranging the elements found in *Odyssey* 11. In some respects he turns *the vision* inside out, using techniques similar to those employed in satire. Plato reverses the usual planes of existence that *the vision* juxtaposes. The *Odyssey* and the *Aeneid* depict their protagonists leaving the mortal plane, undergoing a *catabasis* to reach the underworld in order to witness their visions. Cicero's "Scipio's Dream" and the Book of Revelation conversely depict their protagonists undergoing an *anabasis* from the mortal plane to a heavenly

---

[29] Cf. More, *Utopia* (II.184.25–7) "*Aliud servorum genus est: quum alterius populi mediastinus quispiam laboriosus ac pauper elegerit apud eos sua sponte servire*," in Surtz (1965).

setting to witness their visions. Plato's *Allegory opens* in an underworld setting, establishing it as the "normal" mode of human existence.[30] This is an example of displacement, often used in satire, whereby a common element of a narrative is distorted, magnified, shrunk, or moved to another setting, creating a different kind of relationship between the element and its new context, Swift's basic technique throughout *Gulliver's Travels*. As a consequence of his displacement, the protagonist must undergo an *anabasis* (*Rep.* 515e7, cf. 517b4, 519d1), an ascent, just to reach the earth's surface. What his protagonist now sees in *the vision*, the world outside the cave, is the usual mortal plane of existence, the earth, its flora and fauna, the sky, and heavenly bodies, including the sun. But since it is reached by means of an *anabasis*, which, in the related verb, is already used in Homer of an ascent to the gods' heavenly abode on Olympos (ἀνέβη: *Il.* 1.497, of Thetis' ascent), Plato conflates the normal mortal plane with a heavenly existence.

In a further innovation, Plato has his *narrator*, Socrates, through his act of narrating, serve as the protagonist's otherworldly guide for *the vision*. It is Socrates who gives the visual imperatives, "look" (ἰδέ: *Rep.* 514a2, ὅρα: 514b8, σκόπει: 515c3), as Antikleia does for Odysseus (ἴσθ': *Od.* 11.224), Anchises for Aeneas (*Aen.* 6.760: *vides*, 6.779: *viden*, 6.788: *aspice*, 6.818: *videre*, 6.825: *aspice*, 6.826: *cernis*, 6.855: *aspice*), Scipio the Elder for the Younger, and Christ and the unnamed angel for John in Revelation (discussed below). But in his narrator Plato combines what are two such guides in the *Odyssey*, Teiresias and Antikleia (Sibyl and Anchises in the *Aeneid*). Throughout the Platonic corpus, Socrates has thematic ties to the figure of the prophet. The theory of ideas is predicated upon having Socrates serve literally and figuratively as a *seer*,[31] who reports back to his audience what he has witnessed. In his relationship to Plato, Socrates also exhibits, to some degree, a paternal dimension, thus suggesting the parental or paternal aspect of the second otherworldly guide, as in the *Odyssey*'s Antikleia (cf. the *Aeneid*'s Anchises).

Plato further innovates in the identity of his protagonist. From the standpoint of *Odyssey* 11, Plato's protagonist combines in one character the perspectives of two separate characters, Odysseus and Akhilleus. Like Odysseus, Plato's protagonist witnesses *the vision*, but like Akhilleus he comments on the stark disparity between the two different planes of existence, life within the cave and life in the world outside. Plato inserts a further difference in his protagonist's relationship to his culture. Odysseus

---

[30] Cf. Nightingale (2004: 102), on the *Allegory* as essentially starting out in the underworld (516e).
[31] Defined in the *OED* as "One to whom divine revelations are made in visions."

and Akhilleus are famous heroes, but Plato's protagonist is anonymous (a further thematic link to the *Odyssey*, as discussed below). Plato's protagonist (and Cicero's) wants *to remain* on the other plane of existence where he witnesses *the vision*, whereas both Odysseus and Aeneas are intent on returning to their cultures. We can characterize the opposite reactions of Odysseus and Aeneas, on the one hand, and Plato's protagonist and Scipio the Younger, on the other, as centripetal vs. centrifugal.[32]

Plato's *Allegory* intersects other episodes in the *Odyssey*, not just Book 11, as Nightingale's study helps bring into focus. Nightingale describes a specific subtype of *theoria* which requires the *theoros* to journey to a foreign land to acquire sacred knowledge that he will then bring back to his own city (2004: 63), "A third kind of *theoria* takes the form of a journey to foreign lands in order to see the world. Here, the *theoros* travels abroad in pursuit of knowledge."[33] This subtype in which the protagonist travels to foreign lands to witness *the vision* offers considerable common ground with the *Odyssey*. Nightingale also notes two historians who traveled in search of wisdom, but where she relates them to *theoria*, I relate again to the *Odyssey* (2004: 67):

The proto-historian Hecataeus claimed to be "a man of much wandering" (*aner poluplanes*), and numerous historians wrote on topics that must have involved traveling. Among these wandering thinkers, I find especially interesting the claim of Democritus: "I covered more of the earth as a wanderer... than any of the men of my time, making the most extensive investigations... and I saw more regions and lands and listened to more men of learning."

Both passages not only suggest the *Odyssey* in general, but use phrases close to its proem (Ἄνδρα... ὃς μάλα πολλὰ / πλάγχθη: 1–2, πολλῶν δ' ἀνθρώπων ἴδεν ἄστεα καὶ νόον ἔγνω: 3). Taken together, the passages imply that thinkers of the period, proto-historians or philosophers, framed their own quests for knowledge in terms close to the *Odyssey*'s themes.

Much of the common ground Nightingale sees between Plato's *Allegory* and *theoria* also has a distinct Odyssean ring to it (2004: 36):

Building on the model of traditional *theoria*, Plato constructs a philosophic *theoros* who detaches himself from the social world and "journeys" to see the divine Forms. He is altered and transformed by this contemplative activity, and returns to the city as a stranger to his own kind.

---

[32] Cf. W. B. Stanford (1961: 50) on the stark differences between the Homeric Odysseus and that of later writers, particularly Dante. The movement of the *Odyssey* is essentially inwards, homewards, towards normality. As conceived later by poets like Dante, Tennyson, and Pascoli, Ulysses' urge is centrifugal, outwards towards the exotic or abnormal.
[33] Cf. Nightingale (2004: 36, 42, 67).

In all types of *theoria* Nightingale notes the difficulties the *theoros* experiences on returning to his city. Witnessing the vision has transformed him, alienating him from his own city, making him a virtual stranger (2004: 5), "He thus 'returns' as a sort of stranger to his own kind, bringing a radical alterity into the city."[34] Odysseus' main objective throughout the *Odyssey* is to return to Ithaka, disguised as a foreigner, or stranger (*xeinos*) for most of Books 14–24. The more Nightingale says about the transformation the *theoros*/philosopher undergoes, the closer he resembles Odysseus in Ithaka (2004: 20), "The contemplative philosopher, according to this account, lives as a '*xenikos*' – a (virtual) foreigner who is a sort of stranger in the polis."

Plato pointedly maximizes the protagonist's change, depicting him as alienated from his own society to such a degree that his alterity makes him the target of violence, as Nightingale sums up (2004: 79):

If the philosopher returns to a bad city and communicates his visions to the people there, Socrates says, they will mock and revile him and perhaps even put him to death: the return and reentry of the philosophic *theoros* from the foreign realm of the Forms is a potentially dangerous operation.

Elaborating, Nightingale offers a description close to the *Odyssey*'s depiction of how the suitors treat the disguised Odysseus (2004: 131):

According to Socrates, when the philosophic *theoros* reenters the social and political realm after a period of contemplation, he runs the risk of mockery and even violence at the hands of his fellow citizens (517a). If he returns to a bad city, he will be scorned and maligned, and his fellow citizens will see him as foolish and possibly even dangerous.

Is this not very like Odysseus' situation in Books 17–22 of the *Odyssey* as he, seemingly a *xeinos*, a stranger, is the target of the suitors' abuse and violence?

When Socrates describes the cave dwellers attempting to slay his protagonist on his return, his description suggests not only Odysseus, threatened by the suitors, but matters at the core of New Testament myth. Socrates says that if they could, they would kill "the one who is trying both to free them and lead them up" (*Rep.* 517a5: *ton epikheirounta luein te kai anagein*). Socrates' formulation resembles Odysseus among the suitors, but also unexpectedly suggests Christ in his ability to transcend death and in

---

[34] Cf. Nightingale (2004: 117): "In philosophic *theoria*, this change is quite extreme: the theoretical philosopher becomes a sort of stranger to his own kind."

the hostility that he provokes (analyzed in Chapter 12, *The king returns, unrecognized and abused in his kingdom*).

One exchange in Book 18 between the suitors and the unrecognized Odysseus is particularly relevant to Plato's larger agenda, if we are correct that he references Book 11 of the *Odyssey* and Odysseus' reception by the suitors. Having won the right to beg in the palace by defeating Iros (*Od.* 18.1–116), the disguised Odysseus, shooing away the women servants, asserts *he* will now maintain the fire in the palace, "for I will provide light for all of these" (αὐτὰρ ἐγὼ τούτοισι φάος πάντεσσι παρέξω: *Od.* 18.317). Thereafter he stands near the flaming tripods, gleaming, as he gazes at the suitors (αὐτὰρ ὁ πὰρ λαμπτῆρσι φαείνων αἰθομένοισιν / ἑστήκειν ἐς πάντας ὁρώμενος: *Od.* 18.343–4). Eurymachos, however, noting the gods surely must attend Odysseus, contends that his apparent divine aura emanates from his bald head.

The *Odyssey* uses Odysseus' alterity at several different levels. The audience knows Odysseus actually is accompanied by the gods,[35] attended by an aura which shines its brightest in the following episode (*Od.* 19.34–40).[36] Given the importance of light in Plato's *Allegory*, its association with the world outside the cave that only the protagonist has seen, and the protagonist's ability to lead others to the light, this exchange is quite relevant to Plato's dynamic. Eurymachos' attempt at irony is exposed as an *ad hominem* attack, verbal abuse suggestive of the reception of Plato's protagonist on his return to the cave. The passage's likely connection with Plato is strengthened by Eurymachos' further remarks to Odysseus. Pretending to offer the disguised hero opportunity for work, he concludes, predictably, with another personal attack. The verb he uses for "work," however, is the same verb Akhilleus uses in the passage Socrates quotes in the *Allegory* (*Rep.* 516d5–6). In all of Homer the verb only occurs in the infinitive (θητευέμεν) in these two passages (*Od.* 11.489, 18.357).

THE VISION IN "SCIPIO'S DREAM"

In perhaps the most potent surviving fragment of Cicero's *De Republica*, Publius Cornelius Scipio Africanus the Younger, an as yet undistinguished military man, is in Africa, outside of Carthage, visiting with King Masinissa. His grandfather, a key Roman general in the Punic Wars, had restored hereditary lands to King Masinissa. That night, he dreams of his

---

[35] Cf. de Jong (2001: 455).
[36] See Russo (1992: 70). Cf. Whitman (1958: 121–2) on how the passage at *Od.* 19.34–40, the climactic description of Odysseus' divine glow, presages his victory over the suitors.

grandfather, Cicero's version of *the vision*. We earlier noted that *the vision* often has a dream-like quality. In his dream he is in the heavens, gazing down on earth, his grandfather serving as the otherworldly guide who repeatedly directs his gaze at the Milky Way, whose wonders constitute this vision (*De Rep. videsne*: 6.11; *aspicis, vidi*: 6.14; *vides*: 6.15; *videbantur*: 6.16; *intuerer, aspicis*: 6.16; *intuerer stupens, admirans*: 6.18; *vides*: 6.19; *cernis, cerne, vides, cernis*: 6.20). As in the *Odyssey* and the *Aeneid*, the protagonist meets with his parent, but here the far greater role as otherworldly guide is given to his grandparent, Africanus.

Compared to Plato's *Allegory*, this is a straightforward *anabasis*, in which the earth's surface remains the usual habitat of mortals, and the protagonist, in a dream, ascends to the heavens to witness *the vision*. But the reversal of values the protagonist undergoes is reminiscent of Plato's complicated displacements and alterations. Scipio Africanus reveals to his grandson that what he thinks is important on earth is trivial from the cosmic vantage point their heavenly position affords. Fame, even eternal fame on earth, is inconsequential from the perspective of eternity and infinity (*De Rep.* 6.19). Like Plato's *Allegory* he demonstrates that what Scipio the Younger thinks of as life is really death, his soul imprisoned in his body, whereas death, when his soul will have infinite freedom, is really life (*De Rep.* 6.14–15). Scipio the Elder explains the entire cycle of life, that our souls are made of the same stuff as the stars, that one gigantic soul governs the universe as individual souls govern our bodies, that upon death, our individual souls rejoin with the great soul of the universe (*De Rep.* 6.24–6). In short, Africanus gives perhaps the most concise version of "the big picture" that anyone ever has, to my knowledge, literally explaining the meaning of life in a way that satisfies his audience on a number of levels. In a further link with Plato's *Allegory*, Scipio the Younger, on learning these new values, would prefer to remain in heaven rather than return to his usual existence on earth (*De Rep.* 6.15), until Africanus reminds him of the traditional Stoic virtue of duty.

THE VISION IN THE BOOK OF REVELATION

After a brief address to the Churches in Asia (Chapters 1–3), virtually all of the Book of Revelation is an extended instance of *the vision* (Chapters 4–22).[37] In its use of *the vision* (I distinguish between *the vision* and

---

[37] Though it also builds on the traditional motif in OT myth of the prophet appearing in a divine council, as at Jer. 23:18 and Amos 3:7. For further instances, see Mullen (1980: 209–25).

apocalypse in Chapter 13), the Book of Revelation could hardly conform more closely to the traditional motifs we have observed in the *Odyssey*, Plato's *Allegory*, "Scipio's Dream," and the *Aeneid*. Even particulars of the introductory frame employ details already noted. The protagonist declares at the beginning that he is narrating all that he saw (ὅσα εἶδεν: Rev. 1:2), quite close to Antikleia's admonition to Odysseus at the start of his vision to remember all that he sees (πάντα / ἴσθ': *Od.* 11.223–4).

The closest OT model for Revelation's use of *the vision* is Zechariah. His vision begins at night (Zech. 1:8), supporting our observation of the close ties between *the vision* and a dream, explicit in "Scipio's Dream." His otherworldly guide is an unnamed angel who repeatedly answers Zechariah's questions about what he sees (Zech. 1:9–10, 18–19, 20–1; 2:2; 4:4–14; etc.). Zechariah's vision uses many of the images that will become central to Revelation: riders on different colored horses, an object with numerous eyes, a lamp stand, a scroll, and so forth.

The protagonist of Revelation refers to himself as a servant (δοῦλος) who has had a vision (Rev. 1:1). Like "Scipio's Dream," the narrative, once *the vision* is underway, is a straightforward *anabasis*, in which the protagonist, summoned by an otherworldly guide, ascends to the heavenly realm (Rev. 4:1):

After this I had a vision: a door stood open in heaven, and the voice that I had first heard speaking to me like a trumpet, said, "Come up here (Ἀνάβα ὧδε), and I will show you (δείξω σοι) what must take place hereafter."

The figure who summons him, serving as the otherworldly guide, is Christ, as is evident from the earlier description at Revelation 1:12–13, 17.[38] Christ twice repeats the formulaic admonition we first associated with Antikleia (*Od.* 11.223–4), though Revelation now casts it in a more literate form, telling the protagonist to *write down* what he has seen,[39] so that he may tell others (Rev. 1:11, 1:19). Jesus' direction for the ascent, "Come up here," uses the very verb from which our term for ascent, *anabasis*, derives (cf., *Rep.* 515e7, 517b4, 519d1). The phrase that the *Oxford Study Bible* translates above as "I had a vision" is simply εἶδον, "I saw," repeated through Revelation when the protagonist sees a new sight. In its full form the phrase καὶ εἶδον, "and then I saw," occurs an additional thirty-one times,

---

[38] Cf. Ford (1975: 385): "That the celestial personage is the resurrected Christ is clear from the words which he speaks to the prostrate seer."
[39] On early Christianity's emphasis on the *written* word, and its close association with the new form the *codex*, see Stroumsa (2003).

emphatically reiterating the visual nature of Revelation.[40] This closely mirrors the *Odyssey*'s use of virtually the same form of the same verb ἴδον, as Odysseus notes each of the women he sees in his vision (*Od.* 11.235, 260, 266, 271, 281, 298, 306, 321, 326; 11.281 and 298 actually use the same form as in Revelation, εἶδον). Ford refers to the protagonist, the witness of the vision who introduces himself as John, as "the seer" (1975: 76, 119, 143, 149, 161, 165, 385), further underscoring the visual nature of his experience.

The reversal of values which the protagonist experiences is strongest in Plato's protagonist, who experiences a complete transformation, whereas for Odysseus the transformation is more external, than internal, transformed more in appearance than in nature. In an extension and transformation of tradition typical of Christianity, Revelation intends its *audience* to undergo the transformation, "Happy is the man who takes to heart the words of prophecy contained in this book," used in ring composition around the entire book (Rev. 1:3 = 22:7).

Book 11 of the *Odyssey* underscores the climactic nature of *the vision* by placing the *Intermezzo* (*Od.* 11.330–84) immediately after it. When that unique segment, with Arete's crucial declaration (*Od.* 11.336–41), concludes, Odysseus resumes a narration of what he experienced in Hades, his dialogues with Agamemnon (*Od.* 11.383–466), Akhilleus (*Od.* 11.467–540), and attempted dialogue with Aias (11.543–67). He concludes with a resumption of the "and then I saw" formula (ἴδον/εἶδον: *Od.* 11.568, 576, 582, 593) to describe seeing Minos, Tityos, Tantalos, and Sisyphos (Orion, *Od.* 11.572–5 is introduced instead by *eisenoêsa*). His dialogue with Herakles (11.601–27) caps the entire *catabasis*, the *Odyssey*'s way of implicitly acknowledging the greatness of the hero most closely associated with the triumph over death.

There is cause for regarding the post-*Intermezzo* half of Book 11 as a distinct genre of myth, *The hero speaks with the shades of other heroes*. Bacchylides uses a similar form to depict Meleager, having descended to Hades, in dialogue with Herakles (5.56–169). Other myths, such as Herakles' rescue of Theseus when he is imprisoned in Hades (Gantz 1993: 292–5), may also presume such a form, though I am unaware of parallels in Near Eastern myth.[41]

The *Odyssey* suggests additional, indirect evidence for this subgenre in Odysseus' earlier dialogue with Elpenor (*Od.* 11.51–83). We noted above

---

[40] Book of Revelation 5:1, 6, 11; 6:1, 2, 9 (7:1, 9); 8:2, 13; 9:1, 17; 10:1; 13:1, 11; 14:1, 6, 14; 15:1, 2, 5; 16:13; 17:3; 19:11, 17, 19; 20:1, 4, 11; 21:1, 22. Cf. also the passive, ὤφθη: 12:1, 3.

[41] I classify as quite different types of myth the descents of Ishtar and Nergal, because they are gods not heroes.

common ground between Elpenor's circumstances and Gilgamesh's dialogue with Enkidu (*Gilg.* 12.90–153), particularly the issue of unperformed burial rituals. Enkidu, however, plays a key role in Gilgamesh's greatest exploits, the defeat of Humbaba, and the slaying of the Bull of Heaven. He is a fully heroic figure. Not so Elpenor, who has more in common with Enkidu's example of the man who had been struck by a mooring pole (*Gilg.* 12.144–5). In some respects Odysseus' dialogue with Elpenor is rather like a parody of *The hero speaks with the shades of other heroes*. Though Elpenor, who has fallen to his death, drunk, off Kirke's roof, requests a full hero's burial, as Heubeck well notes (1989: 81) "his birth, station in life, achievements, as well as the manner of his death, are profoundly unheroic." Odysseus nonetheless agrees to his request, dutifully executing it on his return to Aiaia (*Od.* 12.9–15). Though Elpenor serves key structural functions in the *Odyssey* (Louden 1999: 31–49), he embodies much that the poem thematically inveighs against – excessive consumption, ignorance of his own identity (Heubeck 1989: 81). In these ways, and more, he is a decided antitype to Herakles or Akhilleus, natural and expected participants in dialogues with a hero in his *catabasis* in the underworld.

CHAPTER 10

Thrinakia and Exodus 32: Odysseus and Moses
The people disobey their leader and rebel against god

The crew's rebellion on Thrinakia is the final episode and climax of Odysseus' wanderings as he narrates them to the Phaiakians. The only incident mentioned in the proem,[1] a sign of its climactic nature and function, at its conclusion Odysseus is the only surviving member of his once large crew. To depict these key events the *Odyssey* employs a genre of myth also extant in the Old Testament, the Israelites' rebellion against Moses and Yahweh in Exodus 32. We can initially characterize the two myths' common ground as follows. *While in the middle of an arduous journey that takes years, the followers of a leader, who has a personal relationship with god, chafe at being delayed for a month in the same place, unable to continue the journey toward their long sought goal. In his absence, while he communicates with god, they violate a god's commandment, and perform a perverse religious ritual, offending the god. They die as a result of the subsequent divine wrath, but a divine council mediates the wrathful god's anger preventing him from causing even greater destruction. The leader, who had no part in the disobedience, is spared.* Specific parallels exist between Odysseus and Moses as leaders, between the crew and those Israelites who rebel, between Eurylochos and Aaron as leaders of the rebellion and inappropriate rituals, between Helios[2] and Yahweh in their divine wraths against the rebels, and between Zeus and Moses (!) in their successful mediations in divine councils with the wrathful Helios and Yahweh.

There are key distinctions in *context* and *modality*. Though both are on lengthy journeys home, the Israelites travel to a new homeland, whereas Odysseus' crew tries to return to their former homeland, Ithaka. As protagonist, Odysseus is a warrior and hero, Moses a prophet. The *Odyssey* throughout employs the mythic type as part of a heroic, epic modality,

---

[1] See Louden (1999: 69–70, 89–94) for discussion on why the proem singles out Thrinakia.
[2] On the Sun in Indo-European myth and Helios' Indo-European background, see West (2007: 194–209).

whereas Exodus, less concerned with heroic success and failure, employs the episode for its favorite emphasis, a polemic supporting Yahwist religion. The mythic genre occupies a pivotal position, foundational for Israelite religion and cultural identity. The *Odyssey* employs the myth for more modest purpose, more specific to Odysseus the character, than to Greek culture as a whole. But, as Heubeck notes, the episode at Thrinakia has an overtly religious focus unique within the *Apologue*, and explores issues with which modern audiences do not typically associate the *Odyssey* (1989: 132–3),

The episode as a whole is more closely related to religious beliefs. Divine commandments against use of that which properly belongs to the gods, and fearful punishments for men who transgress divine taboos are rooted in ancient belief; and stories of sinners who infringed the privileges of the gods, and were punished for their sacrilege, must at an early date have been attached to various figures.

The episode contains one of the only references in all of Homer to Greeks building a temple (*Od.* 12.346–7). The rebellion on Thrinakia thus explores issues more typically associated with OT myth.

Each episode, through its unexpected parallels, provides a context for the other, each helping us better understand the other, the rebellion of the Israelites a hermeneutic for the crew's disobedience and rebellion on Thrinakia. OT myth has additional instances of the same mythic genre in Numbers 11, 14, 16, and 25, and the rebellion of the Trojan women in Book 5 of the *Aeneid* will be briefly adduced. The time in which the two myths are set offers a further broad parallel, as Bryce notes (2006: 70), "If we accept this story [the Exodus] as historically authentic, then Moses... led his people from the land of the Nile about the time Troy fell to the Greeks."

ODYSSEUS AND MOSES: THE LEADER OF A PEOPLE ON AN ARDUOUS, MULTI-YEAR JOURNEY HOME, HAS A PERSONAL RELATIONSHIP WITH GOD

Both myths thematically depict the leaders, Odysseus and Moses,[3] as having special, privileged relationships with the gods, whereas their followers' are considerably more distant. Though Books 9–12 present Odysseus as largely on his own, the epic thematically portrays him as having special relations with the gods,[4] from Zeus' key remark in the opening divine council

---

[3] On how close the myth of Moses' exposure is to the much earlier Sargon Birth Legend, see Sparks (2005: 280).

[4] For further discussion of the hero's special relations with the gods in heroic Greek and OT myth, see Louden (2006: 167–70).

(*Od.* 1.65–7), to Athena's thematic interventions on his behalf, and theophanies before him (*Od.* 13.221–439, 16.157/–/6, 22.205–40; cf. 1.48–62, 7.18–78).[5] Hermes appears to him giving crucial aid and advice (*Od.* 10.277–307), all incidents setting him quite apart from the crew, who lack such close relations. Parallel to his close relations, Odysseus tends to act in accord with the gods' instructions. He does as Hermes instructs in his approach to Kirke. He carries out Kirke's orders when he goes to Hades and meets with Teiresias. It is part of his character, then, that he will do as she instructs, avoiding the desecration of Helios' cattle on Thrinakia.[6]

In the larger myth of Moses, his special relationship with Yahweh is evident throughout. Beginning with his speaking from the burning bush (Exod. 3:2–4:17), Yahweh makes frequent appearances throughout Exodus, as he advises and instructs Moses in how to deal with Pharaoh. Part of Yahweh's special relationship with Moses is his assurance, when the latter is hesitant to speak before the other Israelites, that Yahweh himself will advise him what to say (Exod. 4:10–12). The *Odyssey* employs this same motif not of Odysseus but in Athena's similar reassurance to the youthful Telemachos, hesitant to speak in Nestor's presence (*Od.* 3.14–28). Athena's considerable aid to Telemachos throughout the epic should be seen as a subset of her thematic aid to his father. In the scenes shortly before Exodus 32 the disparity between Moses' intimate relationship with Yahweh and the distance between the god and the other Israelites becomes even more pronounced. Yahweh commands Moses to ascend Mount Sinai to receive his revelation, "then Moses is to approach the Lord by himself, but not the others" (Exod. 24:2). Moses does so, vanishing from the others' sight within the cloud.

THE PEOPLE CHAFE AS A LENGTHY DELAY IN ONE PLACE EXACERBATES THEIR DIFFICULTIES

Forced to remain in the same location, unable to continue their journey, the people chafe at the delay. The delay is key in both myths because the crew and the Israelites, forced to remain in the same place for a considerable spell, having earlier demonstrated a tendency toward rebellion (discussed below), are now presented with a situation that exacerbates frictions they already feel toward their leaders, Odysseus and Moses. Since it takes both

---

[5] See Louden (2005: 90–6) on how epic typically employs theophany as a type-scene to indicate the relations of the mentor god with the epic hero.
[6] On cattle raids in Indo-European myth, see West (2007: 451).

groups years to travel a comparatively short distance (from Troy to Ithaka, from Egypt to Canaan), the delay also serves as a miniature of their larger difficulties in finishing their treks. The period of delay is basically the same for both groups, a month on Thrinakia (*Od.* 12.325), forty days in Exodus 32, each figure a recurring number in the respective mythic traditions.[7]

UNUSUAL METEOROLOGICAL PHENOMENA ACCOMPANY
THE LENGTHY DELAY

Unusual meteorological phenomena, explicitly attributed to the gods, are connected with the delay. In the *Odyssey*, once the crew land on Thrinakia, adverse winds prevent them from leaving. Menelaus, unable to leave the island Pharos, earlier offers a variation on this theme when no winds come. He is held there for twenty days, his provisions run out, and his men grow hungry (*Od.* 4.360–3). On Thrinakia the winds prevent the crew from leaving by blowing too fiercely. After they land, courtesy of Eurylochos' rebellion, and have taken their dinner, a ferocious storm erupts (*Od.* 12.313–15). The storm is described largely in formulas also used of the storm at 9.67–9. I follow Heubeck (1989: 135–6) in regarding the repetition as significant. The *Odyssey* thematically links the first and last storms in the *Apologue*. The first storm, signaling that Odysseus and crew will experience considerable difficulty in achieving their homecoming, serves as an anticipatory echo of the final, climactic storm,[8] prelude to the destruction of the remaining members of the crew, whose homecoming is never granted. The winds do not relent, continue blowing for a whole month, leading to the same outcome as for Menelaus: their provisions exhausted, the crew grow hungry.

The larger myth of the Exodus regularly employs divine meteorological phenomena, from the pillar of cloud and pillar of fire that accompany the Israelites on their journey (Exod. 13:21–2), to the thick cloud, peals of thunder, and flashes of lightning that attend Yahweh's theophany on Mount Sinai (Exod. 19:9, 16, 18; 20:18, 21; 24:16–18). When, before their rebellion, the Israelites last see Moses, Yahweh has summoned him by calling to him from a cloud atop the mountain (Exod. 24:15–16). Moses then enters the cloud, which keeps him from their sight for the next forty days (Exod. 24:18).

---

[7] Cf. *Od.* 10.14, Menelaus' twenty days at *Od.* 4.360. See Propp (1998: 300) on forty as a "stereotypical number" in the Bible.

[8] See de Jong (2001: 594–5) for analysis of the components that comprise all of the storms in the *Odyssey*.

THE FOLLOWERS EXHIBIT REBELLIOUS TENDENCIES IN EARLIER EPISODES; BOTH GROUPS HAVE DIFFICULTY ENDURING HUNGER OR THIRST

In both the *Odyssey* and the larger Exodus myth, the followers' less intimate relation to the deity, which will culminate in their uprising against him, is paralleled in their tendency to rebel against their leader. Both traditions feature earlier instances of rebellion, which prefigure the climactic episodes in *Odyssey* 12 and Exodus 32, when they question their leader's authority. The *Odyssey* dramatically foregrounds this tendency in the crew by highlighting it in the proem, which declares, unequivocally, that the crew perish through their *own* recklessness, though Odysseus tries to save them (*Od.* 1.6–8). Three previous episodes in the *Apologue* depict the crew exhibiting the rebellious characteristics that will flower into full mutiny on Thrinakia. Ismaros, the first stop, serves as a miniature of the crew's tendency toward mutiny, an even more important link with Thrinakia than the storms. After sacking the Cicones' city, Odysseus commands the crew to leave but they refuse (*Od.* 9.43–4), insisting on a feast, for which they slaughter many sheep and cattle (*Od.* 9.45–6). Because they do so, the Cicones have time to summon allies, launching a counter-attack that results in the deaths of seventy-two members of the crew (*Od.* 9.60–1). Their deaths result from their failure to follow Odysseus' directive, their reckless decision to engage in a feast at an inappropriate time and place, an act of excessive consumption, a lack of self-control that predicts their behavior on Thrinakia.[9]

On the return from Aiolos' isle, the crew is again insubordinate in ways that predict their rebellion over Helios' cattle. Close enough to Ithaka to see people tending fires, an unnamed member of the crew persuades the others, with no evidence, that Odysseus is withholding gold and silver from them. With Odysseus asleep, the crew member opens the bag Aiolos had given Odysseus. Storm winds rush out, blowing them all the way back to Aiolos' isle (*Od.* 10.29–45). As on Thrinakia, one member of the crew persuades the others to revolt against Odysseus. As a consequence of their revolt, the crew lose their homecoming. The brief rebellion is carried out while Odysseus is asleep, as he will be again on Thrinakia.[10] In a third anticipatory episode, Eurylochos attempts to dissuade the rest of the crew from following

---

[9] Heubeck (1989: 16): "Odysseus' companions are responsible for their own downfall by their folly and insubordination." Louden (1999: 4): "The first episode of the Apologue thus establishes a general pattern of the crew's insubordination and inability to control themselves." Cf., 14, 39, 76–7.

[10] See de Jong (2001: 308–9) on the parallel.

Odysseus back to Kirke (*Od.* 10.429–45). Though unsuccessful on this occasion, Eurylochos establishes himself as an opposition spokesman, a voice for those members of the crew who will revolt on Thrinakia.

The crew's penultimate rebellion brings them ashore on Thrinakia, putting them in the proximity of Helios' sacred, inviolate cattle (*Od.* 12.261–303). Both Teiresias (*Od.* 11.107–15) and Kirke (*Od.* 12.137–41) have warned Odysseus not to harm them. Commentators have tended to criticize the repetition on various grounds without considering what effect the repetition might have, if it is, in fact, intentional. When the goddess Kirke repeats some of the same information Teiresias earlier gave, the prohibition against harming the cattle now becomes a divine interdiction, equivalent to Yahweh's commandment against eating from the tree of knowledge in the Genesis creation myth. Violation of a divine interdiction always results in severe punishment, typically death, as when Lot's wife violates the angel's command against looking back at the destruction of Sodom and Gomorrah (Gen. 19:17–26). Accordingly, Odysseus urges his crew not to land on Thrinakia (*Od.* 12.266–76). But Eurylochos, ignoring the warnings, argues that the crew deserve to have one meal on shore rather than risk sailing, tired as they are (*Od.* 12.278–93). Odysseus, recognizing that he has no choice but to yield to the effected mutiny, has them swear an oath not to harm Helios' cattle (*Od.* 12.297–302).

In earlier episodes of the Exodus myth the Israelites rebel against Moses, demonstrating the same tendencies that will culminate in the climactic revolt in Exodus 32.[11] When Moses first asks Pharaoh to let the Israelites leave to perform their ritual, he makes their work harder. The Israelites subsequently blame Moses (not Pharaoh) for their hardships (Exod. 5:20), the first challenge to Moses' authority, as Coats observes (1999: 52), "a crisis develops around the challenge to Moses' leadership in 5:20–21." When Pharaoh pursues them to the Red Sea, the Israelites blame Moses, and wish they had died back in Egypt (Exod. 14:11–12). Reaching Mara, they find only bitter water, and complain to Moses (Exod. 15:23–5). In the wilderness of Sin, only their second month out of Egypt, the Israelites complain of their hunger, the issue that prompts the crew's rebellion on Thrinakia:

If only we had died at the Lord's hand in Egypt, where we sat by the fleshpots and had plenty of bread! But you have brought us out into this wilderness to let this whole assembly starve to death. (Exodus 16:3)

---

[11] Propp (2006: 565–6): "At each setback – the intensification of their servitude (chap. 5), being hemmed in at the Sea (chap. 14), dire hunger (chap. 16) and thirst (15:22–6; 17:1–7) – the Israelites have despaired and rebelled."

Each point resembles the crew's complaints on Thrinakia, especially their assumption that they will now starve to death (*Od.* 12.340–2), like Eurylochos' defeatist attitude, that to die of hunger is the worst of all deaths (*Od.* 12.341–2; cf. 12.350–1). Shortly thereafter when they encamp at Rephidim and find no water, another dispute springs up between the people and Moses over their thirst (Exod. 17:1–7). Moses equates their rebellion from him with a revolt against god, "Why do you dispute with me? Why do you challenge the Lord?" (Exod. 17:2).

WITH THEIR LEADER ABSENT, THE PEOPLE REBEL

In both myths the leader's absence is a key factor in the rebellion. Unable to leave Thrinakia for thirty days, Odysseus goes off by himself, apart from the crew, to pray to the gods (*Od.* 12.333–4). In his absence the crew will more easily go against his directives, to pursue their own agenda, opposite his. But Odysseus should not be seen in any way as responsible for their revolt, as commentators on occasion argue.[12] Such a view ignores, even contradicts, Zeus' central statement about mortals' responsibility (*Od.* 1.32–4). Such a view also ignores the thematic parallels the *Odyssey* establishes between the crew and the suitors, particularly how both groups commit *atasthala*, reckless acts, singled out by Zeus (*Od.* 1.34). Both groups thematically fail to demonstrate self-control (discussed below).

Quite the contrary, Odysseus' absence should be understood for what it reveals about him, and how he differs from the crew. Though these may not be the qualities that a modern audience expects to find, as Heubeck notes (1989: 136), his desire to pray to the gods denotes his morality and leadership, "the captain's piety and good intentions." Perhaps even less expected is the common ground his act suggests with characters in OT myth, as Stanford (1962, Vol. I: 415) notes:

> [Odysseus'] departure to seek the gods in prayer from a solitary place is more in the individualistic manner of a Hebrew prophet than typical of the very communal and ceremonial religion of the Homeric hero.

Though within the *Odyssey* the act may not be as unique as Stanford supposes, Menelaus, in his encounter with Proteus, supplies a relevant parallel. Trapped on Pharos from lack of winds, Menelaus is wandering by himself, when the goddess Eidothea takes pity on him and approaches (*Od.* 4.364–9). Though it does not specify that Menelaus is praying, he

---

[12] Stanford (1962, Vol. I: 415); Heubeck (1989: 136).

is looking for divine aid, and the same otherwise unique full-line formula describing his men desperately fishing occurs as Odysseus goes off to pray (*Od.* 4.369 = 12.332).

In Exodus 32 Moses' absence constitutes the delay which makes the Israelites chafe (whereas on Thrinakia the winds have already kept them there before Odysseus goes off by himself to pray). The connection between the leader's absence and the Israelites' subsequent rebellion is even more explicit than in the *Odyssey*, "the people saw that Moses was so long in coming down from the mountain" (Exod. 32:1). Moses is absent for forty days because between Exodus 24, when Moses goes off to consult with Yahweh, and 32 when he returns, the OT writers have inserted a very different kind of episode, not directly connected with the people's rebellion.[13] Moses' encounter with Yahweh atop the mountain, depicted in Exodus 25–31, is a mixture of two of the mythic types analyzed in Chapter 9, *anabasis* and *the vision*. Moses' ascent up the mountain, literally an *anabasis* in the Septuagint (Exod. 24:1: ἀνάβηθι; 24:9: ἀνέβη; 24:12: ἀνάβηθι; 24:15: ἀνέβη; 24:18: ἀνέβη), is like an approach to heaven (cf. Propp 2006: 300, "When Moses climbs the mountain, he approaches Heaven itself"), where he receives an adapted form of *the vision*, Yahweh himself his otherworldly guide. In both myths the leader is absent because he is communicating with god (Moses), or attempting to do so (Odysseus), while his followers act contrary to the deity's will.

THE PEOPLE FOLLOW ANOTHER LEADER: EURYLOCHOS AND AARON

With their impatience exacerbated by delay, the people follow another leader who, lacking a personal relationship with god, will act contrary to divine decrees to carry out the malcontents' desire. Eurylochos has several times intimated that he would play such a role.[14] He is probably the unnamed member of the crew who opens Aiolos' bag (a close parallel

---

[13] On Exodus 25–31 as inserted into the narrative at a later date, see Suggs (1992: 87): "This material, inserted during the last (priestly) stage of tradition collection and information, ascribes the cultic practices of the postexilic period to the Sinai period. The wealth (and technology) required for such a structure as described would have been an intolerable strain during the wilderness period." Cf. Alter (2004: 460): "The strong scholarly consensus is that these chapters are the work of the Priestly writers (P), and the fascination with all the minute details of cultic paraphernalia seems a clear reflection of P's special interests."

[14] Cf. de Jong (2001: 255–6): "He will oppose Odysseus in a series of increasingly serious confrontations (10.261–73, 428–48, 12.278–303), and in the end make the fatal suggestion to slaughter Helius' cattle (12.333–52). At first he stands alone in his opposition, but gradually he gets the other companions to side with him; then it is Odysseus who stands alone (but survives)."

since both occur while Odysseus sleeps).[15] He openly challenges Odysseus on Aiaia (*Od.* 10.263–73, 429–48), and is responsible for bringing their ship ashore on Thrinakia (*Od.* 12.261–302). In Exodus 32 Aaron, brother of Moses, and the priest who often leads them in sacrifice, assumes this role. Aaron is not originally a leader of the malcontents. In earlier episodes he is their target. The Israelites blame him, along with Moses, for their difficulties with Pharaoh (Exod. 5:20–1), and their hardships on the journey to Canaan (Exod. 16:2). Only when they have remained at the foot of Mount Sinai for forty days, with Moses absent, does Aaron become the leader of the rebellious faction. This difference in degree (that Eurylochos *repeatedly* challenges Odysseus, whereas Aaron does not go against Moses prior to Exodus 32) will be even more visible in their subsequent fates at the conclusion of each myth.

HE IS A RELATIVE OF THE MAIN LEADER

Eurylochos is a relative of Odysseus, closely related to him by marriage, as Odysseus earlier recounts (*Od.* 10.441: καὶ πηῷ περ ἐόντι μάλα σχεδόν). Odysseus notes the connection when Eurylochos unsuccessfully attempts to dissuade the crew from accompanying him to Kirke's palace, his point being that he would have slain even his own relative for such disloyalty. Though not as closely related to Odysseus as Aaron to Moses, the underlying dynamic is parallel: neither the audience nor the leader expects his relative to be disloyal to him.

Aaron is not mentioned at all in the larger narrative of Moses, only after the prophet has married and spent years with the Midianites, at the end of the episode of the burning bush, where Yahweh declares that Moses' brother shall serve as his spokesman (Exod. 4:14). Moses' sister is mentioned, though not named, in the original narrative (Exod. 2:4), making omission of Aaron all the more unusual, given his much larger role in the subsequent narrative. Alter (2004: 328) notes the unusual delay in this first mention, "no previous report of Aaron's existence had been made."[16] As often in OT myth, the stark contradictions in his character, that he becomes leader of the rebels but founder of the priestly line, probably

---

[15] Cf. de Jong (2001: 250) on 10.1–79: "their foolish behavior forms an anticipatory doublet of their slaughter of Helius' cattle." Cf. Heubeck (1989: 10): "There is thus a clear line of development from the encounter with the Cicones to the destruction of the offending company in the final storm."

[16] Cf. Coats (1999: 38) "4:13–17... introduce Aaron into the narrative rather abruptly... the discussion about Aaron subordinates him to Moses."

result from once separate, very different, narratives having been combined, with inevitable inconcinnity.[17]

IN EARLIER EPISODES EURYLOCHOS AND AARON WORK WITH THE PROTAGONISTS

Though Eurylochos repeatedly challenges Odysseus, and leads revolts or mutinies against him, prior to Thrinakia he is also depicted assisting him, particularly in the performance of religious rituals. In Hades two members of the crew, Perimedes, of whom little else is said, and Eurylochos assist in the sacrifice of two rams (*Od*. 11.23–4) in accord with Kirke's earlier instructions (*Od*. 10.527–33). When they approach the Sirens after departing Aiaia, Odysseus relays Kirke's detailed instructions on how he can hear their song and survive, including the crucial point that if he asks the crew to set him free, they are to tighten his restraints (*Od*. 12.53–4, 163–4). When Odysseus, succumbing to the Sirens' song, does signal to the crew to set him free, it is again Perimedes and Eurylochos who tighten his restraints (*Od*. 12.195–6), executing Kirke's instructions, which, as a goddess' behest, suggests ritual, as the sacrifice in Hades.

Aaron broadly parallels Eurylochos with Odysseus, in that, while eventually serving as leader of the rebellion in Exodus 32, in earlier episodes he acts in conjunction with Moses. When Aaron is first mentioned in Exodus (Exod. 4:14–16), Yahweh declares that the two brothers will work as a team, Aaron serving as Moses' spokesman (Exod. 4:30; cf. 7:1). Throughout Moses' meetings with Pharaoh, Aaron repeatedly works in conjunction with his brother (Exod. 5:1–5; 8:25; 9:27–8; 10:16–17). As Israel's first high priest (Metzger and Coogan 1993: 3), Aaron is closely involved with sacrifice. In their first appearance before Pharaoh, Moses and Aaron ask for permission to leave to perform a sacrifice to Yahweh (Exod. 5:3). When Pharaoh refuses to let the Israelites do so, it is Aaron who performs most of the subsequent feats of magic, such as making the Nile's water turn into blood (Exod. 7:20–1). All such feats ironically look ahead to his later being able to make the golden calf.

EURYLOCHOS AND AARON LEAD THE PEOPLE IN A RITUAL OFFENSIVE TO GOD

Declaring that to die of hunger is the worst of all possible deaths, Eurylochos proposes that they sacrifice Helios' best cattle to the Olympian gods,

---

[17] See Propp (1998: 231–2) for an intriguing summary of the relevant source analysis.

and perform further rites for Helios on their return home (*Od.* 12.340–7). He glosses over their offense by enclosing it within the performance of ritual.[18] With Odysseus still asleep (*Od.* 12.338), Eurylochos and the crew drive off a number of Helios' cattle, pray to the gods, and proceed to slay and skin the cattle, roast their thighs, and spit the remainder of their meat. Unnamed Israelites (much as the remainder of Odysseus' crew remain anonymous except Perimedes) approach Aaron asking him to conduct a ritual of a very different sort, fashioning images of and worshipping non-Yahwist gods. Gathering their gold earrings, Aaron fashions an image of a bull-calf, and builds an altar for it (Exod. 32:1–5). Just before leaving Egypt the Israelites get gold and silver jewelry from their neighbors (Exod. 11:2). Though Exodus 32: 2–3 mentions only the Israelites' nose rings as the material for the golden calf, the episode may look back to the jewelry at Exodus 11:2.

PERFORMING THE RITUAL VIOLATES A DIVINE INTERDICTION

Divine interdictions are repeatedly pivotal in Greek and OT myth. Adam and Eve transgressing the prohibition against eating of the tree of knowledge parallels Epimetheus told not to accept gifts from Zeus and Pandora told not to open the urn (*Works and Days* 85–7, 94–5),[19] as Israelite and Greek first couples. Both mythical traditions depict the first mortals' general failure to abide by agreements with the gods in their failure to uphold divine interdictions. The angel commands Lot's party not to look back while fleeing the destruction of Sodom and Gomorrah (Gen. 19:17). When Lot's wife breaks this command, she is turned to a pillar of salt (Gen. 19:26). Kirke, by repeating Teiresias' prohibition against harming Helios' cattle (*Od.* 11.105–13, 12.127–40),[20] converts a prophet's command to a divine interdiction. The Decalogue itself, central to the Exodus myth, is composed entirely of divine interdictions. In fashioning the icon(s) and performing the ritual, Aaron and the rebellious Israelites violate three of the commandments:[21]

---

[18] Cf. de Jong (2001: 309–10), "Eurylochus tries to give their act an air of piety by mentioning the sacrifice and leaving out their eating of the meat"; and Heubeck (1989: 137): "the sacrilege of slaughtering the cattle is justified and recommended not as a necessity to still the pangs of hunger, but as a pious act, a sacrifice to the gods."

[19] Epimetheus' divine interdiction is quite explicit, while Pandora's is implicit, not preserved in the actual wording as we have it, but clear enough in the logic of the story.

[20] Both Teiresias and Kirke technically phrase their warnings as conditions, "If you leave them (Helios' cattle) unharmed." However, these reflect a simple interdiction, "do not harm Helios' cattle."

[21] Cf. Clements (1972: 206).

> You must have no other god besides me.
> Exodus 20:3

> You must not make a carved image for yourself, nor the likeness of anything in the heavens above.
> Exodus 20:4

> You must not bow down to them in worship.
> Exodus 20:5

After this first version of the Decalogue, Yahweh specifically tells Moses "You must not make gods of silver to be worshipped besides me nor may you make yourselves gods of gold" (Exod. 20:23).[22] Aaron and the rebelling Israelites break this additional divine interdiction as well. In both myths the respective gods, Kirke and Yahweh, state the divine interdiction in person to the leaders, Odysseus and Moses.

THE RITUAL, WHICH ACCOMPANIES A FEAST, IS A PARODY OF A TRUE RITUAL

In both myths the ritual the rebels perform is a parody of a true ritual. Eurylochos and the crew have as their main motive satisfying their hunger, the sacrifice to Helios a mere pretext. The sacrifice's validity is further undercut by their use of improper elements: lacking barley they sprinkle oak leaves; lacking wine they pour libations of water (*Od.* 12.357–63). It is doubtful they perform a valid ritual, even if the cattle had not been forbidden. Their accompanying feast lasts six days (*Od.* 12.397–8), marked by frightening portents, the hides of the cattle crawling, the meat on the spits mooing. As commentators have noted,[23] the final feast and its frightening portents thematically parallel the suitors' final feast and Theoklymenos' vision of the palace swimming in their blood, and haunted by their shades (*Od.* 20.345–70). Aaron and the Israelites offer close parallels. Their making of the golden calf breaks divine interdictions. Their subsequent activities include an all-day feast, "After this they sat down to eat and drink and then gave themselves up to revelry" (Exod. 32:6). Propp (2006: 553) notes the incongruity between the ritual and the revelry, "The people's activities parody the Covenant ratification in chap. 24, which also featured sacrifices and a sacred meal before a visible Deity."

---

[22] Propp (2006: 182) regards this as part of what would have been an earlier version of the Decalogue in the E source.
[23] E.g., de Jong (2001: 310): "Like the Suitors, the companions ignore the portent and spend six days . . . consuming the meal."

In both myths the rituals involve essentially the same animal, a cow, bull, or bull-calf. While these are common enough as sacrificial animals and divine icons, it is yet a further parallel, if generic. In Exodus 32 the idol's bovine associations are another element of parody: the Israelites, after familiarity with Yahweh, revert to worship of a god associated with animal form. It is also a reminder of the common ground Greek and Israelite sacrificial practise share, visible throughout the Mosaic Books.

THE REBELS ARE FULLY AWARE THAT THEY ARE COMMITTING A WRONG

When Teiresias prophesies destruction of all the crew if they harm Helios' cattle (*Od.* 11.107–13), Eurylochos and Perimedes are also present, alongside Odysseus. Odysseus repeats the gist of Teiresias' decree to the whole crew while they are sailing by Thrinakia (*Od.* 12.267–76), and has them swear an oath not to slaughter any ox or sheep, and they so swear (*Od.* 12.298–304). As Cook notes (1995: 115), they are fully informed of the dangers connected with violating Helios' cattle, "the very words with which Eurylochos justifies his proposal to eat the cattle demonstrate his understanding of the situation (*Od.* 12.348–51)."[24] Compare Crane (1988: 152), "Still, the men know the significance of their actions: they formally decide that they would rather die at sea than starve to death on Thrinacia... Their wish is fulfilled."[25] The term Odysseus uses, should anyone slay the cattle, is ἀτασθαλίῃσι κακῇσιν (*Od.* 12.300), the first word being thematic in the *Odyssey* for mortals' behavior offensive to the gods (as at *Od.* 1.7, 34; 22.437; etc.).

Given the continual polemics OT myth exercises against the worship of any non-Yahwist god, it would be clear to the Israelites, at some level, that they are engaging in apostasy, an act which the audience knows thematically provokes Yahweh's wrath (see especially Exod. 20:5).

BOTH MYTHS FEATURE DISCUSSION OF A TEMPLE TO BE BUILT

When he urges the crew to sacrifice some of Helios' cattle, Eurylochos pledges they will build a temple to the god should they return home (*Od.* 12.346–7). This is a rare topic in Homeric epic, as Heubeck notes at length (1989: 137):

---

[24] Cf., Cook (1995: 113): "the crew knowingly commit a crime in slaughtering the cattle of the sun."
[25] Cf. Heubeck (1989: 137): "Despite the pressure of circumstances the crew make their decision to do wrong in full knowledge of what is involved."

The vow to dedicate a νηός is all the more remarkable because, with one exception (the νηός of Athena at Athens, *Il.* 2.549), there are no references to Greek temples in Homer. (However, there is a temple of Athena in Troy *Il.* 6.88 etc.), . . . there are among the Phaeacians (*Od.* 7.10). The poem mirrors historical developments: the "Dark Age" Greeks began only relatively late to build temples to the gods, possibly under foreign influence.

Eurylochos' vow, made in conjunction with his exhortation to violate the same god's sacred herd, has an air of unreality in its unthinking incongruity.

The Exodus myth, in the episodes immediately preceding Chapter 32, depicts at length the specifications of the Tabernacle and relevant offerings (Exod. 25:8–27:20, 31:1–9), a climax of the Mosaic Books. Though used quite differently, it is nonetheless another specific motif in common between the two myths, occurring in essentially the same place in the respective sequences.

As Heubeck (*ibid.*) notes, Eurylochos describes the temple he would build for Helios as rich (*piôn*), "The νηός is πίων on account of the ἀγάλματα which will be brought to it." *Agalmata* are offerings the god will find pleasing, whether sacrificial animals, or artifacts, apparently including idols (for which the Septuagint also uses *agalmata*: Isa. 19:3, 21:9; Muraoka's lexicon [2002] compares the term to εἴδωλον). Eurylochos' reference (*Od.* 12.347) is intentionally broad, probably meant to include offerings of several different kinds.

The *Odyssey*'s first use of *agalmata* gives an idea of the range of the term, and offers a thematic parallel for Eurylochos' use. As Nestor narrates to Telemachos, Aigisthos, a typological parallel to the suitors and the crew (by virtue of Zeus' paradigmatic mention at *Od.* 1.32–43), after sacrificing animals, offers *agalmata* (*Od.* 3.274), some of gold, some woven, to express his gratitude for having won Klytaimnestra. Like Eurylochos at *Od.* 12.346–7, Aigisthos offers *agalmata* after having committed acts the gods condemn (as Zeus makes clear: *Od.* 1.32–43). When Nestor correctly deduces that Athena has been before him, he offers to sacrifice a yearling cow to her, after having gilded its horns (*Od.* 3.382–4). The next day the offering is described in detail (*Od.* 3.421–38), the gilding of its horns, now specified as an *agalma* for Athena (*Od.* 3.437–8), the same form as the idol Aaron and the rebellious Israelites offer in Exodus 32, a gilded calf. Demodokos' third song, the only one of the *Odyssey*'s three mentions of the Trojan Horse to give the Trojans' perspective, as de Jong notes (2001: 216), offers intriguing parallels. After some debate, the Trojans decide the Wooden Horse is an *agalma* of the gods (*Od.* 8.509), and bring it within their city.

Somewhat like the Israelites in Exodus 32, then, the Trojans embrace their own destruction in associating the wooden image with the gods.

ODYSSEUS AND MOSES, RETURNING, PERCEIVE THE PEOPLE'S TRANSGRESSION FROM A DISTANCE

Awakening from his sudden sleep, Odysseus heads back to the ship, first smelling the savor of cooking meat as he approaches (*Od.* 12.366–9). As Moses makes his way down the mountain, bearing the tablets Yahweh has fashioned, Joshua thinks he hears the sound of people fighting, but Moses is more correct:

> This is not the sound of warriors,
> nor the sound of a defeated people;
> it is the sound of singing that I hear.
> Exodus 32:17–18

The Septuagint's suggestion of revelry among the Israelites is even closer in tone to *Odyssey* 12, where the feast goes on for six days, "I hear their voice leading by wine" (φωνήν ἐξαρχόντων οἴνου ἐγὼ ἀκούω: Exod. 32:18).

THE WRATHFUL GOD THREATENS APOCALYPTIC DESTRUCTION IN A DIVINE COUNCIL

Enraged over the transgression, a wrathful Helios threatens to Zeus that he will withhold his light from the earth,

> If then they will not requite me with just recompense for my cattle,
> I will go down into Hades and shine among the dead.
> *Odyssey* 12.382–3

As noted in Chapter 1, this is the specific subtype of divine council in which the sky father, Zeus, mediates the god who in his wrath threatens large-scale destruction. *Gilgamesh* features an instance of this same subtype when a wrathful Ishtar meets with Anu. As commentators have noted, Ishtar's threat to Anu in *Gilgamesh* is quite similar:

> I shall set my face toward the infernal regions,
> I shall raise up the dead and they will eat the living,
> I shall make the dead outnumber the living.
> *Gilgamesh* VI.iii

Were he to shine in Hades and not on the earth, Helios would bring about a full apocalypse, the destruction of all life on earth. Zeus, however, successfully mediates his wrath, getting Helios to agree that only those mortals who desecrated his cattle shall die.

When he learns of the revolt, Yahweh reacts much as Helios, so enraged over their transgression that he wishes to slay all of the Israelites (Exod. 32:7–10), not just those who took part in the ritual. Why does he not do so? Moses talks him down to a much lower level of destruction, mediating his wrath much as Zeus with Helios. As noted in Chapter 1, Moses here engages in a dialogue (Exod. 32:7–14) with Yahweh that is a modified divine council, the same specific subtype as that between Zeus and Helios. Their modified divine council has two radical innovations. First, it is between a god and a mortal.[26] Moses, here and elsewhere in Exodus, serves functions typically associated with a god, as Hauge interprets of several Exodus episodes, "a corresponding parallelism between YHWH and Moses is reflected in this episode" (2001: 266–7); "Moses... has been assigned a role which transcends the level of a human being" (pp. 311–12); "He can be presented as the substitute of the divine actor" (p. 313). In an even more radical change, Moses acts as the sky father would (Zeus, Anu), and Yahweh acts as the lesser god with a wrath against a mortal (Helios, Ishtar). Moses successfully mediates Yahweh's wrath, talking him down from an apocalyptic level of destruction, slaying all of the Israelites (600,000 according to Exod. 12:37, 603,550 according to Num. 1:46),[27] to destroying a small percentage, three thousand (Exod. 32:11–14).

There are larger thematic parallels between the wraths of Poseidon in Homeric epic and Yahweh in these OT episodes. Each exemplifies the traditional motif of a god complaining of a lack of respect, as Poseidon does at *Od.* 13.127–45 and *Il.* 7.446–63.[28] Although the motif is generic, given that we noted other parallels between Yahweh and Poseidon in Chapter 7, the two deities share considerable common ground. A possible explanation lies in E. L. Brown's (2000) tantalizing, but conjectural, argument that the -daon of Posei-daon (Homeric) is related to Dagon, the Philistines' main god according to OT myth. Since many archeologists now associate

---

[26] OT myth makes this same innovation at Genesis 18: 22–33, the dialogue between Yahweh and Abraham, also an adapted divine council, discussed in Chapter 13.
[27] See Propp (1998: 414) on interpretation and significance of the number.
[28] On Yahweh here as complaining of a lack of respect, see Propp (2006: 555), "Despite his theoretically limitless might, the anthropomorphized Yahweh still worries about his reputation among the nations (see also Deut. 9:28; Josh. 7:9; Ezek. 20:14; 36:22–3; Joel 2:17."

the Philistines with Mycenaean Greek culture,[29] connection between the two names is not out of the question.

ODYSSEUS AND MOSES ARE SPARED, HAVING TAKEN NO PART IN THE RITUAL

Both myths depict a test of the people, which they categorically fail. But Odysseus, away, praying to the gods when Eurylochos and the crew sacrifice Helios' cattle, neither participates in the sacrifice (as Helios also notes), nor takes part in the subsequent feasting (*Od.* 12.397–8). The *Odyssey* thus uses the episode to instantiate his thematic self-control and the crew's thematic lack of the same, his thematic observance of the god's behests, and the crew's failure to do so, as Crane explains (1988: 152–3):

> In the end, the companions cannot meet the demands made upon them... Their failure underlines Odysseus' success and the gulf that separates him from ordinary mortals such as his men.

The Exodus myth depicts a similar opposition between Moses and the rest of the Israelites, as Alter (2004: 459) notes, when Moses disappears into the cloud for the forty-day meeting with Yahweh,

> The terrifying gap between Moses and the people is beautifully registered. They quail down below, seeing pulses of consuming fire from within the cloud... the assembled people at the foot of the mountain who look up awestruck as Moses disappears in the cloud.

Earlier, Moses had told the Israelites, "Do not be afraid. God has come only to test you" (Exod. 20:20).[30] Much like Odysseus' crew on Thrinakia, the rebelling Israelites fail the test.

The rebels are subsequently destroyed, in accord with divine decree. Normal winds having resumed, they are now able to sail away from Thrinakia. But Zeus shatters their ship with lightning, leaving Odysseus the lone survivor. In Exodus 32 the destruction is carried out by mortals. In one of the more unsettling episodes in OT myth, Moses carries out Yahweh's will by directing the Levites to slay those who took part in the ritual:

---

[29] Though OT depiction of Philistine religion is highly problematic not only because the OT writers distort the narratives, making them polemics for the worship of Yahweh, but they consistently depict the Philistines as monotheistic (the authors probably retrojecting their own monotheism), whereas we know they were polytheistic. For some evidence of Philistine religion, see Laffineur and Hägg (2001).

[30] See Propp (2006: 182, 566), on Moses' subsequent disappearance as "the test."

The Lord the God of Israel has said: "Arm yourselves, each of you, with his sword. Go through the camp from gate to gate and back again. Each of you kill brother, friend, neighbor." The Levites obeyed, and about three thousand of the people died that day. (Exodus 32:27–8)

Exodus 32 has mortals serve as the agents of the divine justice, carrying out the demanded destruction. The *Odyssey* uses this same means not on Thrinakia, but on Ithaka, where Odysseus, a mortal, carries out the divine destruction required against the suitors for their having offended Athena in the negative theoxeny in Book 1. We postpone more specific discussion of the apocalyptic destruction in both myths until Chapter 13.

THOUGH A PARTICIPANT IN THE REBELLION, AARON LIVES WHILE EURYLOCHOS DIES

In a key difference, however, Aaron is not held responsible for his leading role in the rebellion as Eurylochos is. He survives the contained apocalypse, retains his position as Israel's priest. When Moses questions him, Aaron downplays his own role, blaming it on the people's wickedness, claiming he merely threw their gold jewelry into the fire and out came the bull-calf (Exod. 32:21–4). Though Moses appears to blame him to some extent ("Moses saw that the people were out of control and that Aaron had laid them open to the secret malice of their enemies": Exod. 32:25), Aaron is conspicuously absent from later parts of the narrative until Exodus 32:35, "Then the Lord punished the people who through Aaron had made the bull-calf."

Biblical commentators have posited a number of factors to account for Aaron's starkly different roles. As Propp argues, Aaron's role in the Exodus myth, in chapter 32 and earlier episodes, has been adapted to reflect later tensions in Israelite culture (2006: 566):

Like other biblical stories of rebellion, Exodus 32 appears to be addressed to later generations... The rebellion stories can be read as advocating obedience to some theocratic authority, a person or group that in future times stands in for Moses and Yahweh.

The depiction of Aaron also serves as an etiology for the priesthood, and its connection with the Levites, which receives extensive focus in Exodus 28–9 (Propp 2006: 567). Scholars have determined there was a conflict in Israelite culture, spanning generations, over who was seen as a proper priest (Propp 2006: 567–74). In later times, "only those claiming Aaronic pedigree were considered legitimate priests" (Propp 2006: 567), for which view Exodus 32 offers a foundational account, and requires Aaron's survival.

It has long been recognized that Exodus 32 makes reference to the reign of Jeroboam I.[31] Jeroboam had gold calves fashioned, as images of Yahweh and objects of ritual. Thus Aaron's causing the gold calf to be fashioned may serve as the authors' comment on Jeroboam's practice.[32] Propp also allows that greater blame may once have been associated with Aaron (which would bring the myth closer to the *Odyssey*'s portrayal of Eurylochos) than our version of Exodus 32 offers (2006: 568), "I think it likely that in a version of the Gold Calf story more complete than that preserved in Exodus, Levite followers of Aaron also fell in the purge."

THE *ODYSSEY* MAY OFFER THE MORE TRADITIONAL FORM OF THIS MYTHIC TYPE

Given the homologies consistent between the other characters, and the larger narratives of the two myths, Aaron's surprising avoidance of punishment and destruction suggests that the OT authors have significantly altered the traditional form of the myth that they inherited.[33] There is no question that such is the case in the radically altered divine council that mediates Yahweh's wrath. While retaining the recognizable structure of the specific subtype of divine council in which the sky father mediates the wrath of a lesser god, the authors of Exodus innovate considerably in assigning Moses the role traditionally occupied by a culture's principal deity, and Yahweh the role of the wrathful lesser god.

The myth presented in *Odyssey* 12 is more difficult to place within a historical context, aside from its reference to a Greek temple (*Od.* 12.346–7). Accordingly, the *Odyssey* may therefore present the more traditional version of this mythic type, less interested in advancing religious polemics. Though the *Odyssey* does not employ the Thrinakia episode as part of an agenda in a holy war, it has, nonetheless, subordinated this genre under the larger influence of Argonautic myth, which, as we have seen in Chapter 6, colors and governs much of Books 6–12. Thus, Helios, the god who

---

[31] Among other commentators, see Propp (2006: 574–778), and Cody's article on Aaron in Metzger and Coogan (1993).
[32] Propp (2006: 578), "[J]ust as Exodus 32 must be read in the context of ancient debates over who was a priest, so it also addresses the question of whether a gold calf is an appropriate Yahweh symbol and perhaps whether Jeroboam's secession from David's hegemony was legitimate."
[33] On Exodus 32 as essentially a "late" part of Genesis, see Sparks (2005: 303), "it is clear enough from the Near Eastern evidence that many legends were designed to look much older than they were... the story of the Golden Calf in Exod. 32." Cf. Carr (1996: 129–30).

becomes wrathful because of the improper ritual, is simultaneously the figure of the angry father-in-law, Aietes, in the *Argonautica* (cf. Laban in Gen. 29–31). Kirke, advising Odysseus how to deal with her potent father, is even more obviously a Medea figure. In these ways, and possibly others, the *Odyssey* may alter the mythic type we have noted in this chapter to accommodate the over-arching trajectory of Argonautic myth.

OTHER OT INSTANCES OF THE SAME GENRE OF MYTH

Several other episodes in Numbers can be seen as miniatures, partial instances, of the same mythic type as that presented in greater detail in Exodus 32, *The people disobey their leader and rebel against god*.[34] These narratives also offer thematic parallels with events on Thrinakia, and other episodes of the crew's insubordination. Numbers 11, like *Odyssey* 12, situates the rebellion in an act of eating, eating meat in particular.[35] The Israelites make a general complaint and an angry Yahweh causes fire to break out on the edge of the camp (Num. 11:1–2). When Moses intervenes, however, the fire lessens. Essentially these two verses are a miniature of Exodus 32, Moses mediating Yahweh's wrath when the Israelites offend him, but without an idol. In a second complaint, the Israelites wish they had meat, cucumbers, watermelon, leeks, onions and garlic, instead of manna (Num. 11:4–13). This complaint arises partly as a result of a company of strangers who have joined them. From the perspective of Exodus 32 the non-Israelites function like the rebels who turn away from Yahweh. Yahweh tells Moses he will give them so much meat, a month's worth, they will be sick of it. He then causes the winds to drive quail to them. But when they eat the quail, he strikes them with a plague. The Israelites' inability to restrain their desire to eat meat, and a wrathful god sending plague, restates some but not all of the motifs found in Exodus 32 and the crew's rebellion on Thrinakia.

Numbers 14 presents an etiology for why it takes the Israelites forty years to travel the comparatively short distance from Egypt to Canaan (Num. 14:22–35). When the Israelites learn from scouts that Canaan is inhabited by warrior peoples, they complain that they would rather have died in Egypt than in Canaan (cf. Eurylochos preferring to die at sea rather than on land). Their complaint again provokes a divine wrath in Yahweh, who declares that all who have turned against him will die before reaching

---

[34] See also Carr (1996: 120).
[35] As Ackerman (1987: 80 in Alter and Kermode) notes, the narrative combines what must originally have been two separate tales, the rebellion, and a depiction of divinely inspired prophecy. I here only consider elements of the rebellion narrative.

Canaan (rather as the crew on Thrinakia), and that it will take the others forty years to reach it, for the forty days the scouts spent exploring the land. Only Caleb and Joshua will live to see the promised land, much as only Odysseus returns to Ithaka. Here Yahweh's wrath again functions very like Poseidon's in the *Odyssey* as the main factor behind the extraordinary delay in reaching their goal (ten years for Odysseus and crew, forty years for Moses and the Israelites).

Numbers 16 presents a more direct challenge to Moses' leadership, when Korah, and 250 others, charge that Moses and Aaron have set themselves above the rest of the people. The next day the earth opens and swallows Korah's family; a fire consumes the 250 others. The following day when other Israelites blame Moses and Aaron for the deaths of the 250, a plague breaks out killing 14,700 more until Aaron and Moses intervene. The mistrust of Moses and Aaron is reminiscent of the false charge from the unnamed crew member (thematically Eurylochos' role) who, claiming Odysseus always takes a disproportionate share (*Od.* 10.34–49), then unleashes the storm winds, blowing them back to Aiolos' island. Both episodes occur as the respective groups are physically close to their destinations (Ithaka, Canaan). Both episodes predict that many of the followers will never reach their home. In its conclusion, with a wrathful god destroying large numbers of mortals, Numbers 16 shares common ground with Zeus' destruction of the crew in *Odyssey* 12, and Poseidon's of the Phaiakian crew in *Odyssey* 13.

Numbers 21:4–7 offers a very effective miniature. Here the Israelites again complain of hunger (as the crew on Thrinakia) and thirst, and assume they will die in the desert (cf. the crew accepting death at sea). In response, Yahweh sends poisonous snakes among them, causing many to die. Others then plead with Moses to intervene, and he intercedes on their behalf. The episode works as a stripped-down, four-verse miniature of several of the main motifs present in Exodus 32: rebellion, divine wrath, destruction, Moses' mediation of further destruction.

REBELLION OF THE TROJAN WOMEN AT *AENEID* 5.604–745

Much of Books 1–6 of the *Aeneid* employs the same genres of myth OT myth uses in Exodus-Deuteronomy to depict the Israelites' journey from Egypt to Canaan. Aeneas, who has a close personal relationship with god, fulfills several of the functions Moses serves. Books 7–12 of the *Aeneid*, on the other hand, parallel the mythic genres used in Joshua: the people, having followed divine dictates, arrive in the promised land only to find it already inhabited. In Book 5 Vergil employs an instance of the mythic type this chapter explores to depict the revolt of the Trojan women on Sicily. In a parallel with events on Thrinakia, Vergil situates his rebellion on an island. Somewhat as in Exodus 32, the Trojans are engaged in elaborate ritual, funeral games to mark the anniversary of Anchises' death, when the rebellion occurs. Juno, who throughout embodies rebellion against Jupiter, sends Iris to incite the Trojan women to burn the ships. Very like Moses, Aeneas despairs, praying to Jupiter to either help them, or destroy them once and for all (*Aen.* 5.664–99). Jupiter responds with a thunderstorm, saving all but four of the ships. When Aeneas continues to despair over abandoning their mission, Nautes, whose connections with prophecy are here emphasized, suggests that those who prefer not to go on be allowed to stay on Sicily (*Aen.* 5.700–45). As in *Odyssey* 12, the Aiolos episode (*Od.* 10.34–49), and Numbers 16, the people are close to their eventual goal when instead they act in a way that prevents them from reaching it.

As between *Odyssey* 12 and Exodus 32, we have a close homology between Aeneas and Moses, the disgruntled Trojan women and the rebellious Israelites, and even a partial one between Nautes and Aaron. As in *Odyssey* 12, two gods, Juno and Jupiter separately perform Yahweh's roles of wrathful god, and beneficent god, as do Helios and Zeus. Quite opposite to the OT myths, however, and *Odyssey* 12, in Vergil's episode none of the rebels is slain. Juno's wrath, the only divine wrath expressed in the episode, does not result from and punish the rebels' action but *prompts* it, and is directed more at Aeneas, less at the Trojans as a group. Since those who elect to remain are the elderly, the sick, or the disgruntled, the Trojans as a whole are better off as a result of the incident. They emerge as a group more fit to face the challenges that await them in Italy. By blunting or softening some of the usual motifs, Vergil thus presents a milder, more humanized version of the same mythic type.

CHAPTER 11

The suitors and the depiction of impious men in wisdom literature

After Odysseus' narration of his wanderings concludes with the events at Thrinakia, the principal narrator describes his return to Ithaka (discussed in Chapter 13). Once he has returned, the principal focus of the *Odyssey* becomes, directly or indirectly, the destruction of the suitors.[1] As our analysis of negative theoxeny in Chapter 2 demonstrates, the suitors have already brought death upon themselves by offending the disguised Athena (*Od.* 1.227–9), provoking her divine wrath in violating hospitality. Once a disguised Odysseus is among them, the *Odyssey* continues to depict their failings not only through the lens of theoxeny, but through other forms of misconduct. Zeus' assertion in the opening divine council, that mortals bring suffering upon themselves through their own recklessness, establishes the *Odyssey*'s concern with depicting relevant forms of inappropriate behavior.[2]

His paradigmatic example of such behavior is Aigisthos' transgression of a divine interdiction. Hermes had told him not to marry Klytaimnestra, and not to kill Agamemnon (*Od.* 1.39). Aigisthos embodies a traditional type of immoral behavior common in Old Testament myth, the mortal who does not fear the gods. The suitors, by violating hospitality in Athena's presence, replicate Aigisthos' stance toward the gods, as do the crew when they transgress the divine interdiction on Thrinakia. But the *Odyssey*'s favored form of recklessness is depicted in mortals who perish because of excessive or inappropriate consumption. In these ways the *Odyssey* resembles depictions of wicked mortals found in ancient Near Eastern wisdom

---

[1] See Sparks (2005: 56, 58, 64, 70, 72) on wisdom literature, and Near Eastern texts relevant to OT wisdom literature.
[2] See Louden (2006: 183–201) on how the *Iliad* figures the Trojans' wrongdoing. Lowe aptly sums up the *Odyssey*'s focus on moral behavior, "In the *Odyssey*, these rules are above all *moral* rules, and their sole and sufficient enforcer is Zeus... the subjection of that entire universe to a set of *global rules of moral behaviour*... the gods ensure human responsibility by warning of the sin and its consequences in time to allow the perpetrator an escape. Inexorably, wilful transgression by mortals brings first a warning and then, if the warning is unheeded, disaster." Cf. Lowe (2000: 141–2).

literature. Though examples survive from Egypt and Mesopotamia, the Bible, particularly Proverbs, passages in Psalms,[3] and others sprinkled throughout the OT, offers many relevant instances. The *Odyssey*, in its depiction of the suitors, is aware of and consciously draws upon a wisdom literature tradition (but probably does not draw upon OT instances), as does Hesiod in the *Works and Days*.

Wisdom literature seeks to illustrate how the gods reward mortals for good behavior, and punish them for offensive acts, often summing up these tendencies in concise couplets.[4] A typical couplet from Proverbs voices a central thrust of the *Odyssey*, evident in Odysseus' triumphs over Polyphêmos and the suitors (Prov. 24:5–6):

> Wisdom prevails over strength, knowledge over brute force;
> for wars are won by skilful strategy and victory is the result of detailed planning.

Perhaps the governing principal behind such a view is a conception of divine retribution, as James G. Williams argues (1987: 263), "The world is viewed as an order informed by a principle of retributive justice."[5] Homeric epic has two ways of figuring and personifying divine retribution, *opis*, and *nemesis* (discussed below). While the *Odyssey*'s use of theoxeny and romance also embodies a similar dynamic, that the gods reward the good and punish the wicked, Books 17–22 broaden the palette to depict other forms of behavior offensive to the gods: lack of respect for the gods and for prophecy, unnecessarily abusive acts toward others, and the like, all of which occur in Proverbs.

In Books 17–22, Odysseus, Penelope, and even the suitors, speak, on occasion, in the figures used in wisdom literature – proverbs.[6] Wondering how her mysterious guest could know if she surpasses other women, Penelope uses wisdom tropes to illustrate how one's behavior determines one's reputation:

> When a man is unyielding and has an unyielding character,
> all mortals curse him with evils while he
> lives, and all will mock him when he dies,

---

[3] Cf. Williams (1987: 263): "we find Wisdom compositions among the psalms."
[4] Cf. Dell (2001: 418): "The thought-world of Proverbs is . . . the principle that good and bad deeds have consequences that can be known through the study of patterns of human behavior. This principle and various other insights into human characteristics are summed up in pithy proverbial sayings."
[5] On retribution as a principle of Near Eastern wisdom literature in general, see Williams (1987: 263–6).
[6] Dell (2001: 423): "Wisdom literature is easily recognized by the use of certain forms, most notably the proverb, which lies at the heart of the Wisdom enterprise."

> but when a man is blameless and has a blameless
> character, his guests bear tidings of his wide fame
> through all mankind, and all say he is noble.
>
> *Odyssey* 19.329–34

When the disguised Odysseus is the cause of friction among them, the suitors Amphinomos and Agelaos both use a wisdom trope to defuse the tension:

> Friends, let no one threaten violence, accosting
> with squabbling words, when something was said justly.
>
> *Odyssey* 18.414–15=20.322–3

PARALLELS BETWEEN THE SUITORS AND HESIOD'S PERSES

Many of the suitors' defining characteristics are also shared by Perses in Hesiod's *Works and Days*. Much of Hesiod's poem, which should also be classified as wisdom literature, is organized around the opposing figures of Hesiod and the contentious Perses. Each embodies an opposing form of strife (*eris*): Hesiod, that which helps strengthen and give order to a community by encouraging competition (*Works and Days* 17–26); Perses, that which tears it apart and leads to war (*Works and Days* 14–16). Similarly, Hesiod implicitly embodies *dikê*, justice, while Perses embodies *hubris* (*Works and Days* 213–14), overweening arrogance. Much of the *Works and Days* presents an explanation for why human existence is so difficult (*Works and Days* 42–201). Implicitly this serves as an etiology for the necessity of work: no longer living a golden age existence, mortals must work hard and plan ahead if they are to survive winter and other hardships. Within the framework of the necessity of hard work, the two brothers also serve as polar opposites. Hesiod's character embodies an ideal of conscientious hard work, while Perses avoids work, attempting to live off the fruits of others' toils (*Works and Days* 27–34).

A confrontation between the suitors and the disguised Odysseus highlights a depiction of similar attitudes toward work (*Od.* 18.357–86). When Odysseus begs in his palace, Eurymachos taunts him for being bald (*Od.* 18.350–5; discussed below), then insults him, alleging he is lazy and avoids hard work, a formula Melanthios earlier directed at him (*Od.* 18.362–4=17.226–8). With unintended irony and hypocrisy, typical of the suitors,[7]

---

[7] On sarcasm in wisdom literature, see Sparks (2005: 64).

Eurymachos has been eating all of his meals at the palace for three years now, never paying or contributing anything for them. It is he and the other suitors who are avoiding work entirely, and now unnecessarily provoking strife with the disguised Odysseus.

Perses' defining characteristics are also present in some details in Hesiod's account of the silver race (*Works and Days* 127–37). Though the suitors may not share the silver race's more fantastic traits (their very lengthy childhood), the final characteristic closely fits them, and is typical of wisdom literature figures. Men of the silver race cannot keep from committing *hubrin atasthalon* (*Works and Days* 134). The *Odyssey* frequently applies both terms to the suitors (*hubris*: *Od.* 1.368, 4.321, 4.627, 15.329, 17.565, etc.; *atasthalos, atasthalie*: *Od.* 18.143, 21.146, 22.314, 22.416, etc.). Hesiod concludes his discussion of *hubris* with another passage reminiscent of the *Odyssey*'s depictions of the suitors, the apocalyptic destruction that awaits those who commit violent acts (*Works and Days* 238–41).

MORTALS WHO DO NOT FEAR THE GODS

Fear of the gods is central to wisdom literature's depiction of moral behavior. Proverbs articulates this view almost immediately, "The fear of the Lord is the foundation of knowledge" (Prov. 1:7; cf. 1:29; 2:5; 3:7, etc.). Again, in Zeus' paradigmatic example, Aigisthos acts in a manner revealing he does not fear the gods, nor do the suitors, implicitly and explicitly. Homeric epic has a specific term to express this concept, *opis* (ὄπις), which Cunliffe (1963) renders as "The watch (kept by the gods) on the deeds of men, their regard for righteousness and reprobation of evil-doing." Hesiod uses it in the *Works and Days* as an instance of a type of mortal behavior the gods punish, θεῶν ὄπιν οὐκ ἀλέγοντες (*Works and Days* 251), which Sinclair (1966: 29) renders, "not heeding the vengeance of the gods." He elaborates:

The phrase occurs in a similar connexion in *Il.* 16.388... The word therefore means "notice," "regard," whether paid by gods to men or by men to gods. The gods may take "notice" of a man either for good or evil, hence the meaning "divine visitation," "vengeance."

Eumaios tells the disguised Odysseus that the suitors are pitiless, caring nothing for anyone (*Od.* 14.82: οὐκ ὄπιδα φρονέοντες). From that phrase he proceeds with a few wisdom literature tropes that could be right out of the *Works and Days* (esp. as at 237 ff.) or Proverbs, that the gods do not love pitiless acts, and so on (*Od.* 14.83–8). Philoitios utters the *Odyssey*'s key instance of the suitors' lack of *opis*. Delineating their abusive behavior toward him, Telemachos, and Odysseus' possessions, he sums up their outrages by noting, "they do not fear the gods' vengeance" (*Od.* 20.215: οὐδ' ὄπιδα τρομέουσι θεῶν). When Telemachos asks the other Ithakans to help rid him of the suitors, he urges them to θεῶν δ' ὑποδείσατε μῆνιν (*Od.* 2.66), "be afraid of the gods' wrath," lest they seem to condone the suitors' outrages.[8] Peisistratos' declaration to Telemachos, "all men need the gods" (πάντες δὲ θεῶν χατέουσ' ἄνθρωποι: *Od.* 3.48) is, in effect, the positive complement of the same belief.

WICKED MEN INSULT THOSE WHO WOULD CORRECT THEM

Proverbs repeatedly asserts that those most in need of correction will insult anyone who attempts to do so, "Correct an insolent person, and you earn abuse" (Prov. 9:7); "the arrogant will not listen to rebuke" (Prov. 13:1). The *Odyssey* thematically portrays the suitors and their party behaving in the same manner. In his first appearance Melanthios embodies the traditional type (*Od.* 17.247–53). Eumaios prays to the nymphs of the fountain that if Odysseus ever sacrificed to them, a god might lead him home to scatter Melanthios' glories, since wicked shepherds are ruining Odysseus' herds (*Od.* 17.240–6). In response Melanthios calls him a dog, threatens to sell him into slavery, and hopes either Apollo or the suitors slay Telemachos (*Od.* 17.248–53).

Directed by Athena to test the suitors' hospitality (*Od.* 17.360–4), Odysseus does so by narrating his fictive life as a suffering wanderer, as an exemplum. When he articulates the first such exemplum to Antinoös (*Od.* 17.415–44), which has as its implicit moral, that Zeus punishes mortals who act recklessly, Antinoös responds with an insult, accusing him of spoiling the feast, among other taunts (*Od.* 17.446–52). When Iros tells the disguised Odysseus to vacate the forecourt willingly or be forced to, Odysseus replies that if Iros wants a fight, he faces a defeat so decisive he will never be able to return to the palace. In response Iros compares Odysseus to an old woman at an oven, and threatens to knock his teeth out (*Od.* 18.15–31).

Proverbs, and other wisdom literature, employ insults as a subset of broader behavior: the wicked speak abusively. Psalms offers one of the most salient descriptions, "The wicked person's mouth is full of cursing,

---

[8] Cf. the disguised Odysseus' remark to Eumaios, *Odyssey* 20.169–71.

deceit, and violence; mischief and wickedness are under his tongue" (Ps. 10:7). A later passage in Psalms could easily be used of the suitors:

> Their talk is all mockery and malice;
> high-handedly they threaten oppression.
> Their slanders reach up to heaven,
> while their tongues are never still on earth.
>
> Psalms 73:8–9

Throughout, the suitors' modes of speaking reflect how they shirk responsibility and blame others. In a typical example in the assembly in Book 2, Antinoös blames Penelope for all the harm they do to Telemachos' estate (*Od.* 2.85–128).[9] Eurymachos, after ridiculing Halitherses' augury (*Od.* 2.178–84, discussed below), threatens him (*Od.* 187–93). When Mentor speaks up in support of Telemachos, the suitor Leokritos insults him (*Od.* 2.243), adding an implicit threat of force, that no one will be able to drive them out of the palace (*Od.* 2.244–51). All such statements by the suitors instantiate a tenet in Proverbs, "the speech of the wicked conceals violence" (Prov. 10:6 = 10:11). In all these ways the brother and sister Melantho (*Od.* 18.321–36; 19.65–9) and Melanthios (*Od.* 17.217–32, 248–53; 20.178–82) function almost as a tag team, partners in verbally abusing the disguised Odysseus. Proverbs sums up the general tendency, "The insolent delight in their insolence; the stupid hate knowledge" (Prov. 1:27).

THE WICKED TAUNT A BALD PROPHET

The suitors employ one specific form of insult also found in OT myth. When Eurymachos makes fun of the disguised Odysseus for being bald he parallels an episode in the myth of the prophet Elisha. The *Odyssey* employs the insult as one of several references to Odysseus providing light for the palace. After he has defeated Iros, and established a presence in the palace, Odysseus tells the maids to attend to the queen, for he, by tending the cressets, will provide light for everyone (*Od.* 18.313–19). Eurymachos responds that the gleams coming from his bald head can illuminate the palace, and surely the gods must have led him (*Od.* 18.353–5). I quote Russo's analysis at length (1992: 70):

The connection in thought is not at first sight obvious. Eurymachus, seeking to be ironic at Odysseus' expense, pretends to voice the traditional sentiment expressed

---

[9] Telemachos later offers a succinct characterization of Antinoös' speaking style (*Od.* 17.394–5). Cf. Russo (1992) on *Odyssey* 17.450–2.

by the suitors earlier at 17.483–85, that gods go among men in disguise. But then abruptly... he turns to mocking the idea of a divine presence, asserting that the light apparently radiating from Odysseus (cf. 317, 434–4) must come from his bald head. Since Homer has been giving increasing emphasis to the symbolic equation of light = victory (see note to 317–19), the attempted irony he puts in the mouth of Eurymachus turns around and becomes an irony at the suitor's expense.

Odysseus does not directly respond to Eurymachos' insult, for the suitor first launches into another, hypocritical claim (*Od.* 18.357–64), that Odysseus is avoiding work, discussed above. As is typical in wisdom literature, the taunt reveals more about the man who utters it and the consequences he faces, than it fits its supposed target.

The myth of the prophet Elisha, Elijah's successor, includes the following brief episode:

From there he went up to Bethel and, as he was on his way, some small boys came out of the town and jeered at him, saying "Get along with you, bald head, get along." He turned round, looked at them, and cursed them in the name of the Lord; and two she-bears came out of a wood and mauled 42 of them. (2 Kgs. 2:23–4)

While Odysseus is not a prophet in the sense that Elisha is, he is in tune with the gods' will, and he does offer the suitors warnings very like those a prophet would utter, as discussed below. The boys are immediately destroyed, whereas the suitors will perish the following day. Both groups perish at least in part because they offend the man who is observing the gods' will.

ATTEMPTED MURDER

The suitors' plot to murder Telemachos also overlaps with sentiments found in wisdom literature. Particularly apropos is Proverbs' account of a band of would-be murderers, whose acts ironically further their own demise:

They may say: "Join us and lie in wait for someone's blood;
let us waylay some innocent person who has done us no harm...
We shall take rich treasure of every sort and fill our houses with plunder.
Throw in your lot with us and share the common purse..."
It is for their own blood they lie in wait;
they waylay no one but themselves.
                                                            Proverbs 1:11–18

Though ultimately unsuccessful, the suitors, at Antinoös' suggestion (*Od.* 4.667–72), plot to murder Telemachos on his return from Sparta and Pylos, hoping to ambush him (*Od.* 16.364–9). When he eludes them with

The suitors and the depiction of impious men

Athena's aid, they plot again to murder him in Ithaka (*Od.* 16.371–86), in much the same way that Proverbs sketches out:

> But let us catch him by surprise, seizing him in the field away
> from the city on the way, and let us have his possessions ourselves,
> dividing them up among us.
> *Odyssey* 16.383–5

Their scheme remains in play until Amphinomos, after interpreting an augury (*Od.* 20.241–7), convinces them to give it up. The contest with Iros suggests the other specific situation hinted at in Proverbs 1:11–18, inviting a man to join the wicked band. While encouraging the fight, Antinoös invites the winner to dine with them, promising he shall always be entitled to do so (*Od.* 18.43–9).

THE GODS ENCOURAGE THE WICKED TO WORSEN THEIR OWN CIRCUMSTANCES

In a few scenes the *Odyssey* depicts Athena encouraging the suitors to continue to commit acts offensive to the gods. Though modern audiences often misunderstand these scenes, OT myth offers instructive parallels for them. In the first such passage Athena encourages Odysseus to beg from the suitors to tell which are just and which are not, with the narrator noting that, nonetheless, she will not spare any of them from destruction (*Od.* 17.360–4). Two additional passages make Athena's intent more specific:

> But Athena did not altogether let the arrogant suitors
> keep from heart-hurting outrage, so that yet more pain
> would pierce the heart of Laertes' son, Odysseus.
> *Odyssey* 18.346–8 = 20.284–6

Russo comments on the last two passages (1992: 69), "A modern reader may puzzle over the desire of a deity to incite the suitors so that Odysseus may be caused more pain." He then speculates (*ibid.*) that it is to help justify what he views as "total, unsparing revenge Odysseus will later take against the suitors." But such a view, that revenge is the main factor, downplays, even ignores, the gods' larger role in upholding the sanctity of hospitality, and punishing the suitors for their violations of it, the inevitable conclusion of a negative theoxeny.

In the account of the plagues, Exodus employs a more prominent, fully developed instance of the same dynamic. As Moses is about to return to

Egypt, Yahweh tells him how he will encourage Pharaoh not to let the Israelites leave Egypt, "But I on my part *shall toughen his heart* and he will not send the people away" (Exod. 4:21). The formulaic phrase, in a few variants, runs throughout the plagues account (I count eleven such expressions: Exod. 4:21; 7:22; 8:11, 8:28; 9:7, 9:12, 9:35; 10:20, 10:27; 11:10; 14:4). Three of these (Exod. 4:21, 7:22, 14:4) are further linked in specifically highlighting Yahweh's involvement or agency. Alter (2004: 329–30) offers an interpretation of the phrases and the phenomenon:

> This phrase, which with two synonymous variants punctuates the Plagues narrative, has been the source of endless theological debate over whether Pharaoh is exercising free will or whether God is playing him as a puppet and then punishing him for his puppet's performance. The latter alternative surely states matters too crudely... God needs Pharaoh's recalcitrance in order that He may deploy the plagues... thus humiliating the great imperial power of Egypt... But Pharaoh is presumably manifesting his own character: callousness, resistance to instruction, and arrogance would all be implied by the toughening of the heart. God is not so much pulling a marionette's strings as allowing, or perhaps encouraging, the oppressor-king to persist in his habitual harsh willfulness and presumption.

In assigning separate but joint motivations to the god and the mortal, Alter essentially arrives at an independent formulation of Dodds' (1960) rubric of overdetermination. His comments apply well to Athena's treatment of the suitors.

Greco-Roman myth is full of many relevant instances. Does Aphrodite compel Phaedra to desire her stepson Hippolytos? Does Cupid compel Dido to fall in love with Aeneas? What causes the dust storm that accompanies Antigone as she breaks Creon's edict against performing funeral rites for Polyneices? In each case a god encourages a mortal to act in a way that the mortal is already inclined to pursue. It is not a question of free will (a later concept, in any case) vs. puppetry. In these scenes Athena acts with the suitors precisely as Yahweh does with Pharaoh.[10] Additional specific motifs are used of both "hard-hearted" bands. Both the suitors and Pharaoh's followers are tricked into giving away costly jewelry to the protagonists (Exod. 11:2, 12:35–6, cf. 3:22; *Od.* 18.276–82); both face apocalyptic destruction that none survives (Exod. 14:28).

---

[10] Cf. Alter (2004: 345) (on Exod. 7:22): "Whatever the theological difficulties, the general aim of God's allowing, or here causing Pharaoh to persist in his harshness is made clear: without Pharaoh's resistance, God would not have the opportunity to deploy His great wonders and so demonstrate His insuperable power in history and the emptiness of the power attributed to the gods of Egypt... three different verbs are used in the story for the action on or in Pharaoh's heart... The force of all three idioms is to be stubborn, unfeeling, arrogantly inflexible."

The suitors and the depiction of impious men

Wisdom literature is also fond of displaying the same tendency from a broader perspective, focusing more on the human agency than the divine, to show that the wicked will not refrain from being wicked:

> He who is wicked is caught in his own iniquities, held fast in the toils of his own sin;
> for want of discipline he will perish, wrapped in the shroud of his boundless folly.
>
> Proverbs 5:22–3

> but the wicked are brought down by their own wickedness.
>
> Proverbs 11:5

> The wicked are caught up in their own violence.
>
> Proverbs 21:7

> the wicked are trapped in their own devices.
>
> Psams 9:16

All such appraisals of human behavior resemble Zeus' programmatic assertion that mortals bring disaster upon themselves through their own recklessness (*Od.* 1.34: ἀτασθαλίῃσιν), an anticipation of the suitors' thematic tendencies.

THE WICKED IGNORE PROPHETS' WARNINGS OF THE CONSEQUENCES OF THEIR BEHAVIOR

In our investigation of theoxeny in Chapter 2 we noted that the suitors and Lot's sons-in-law scorn prophecies of their coming destruction. The motif is not restricted to theoxenic myth, but is a given in many myths that highlight prophecy. In wisdom literature we have noted the larger tendency for the wicked to not fear god, to abuse those who would correct them. Disrespect for prophecy is thus a natural subset of such behavior. The *Odyssey* has four broad types of prophecy that the suitors reject or ridicule. There are general prophecies, such as Halitherses' in the Book 2 assembly (*Od.* 2.161–76). While Odysseus' *exempla* also implicitly serve as a second kind of prophecy of the suitors' destruction (*Od.* 17.415–44, 18.125–50, 19.75–88), Theoklymenos delivers the poem's climactic instance of this traditional motif, and that most like those in many OT prophecies (*Od.* 20.351–7, 365–70). In Leodes the suitors also have one of their own as a seer who predicts their destruction (*Od.* 21.152–62). In the assembly in Book 2 Eurymachos not only ridicules Halitherses' prophecy that Odysseus will soon return home, but threatens him for having made it

(*Od.* 2.178–207). Theoklymenos has earlier validated his credentials for the audience, who knows he is descended from an illustrious line of prophets (*Od.* 15.225–56), and observed him accurately prophesy that Odysseus was already nearby, plotting destruction for the suitors (*Od.* 17.152–71). Thus the audience knows how accurate is his prophecy of their apocalyptic destruction (discussed in Chapter 13), his chief reason for being in the poem.

THE GODS STRIKE WICKED MEN WITH MADNESS OR BLINDNESS

In a common traditional motif the gods intervene to temporarily incapacitate the wicked, so god-fearing mortals may make their escape. We noted this motif in our exploration of negative theoxeny as used against the mob in Sodom (Gen. 19:11). Such interventions parallel the common motif of the gods striking panic or terror into the foe in military settings.[11] A typical instance is used to rescue the prophet Elisha:

As the Aramaeans came down towards him, Elisha prayed to the Lord: "Strike this host, I pray, with blindness"; and they were struck blind as Elisha had asked. (2 Kings 6:18)

Deuteronomy includes similar interventions among the afflictions god will bring on those who do not serve him:

May the Lord strike you with madness, blindness, and stupefaction; so that you will grope about in broad daylight, just as a blind man gropes in darkness. (Deuteronomy 28:28–9)

In a general judgment against Egypt Isaiah articulates a more general sense of divine intervention:

> The Lord has infused into them a spirit that distorts their judgment;
> they make Egypt miss her way in all she does,
> as a vomiting drunkard will miss his footing.
>   Isaiah 19:14

In the *Odyssey* Athena interacts with the suitors twice in much the same way, once so they will not notice Telemachos as he prepares to leave for Pylos:

---

[11] On which see Louden (2006: 225–6), *God panics the army by hurling lightning, reversing the tide of battle.*

> She went on her way, into the house of godlike Odysseus
> and there she drifted a sweet slumber over the suitors,
> and struck (πλάζε) them as they drank, and knocked the goblets
>   from their hands.
>
> *Odyssey* 2.394–6

Though a milder form than either madness or blindness, this temporary incapacitation works much the same as in the OT passages. Athena incapacitates them a second time right before Theoklymenos' climactic prophecy, again while they are feasting:

> In the suitors Pallas Athena
> stirred up uncontrollable laughter, and addled (παρέπλαγξεν) their
>   thinking,
> Now they laughed with jaws that were no longer their own.
> The meat they ate was splattered with blood; their eyes were bursting
> full of tears, and their laughter sounded like lamentation.
>
> *Odyssey* 20.345–9

Possessed by the giddy madness of the doomed,[12] the suitors embody wisdom literature's tendency to depict the wicked as willingly seeking damnation.[13] In one of the most ironic lines in the *Odyssey*, Eurymachos subsequently accuses Theoklymenos of being mad (ἀφραίνει: 20.360).[14]

The *Odyssey* also presents what should be thought of as a "positive" instance of the motif, when Athena prevents Penelope from perceiving Eurykleia's recognition of Odysseus. As noted in Chapter 3, romance does not permit a premature recognition of Odysseus by Penelope at this point. Consequently, Athena intervenes to induce something like a momentary blindness in Penelope to prevent her from perceiving Eurykleia's recognition of Odysseus (*Od.* 19.478–9).

THE WICKED ARRIVE IN THE UNDERWORLD

Though criticized for a number of reasons,[15] Book 24's portrayal of the suitors' arrival in Hades is nonetheless quite close to several passages in OT

---

[12] Cf. Rutherford (1992: 231): "macabre form of hysteria."
[13] Cf. *Odyssey* 18.406–7, where Telemachos, assuming some god agitates the suitors, notes how they are mad in their feasting.
[14] Cf. West's (2007: 488) quotation of *Mahabhârata* 2.72.8–10: "When the gods deal defeat to a person, they first take his mind away, so that he sees matters wrongly. When destruction is imminent and his mind is beclouded, the wrong course appears as the right one and cannot be dislodged from his heart. When his destruction is near, evil takes on the appearance of good, the good appears as evil."
[15] Starting at least as far back as Aristarchus. See Heubeck (1992: 356) for a brief summary.

myth in its specific combination of traditional motifs. Some elements and details in the depiction of the suitors' descent are prefigured in Theoklymenos' apocalyptic prophecy in Book 20. There he essentially sees them as the ghosts they become in Book 24.[16] His word for them as ghosts, *eidolon* (εἰδώλων: *Od.* 20.355), is the standard term in Homeric epic for the denizens of Hades (*Od.* 11.83, 213, 602). As in Greek and other Near Eastern myth, the OT tradition conceives of the underworld, Sheol, as a city.[17] Like Hades, the OT Sheol has gates (Isa. 38:10), and is inhabited by phantoms (Dahood 1968: 193, on Psalm 73:20).

Like *Odyssey* Book 24, OT myth has depictions of the wicked as they enter Sheol. The key passage, for our purposes, is in Isaiah:

Sheol below was all astir to greet you at your coming. All greet you with these words: "So you too are impotent as we are, and have become like one of us!" Your pride has been brought down to Sheol. (Isaiah 14:9)

Like *Odyssey* 24, Isaiah notes the noise accompanying their arrival,[18] though the former focuses on the suitors' noise in flight, while Isaiah does so on the arrival of the wicked. In both episodes the newly arrived wicked become the focus of attention, and are then directly addressed by those already occupying the infernal regions.

Proverbs offers other episodes that supplete Isaiah's depiction, and parallel the suitors' plight in specific details. The suitors are convinced that Penelope intentionally misled them, and bears direct responsibility for their descent to Hades. Thus when Amphinomos replies to Agamemnon's query about why such a large band of men is arriving simultaneously, he blames Penelope (ἡμῖν φραζομένη θάνατον καὶ κῆρα μέλαιναν: *Od.* 24.127). Proverbs' Lady Stupidity is repeatedly depicted in hospitality settings, leading her guests down to Sheol, much as Amphinomos, albeit mistakenly,[19] believes Penelope has done for the suitors:

> For her house is the way down to death,
> and her course leads to the land of the dead.
> Proverbs 2:18

---

[16] Cf., Rutherford (1992: 233): "The image of ghosts descending to Hades foreshadows the episode which opens Book 24, in which Hermes guides the suitors there."
[17] See Dahood (1968: 194): "Among the numerous texts which depict the realm of the dead as a city with gates (Isa. 38:10; Job 24:12, 38:17; Eccl. 51:9, Matt. 16:18) ... In Canaanite mythology, Death's subterranean domain is termed *qrt*, 'city.'"
[18] Cf. Heubeck (1992: 359), on "The noisy flight of the souls."
[19] Heubeck (1992: 374) "The suitor remains unaware of the real reason for Penelope's indecision, and gives his own interpretation of her behavior (which from his point of view is entirely plausible)."

> Her feet tread the downward path towards death.
> Proverbs 5:5

> He followed her, the simple fool,
> like an ox on its way to be slaughtered.
> Proverbs 7:22

> Her house is the entrance to Sheol,
> leading down to the halls of death.
> Proverbs 7:27

> Little does he know that the dead are there,
> that her guests are in the depths of Sheol.
> Proverbs 9:18

This last passage, though for different narrative purposes, arrives at a similar juxtaposition as the *Odyssey* so forcefully places in Theoklymenos' prophecy (discussed in Chapter 13). While the suitors in their drunkenness, mistakenly think they are courting Penelope, Theoklymenos sees them already in Hades.

CHAPTER 12

Odysseus and Jesus
The king returns, unrecognized and abused in his kingdom

As the hero who thematically triumphs over death, and can bring other mortals back from the underworld, Odysseus shares several traditional motifs with Christ as he is depicted in New Testament myth. Implicit in the episode of the Lotus Eaters, from which island Odysseus successfully brings all his men back alive, though against their will, Odysseus' ability to triumph over death is thematic throughout the *Odyssey*. The escape from Polyphêmos' cave, which suggests a miniature of the underworld, is perhaps the most emphatic instance. Odysseus saves all of his crew who entered the cave with him, except the six the Cyclops ate. On Aiaia, where half the crew had been turned into swine, he saves them by having Kirke restore their proper form. They would have otherwise been slaughtered, possibly eaten, if remaining in their porcine state, shut in pens to be fattened. Odysseus brings all his crew back from Hades (other than Elpenor, who had earlier gone by himself) after consulting Teiresias, a literal return from death.[1] But the ability to triumph over death typifies most ancient heroes, and is thus a somewhat generic parallel between the Homeric Odysseus and Christ. The *Odyssey* depicts Odysseus' triumphs over death as heroic acts, fitting an epic modality, whereas NT myth depicts Christ's triumphs over death less as heroic acts, more as how a god, Dionysus, for instance, would accomplish such acts.

But parallels of a much more specific nature emerge once Odysseus returns to Ithaka, and, under Athena's direction, proceeds to his palace disguised as an old beggar. Christ's approach to Jerusalem, and his treatment therein, as depicted in roughly the last third of each of the synoptic gospels (Mark 11–16; Matt. 21–8; Luke 9:51–24:31 and much of John), employs many of the same motifs as the second half of the *Odyssey*. The particular

---

[1] The Laistrygones episode is the big exception to his being able to save his crew. Here Poseidon's curse is shown absolutely dominant; there is no escape from these giants who have much greater technology than the Cyclopes. At Thrinakia, on the other hand, the crew themselves are to blame for their destruction.

concatenation of motifs can be taken together as a genre of myth: *The king returns, unrecognized and abused in his kingdom.* Parallels between Greek myth and the NT should not be unexpected given the very broad spread and deep influence of Hellenistic culture, and that the authors of the gospels know the Old Testament only in the Greek Septuagint (as demonstrated below).

While the specific motifs are analyzed below, we here note some larger thematic concerns. This mythic genre is less heroic, divergent from typical epic modality. The protagonist associates with the *least* powerful members of his society, not the warriors and kings common to epic. In its focus on the least powerful, often on slaves, this genre of myth offers implicit models of what it regards as the proper acquisition of material goods, inveighing against those who seize others' goods, and how wealth corrupts. This genre of myth subverts what is usually a culture's dominant ethical paradigm, arguing, through repeated examples, that the poor and less powerful can be the more moral members of a society, that the most powerful elements tend to be the most corrupt. Each protagonist is able to penetrate the core of the powerful because they underestimate him, owing to his unassuming, non-heroic appearance.

I would analyze the gospels' *overall* depiction of Christ (as opposed to the specific sections with which we are here concerned) as a broad synthesis of five traditional types of mythical figures extant in ancient myth:

1 The prophet who can perform miracles (Melampous; Elijah and Elishah in OT myth).[2]
2 The prophet who predicts the coming apocalypse (Theoklymenos in the *Odyssey*, and most OT prophets).
3 The healer who can bring mortals back from death (Asclepius in Greek myth).[3]
4 The hero who can bring mortals back from death (Herakles in Greek myth,[4] and Odysseus, as noted above).
5 A god, the son of god, who founds a new religion (Dionysus in Greek myth).

Christ's treatment at the hands of the imperial and religious elites resembles Odysseus' treatment at the hands of the suitors, and Dionysus' treatment at the hands of Pentheus and, to a lesser extent, Cadmus, in the *Bacchae*.

---

[2] Mark repeatedly likens Christ to Elijah (Mark 6:15, 8:28, 9:4, 15:35–6).
[3] There is brief, elliptic mention of Asclepius in the *Alcestis* (*Alc.* 4, 124, 970). For fuller treatment, see Edelstein's (1998) monumental study.
[4] The myth of Lazarus in John 11 is the same genre of myth as the *Alcestis*, with Christ in Herakles' role, Lazarus in Alcestis' and Mary in Admetos'.

Christ's androgynous characteristics also evoke some of Dionysus' defining qualities, as does his turning water into wine as the first sign in John. Though contemporary audiences may regard Dionysus' punishment of Pentheus and Thebes as excessively violent,[5] the gospels' depictions of Christ conclude with similar violence, though set in the future at the Day of Judgment, or Second Coming (discussed in Chapter 13).

There are very different chronologies or sequences, however, in the larger myths of the *Odyssey* and the gospels. Some of these result from the different ages of the respective heroes. Odysseus is a middle-aged man who has spent ten years at war, a further ten years wandering before enduring the suitors' abuse. Christ is a slightly more youthful figure whose previous heroic experiences are limited, chiefly, to the temptation. Odysseus goes to the underworld and triumphs over death *before* he returns to Ithaka, whereas in NT myth Christ undergoes these motifs *after* his abusive treatment in Jerusalem. On Thrinakia Odysseus has already undergone an apocalypse in which his followers were unable to maintain the required discipline, whereas Christ's disciples will fail in Gethsemane, after his return to Jerusalem. As a result of these key differences in sequence, some motifs used of Christ, as analyzed in this chapter, offer closer parallels to what Odysseus undergoes in Books 9–12 than to his experiences after returning to his kingdom of Ithaka. Both myths depict wicked mortals who, by abusing the unrecognized king, provoke divine wraths directed at themselves, resulting in their destruction at the hands of the gods or their agents. But in the gospels the apocalyptic destruction that awaits those who have abused the king is postponed until a future date, the Day of Judgment, or the Second Coming, whereas in the *Odyssey*, as in Genesis 19, Exodus 32, and the *Bacchae*, the destruction comes that day.[6]

As noted in Chapter 9, Odysseus' return to Ithaka presents thematic parallels with the philosopher's return to his society in Plato's *Allegory*. The *Allegory of the Cave* also sheds light on the *Odyssey*'s parallels with Christ's approach to Jerusalem. I repeat Nightingale's analysis, shaped around an observer at a *theoria* (2004: 79):

If the philosopher returns to a bad city and communicates his visions to the people there, Socrates says, they will mock and revile him and perhaps even put him to death: the return and re-entry of the philosophic *theoros* from the foreign realm of the Forms is a potentially dangerous operation.

---

[5] Cf. Dodds (1960: xxv): "The story of Pentheus and Agave is one of a series of cult-legends which describe the punishment of those rash mortals who refused to accept the religion of Dionysus."

[6] Though as noted in Chapter 2, from the perspective of the negative theoxeny initiated in Book 1, the suitors' destruction is postponed to coincide with Odysseus' return.

And again (2004: 131),

> According to Socrates, when the philosophic *theoros* re-enters the social and political realm after a period of contemplation, he runs the risk of mockery and even violence at the hands of his fellow citizens (517a). If he returns to a bad city, he will be scorned and maligned, and his fellow citizens will see him as foolish and possibly even dangerous.

As we note below, Plato employs several of the same motifs that the *Odyssey* uses to depict Odysseus' treatment by the suitors and that the gospels use of Christ's abusive treatment in Jerusalem. In a key difference, Plato lacks a divine agency, though the Forms themselves may serve in a similar capacity.

THE KING'S RETURN HAS LONG BEEN PROPHESIED

In the assembly in Book 2 Halitherses relates how he had prophesied, as Odysseus and the others were leaving for Troy, that Odysseus would return twenty years later, having suffered many evils, all of his companions destroyed (*Od.* 2.171–6). Halitherses suggests a combination of the functions visible in Anchises and John the Baptist. He is an aged hero (*gerôn*: *Od.* 2.157), closely associated with Odysseus (*Od.* 2.253–4), separate from the suitors' contingent (*Od.* 17.68–70), a paternal prophetic figure, something like what Anchises will become in the *Aeneid*, or Scipio the Elder in "Scipio's Dream." His name, "Sea-Bold,"[7] suggests further thematic parallels with Odysseus, a more aged version of the protagonist. Declaring that the destruction of the suitors is their own fault, he later tries to talk their relatives out of storming the palace, predicting their doom if they should (*Od.* 24.451–65).

While in disguise, Odysseus himself also "prophesies" to Eumaios that he will return, and for having done so, asks Eumaios for an *euangelion* (εὐαγγέλιον), a "(reward for) *good news*" (*Od.* 14.152, cf. 14.166). *Euangelion* is the same basic word as that of which "gospel" (originally "good tidings") is the English translation, and from which English "evangelist" and similar derivatives are formed. In the *Odyssey*, as in some respects in the gospels, the good news is *the return of the king to his kingdom*.

While the gospels depict Christ as fulfilling ancient prophecies from OT myth, too numerous to mention, John the Baptist, like Halitherses in the *Odyssey*, prophesies his coming shortly before he does so (Matt. 3:11, Mark

---

[7] Von Kamptz (1982: 88): "auf dem Meere Mut habend." S. West (1988: 142): "Sea-bold."

1:7, Luke 3:16–17). The Baptist plays a larger, and more dramatic role than does Halitherses, with his own death depicted in what might be regarded as an anticipatory echo of Christ's treatment and suffering.

HE IS THE AGENT OF GOD

Once returned to Ithaka, Odysseus executes an agenda explicitly directed by Athena (*Od.* 13.365, 373, 393–411), who, in so doing performs the typical functions of the mentor god. Even earlier Zeus declares his overall support (*Od.* 1.65–79), and prophesies that Odysseus will return to his country and home, and punish the suitors (*Od.* 5.23–4, 30–42). In the gospels Christ explicitly asserts that he has been sent by his Father, and executes his purpose. John 12:49 offers a typical example, "I do not speak on my own behalf, but the Father, having sent me, He gave me the charge, what I should say and what I should speak."[8] The gospels also repeat this theme after the resurrection by having (an) angel(s) appear to Christ's followers to reveal what has happened (Matt. 28:2–3, Mark 16:5, Luke 24:4). In Mark the angel's form as a white-robed young man is particularly close to Athena's appearance to Odysseus in Book 13 (Mark 16:5: νεανίσκον: cf. Athena, νέῳ: *Od.* 13.222). Matthew instead has an angel of the Lord descend from heaven (Matt. 28:2 ἄγγελος γὰρ Κυρίου καταβὰς ἐξ οὐρανοῦ), like a star, in a cloak white as snow, while Luke has two "men" in lightning-flashing garments (Luke 24:4: ἄνδρες δύο ἐπέστησαν αὐταῖς ἐν ἐσθῆτι ἀστραπτούσῃ).

HE IS ASSOCIATED WITH LIGHT

Chapter 11 briefly notes the passages associating Odysseus with light, and with providing it to others (*Od.* 18.317, 354–5; 19.33–40). The *Odyssey* also implies Odysseus' association with light in the events on Thrinakia. Since Homeric epic equates seeing the sun with being alive (*Od.* 4.540, 8.33, 9.498, 11.93, 13.44, 20.207; *Il.* 18.61, 442), Odysseus is to some extent identified with the sun when he survives the ordeal on Helios' island. By not offending the god of the Sun, he remains alive; in offending Helios, the crew implicitly choose death, and a descent to the darkness of Hades, over life. In the gospels, John repeatedly connects Christ with light and with providing it to others (John 1:4–9, 3:19, 8:12, 9:5, 12:35–6, 46). Implicitly, when Christ restores vision to a blind man, he leads him to the light (Matt. 9:27–31,

---

[8] Cf. John 5:37, 8:16, 8:18, 14:24, 20:21; Matt. 28:18; Luke 22:29.

11:5; Mark 8:22–6; John 9:1–40). Given their very different valences, the heroic *Odyssey*, and the miracle and prophecy-centered gospels, Christ's miraculous restoration of eyesight is a functional equivalent to Odysseus being the only survivor of the ordeal on Thrinakia. As noted in Chapter 11, Odysseus' association with light prefigures aspects of Plato's *Allegory* and the theory of ideas. One passage in John is suggestive of Plato's *Allegory of the Cave*, "but the people preferred the darkness to the light" (John 3:19: καὶ ἠγάπησαν οἱ ἄνθρωποι μᾶλλον τὸ σκότος ἢ τὸ φῶς).

HE ATTRACTS A BAND OF LOYAL FOLLOWERS

Directed by Athena (*Od.* 13.404–11), Odysseus goes first to the hut of the swineherd, Eumaios, the first loyal follower he meets with on Ithaka. Here the process is only initiated: Eumaios develops a bond with his mysterious guest, but does not complete his transformation into a follower of Odysseus until the hero later reveals himself (*Od.* 21.188–227). Having directed the returning Telemachos to go first to Eumaios' (*Od.* 15.38–40), Athena also helps Odysseus add his most important follower, his son, also at Eumaios' hut (*Od.* 16.156–219). Eurykleia and Philoitios swell the band to five. The gospels likewise depict Christ in the act of acquiring his disciples, an initial encounter when he comes upon the first few (Matt. 4:18–22; Mark 1:16–20, 3:13–19; Luke 5:1–11), and subsequent episodes until he has gathered twelve.

In both myths the band of followers is largely composed of laborers of low economic status. In the gospels this is explicit in the first two followers, Simon and Andrew, who thus broadly parallel Odysseus' followers Eumaios, Philoitios, and Eurykleia (Matt. 4:18–22; Mark 1:16–20, 3:13–19; Luke 5:1–11, 6:12–19; John 1:40–42). The gospel of Luke lays particular stress on Christ's association with the poor,[9] beginning even with its version of the nativity narrative, in which Mary praises Christ because "He has filled the hungry with good things, and sent the rich away empty" (Luke 1:53). When he first returns to the synagogue at Nazareth after the Temptation, he reads aloud a passage from Isaiah, "He anointed me to bring good news to the poor" (Luke 4:18: ἔχρισέν με εὐαγγελίσασθαι πτωχοῖς), proclaiming that today the prophecy has become true. The word Christ uses for the poor is *ptôkhos*, the same word the *Odyssey* uses of Odysseus in his beggar guise (*Od.* 16.209, 16.273, 17.202, 17.337). In a sermon to his disciples Christ proclaims, "Blessed are the poor, because yours is the kingdom of God"

---

[9] See Fitzmyer (1981: 248–51, 532) on attention to the poor in Luke.

(Luke 6:20: Μακάριοι οἱ πτωχοί, ὅτι ὑμετέρα ἐστὶν ἡ βασιλεία τοῦ Θεοῦ). The sentiment shares considerable common ground with Eumaios' declaration to Odysseus, while in his *ptôkhos* disguise:

> Stranger (ξεῖν'), it is not right to dishonor a guest (ξεῖνον), not even if one
> poorer than you were to come, for from Zeus are all
> the strangers (ξεῖνοί) and beggars (πτωχοί).
>
> *Odyssey* 14.56–8

Christ's tale of Lazarus who is a πτωχός (Luke 16:20), concludes with the poor man dying, then carried by angels to Abraham (Luke 16:22: ἐγένετο δὲ ἀποθανεῖν τὸν πτωχόν, καὶ ἀπενεχθῆναι αὐτὸν ὑπὸ τῶν ἀγγέλων εἰς τὸν κόλπον Ἀβραάμ).[10]

In both myths the followers are not fully aware that he is the king, or that he fulfills a divine agenda. In the *Odyssey* only Telemachos knows Odysseus' status in Books 16–18, after which Eurykleia is added to the inner circle, in Book 19.

THE TRANSFIGURATION: THE KING BRIEFLY APPEARS IN HIS TRUE FORM TO HIS CLOSEST FOLLOWER(S)

After having directed Odysseus and Telemachos separately to Eumaios' hut, Athena arranges a dramatic reunion of father and son (*Od.* 16.156–219). One of the many recognition scenes in the second half of the *Odyssey* (as analyzed in Chapter 3), the episode depends not on a recognition token, such as a scar, but on Odysseus' sudden metamorphosis away from seeming beggar to his true form. His sudden visual transformation is a simpler version of the *Transfiguration* in the gospels, for which, *mutatis mutandis*, there is a homology between the principal characters and the functions they perform: the king: Odysseus and Christ; the supernatural beings that accompany him: Athena on the one hand, Moses, Elijah, and god's voice in the cloud on the other; his followers who witness the event: Telemachos (and Eumaios' hounds), Peter and other disciples.

Part of the king's true identity and status are shown in his personal relationship with supernatural beings that do not associate with the other characters. Athena is Odysseus' mentor throughout the *Odyssey* (other than in Books 9–12), personally appearing to him on several occasions (*Od.* 7.18–28, 13.221–439, 16.157–76, 22.205–40), as well as mentoring Telemachos in

---

[10] Further Lucan passages focusing on the poor: 7:22: πτωχοὶ εὐαγγελίζονται; 14:13: ἀλλ' ὅταν δοχὴν ποιῇς, κάλει πτωχούς; 14:21: τοὺς πτωχοὺς ... εἰσάγαγε ὧδε; 18:22: πάντα ὅσα ἔχεις πώλησον καὶ διάδος πτωχοῖς; 21:3: ἡ χήρα αὕτη ἡ πτωχὴ πλεῖον πάντων ἔβαλεν.

Books 1–3, and 15. She approaches, once Eumaios has left, in the form of a woman knowing splendid crafts (*Od.* 16.157–8). Telemachos does not perceive her, only Odysseus and Eumaios' dogs. When she draws nears, Eumaios' hounds register her approach and status by giving way, "with a whimper they cowered to the other side of the hut" (κνυζηθμῷ δ' ἑτέρωσε διὰ σταθμοῖο φόβηθεν: *Od.* 16.163).[11] When he has seen the transformed Odysseus Telemachos reacts with a sense of awe, "His own son was amazed at him, and frightened, cast his glance away lest he was a god" (*Od.* 16.178–9: θάμβησε δέ μιν φίλος υἱός, ταρβήσας δ' ἑτέρωσε βάλ' ὄμματα, μὴ θεὸς εἴη). In the gospels' *Transfiguration* scene, Moses and Elijah are suddenly visible, conversing with Christ, and then the voice of god speaks from a cloud (Matt. 17:5, Mark 9:7, Luke 9:34–5). Peter and the other disciples cower when they see Christ in such company (Luke 9:34: ἐφοβήθησαν δὲ ἐν τῷ εἰσελθεῖν αὐτοὺς εἰς τὴν νεφέλην; Matt. 17:6: καὶ ἀκούσαντες οἱ μαθηταὶ ἔπεσαν ἐπὶ πρόσωπον αὐτῶν καὶ ἐφοβήθησαν σφόδρα; Mark 9:6: ἔκφοβοι γὰρ ἐγένοντο).

In both myths a marked change of clothing is key to designating the king's transformation. Athena, striking Odysseus with a golden wand (as when she disfigured his form at *Od.* 13.429; cf. Judg. 6:21, where an angel makes fire spring out from his wand), first places a tunic and a well-washed cloak (in place of the rags he was wearing) around his chest (*Od.* 16.173–4). Telemachos notes that his clothes are now quite different (*Od.* 16.182: ἄλλα δὲ εἵματ' ἔχεις). The gospels underscore the dazzling whiteness of Christ's garments in his scene, "his clothes became as white as light" (Matt. 17:2: τὰ δὲ ἱμάτια αὐτοῦ ἐγένετο λευκὰ ὡς τὸ φῶς); "his clothes became an exceedingly gleaming white, such as no bleacher on earth could whiten as much" (Mark 9:3: καὶ τὰ ἱμάτια αὐτοῦ ἐγένετο στίλβοντα λευκὰ λίαν οἷα γναφεὺς ἐπὶ τῆς γῆς οὐ δύναται οὕτως λευκᾶναι); "and his white clothing was flashing lightning" (Luke 9:29: καὶ ὁ ἱματισμὸς αὐτοῦ λευκὸς ἐξαστράπτων). Mark's mention of a hypothetical bleacher having treated Christ's robe (Mark 9:3) is close to the *Odyssey*'s specific detail that Athena places a well-washed (ἐϋπλυνές: *Od.* 16.173) robe around Odysseus.

Both myths also highlight a change in the king's bodily form. After altering his clothing, Athena increases Odysseus' stature and youthfulness (*Od.* 16.174: δέμας δ' ὤφελλε καὶ ἥβην), darkens his skin color (*Od.* 16.175: ἂψ δὲ μελαγχροιὴς γένετο), and turns his beard from gray to black (*Od.* 16.176: κυάνεαι δ' ἐγένοντο γενειάδες ἀμφὶ γένειον). Telemachos' reaction sums up the overall effect:

---

[11] A thematic parallel to Argos being the only character to recognize Odysseus (*Od.* 17.290–327).

> Stranger, you appear different to me, younger than before,
> you have different garments, and your body is not the same,
> truly, you are some god.
>
> *Odyssey* 16.181–3

Though the gospels do not depict Christ undergoing as distinct a bodily transformation as Odysseus undergoes, from old man to young, they use the verb *metamorphoô* to describe his transformation (Matt. 17:1 = Mark 9:2: μετεμορφώθη ἔμπροσθεν αὐτῶν). In Matthew his face now shines like the sun (Matt. 17:2: καὶ ἔλαμψεν τὸ πρόσωπον αὐτοῦ ὡς ὁ ἥλιος). Both kings give off a heavenly aura to their followers, as Drury notes of Christ (1987: 411): "At the Transfiguration Jesus' garments radiate heavenly light." In each myth the transfiguration is dramatic because the king's true form remains a secret identity.[12]

HIS KINGDOM IS UNDER THE CONTROL OF HIS ENEMIES, WHO THREATEN AND INTIMIDATE HIS FOLLOWERS

For several years the suitors and their agents, such as Melanthios, have been having their way in the palace, taking their meals there each day, giving orders to the staff, having sex with the female servants (*Od.* 1.245–51, 2.50–79, 3.205–7, 4.318–21, 17.532–40, 18.220–4, 325, 20.7–12). Their manipulation of the assembly in Book 2 suggests they also exercise considerable power over the rest of Ithaka. Though the assembly opens with Telemachos receiving some support, the suitors easily thwart his every move. In *proto* blame-the-victim fashion, they deny they are at fault, asserting Penelope is entirely to blame, that she leads them all on (*Od.* 2.91–2), then stalls, putting off the inevitable wedding through her ruse of the funeral shroud for Laertes (*Od.* 2.93–110). They declare they will leave the palace (and stop devouring his possessions) when she marries one of them (*Od.* 2.110–28). In Antinoös' forceful, but sophistic, presentation, Penelope is held responsible for *their* conduct. When a dissenting voice is raised, Halitherses' augury predicting Odysseus' return and their destruction, Eurymachos ridicules his powers of augury (*Od.* 2.178–84), and threatens him (*Od.* 2.187–93). Through this example the suitors intimidate opposition and dominate the assembly. Later Eumaios makes a similar target for the suitors, first Melanthios (*Od.* 17.215–32), then the suitors themselves, as they threaten to give

---

[12] On this aspect of the gospels' handling of the *Transfiguration*, see again Drury (1987: 409): "Jesus' secret identity is displayed and bound into his coming sufferings."

his body to his own dogs to feed on when he attempts to hand the bow to the disguised Odysseus (*Od.* 21.360–7).

In the gospels two groups hold sway over different aspects of the kingdom, religious officials, with whom Christ comes into frequent contact, and the Roman Empire, whose agents exercise increasing power over him as he approaches Jerusalem. As the founder of a new religion, Christ represents a considerable threat to the pre-existing religions, somewhat as Dionysus does to Pentheus, king of Thebes, and embodiment of its more traditional religious practices in the *Bacchae* (e.g., *Bacch.* 272–4, 516–17). Perhaps four distinct subgroups of religious officials may be identified, the chief priests, the scribes, the Pharisees, and the Sadducees, each of which repeatedly attempts to ensnare him. These groups also abuse argument, somewhat as the suitors in the assembly, in trying to catch Christ in a fine point of theology. The Pharisees complain that everyone is starting to follow Christ (John 12:19), somewhat as Odysseus gradually gains a foothold in the palace, winning over Eumaios and Penelope, defeating Iros, and causing fissures between the suitors (as at *Od.* 17.460–88). More would follow Christ but fear reprisals from the Pharisees if they did (John 12:42), paralleling the suitors' use of intimidation in the Book 2 assembly. Judas is on close terms with the chief priests (Mark 14:3, Matt. 26:14–15). From the perspective of *Odyssey* Books 14–24, Judas suggests a combination of Melanthios and Eurymachos. Like the suitors with Telemachos, the chief priests plot to do away with Christ. In John they want to do away with Lazarus as well (John 12:9–11). Drury sums up the religious opposition (1987: 412), "The chief priests are wicked, the Pharisees and scribes hostile and wrong, the Sadducees just wrong." The Roman Empire, through Pontius Pilate and others, exercises the power of life and death over Christ, though depicted as acting under the influence of the religious opposition. The gospels do, however, offer positive counter-examples in the Roman centurion (Matt. 8:5–13; Luke 7:1–10), and the centurion at the cross (Mark 15:39). In both myths the powerful opponents are unable to recognize the king in their midst.

HIS ENEMIES APPROPRIATE OTHERS' MONEY AND PROPERTY FOR THEMSELVES

The *Odyssey* thematically depicts the suitors devouring Odysseus' estate without payment or requital (*Od.* 1.160, 1.377 = 2.141, 14.377, 14.417, 18.280; cf. 1.250–1, 2.55–79, 21.331–3, 22.36). They treat Odysseus' property and possessions as if their own. Much of what the gospels suggest about the acquisition of material goods resembles the *Odyssey*'s depiction of Ithaka under the suitors' control, in which characters such as Eumaios, Eurykleia, and Philoitios display their honesty and morality, but the well-to-do suitors demonstrate corruption and immorality. The gospels depict Christ having greater empathy with the poor than with the wealthy, as in the episode of the poor widow (Luke 21:1–4). After wealthy people make offerings to the treasury, Christ observes a poor widow contributing two brass coins, and declares she has given more than everyone else. The gospels particularly associate Christ's religious opponents with having an excessive, improper focus on money. Luke characterizes the Pharisees in general as "money-loving" (Luke 16:14: Φαρισαῖοι φιλάργυροι). Judas, who is associated with the high priests, is depicted pilfering money from the common purse (John 12:4–6).

Perhaps the central episode for the gospels' depiction of the financial corruption of Christ's enemies, in a way that parallels how the *Odyssey* figures the suitors' greed and appropriation of others' goods, is the Cleansing of the Temple (Matt. 21:12–17; Mark 11:15–19; Luke 19:45–8; John 2:14–16). Entering the Temple, Christ instantly disrupts all those engaging in various financial activities, throwing the buyers and sellers out of the temple (πωλοῦντας, ἀγοράζοντας), overturning the tables of the money-changers (κολλυβιστῶν). The synoptic gospels all use an expression which alludes to Jeremiah 7:11, when Christ declares, as it is written, that they have made his house into a "cave of thieves," σπήλαιον λῃστῶν (Matt. 21:13; Mark 11:17; Luke 19:46). In Greek myth a cave often has an underworld association – Polyphêmos' cave (cf. Plato's *Allegory*, as we have noted more than once) – and in the OT also has associations with a place of the dead (σπήλαιον is a family cemetery in the Septuagint at Gen. 23:9, 49:29). Christ's triumph over his enemies by foiling their financial corruption in a place that has underworld associations foreshadows his own triumph over death, but also suggests another parallel with the *Odyssey*. In Theoklymenos' prophecy (*Od.* 20.347–70), he sees the suitors as if already in Hades. In a sense they have turned the palace into an underworld through their various behaviors, somewhat as the crew choose death over life on Thrinakia. The day before the suitors' final day, Penelope tricks them into giving her gifts so valuable that they compensate for their years of depredations (*Od.* 18.274–303). Her luring them into giving her costly gifts is thus thematically similar to Christ expelling the buyers and sellers and upsetting the tables of the money-changers. In both myths, then, the king, or his agent, effects a reversal of the enemies' unjust appropriation of others' wealth. Christ's triumph foreshadows

Odysseus and Jesus

his eventual triumph over death, and his enemies' association with the underworld.

A FEMALE FOLLOWER ANOINTS HIM WITH OIL

In both myths a female follower anoints the king shortly before events reach a crisis.[13] In the *Odyssey*, Eurykleia gives Odysseus a bath (*Od.* 19.363–91) as the last stage of the hospitality Penelope has earlier granted him (*Od.* 19.318–23). Reece notes the transformative quality of this bath (1993: 34),

> The transformative function of the bath is a key to the theme of disguise and recognition in the *Odyssey*. Often the guest rises from the bath with an enhanced appearance, sometimes "looking like a god"... causing those who see him to "marvel"... His eventual restoration as master of the house is symbolically realized later through the transformative function of a proper bath (23.153–64).

During the bath Eurykleia recognizes her long-lost king (*Od.* 19.467–75). Moments after recognizing Odysseus, Eurykleia anoints him with oil (19.505: ἤλειψεν λίπ' ἐλαίῳ).[14] Originally, however, Penelope had said the anointing (*Od.* 19.320: χρῖσαι) was to be the next morning, so the stranger could then dine with Telemachos. Did Eurykleia move the anointing up as a result of having recognized Odysseus?

In OT myth a prophet anoints the king, pouring oil on his head, in a ceremony that cements his status as king of Israel. Five passages depict David so anointed as king (2 Sam. 2:4, 2:7, 5:3, 5:17, 12:7; cf. 1 Sam. 16:12, 13). Saul is anointed as first king of Israel (1 Sam. 9:16, 10:1, 15:1, 15:17, 16:3; cf. Absalom, at 2 Sam. 19:10, and Solomon, at 1 Kgs. 1:34, 1:39, 1:45, 5:1). The gospels all include scenes of Christ being anointed, but with significant differences. All five such episodes occur in social contexts, at feasts, bringing them close to the connection with hospitality that underlies Eurykleia's anointing of Odysseus.[15] Because of the connection between the epithet "Christ" and the act of anointing (discussed below), all such episodes also draw on or allude to the OT episodes of the anointing of the king, but with a difference. Christ is recognized as a king in a figurative sense, of the common people, rather than of a powerful government.

---

[13] MacDonald (2000: 111–19) pursues tenuous parallels between Eurykleia's bathing and anointing of Odysseus and three episodes in Mark, but does not comment on the episode in Luke.

[14] Eurynome, who functions as a doublet of Eurykleia,, also anoints Odysseus before he meets with Penelope for their climactic recognition scene (*Od.* 23.154: Εὐρυνόμη ταμίη λοῦσεν καὶ χρῖσεν ἐλαίῳ).

[15] Cf. Suggs (1992) on Matt. 26:7, "*Pour*: an act of social courtesy."

In the gospels it is not a prophet who anoints him, but, as with Eurykleia and Odysseus, a woman. She anoints Christ not with oil, as in the Homeric and OT instances, but with perfume. In Matthew and Mark an unnamed woman anoints Christ with myrrh at a feast two days before Passover (Matt. 26:7; Mark 14:3: τὴν ἀλάβαστρον κατέχεεν αὐτοῦ τῆς κεφαλῆς).[16] In Luke, while Christ has dinner with Simon the Pharisee, another unnamed woman anoints his feet with perfume (Luke 7:36–50). In John, Lazarus' sister, Mary, anoints Christ's feet with a costly perfume; then wipes them with her hair (John 11:2, 12:1–8). In all four episodes observers of the incident complain (unnamed disciples in Matthew, anonymous guests in Mark, a Pharisee in Luke, and Judas in John) that the perfume was so costly, it would have been better to have sold it and given the proceeds to the poor.

Though the episode in Luke occurs much earlier in Christ's myth than in the others, it shares a number of parallels with Odysseus' scene with Eurykleia in Book 19. Christ having dinner with a Pharisee resembles the tension present with Odysseus being in the company of the suitors. The unnamed woman who anoints Christ is explicitly a "sinner" (ἁμαρτωλός), in some respects thus approximating Eurykleia's servant status. Simon the Pharisee criticizes him for letting himself be anointed by such a woman. Christ replies that the woman has offered him those aspects of hospitality Simon himself had failed to offer – water to wash his feet, a kiss, and an anointing (Luke 7:44–6) – rather like the disguised Odysseus' rebukes of Antinoös, and Eurymachos. As does Eurykleia with Odysseus (*Od.* 19.361–2, 471–2), the woman cries while anointing Christ (Luke 7:38).

Jesus' epithet "Christ" comes from the past participle of the Greek verb used for anointing the king, *khristos*, *khriô* (χρίω), underscoring the thematic importance of the anointing episodes. Five passages suggest etymological wordplays on his epithet and the verb from which it derives. Two such passages allude to OT readings, Luke 4:18, which quotes Isaiah 61:1–2, and Hebrews 1:9, which quotes Psalms 45:6–7. Both quotes are identical to the passages in the Septuagint because the NT writers read the OT in Greek, not Hebrew.[17] The passage in Luke, explaining why god anointed his son, reiterates the gospels' concerns with the acquisition of material goods, "He has anointed me to give good news to the poor" (Luke 4:18: ἔχρισέν με εὐαγγελίσασθαι πτωχοῖς). Since "me" in a NT context

---

[16] Cf. the Homeric formula: κατέχευε χάριν κεφαλῇ τε καὶ ὤμοις (*Od.* 6.235, 8.19).
[17] Cf. Stroumsa (2003: 161).

now designates Christ, "has anointed", *ekhrisen*, echoes his epithet, and forms a wordplay. The passage in Hebrews gives the reason for god having anointed Christ as being that he loves justice and hates lawlessness: "because of this your God has anointed you" (Heb. 1:9: διὰ τοῦτο ἔχρισέν σε ὁ Θεός, ὁ Θεός σου). Two passages in Acts contain additional wordplays, "whom you anointed" (Acts 4:27: ὃν ἔχρισας), and "you know... Jesus the one from Nazareth, how God anointed him" (Acts 10:37–8: οἴδατε... Ἰησοῦν τὸν ἀπὸ Ναζαρέθ, ὡς ἔχρισεν αὐτὸν ὁ Θεός). In this last passage the name "Jesus" is pronounced in close proximity to the verb from which "Christ" derives. Since Acts is written by the same author as Luke, the three wordplays suggest a stylistic tendency on his part. But a passage in 2 Corinthians offers the most explicit etymological wordplay on Jesus' epithet "Christ," "and God has anointed us into Christ" (2 Cor. 1:21: εἰς Χριστὸν καὶ χρίσας ἡμᾶς Θεός).[18] The *Odyssey* uses the same verb, *khriô*, of Odysseus being anointed by Kirke, Eurykleia, and Eurynome (*Od.* 10.364: ἔχρισεν, 19.320: χρῖσαι, 23.154: χρῖσεν).[19]

HE PREDICTS A COMING APOCALYPSE

In both myths, the king serves as an instrument of god to punish those who have provoked a divine wrath through their offensive acts. Consequently, in both myths he warns others of the coming apocalypse. Though the *Odyssey* has, in Theoklymenos, a separate figure of the prophet who articulates the climactic prophecy of the coming apocalypse (*Od.* 20.345–71), Odysseus himself does so earlier, if less explicitly, through his *exempla* to the suitors. Separately to Antinoös (*Od.* 17.415–44), to Amphinomos (*Od.* 18.125–50), and to Melantho (*Od.* 19.75–88), the disguised Odysseus gives implicit warnings of divine dispensation coming for the suitors should they continue to act as they do. Christ prophesies the destruction of the Temple, subsequent wars, suffering, earthquakes, and the Second Coming (Matt. 24, Mark 13, Luke 21). He also prophesies signs in the heavens that will mark the Second Coming, "the sun will be darkened, and the moon will not give forth its light, and the stars will fall down from heaven" (ὁ ἥλιος σκοτισθήσεται, καὶ ἡ σελήνη οὐ δώσει τὸ φέγγος αὐτῆς, καὶ οἱ ἀστέρες πεσοῦνται ἀπὸ τοῦ οὐρανοῦ: Matt. 24:29; cf. Mark 13:24–5, Luke 21:25). The signs are traditional, extant not only in OT myth (Amos 8:9, Joel 2:10,

---

[18] See Louden (1995: 34–41), on puns on the name Odysseus in the *Odyssey*.
[19] Since NT Greek has several other verbs also used for anoint (ἀλείφω, μυρίζω; cf. καταχέω), the passages here discussed seem to be deliberate wordplays in their use of χρίω.

31; cf. Isa. 13:10), but close to Theoklymenos' prophecy of the apocalypse that awaits the suitors, "the sun has vanished from heaven, and a foul mist has spread over" (*Od.* 20.356–7).

Perhaps most intriguing of Christ's prophecies of the coming apocalypse, for its thematic parallels with the *Odyssey*, is the parable of the vineyard owner (Matt. 21:33–46, Mark 12:1–12, Luke 20:9–19).[20] I summarize the three versions as follows:[21]

> A man plants a vineyard, then leases it out to winegrowers. After a certain time he sends servant(s) to receive part of the fruits, only to have the lessees beat, stone or kill him/them. He sends another servant or group, with the same result. He sends his beloved son, and they cast him out and slay him. Now he will destroy the winegrowers, and give the vineyard to others. The son, the stone the builders rejected, is now the cornerstone.[22]

While commentators have sometimes sought a specific reading in which the vineyard is Israel and the story figures Christianity separating from Judaism (see Mann 1986: 460), the parable/allegory works on more than one level. The tale's basic elements are those that comprise, in our terms, a contained apocalypse, a band of mortals performing acts offensive to god, prompting a divine wrath that destroys them. The winegrowers have more than a little in common with the suitors, who, in their conspiracy to murder Telemachos, also plot to kill the son. Though on its own terms the parable is a contained apocalypse, it also points to the full-scale apocalypse that is the Second Coming, since the detail of the son having been cast out to be slain, as given at Matt. 21:39, clearly alludes to Christ's death (Albright and Mann 1971: 264). All three versions depict god destroying the winegrowers with the same form of the verb Hesiod uses for the impending apocalyptic destruction of the iron age "and Zeus will destroy (ὀλέσει) this race" (*Works and Days* 180; cf. ἀπολέσει αὐτούς: Matt. 21:41; ἀπολέσει τοὺς γεωργούς: Mark 12:9; ἀπολέσει τοὺς γεωργοὺς τούτους: Luke 20:16). Drury notes Matthew's tendency to intend his parables to have a broad application (1987: 432), "Matthew, still using historical allegory, more often makes the 'elsewhere' to which they [the parables] refer into the day of doom at the end of time."

---

[20] The Gospel of Thomas contains a fourth version of the parable. See Mann (1986: 458–67) on its resemblance to the versions in the synoptics.
[21] Partly based on Mann's summary (1986: 459).
[22] Albright and Mann note (1971: 265) that the last sentence is a quote from the Septuagint version of Psalm 118:22–3.

HIS ENEMIES ACCUSE HIM OF BEING MAD

Because he represents such a threat through his forthright speech, and because they fail to discern his true identity, the king's enemies perceive him as mad. In the *Odyssey* this again applies to both Odysseus and Theoklymenos. When Odysseus tells the maids to tend to Penelope since he will provide the light in the palace, Melantho accuses him of being crazy, "you have been driven out of your mind " (φρένας ἐκπεπαταγμένος ἐσσί: *Od.* 18.327). She assumes excessive drinking is the likely explanation for such seemingly irrational behavior (*Od.* 18.331), as members of the suitors' party do repeatedly of Odysseus' interactions with them. The next day, when Theoklymenos prophesies the suitors' apocalyptic destruction, Eurymachos declares he is mad, "the stranger is out of his mind" (ἀφραίνει ξεῖνος: *Od.* 20.360). A nameless suitor then ridicules his prophecy (*Od.* 20.380), and mockingly threatens to sell all such guests/strangers into slavery (perhaps a virtual negative theoxeny).

Because they are aware that Christ can cast out demons (an anticipatory echo of coming victory over all his opponents), the scribes, a specific subset of his religious opposition, think he is possessed by Beelzebul (Βεελζεβοὺλ ἔχει: Mark 3:22). By virtue of the worldview to which NT authors subscribe, demonic possession constitutes madness, as generally denoted by the verb, δαιμονίζομαι (Mark 5:18, Luke 8:36, John 10:21). In his enemies' view Christ's ability to cast out demons suggests he does so in Beelzebul's name (cf. Matt. 12:24; Luke 11:15; John 7:20, 8:48–9, 8:52, 10:20). In the gospels, attributing demonic possession to the king is thus a rough equivalent to members of the suitors' party attributing excessive consumption of alcohol to Odysseus.

HIS ENEMIES PREFER A PARODIC DOUBLET OF THE KING (IROS AND BARABBAS)

The suitors already tolerate a beggar among them, Iros, who runs various errands. His real name is Arnaios (*Od.* 18.5), Iros being a nickname or ironic epithet because he serves as their messenger. As with many proper names in the *Odyssey*, Arnaios appears to have a clear derivation and literal meaning, as Russo (1992: 47) notes, "'Getter', from ἄρνυμαι, 'to acquire.'" While Russo (1992: 47) interprets the name's meaning as applying to his acts as a beggar, and de Jong (2001: 437–8) that he instantiates the suitors' chief qualities, in other respects he suggests a parodic doublet of Odysseus. If the derivation of Arnaios from *arnumai* is correct, we note that the verb's only instance in the *Odyssey* is used of Odysseus, set prominently in the proem (*Od.* 1.5). Iros has an insatiable belly (de Jong 2001: 438), but so does Odysseus, as he repeatedly claims (*Od.* 7.216–21, 15.344–5, 17.286–9, 470–4). Further linking Odysseus, Iros, and belly is the sausage, literally "bellies of goats" (γαστέρες αἵδ' αἰγῶν: *Od.* 18.44–7), which Antinoös declares will be the victor's prize in the contest between them. A simile will shortly compare Odysseus to a sausage being cooked (*Od.* 20.25–30, discussed below under: *The king is full of anxiety the night before the climactic events*; see Russo 1992: 50, on the link). As Odysseus defeats Antinoös, the suitors die of laughter (γέλῳ ἔκθανον: *Od.* 18.100), adding to the episode's burlesque feel (cf. de Jong 2001: 437), but also looking ahead to their mad laughter (*Od.* 20.347: γναθμοῖσι γελώων ἀλλοτρίοισιν) before Theoklymenos' apocalyptic prophecy. Cementing Iros' function as his doublet, Odysseus replaces him, in effect, once he is victorious, and becomes an accepted presence in the palace.

The Barabbas episode, present in all four gospels (Matt. 27:16–26, Mark 15:6–15, Luke 23:18–25, John 18:40), is problematic in a number of respects.[23] As with Iros, "Barabbas" is an epithet, not a proper name (Mann 1986: 637). At Matt. 27:16 and Mark 15:7 the participle *legomenos* precedes "Barabbas," as it normally does a nickname or epithet, as Mann notes (Matt. 27:17: Ἰησοῦν τὸν λεγόμενον Χριστόν). Literally *bar abba* is "son of the father" in Aramaic (Mann 1986: 637). Mann (*ibid.*) goes on to note a further peculiarity:

In Matt. 27:16, 17 there are in two groups of manuscripts two readings: *Iêsoun Barabban* and *Iêsoun ton Barabban* = "Jesus Bar-abbas"... we may reasonably conjecture that originally some form of "Jesus Bar-abbas" was found in both gospels [Matt. and Mark].

That is, Barabbas' actual name, according to the groups of mss. Mann cites, was Jesus (cf. Fitzmyer 1985: 1490). Some commentators, as a consequence, think the episode is a later addition arising from confusion over the name, as R. Brown notes (1970: 856):

Others have thought of Barabbas as a fictional creation. Riggs *JBL* 64 (1945): 417–56 thinks that originally Jesus Barabbas ("Son of the Father") was another designation of Jesus the Messiah and that the two names express the religious and political charges against Jesus.

---

[23] R. Brown (1970: 870–1) summarizes the similarities and differences in how the four gospels depict the incident.

Odysseus and Jesus

The depiction of the custom *privilegium paschale*, that a prisoner would be freed during the Passover, has also attracted a wide variety of criticisms.

As it stands, the episode is one of the most ironic in the gospels (Fitzmyer 1985: 1489, R. Brown 1970: 872): Barabbas, the crowd's favorite, but a notorious prisoner (Matt. 27:16), or insurrectionist (Mark 15:7: μετὰ τῶν στασιαστῶν), "defeats" Christ. Pilate adjudicates the dispute somewhat as Antinoös acts as umpire between Odysseus and Iros. In Mark the chief priests incite the crowd, a thematic parallel for the suitors' easy manipulation of the assembly in Book 2. Albright and Mann (1971: 345) note the mob psychology that prevails in the episode, "we are dealing here not with the studied calm of a dispassionate legal examination, but with a mob scene outside the crowded city of Jerusalem at Passover." This again suggests not only parallels with the suitors in the assembly, but their victimization by Athena before Theoklymenos prophesies their destruction. As with Odysseus and Iros, one ends up substituting for, or replacing the other, though with the opposite outcome: Barabbas is freed. The abuse now directed at Christ resembles that which the suitors direct at Iros after Odysseus defeats him (*Od.* 18.114–16).

THEY MOCK, JEER AT, AND STRIKE THE KING

Odysseus, dressed in rags, in his own kingdom, seemingly a nameless wanderer, is contrary to the traditional behavior of an epic hero. As commentators note, one cannot imagine Akhilleus willingly enduring the abuse that Odysseus receives from the suitors and their agent, Melanthios. But Athena herself directs him to proceed in just such a fashion (*Od.* 13.306–10), specifying that "he is to suffer many pains in silence" (πάσχειν ἄλγεα πολλά: 13.310).[24] Odysseus' first such encounter is the run-in with Melanthios on the way to the palace, a miniature of what he later experiences from the suitors themselves. Unprovoked, Melanthios insults Eumaios and the disguised Odysseus, then strikes the king, kicking him as he passes (*Od.* 17.233–4). In Chapter 11 we noted forms of verbal abuse that Antinoös, Eurymachos, Ktesippos, and Melantho all hurl at Odysseus, the first three of whom also strike or attempt to strike him (*Od.* 17.462–3, 18.394–8, 20.299–301).

Christ not only endures similar forms of abuse, but the same basic phrase is used to predict that he will undergo such suffering, "to suffer

---

[24] Cf. Lowe (2000: 153–4): "Odysseus will have silently to endure abuse in his own palace ... he will be disguised"; (p. 155): "Outrage upon outrage is heaped on Odysseus by his enemies, with retaliation postponed."

many things," πολλὰ παθεῖν, *polla pathein* (Matt. 16:21, Mark 8:31, Luke 9:22). It is worth emphasizing that there are no OT precedents for the phrase, as commentators have pointed out,[25] whereas *Od.* 13.310 employs a very similar phrase. There are further specific parallels in who pronounces the phrase and when it is articulated. In both myths the phrase is uttered as a prophecy, by the goddess Athena in the *Odyssey*, by Christ himself in the gospels, before the king undergoes such abuses.

The abuse Christ encounters reaches a crescendo when he is arrested (Matt. 26:47–56, Mark 14:43–52, Luke 22:47–53, John 18:2–12). After a trial before religious authorities, he is in the custody of guards when they, and in some cases, others who have been watching the trial, mock and abuse him:

Then they spat in his face and they struck him; then they seized him, saying, "Prophesy for us, Anointed One/Christ! Who just struck you?" (Matt. 26:67–8)

Some began to spit at him and, covering his eyes with a blindfold, they hit him, and said to him, "Prophesy!" And the attendants struck him with blows. (Mark 14:65)

Then the men who were holding him began to mock him, beating him; then having blindfolded him, they began to question him, saying, "Prophesy! Who just struck you?" (Luke 22:63–4)

In Mark there is a second cycle of abuse after Christ has been taken before Pilate and is now in the soldiers' custody:

Then they dressed him in purple, and having braided a crown of thorns, they set it on him; and they began to salute him, "Hail the King of the Jews." And they began to strike him in the head with their staffs, and they spat on him, and getting on their knees, they bowed to him. (Mark 15:17–19)

The irony and sarcasm the guards hurl at Christ is quite close to that hurled at Odysseus by Melantho (*Od.* 18.327–33), Eurymachos (*Od.* 18.357–64, 389–93), and Antinoös (*Od.* 21.288–310). The mocking of Christ's prophetic powers essentially combines the suitors' treatment of Odysseus *and* Theoklymenos. The physical abuse Christ receives after being taken into custody resembles the suitors' repeated threats to have the disguised Odysseus mutilated and sold into slavery (*Od.* 18.84–7, 448–9; 20.381–3; 21.307–9).

---

[25] Fitzmeyer (1981: 780): "There is no suffering Son of Man figure in the OT." Cf. Mann (1986: 346): "So far, no rabbinic parallel has been found for the Greek *polla pathein* in the sense of enduring persecution."

The various opposed religious factions all plot his murder, somewhat as the suitors plot Telemachos' death. In Mark the Pharisees early on meet with some of Herod's men to plot to destroy him (Mark 3:6). In the synoptics the chief priests form a conspiracy to kill him by deceit (Matt. 26:1–5, Mark 14:1–2, Luke 22:1–2). In John it is the Jews who first plot to kill him (John 5:16–18; 7:1, 7:13, 7:19, 7:30, 8:40, 10:39), with Caiaphas and the chief priests forming a subsequent plot against him later (John 11:53).[26]

ONE OF THE KING'S OWN FOLLOWERS BETRAYS HIM

In the *Odyssey* three parallel figures, linked through their parallel names, Eurylochos in the crew, Euryalos of the Phaiakian athletes, and Eurymachos, one of the two ringleaders of the suitors, each betrays Odysseus.[27] Of these three Eurylochos, who is only active in Books 9–12, is the closest match for Judas in the myth of Christ. His desecration of Helios' cattle is a religious crime as well as a betrayal of Odysseus. But Eurylochos lacks Judas' role of doing what he does in the service of someone else, as Judas does for the high priests (Matt. 26:14, Mark 14:10, Luke 22:4). In this sense Melanthios is a closer parallel. Still technically in Odysseus' employ, he has gone over to the suitors' party. While we have noted his abuse toward the disguised Odysseus, his greatest act of betrayal comes after Odysseus reveals his identity, and Melanthios retrieves the arms that Odysseus and Telemachos had hidden away (*Od.* 22.139–52). When Odysseus notices the unfortunate turn of events, he labels it a μέγα ... ἔργον, *mega ergon* (*Od.* 22.149), literally, a "great deed." Fernández-Galiano (1992: 248) is mistaken in arguing that *mega ergon* here has a positive meaning. The *Odyssey* provides two close parallels that remove any ambiguity about how the phrase should be taken. When Odysseus learns that Eurylochos has led the crew to violate Helios' cattle he uses the same phrase, *mega ergon* (*Od.* 12.373), of which Heubeck notes (1989: 139), "μέγα ἔργον: here depreciatory, 'great wickedness'." When Melantho, Melanthios' sister, abuses the disguised Odysseus, Penelope refers to her act as a *mega ergon* (*Od.* 19.92).

In his function as prophet, Christ predicts that one of his disciples will betray him. He prophesies that it would be better for that man if he had never been born (Mark 14:21: καλὸν αὐτῷ, εἰ οὐκ ἐγεννήθη ὁ ἄνθρωπος ἐκεῖνος), on the one hand an almost Sophoclean tragic note, on the other

---

[26] These last two motifs (*His enemies accuse him of being mad; They mock, jeer at, and strike the king*) are also present in Plato's *Allegory of the Cave* (*Rep.* 517a).
[27] See Louden (1999: 19–20) for discussion of the parallels.

suggestive of Melanthios' gruesome fate (*Od.* 22.473–6). Somewhat as Melanthios getting the armor, Judas appears leading a mob to arrest Christ. Actual swordplay immediately follows Judas' betrayal (Matt. 26:51, Mark 14:47, Luke 22:49–50), with an unnamed disciple lopping off the ear of the high priest's servant. In Matthew (26:14–16) and Luke (22:3–6) Satan enters into Judas before his great betrayal, a NT instantiation of Dodds' (1960) principle of overdetermination, rather like Iris sent by Juno to incite the Trojan women to burn the ships, or Allecto sent to Amata.

THE KING'S CRUCIAL CONFRONTATION WITH HIS ENEMIES FALLS ON A RELIGIOUS FESTIVAL (HEORTÊ)

Indirectly, without fanfare, in the way that key details emerge in a Platonic dialogue, the *Odyssey* reveals that the day on which the suitors will die is a religious festival, ἑορτή, *heortê*, for Apollo (*Od.* 20.156, 21.258; cf. 20.276–8). A few earlier passages, particularly Penelope's wish that Apollo would strike dead whoever struck the stranger (*Od.* 17.494), hint at the occasion.[28] She may imply that the next day is a religious festival for Apollo when she announces her decision to hold the archery contest (*Od.* 19.572–80). Austin (1975: 245) quotes a scholiast who believes the feast is that of "Apollo *Noumenios*, Apollo of the New Moon."[29] Even the suitors are aware of the sanctity of the day, when, with typical unintended irony, Antinoös ascribes the suitors' inability to string the bow to the day's being a festive occasion (*Od.* 21.257–68). Contrary to Antinoös' claim, successfully stringing and wielding the bow is a way of showing honor to Apollo on his day. By having the suitors slain on his day, the *Odyssey* suggests that the oft-invoked Homeric trinity of Zeus, Athena, and Apollo (*Od.* 4.341, 7.311, 17.132, 18.235, 24.376; *Il.* 2.371, 4.288, 7.132, 16.97) are working in tandem to bring about the suitors' destruction.

In the gospels the priests and elders plot to seize Christ during the festival of the Passover (Mark 14:1–2; Matt. 26:1–5, Luke 22:1–2). While "Passover" is *to Pascha* in NT Greek, ἑορτή, the *Odyssey*'s term for Apollo's religious festival, is also used (Matt. 26:5, Mark 14:2, Luke 2:41, John 13:1; cf. Luke 22). It is highly ironic that the religious officials do not hesitate to subvert the purpose of the religious festival to pursue their agenda against Christ.

---

[28] De Jong (2001: 498) also lists *Od.* 18.235–42; 19.86; as well as *Od.* 21.257–68, 338; 22.7.
[29] Austin adduces further evidence and interpretations (1975: 246–50), strengthening the festival's likely association with the new moon.

Heortê is also used in the Septuagint of the original Passover (Exod. 10:9, 23:15, 34:25; Deut. 16:16). Passover has particularly violent roots, involving, as it does, the slaying of all the firstborn (other than those of the Hebrews).

In Exodus 11–13 the Passover is the tenth plague, the destruction of the firstborn of Egypt. To slay the Egyptians' firstborn Yahweh sends the Destroyer (Exod. 12:23: ὁ ὀλοθρεύων, in the Septuagint, also at Hebr. 11:28; cf. Homeric ὄλεθρος), very like episodes involving the exterminating angel (e.g., 2 Sam. 24:16: τῷ ἀγγέλῳ τῷ διαφθείροντι).[30] Propp (1998: 409) also compares the Destroyer of Exodus 12:23 with the exterminating angel passages:

> We often read of destructive angels dispatched or restrained by God (Gen. 19; Num. 22:22–35; 2 Sam. 24:16; 2 Kgs. 19:35; Ps. 35:5–6; 1 Chr. 21:15). Sometimes multiple entities act in concert (Ezek. 9; Ps. 78:49). Since in 1 Samuel 13:17; 14:15, *mashit* means "(human) strike force," it is even possible in 12:23 that Yahweh's Destroyer is an angelic host, rather than a single being.

The specific means the Destroyer uses to slay the Egyptians' firstborn is left vague. Could it be with arrows, as Yahweh himself is depicted using at 2 Samuel 22:15? If so, we would have a further parallel with Apollo's *heortê*, where Odysseus, implicitly Apollo's agent, slays the suitors with arrows. The crucifixion also takes place during Passover (Matt. 26:2, Mark 14:1–2, Luke 22:1–2). There thus seems additional irony in that Christ, the (firstborn) Son, is crucified during Passover, when the firstborn of the Hebrews were spared, as if the original dynamics of the Passover are inverted in Christ's crucifixion.

AT A FINAL BANQUET PROPHECIES FORETELL WHAT FOLLOWS

Though in very different roles in the two myths, the king is present at a final banquet at which a prophecy declares the climactic events that are soon to come. The climax of the suitors' final supper, the night before they will be destroyed, is marked by Theoklymenos' prophecy of their apocalyptic destruction (*Od.* 20.247–384). Odysseus is present as the guest of Penelope and Telemachos (*Od.* 20.257–67), but also as provocateur (*Od.* 20.284–302, 322–5). In the tense atmosphere that follows Ktesippos hurling an ox-hoof at him, Athena intervenes against the suitors, incapacitating them

---

[30] For further discussion of the exterminating angel, see John Pairman Brown (2000: 143–5), and Louden (2006: 154–5).

by driving them mad for a brief period.[31] Laughing uncontrollably, they feast on meat sullied with blood, their laughter sounding like lamentation. Now Theoklymenos prophesies their destruction, seeing them as if already dead and in Hades. Never was there a more unpleasant (ἀχαρίστερον: *Od.* 20.392) meal, the narrator asserts.

In the gospels the last supper for Christ and the disciples is the meal on the first day of Passover (Matt. 26:17, Mark 14:12; Luke 22:7). After the meal, Christ prophesies that one of them will betray him, and that "it would be better for him if he had never been born" (Matt. 26:24, Mark 14:21). Though expressed in very different terms, this nicely parallels Theoklymenos' prophecy of the suitors. Christ goes on to prophesy that all of them will "be offended" on his account (σκανδαλισθήσεσθε), that he will later be resurrected and will meet them in Galilee (Matt. 26:31–5, Mark 14:27–8). His prophecy also offers partial parallels with Odysseus repeating to the crew the prophecies of Teiresias and Kirke of what will happen to them should they eat Helios' cattle (*Od.* 12.271–6), which for the crew is their thematic parallel to the suitors' maddened final feast.

THE KING IS FULL OF ANXIETY THE NIGHT BEFORE THE CLIMACTIC EVENTS

In both myths the king is full of anxiety, the night before the climactic events, over what is about to happen to him. Odysseus lies awake, tossing and turning, debating with himself how he, one against many, will be able to confront the suitors (*Od.* 20.24–30). A unique simile (*Od.* 20.25–30) compares him, tossing and turning (ἔνθα καὶ ἔνθα ἐλίσσετο), to a sausage being rolled back and forth, as it is roasted (ὀπτηθῆναι) over a fire. Commentators see the roasting paralleled in Odysseus cooking up his plans (Russo 1992: 110, de Jong 2001: 486). I argue that it also exemplifies his physical and emotional discomfort, that he is in a hot spot: the sausage is full of blood (ἐμπλείην… αἵματος). But Athena comes to him, reassuring him of her divine aid tomorrow. When she then pours sleep on his eyelids, he falls asleep. His sleeplessness should be seen as an inversion of the earlier motif in which he falls asleep before the crew desecrate Helios' cattle on Thrinakia (*Od.* 12.333–8), and when, with Ithaka in sight, the crew open Aiolos' bag (*Od.* 10.29–55). This sleep, the result of divine intervention, breaks the cycle of the two others, in which his being asleep leads to disastrous results.

---

[31] Cf. de Jong (2001: 440): "the Suitors' uncontrolled laughter is that of lunatics."

In the gospels when Christ and the disciples reach Gethsemane he has them sit and wait while he goes off to pray. Distress and anguish over what is about to happen overwhelm him (ἤρξατο λυπεῖσθαι καὶ ἀδημονεῖν: Matt. 26:37; Περίλυπός ἐστιν ἡ ψυχή μου: Matt. 26:38 = Mark 14:34). In Luke (22:24–30) the disciples quarrel among themselves (ἐγένετο δὲ καὶ φιλονεικία) over who is the greatest, making a further parallel with the behavior of Odysseus' crew on Thrinakia, and Eurylochos' mutinous insubordination. Three times he asks his disciples to stay awake for him, and three times they fall asleep. The disciples' repeated failure resembles the crew's failure on Thrinakia.

At this juncture, alone among the four gospels, Luke employs motifs very close to *Odyssey* 20.24–54. Christ's anguish (γενόμενος ἐν ἀγωνίᾳ, "being in agony") is here accompanied by physical symptoms, "his sweat, falling on the ground like drops of blood" (ὁ ἱδρὼς αὐτοῦ ὡσεὶ θρόμβοι αἵματος καταβαίνοντες ἐπὶ τὴν γῆν: Luke 22:44). Only here does an angel from heaven come in response, bringing him strength (Luke 22:43). Fitzmyer (1985: 1,444) notes the passage's unique lexicon, "*agônia* is found only here in the NT... Both *idrôs*, 'sweat,' and *thrombos*, 'drop,' are *hapax legomena* in the NT." The same words are also obscure in the Septuagint, which lacks *thrombos*, has *agônia* only in 2 Maccabees, and *idrôs* once in Genesis, otherwise only in 2 and 4 Maccabees. Fitzmyer (1985: 1,443), noting that many ancient mss. lack Luke 22:43–4, points out (1,437–8) the likelihood that the author must have consulted another source for these unusual details. Homeric epic should be considered a likely source. The unique detail of an angel coming to Christ closely parallels Athena coming to Odysseus at the same point in his anguished night, as noted above, after he is likened to a blood-filled sausage. The *Iliad* offers a relevant parallel for the striking description of Christ's sweat running down to the ground like drops of blood. When his cherished son Sarpedon dies, Zeus pours down bloody tears on the earth, also a scene of unique pathos (*Il.* 16.459).[32]

At about this point the *Odyssey* and the gospels diverge, mainly in the timing of the coming apocalypse. The *Odyssey* now proceeds directly to the climax of its negative theoxeny, the apocalyptic destruction of the suitors. Many other myths have similar sequence and timing, destruction coming that day, that night, or the next day, not only negative theoxenies such as Genesis 19 and Baucis and Philemon, but Exodus 32 and the

---

[32] Lateiner (2002: 49 n. 31) cites the parallel.

Bacchae.[33] But in the gospels the apocalyptic destruction that awaits those who have abused the king is postponed until a future date.[34] In a further key difference in sequence, Odysseus has already gone to the underworld and triumphed over death before returning to Ithaka, whereas Christ undergoes both motifs after his abusive treatment in Jerusalem.

[33] Though as noted in Chapter 2, from the perspective of the negative theoxeny initiated in Book 1, the suitors' destruction is postponed to coincide with Odysseus' return.
[34] Perhaps originally expected to occur shortly after the destruction of the Temple in 70 CE. See discussion in Chapter 13.

CHAPTER 13

Contained apocalypse
Odyssey *12, 13, 22 and 24; Exodus 32 (and Gen. 18–19)*

The word "apocalypse" as the designation of a mythic type comes from its appearance as the first word in Revelation, most subsequent uses of the word descending, one way or another, from this instance.[1] John J. Collins offers a definition that addresses its original use and some subsequent applications (2000a: 146):

An apocalypse is a genre of revelatory literature with a narrative framework, in which a revelation is mediated by an otherworldly being to a human recipient, disclosing a transcendent reality which is both temporal, insofar as it envisages eschatological salvation, and spatial insofar as it involves another, supernatural world.[2]

Most commentators would agree, however, that "apocalypse" as a mythic type, exists earlier than Revelation, and employs motifs absent from Collins' definition.[3] With its focus on "a revelation . . . mediated by an otherworldly being to a human recipient," all of which stays close to the literal meaning of the Greek word, Collins actually designates the mythic type we have earlier noted as *the vision*.[4] Yet as we observed in Chapter 9, *the vision* need not be part of an apocalyptic scenario, as it is not in *Odyssey* 11, Book 7 of Plato's *Republic*, or *Aeneid* 6, all of which antedate Revelation.

Not only Collins, but other commentators typically analyze Revelation delineating motifs we have classified as constituent elements of *the*

---

[1] For discussion of the term and its origin, see de Boer (2000: 350–7).
[2] Cf. Sparks' quotation (2005: 240) of the definition of apocalypse "adopted by scholars from the Society of Biblical Genres Project. See Sparks (2005: 240–3) for discussion of other Near Eastern instances of apocalypse. For a brief overview of apocalypse and eschatology in the Bible, see Nelson (1993).
[3] See Vanderkam (2000: 196) on how commentators tend to approach apocalyptic myth with tremendous selectivity, "The tendency among scholars has been to focus on the eschatological side of teachings in the apocalypses and less on the other kinds of material found in them."
[4] Explored in Chapter 9 in *Odyssey* 11, *Republic* Book 7, *Aeneid* 6, and the Book of Revelation itself.

vision, and minimizing, if not omitting entirely, the destruction that typically results from apocalyptic myths. Vanderkam (2000: 196), for instance, notes a specific subtype of apocalypse, "the 'historical' type which includes a review of history."[5] *Odyssey* 11 has what could be considered a precursor of a historical survey in the *Catalogue of Women* (*Od.* 11.225–330), but again employed as a component in its presentation of *the vision* in Odysseus' *catabasis* to the underworld, not as part of any apocalyptic myth. Vanderkam (*ibid.*) notes other suggestions toward an attempted classification and typology of apocalyptic myth:

> Collins and other authors... distinguished between two major types of apocalypses: some apocalypses have and others lack an otherworldly journey by the individual who receives the revelation. Both those with and without otherworldly journeys can be further subdivided: (a) the "historical" type... (b) apocalypses which... envisage cosmic and/or political eschatology, and (c) apocalypses which have... only personal eschatology.

Clifford, on the other hand, in "The roots of apocalypticism in Near Eastern myth," comes closer to the approach I adopt here. Breaking apocalyptic myth down into such components as divine councils, the combat myth, "prophecies after the fact," and the "Dream vision," he finds antecedents in several ancient Near Eastern texts, including the *Enuma Elish* and *The Baal Cycle*.[6] Collins himself suggests at least partial agreement with such a view (2000a: 129), "the expectation of the end of the world... The ultimate roots of the concept lie in the combat myths that can be found in various cultures of the ancient Near East."

An apocalyptic myth is not a single, seamless entity but a combination of motifs, as Clifford's survey suggests. Absent from Collins' definition are such motifs as divine wrath, divine judgment upon mortals, destruction of mortals, salvation for an elect, and so forth. Yet these *are* prominent motifs in Revelation, and in earlier narratives, such as Genesis 19 and Exodus 32. Though its original Greek name is the source for the term apocalypse, Revelation is in some respects atypical, not representative of apocalyptic myth. It and Israelite apocalypses with which it is often grouped (Dan., 1 Enoch, 2 Baruch, 4 Ezra) differ from the older narratives under discussion in this chapter in their central use of *the vision*, which is a separate type of myth in the older narratives, as we have seen in *Odyssey* 11, *Republic* 7, and *Aeneid* 6. Nonetheless, earlier apocalyptic myths may suggest an

---

[5] Cf. Clifford (2000: 12).
[6] Cf. Cross, who argues that "the origins of the apocalyptic must be searched for as early as the sixth century B.C." (1973: 343), though he limits his analysis to only earlier Israelite texts.

embryonic version of such scenes, Collins' "revelation... mediated by an otherworldly being to a human recipient," in the divine warning of the coming destruction, as in Genesis 19, or in a mortal prophet's prophecy of coming destruction, as at *Odyssey* 20.351–7, 365–70. But in a broader sense, in the earlier myths it is not a prophet or hero who receives the vision of the coming apocalypse, but the *audience* who learns of Troy's coming destruction, or the three contained apocalypses that conclude the *Odyssey*'s three sequences. Revelation also differs from Exodus 32 and the *Odyssey*'s relevant episodes in the *degree* of destruction.

John J. Collins notes common ground between the combat myth and apocalyptic myth, and argues for the latter's evolution from the former (2000a: 129),

> [T]he expectation of the end of the world... The ultimate roots of the concept lie in the combat myths that can be found in various cultures of the ancient Near East. In Israel... the prophets, however, projected the conflict into the future and used the mythology to evoke the judgment of God, both on the Gentile nations and on Israel itself.[7]

By depicting an agent who is identified as god or "good" destroying an opponent who is figured as monstrous or "evil," apocalyptic myth essentially replays the basic dynamic of the combat myth. The defeat of a cosmic, primordial dragon at the beginning of time is re-enacted, but set in a future time. Combat myth typically features a monster as the chief antagonist, Tiamat, Typhoeus, or Leviathan.[8] Revelation replays this motif in its brief description of the defeat and imprisonment of the dragon (Rev. 12), as well as the beast (Rev. 11:7, 13:1–10). In the apocalyptic destruction of the suitors in Book 22, the *Odyssey* implies a connection with the combat myth in the thematic parallels drawn between the suitors and Polyphêmos as outrageous violators of hospitality (discussed below).

In this study I use "apocalypse" in a broader sense, one that works for Revelation, but also designates myths that employ several motifs used in Revelation, but lack others. Since in our era apocalypse primarily denotes the end of the world, my definition centers on god-sent destruction of mortals who have committed offences against the gods. The older myths that I classify as apocalypses may conclude with any of the three levels of destruction, worldwide, the highest level, a whole city, the middle and most frequent level, or contained, the lowest level. Because Christian and

---

[7] Cf. Clifford (2000: 7–12, 15, 17, 22–6).
[8] Clifford (2000: 17): "Another relevant recurrent element of the genre of combat myth is the enemy as monster."

Old Testament myth tend to expand motifs to make them universal, Revelation and Israelite apocalyptic narratives from Daniel on conclude with the highest of the three degrees, intending their divine judgments and punishments as worldwide, not just on a specific city, or smaller unit as in Exodus 32 and the *Odyssey*. Consequently, in this study I employ the term apocalypse to designate *a myth depicting mortals who commit an offence that provokes a divine wrath resulting in large-scale destruction of mortals*. My definition recognizes the parallels between the three degrees of apocalypse, worldwide destruction, destruction of a city, and contained apocalypse as in Exodus 34, *Gilgamesh* VI.iii–iv, and *Odyssey* 12, 13, and 22. The specific form of apocalypse that is the Book of Revelation should be seen as a development, an adaptation of the earlier-attested lower degrees of apocalypse, to which *the vision* has accrued.

DIVINE COUNCILS AND THE THREE DEGREES OF APOCALYPSE

In Exodus 32, when Yahweh learns of the offensive ritual the Israelites have performed, he wants to destroy them all, not just those who took part in the act (Exod. 32:10). But Moses reasons with him, persuading him to exact *only* the deaths of those who took part in the ritual. The process of their dialogue evokes two of the three possible degrees of apocalyptic destruction demanded by a wrathful god.[9] In the full degree of apocalypse a wrathful god destroys all of humanity, leaving only the *one just man* (discussed below) as survivor. OT myth exhibits this full degree of apocalypse in the myth of the Deluge (Gen. 6:5–8:22, inherited from the earlier Mesopotamian story of Atrahasis/Utnapishtim) where Yahweh, in his wrath at all of humanity over unspecified offences, destroys the entire human race, leaving Noah as the first of OT myth's *one just man* figures. Implicitly, Zeus acts in similar fashion to end the Silver Race in Hesiod's *Works and Days* (lines 137–40). The *Homeric Hymn to Demeter* implies a full-degree apocalypse when Demeter, in her wrath over Persephone's disappearance, threatens to stop making crops grow on earth (lines 310–13). Christian myth presumes a coming apocalypse of the highest degree in the Day of Judgment (discussed below), a traditional view earlier expressed in Hesiod's description of the pending destruction of the race of iron (*Works and Days* 174–201), his own age.[10] In Book 12 of the *Odyssey* Helios threatens a similar level of

---

[9] The next two paragraphs expand upon some points made in Louden (2006: 226–35).
[10] On Hesiod's own age as the Iron Age destined for apocalyptic destruction, see Cancik (2000: 105).

destruction, the death of all mortals, when he tells Zeus he will descend to Hades and shine there unless he receives requital for the loss of his cattle (*Od.* 12.377–83).

At least as common in ancient myth is a middle degree, apocalyptic destruction of an entire city. When Gilgamesh rudely rejects her, Ishtar initially seeks to destroy all of Uruk (*Gilg.* VI.iii–iv). Hesiod refers to this level in the *Works and Days* (240–1), when he observes that sometimes a whole city is destroyed for the inappropriate actions of one man (by which he probably means Paris and Troy). The destruction of Troy, ordained by Zeus (*Il.* 4.160–8), the annihilation of Sodom and Gomorrah, with two cities in place of one, Ovid's myth of Baucis and Philemon, in which the city is said to contain 100,000 homes, all conclude with the destruction of a whole city, each narrative leaving a *one just man* (Aeneas, Lot, Baucis and Philemon, respectively) as survivor.[11]

The dialogue between Moses and Yahweh in Exodus 32 is also an adaptation of a divine council,[12] the specific subtype noted in Chapter 1, in which the sky father mediates a divine wrath and establishes the appropriate level of destruction. When such mediation is successful, the wrathful god agrees to a lower level of destruction than initially sought, a contained apocalypse. Such is the case when Anu mediates Ishtar's wrath, after which 600 people die as opposed to the entire city of Uruk. Such is the case when Yahweh agrees to the deaths of only those Israelites who took part in the perverse ritual, resulting in the death of 3,000, rather than the entire aggregate making the exodus. Three times the *Odyssey* employs this same dynamic, a wrathful god who initially seeks to destroy large numbers of mortals, but agrees to the smaller number, Helios (*Od.* 12.376–88), Poseidon (*Od.* 13.125–58), and Athena/Zeus (*Od.* 24.472–88).

Why does the *Odyssey* have three such episodes? Each scene concludes one of the three sequences around which the *Odyssey* has organized its larger structure (discussion in Louden 1999: 1–30). The Ithakan sequence, centered on Odysseus' conflict with the suitors over Penelope, is largest, comprising most of Books 1–4 (but with Telemachos in Odysseus' place in the opening books) and 13.187 – Book 24. The Scherian sequence, comprising Books 6–8, 11.332–81, and 13.1–187, centers on the friction Odysseus encounters as he approaches Arete, and, earlier, Nausikaa. The Aiaian sequence, centered on the friction that develops between Odysseus and his crew, some of which involves Kirke, comprises Books 9–12 (other than

---

[11] See Louden (2006: 235–9) for discussion of the typical figure of the "one just man."
[12] See Clifford (2000: 6) on divine councils as a typical element in Near Eastern apocalyptic myth.

the *Intermezzo*, 11.332–81). Each of the three sequences concludes with the destruction of the parallel body of fractious men who have provoked a divine wrath (the suitors, the Phaiakian athletes, Odysseus' crew). Athena and Odysseus jointly destroy the suitors, who provoke her wrath in Book 1 (1.227–9), Odysseus serving, in effect, as her agent (*Od.* 17.483–7). Poseidon destroys the Phaiakian crew that ferries Odysseus home, which crew consists of the athletes who took part in the games in Book 8,[13] some of whom rudely confront Odysseus (*Od.* 13.159–87). Odysseus' crew, having desecrated Helios' inviolate cattle and provoked his wrath, are destroyed in Book 12 (*Od.* 12.405–19).[14] The three sequences differ in the subgenres of myth they employ to culminate in their respective apocalypses. The Aiaian and Scherian sequences both use Argonautic myth more than any other type, though the Aiaian sequence also incorporates the other subgenres explored in Chapters 7–10. The Ithakan sequence, on the other hand, is largely composed of negative theoxeny (positive theoxeny in Book 3) and romance. Two other subgenres, *The suitors and the depiction of impious men in wisdom literature*, and *The king returns, unrecognized and abused in his kingdom*, also overlap with, and add additional specific colorings to, the larger structures romance and theoxeny provide.

Genesis 18–19, as transition into its negative theoxeny, feature a variant of the kind of dialogue employed in Exodus 32, an adapted divine council that would mediate the level of destruction sought by a wrathful god. But here OT myth innovates not only in having Abraham, a mortal, engage in dialogue with Yahweh (as does Exodus 32) concerning his intended destruction of Sodom and Gomorrah, but also in the chronology, and unique outcome of the scene. *Before* the narrative depicts any offensive behavior, Yahweh is already considering destroying everyone in Sodom and Gomorrah (Gen. 18:20–3), whereas the divine councils in *Gilgamesh*, Exodus 32, and the *Odyssey*, all occur after the mortals commit the offensive act. In a more radical innovation, the mediation, which the type-scene is designed to provide, fails only here.

As Moses in Exodus 32, Zeus at *Odyssey* 12.384–8, 13.140–58, and 24.472–88, and Anu with Ishtar at *Gilgamesh* (VI.iii–iv), Abraham mediates, attempting to talk Yahweh down to a lower level of destruction. His strategy in doing so calls attention to the problematic outcome inherent in most myths of apocalyptic destruction. What if, in the course of destroying all the inhabitants in Sodom and Gomorrah, Yahweh destroys mortals

---

[13] Discussion in Louden (1999: 14–23).
[14] Book 5 is not part of the three sequences, but is designed to insert Odysseus into the Phaiakian sequence; discussion in Louden (1999: 104–29).

who have committed no wrong, but are in the midst of those who have? A unique bartering scene ensues, in which Abraham starts with fifty men who have committed no offence – would Yahweh destroy them along with the rest of the city? – the number diminishing in successive steps, ending with ten (Gen. 18:23–32). Yahweh agrees to spare the cities if ten moral men are found.

While the two angels are inside Lot's dwelling, as discussed in Chapter 2, a mob assembles, "the men of Sodom, both young and old, everyone without exception" (Gen. 19:4). The mob, a close parallel to the suitors in *Odyssey* 1–2, 17–22, all clearly violate hospitality in demanding to have sex with Lot's guests, and in threatening Lot himself, as witnessed by the angels. By the conventions of theoxenic myth, they deserve to die, as the suitors in Book 1 of the *Odyssey* already provoke Athena's wrath (*Od.* 1.227–9). But after the angels stun the mob with temporary blindness (Gen. 19: 11; cf. *Od.* 2.394–6, and 20.345–9, where Athena incapacitates the suitors), there is no further mention of whether any people should be spared. Abraham makes no further appearance in the narrative; the issues raised in his dialogue with Yahweh are left unresolved.

Yahweh's subsequent behavior is unique in ancient myth, to my knowledge. Having participated in a traditional scene of mediation, he nonetheless exacts the full level of destruction he initially sought. Abraham's attempted mediation fails, opposite the outcome of Moses' dialogue with Yahweh in Exodus 32, opposite every instance of the subtype of divine council from which Abraham's dialogue descends. As noted in Chapter 1, divine councils usually feature two members of the epic triangle, the sky father and the mentor god, or the sky father and the wrathful god. In the divine councils in Job (1:6–12; 2:1–6), perhaps as an alteration OT myth's emerging monotheism forces on the traditional epic triangle, Yahweh suggests a combination of the sky father and the mentor god (discussion in Chapter 1). Genesis 18 presents the converse: Yahweh fuses the functions of the sky father and the wrathful deity.

The narrative does not specify that he has a divine wrath, merely that he is offended by the mortals' behavior (Gen. 18:20), "How great is the outcry over Sodom and Gomorrah! How grave their sin must be!" As an opening complaint, Yahweh's censure broadly parallels Zeus' first lines about mortals' irresponsibility and Aigisthos (*Od.* 1.32–6). Both embody the broader outlook, and larger perspective of the sky father, as opposed to the wrathful god, who has a more personal relationship to the mortals' offence, as do Athena (*Od.* 1.227–8), Helios (*Od.* 12.377–83), and Poseidon (*Od.* 13.127–38), the *Odyssey*'s three wrathful deities. In Greek myth a wrathful god cannot usually destroy a city without Zeus' permission, as divine councils in the *Iliad* with Zeus, Hera, and Athena particularly demonstrate (*Il.* 4.1–73, 8.1–37). Implicitly, as the *Odyssey*'s three scenes of mediation and the *Homeric Hymn to Demeter* 310–13 suggest, only Zeus can validate a middle or full-scale apocalypse. In these respects Yahweh's initial position suggests that of the sky father, or principal deity. However, in his attempted mediation, Abraham plays the role elsewhere played by the principal deity, Zeus, in the *Odyssey*'s three thematically related scenes, or Anu in *Gilgamesh*'s instance with Ishtar, in attempting to reason with the god who seeks destruction and to lessen the level of destruction. Abraham doing so places Yahweh in the traditional role of the wrathful lesser god.

The adapted divine council serves a further purpose that also finds a parallel in the *Odyssey*'s negative theoxeny: to emphasize the teamwork between the mortal and the god. Genesis presents Abraham as Yahweh's partner and confidant. Yahweh is twice earlier depicted establishing a covenant with him (Gen. 15; 17:1–22), promising to keep him and his descendants safe. Alter (2004: 88) refers to Abraham as "a human partner" to Yahweh when they discuss the destruction of Sodom and Gomorrah. In these respects the scene parallels *Odyssey* 13.287–440, where Athena and Odysseus plot the destruction of the suitors. The *Odyssey* depicts a similarly close relationship between Odysseus and Athena, given the different modality that heroic epic confers upon such an association.[15] Though no such word as covenant is used of their relationship, she clearly suggests a similar support, if not on a national scale, since Odysseus is not explicitly figured as the father of Greece as Abraham is of Israel. But Athena displays a similar concern for his safety and well-being, reassuring him when he is anxious about facing the suitors in their great number, "I will truly be at your side" (*Od.* 13.393: καὶ λίην τοι ἐγώ γε παρέσσομαι), close to Yahweh's declaration to Abraham at Genesis 15:1 (ὑπερασπίζω σου, in the Septuagint), "I am your shield." In a smaller parallel to Yahweh's concern for Abraham's descendants, Athena also looks after Telemachos' safety and well-being (*Od.* 13.421–2), which is as far into the future as the *Odyssey* takes Odysseus' descendants. The same holds for Yahweh and Moses, with whom the god also forms a covenant (Exod. 24:7), and whom he consults, in an adapted divine council (Exod. 32:7–14), concerning the apocalyptic destruction of the rebellious Israelites.

---

[15] Cf. Hoekstra's comments (1989: 183) on "Athena and her protégé"; cf. 185.

THE SIGN OF THE COMING APOCALYPSE: THE SUN AND MOON ARE DARKENED

In Book 20, after Athena addles the suitors (*Od.* 20.346: παρέπλαγξεν), causing them to laugh hysterically, their eyes well with tears, as they eat meat defiled with blood, a grotesque perversion of a true feast. While their eating meat that oozes blood (*Od.* 20.348: αἱμοφόρυκτα) restates and amplifies how the suitors are figured as ticks in the description of Argos (*Od.* 17.300), the offensive feast as a whole is prelude to an impending apocalypse (cf. Dan. 5:1–4). As many have noted,[16] the frightening signs in Book 20 find a parallel in the sinister portents that attend the crew's perverse feast on Helios' cattle at Thrinakia, and, to a lesser extent, in the rebellious Israelites' feast in Exodus 32. The stage set, Theoklymenos delivers his two short prophecies, his chief reason for being in the epic.[17] Wondering what evil the suitors are suffering, declaring that their heads and faces are shrouded in darkness, the walls and columns splattered with blood, and everywhere are ghosts speeding toward dark Erebos, Theoklymenos ends his first prophecy (*Od.* 20.351–7) with a traditional sign, also frequent in OT myth. The darkness he sees exists on several levels, including a celestial one:

> and the sun has vanished
> out of heaven, and a foul mist has poured forth.
> *Odyssey* 20.356–7

Russo (1992: 124) characterizes the prophecy as "The most eerie passage in Homer," and, as other commentators, cites parallels in folktales, Herodotus, and Aeschylus, but is silent on the eclipse, as is de Jong (2001). As Stanford rightly notes, Theoklymenos clearly describes an eclipse (1962, vol. II: 355), "an eclipse or darkening of the sun was universally recognized as a portent of evil."[18] An eclipse is a standard feature in OT prophecies of

---

[16] E.g., Stanford (1962, Vol. II: 354); cf. de Jong (2001: 501), on 20.345–86, "The supernatural phenomena resemble those of *Odyssey* 12.394–6, where the dead cattle of Helius low on the spit and their hides crawl."

[17] On how Theoklymenos' prophecy is integral to the *Odyssey*'s plot, against the analyst-based argument of critics such as Page, see Daniel Levine (1983); cf. de Jong (2001: 501), "This eerie scene features Theoclymenus' finest hour in the *Odyssey*."

[18] Cf. Austin (1975: 250) on how the eclipse is part of a pattern of solar and lunar references in the *Odyssey*. For further arguments that Theoklymenos' prophecy refers to a solar eclipse, see Baikouzis and Magnasco (2008), who, on the basis of several models, argue that the *Odyssey* here refers to a historical eclipse of the sun over the Ionian Sea, on April 16, 1178 BCE. I thank Charles Louis Roberts for calling my attention to their article.

the apocalyptic destruction of the Day of Judgment, a parallel unnoted in Homeric critical commentary.[19] Perhaps the two passages closest to *Odyssey* 20.356–7 are in Amos and Joel:

> On that day, says the Lord God,
> I shall make the sun go down at noon
> and darken the earth in broad daylight.
>
> Amos 8:9

> The sun will be turned to darkness
> and the moon to blood
> before the coming of the great and terrible day of the Lord.
>
> Joel 2:31

Both passages mark a day of apocalyptic destruction, as Theoklymenos does for the suitors. Both emphasize the sun vanishing during daytime, an eclipse. Since absence of the sun is a sign of impending apocalypse, both passages imply an equation of the sun with life, as is standard in Homeric epic ("to be alive and see the light of the sun"; *Il.* 18.61, 442; 24.558; *Od.* 4.540; 10.498; 14.44; 20.207).

In the Thrinakia episode, when Helios vows to descend to Hades and shine among the dead (*Od.* 12.383), he threatens what would seem to mortals to be a permanent solar eclipse (*Od.* 12.377–83). As Aristotle suggested (Barnes 1984: 2,433, F 175 R 3, quoting Eustathius), Helios' cattle number 350 because allegorically they stand for the number of days in the twelve lunar months.[20] The *Rig Veda* offers *comparanda*, cows likened to rays of the sun or dawn (e.g., *RV* 1.92.1–4, 12, 14). In slaying the cattle, the crew not only desecrate Helios, an ultimate source of life, but allegorically attack life itself. In this respect Helios' threat parallels the crew's act; he would deprive all mortals of seeing the light of the sun, and therefore deprive them of life itself.

In addition to an eclipse of the sun in Amos, Joel, and *Odyssey* 20, the darkness of the New Moon may also portend an apocalypse, as is perhaps suggested in the phrase in Joel "and the moon [turn] to blood." A New Moon is, in fact, "a necessary condition for a solar eclipse" (Baikouzis and Magnasco 2008: 8,823). Two other passages from Isaiah and Ezekiel may also suggest the darkness of the New Moon, along with a solar eclipse, as a traditional phenomenon marking an apocalypse:

---

[19] Though Stanford (1962, Vol. II: 353) notes an unnamed commentator who compares the episode's atmosphere "to that of the Writing on the Wall at Belshazzar's Feast."

[20] Austin (1975: 134, 137): "They [the crew] desecrate the property of the sun or, as Aristotle noted, the days and nights of the year." Cf. West (2005: 57).

> The stars of heaven in their constellation will give no light,
> the sun will be dark at its rising, and the moon will not shed its light.
>
> Isaiah 13.10

> When your light is quenched I shall veil the sky and darken its stars;
> I shall veil the sun with clouds, and the moon will give no light.
> I shall darken all shining lights of the sky above you
> and bring darkness over your land.
>
> Ezekiel 32:7–8

Though Theoklymenos' prophecy makes no mention of the moon, other passages in the *Odyssey* suggest that Odysseus' return coincides with a New Moon, its darkness portending the suitors' apocalyptic destruction.

On his first night in Eumaios' hut Odysseus improvises a tale about an ambush he took part in at Troy on a dark and stormy night, a bad night (νύξ δ' ἄρ' ἐπῆλθε κακή: *Od.* 14.475), with the north wind blowing, snow, and frost. Though his purpose is to test Eumaios, and see if he will give him a cloak (as Odysseus gave him one in the made-up narrative: *Od.* 14.468–502), the tale has additional links with the *Odyssey*'s larger plot. The same formula occurs right before Odysseus begins his tale, "a bad night came on" (νύξ δ' ἄρ' ἐπῆλθε κακή: *Od.* 14.457), with Zeus raining all night, like the inclement conditions in his tale. The principal narrator adds that it was "the dark of the moon" (σκοτομήνιος: *Od.* 14.457), a word occurring only here in Homeric epic. Hoekstra (1989: 226) argues that the *Odyssey*'s emphasis here on the dark of the moon is a traditional theme, "The 'Return of the Hero at New Moon' must have been a theme of the old saga." As earlier noted, Austin (1975: 245) quotes a scholiast who believes the suitors' feast in Books 21–2 is that of "Apollo *Noumênios*, Apollo of the New Moon," adducing further evidence (246–50) to strengthen the festival's likely association with the New Moon. Austin's very title, *Archery at the Dark of the Moon*, alludes to the *Odyssey*'s use of such elements. The first component, *skotos*, "darkness," is used throughout the *Iliad* for the darkness of death.[21] The Septuagint uses the same word for the apocalyptic darkening of solar eclipses in Joel, "The sun will be turned to darkness" (*skotos*: Joel 2:31), and a related verb in Amos, "darken," "I will make the sun go down at noon, and darken the earth in broad daylight" (*suskotazô*: Amos 8:9). The phrase in Joel "the moon to blood" (Joel 2:31) overlaps with Theoklymenos' prophecy of the blood-splattered palace walls and columns (*Od.* 20.354), at the eclipse of the sun. In both prophecies the unexpected

---

[21] Cunliffe (1963) lists *Iliad* 4.461, 503, 526; 5.47; 6.11; 13.575, 672; 14.519; 15.578; 16.316, 325, 607; 20.393, 471; 21.181.

bloody imagery prefigures the violence and destruction to come. The eclipses and the bleeding walls are both reflexes of the so-called pathetic fallacy, the belief that the natural world, in some way, mirrors pivotal events that befall mortals, positive or negative, freakish, prodigious events to mark the murder of a hero, positive harmonious signs accompanying the birth of a savior.

BLOODTHIRSTY DEITIES: ATHENA, ANAT, AND YAHWEH

Theoklymenos sees blood-spattered walls in the palace; Joel's moon is (turned) to blood. In Homeric, Near Eastern, and OT myth, wrathful deities demand apocalyptic destruction for a number of offences, violations of hospitality (Athena, Yahweh in Genesis 19), personal affront (Helios, Poseidon, Yahweh in Exodus 32, Ishtar in *Gilgamesh*), disrupting their relationship as god's chosen people (Phaiakians and Poseidon: *Odyssey* 13, Israelites and Yahweh: Exodus 32), and so forth.[22] When she meets with Odysseus, and vows to aid him against the suitors, Athena invokes their destruction in the most graphic terms:

> When we work together to accomplish these things, I hope that
> your immense floor will be spattered with their blood and brains.
> ὁππότε κεν δὴ ταῦτα πενώμεθα: καί τιν' ὀΐω
> αἵματι τ' ἐγκεφάλῳ τε παλαξέμεν ἄσπετον οὖδας.
>
> *Odyssey* 13.394–5

Seven books earlier Athena thus demands the blood-spattered walls that Theoklymenos sees in his prophecy. In her meeting with Odysseus (*Od.* 13.287–439) she formally initiates the slaughter of the suitors, her response to their role in the negative theoxeny in Book 1 (*Od.* 1.227–9), postponed to coincide with Odysseus' return.

Athena has a thematic association with violence throughout Homeric epic. Three other passages use variants of the formula in *Odyssey* 13.395, αἵματι τ' ἐγκεφάλῳ τε παλαξέμεν, "spattered with brain and blood." After executing the bloodshed Athena directs, the slaughter of the suitors, Odysseus himself is αἵματι καὶ λύθρῳ πεπαλαγμένον (*Od.* 22.402), "spattered with blood and gore." Shortly thereafter, an exultant Eurykleia tells Penelope, that Odysseus has returned, that he was the mysterious beggar, and, having slain the suitors, is now "spattered with blood and gore" (*Od.* 23.48 = 22.402). In the *Iliad* when Hektor leaves the battlefield to

---

[22] The following discussion expands upon material presented in Louden (2006: 72–3, 203–4, 257–61, 281–5).

arrange for a sacrifice to Athena, he declines to take part in the ritual himself because it is not right, he declares, to pray, "spattered with blood and gore," αἵματι καὶ λύθρῳ πεπαλαγμένον εὐχετάασθαι (*Il.* 6.268 = *Od.* 22.402, 23.48). Odysseus, the warrior Athena supports, is covered with blood and gore in victory she devises; Hector, object of her wrath, is covered with blood and gore presaging his death at her hands (*Od.* 22.166–329).[23]

Athena's brief arming scene in which she takes her great spear, employed three times in Homeric epic, projects an undercurrent of violence. The *Odyssey* employs the set piece when she descends from Olympos to meet with Telemachos and witness the suitors' violations of hospitality:

> She seized her mighty spear, tipped with a sharp bronze point, heavy, great, and stout, with which she *subdues* (δάμνησι) the ranks of heroes, those at whom she of the mighty father is angered.
>
> *Odyssey.* 1.99–101

The *Iliad* uses the same set piece twice (*Il.* 5.745–7 and 8.389–91 = *Od.* 1.99–101). In the *Iliad* the Greek verb rendered here as "subdues," δάμνησι, often denotes not just defeat, but a warrior's actual death (*Il.* 5.653, 11.444, 11.820, 16.816, 16.848, 22.55, 22.271, *et al.*).

The verb used of her wrath, *koteô*, "she subdues the ranks of heroes, those at whom she *is angry* (κοτέσσεται)," is especially used of long-term divine anger, the type that will culminate in apocalyptic destruction.[24] The formulaic description thus not only figures Athena threatening warriors with her deadly spear in a general way, but looks ahead to her key role in the climax of each poem, helping slay the warrior Hektor in the *Iliad* (*Il.* 22.166–329), helping slay the warrior band of the suitors in the *Odyssey* (Book 22).

The West Semitic deity, Anat, a virgin war goddess like Athena, also has a similar association with bloodthirsty violence, graphically depicted in a unique episode in the *Baal Cycle*. The passage shares qualities found in Athena's arming scene, in the depiction of the city at war on Akhilleus' shield (*Il.* 18.509–40), and in the spattered-with-blood-and-gore passages both Homeric epics associate with Athena:

> And look! Anat fights in the valley.
> Battles between the two cities.
> She smites peoples of the seashore
> Strikes the populace of the sunrise.

---

[23] On Hektor's appearance at *Iliad* 6.268 as prefiguring his death in *Iliad* 22, see Louden (2006: 72–3, 202–7).
[24] Walsh (2004: 23–9, 50, 52–3, 79, 97, 101).

> Under her, like balls, heads,
> Above her, like locusts, hands,
> Like locusts, heaps of warrior-hands.
> She fixes heads to her back,
> She fastens hands to her belt.
> Knee-deep she gleans in warrior-blood,
> Neck-deep in the gore of soldiers.
> With a shaft she drives away captives,
> With her bowstring, the foe.
> And look! Anat goes to her house,
> The goddess takes herself to her palace,
> For she is not sated with her fighting in the valley,
> With battling between the two cities.
> She arranges chairs for the soldiery,
> Arranges tables for the hosts,
> Footstools for the heroes.
> Hard she fights and looks about,
> Battling Anat surveys.
> Her innards swell with laughter,
> Her heart fills with joy,
> The innards of Anat with victory.
> Knee-deep she gleans in warrior-blood,
> Neck-deep in the gore of soldiers,
> Until she is sated with fighting in the house,
> With battling between the tables.
>   KTU 1.3 II 3–30[25]

While portions of the text defy sure interpretation, and commentators offer different readings,[26] there is a rough consensus that it naturally separates into two parts, as presented above. The first section depicts battle between two cities, and in this respect might be seen as a predecessor for the depiction of the city at war on Akhilleus' shield (*Il.* 18.509–40). The second section, however, depicts fighting in a less expected context, Anat's own palace/temple, connected in some way with a feast or banquet.[27] Both sections present considerable common ground with Homeric epic's more violent depictions of Athena. Gray (1979) refers to the whole text as Anat's Blood Bath. For our purposes, the description of Anat as "Knee-deep she gleans in warrior-blood,/Neck-deep in the gore of soldiers" (lines 12–13)

---

[25] Translation M. Smith (1995: 369).
[26] E.g., M. Smith (1995) argues for actual cannibalism by Anat in the second half; cf. Wyatt (1998: 248). In the *Iliad* Hera is associated with divine cannibalism, but only as an insult from Zeus (*Il.* 4.34–6).
[27] See Kapelrud (1969: 49–54) and Mark Smith (1995) for a sampling of interpretations.

is unexpectedly close to Athena's "spattered with blood and brains/gore" passages (though Athena herself is never so described), and suggests a similar tradition and conception. Details in the second section not only evoke parallels with Athena, but with the specific circumstances of Odysseus as he slays the suitors under her direction.

All of Athena's actions against the suitors take place indoors, inside Odysseus' palace, during feasts. In Book 2 she temporarily incapacitates them, knocking their drinking goblets out of their hands and making them sleep (*Od.* 2.393–8), a premonitory miniature of their slaughter, so Telemachos can leave, unobserved, for Pylos. In Book 20 she induces their hysterical laughter (*Od.* 20.345–6) just before Theoklymenos prophesies their destruction (both episodes marked by forms of *plazô*, *Odyssey* 2.396, 20.346, expressing her divine wrath against them; Louden 1999: 87–8). In Book 22 she repeatedly aids and directs Odysseus in slaying them (*Od.* 22.205–40, 256–9, 273–5, 297–8). However we interpret Anat's actions, the depiction of her employing violence in a feast or banquet setting, "fighting in the house,/With battling between the tables," is unexpectedly close in setting to the gore and bloodshed that is the destruction of the suitors while they feast in Odysseus' palace.[28] The key difference (discussed below) is that Odysseus, a mortal, carries out the violent destruction Athena demands, whereas in the *Baal Cycle* Anat, the goddess herself, battles with and slaughters the warriors.

In the *Odyssey* all the spattered-with-blood-and-gore passages (*Od.* 13.395, 22.402, 23.408) refer to Odysseus' slaughter of the suitors, planned and directed by Athena. Three additional passages further the graphic depiction of bloodshed reminiscent of Anat's slaughter of the warriors in her temple. In his prophecy of the suitors' destruction, Theoklymenos sees the palace's "beautiful walls and columns splashed with blood" (αἵματι δ' ἐρράδαται τοῖχοι καλαί τε μεσόδμαι: *Od.* 20.354). While Odysseus slays the suitors, and again when Amphimedon's ghost, in Hades, narrates to Agamemnon what happened to them, the palace streams with blood, "their horrible cries rose, their heads shattered, the whole floor was running with blood" (τῶν δὲ στόνος ὄρνυτ' ἀεικής / κράτων τυπτομένων, δάπεδον δ' ἅπαν αἵματι θῦε: *Od.* 22.308–9 = 24.184–5). Theano's sacrifice to Athena, refused by the goddess, is an unsuccessful attempt to prevent such god-demanded violence. Hektor's blood-spattered form here (*Il.* 6.267–8) prefigures his

---

[28] To my knowledge, Gordon's comment in passing (1965a: 186–7), is the only earlier mention of these parallels.

own death at Akhilleus' hands, under Athena's direction.[29] Such divine violence is at the core of apocalyptic myth.

OT myth occasionally draws on an unexpectedly similar tradition and conception of divine violence for Yahweh. Perhaps no passage is more startling in its violence than Isaiah 63, in its similarity to the spattered-with-blood-and-gore passages Athena attracts, and Anat, "Knee-deep she gleans in warrior blood." Here the prophet asks Yahweh about his alarming appearance:

> Why are your clothes all red,
> like the garments of one treading grapes in the winepress?
> I have trodden the press alone,
> for none of my people was with me.
> I trod the nations in my anger,
> I trampled them in my fury,
> and their blood bespattered my garments
> and all my clothing was stained...
> I stamped on peoples in my anger,
> I shattered them in my fury
> and spilled their blood over the ground.
> (Isaiah 63:2–3, 6)

Yahweh here describes himself in terms similar to those used for Odysseus after Athena directs him in slaughtering the suitors, or Anat, "knee-deep... in warrior-blood, neck-deep in the gore of soldiers." McKenzie interprets (1968: 187):

This is the theophany of Yahweh the warrior judge... the imagery of Yahweh marching in blood-stained garments is somewhat appalling, but by a literary touch not common in Third Isaiah, one is left to imagine the scene from which Yahweh has come... In this poem we are on the verge of apocalyptic literature... the overthrow as a world cataclysm.

A passage from Psalms again suggests parallels both with Odysseus, directed by Athena as he slays the suitors, and Anat, in the episode from the *Baal Cycle*:

> God himself smites the heads of his enemies,
> those proud sinners with their flowing locks.
> The Lord says, "I shall fetch them back from Bashan,
> I shall fetch them from the depths of the sea.

---

[29] For additional parallels between Athena and Anat, see Louden (2006: 245–85); on the possibility that Hektor's death is influenced by myths of human sacrifice, see Louden (2006: 71–3, 202–7).

that you may bathe your feet in blood,
while the tongues of your dogs are eager for it.

Psalm 68:21–3[30]

In its specific emphasis on striking the enemies' heads, the passage is close to the description of the suitors' heads, struck by Odysseus (*Od.* 22.308–9 = 24.184–5), the palace floor running with their blood. The graphic description of reveling in the victims' blood again suggests Anat, "neck-deep in the gore of warriors," wearing the heads of slain warriors as ornaments.

Isaiah's depiction of the destruction of Edom combines similar bloodthirsty qualities with apocalyptic destruction, probably middle degree:

[F]or the Lord's anger is against all the nations
and his wrath against all their hordes;
he gives them over to slaughter and destruction.
Their slain will be flung out,
stench will rise from their corpses,
and the mountains will run with their blood...
The Lord has a sword sated with blood,
gorged with fat, the fat of rams' kidneys,
and with the blood of lambs and goats;
for the Lord has a sacrifice in Bozrah,
a great slaughter in Edom.

Isaiah 34:2–4, 6[31]

MORTAL AGENTS BRING ABOUT THE DESTRUCTION THE GODS REQUIRE (*OD.* 22 AND EXOD. 32)

Odyssey 22 and Exodus 32 both share an otherwise unique variation on contained apocalypse. In each myth, though the god insists on the destruction of a large number of mortals who have caused offense, mortals, acting as the god's agents, carry out the required destruction. In both myths this is a logical outcome of the close teamwork between the mortal protagonist and god. The two myths employ the motif very differently, reflecting

---

[30] Cf. I shall make my arrows drunk with blood, my sword will devour flesh,
blood of slain and captives,
the heads of the enemy princes.
(Deuteronomy 32:42)

[31] See M. Smith (1990: 63) for additional OT passages offering parallels to the Anat text.

fundamental distinctions between the two different types of characters, Odysseus, warrior and hero, Moses, prophet and patriarch. In the *Odyssey* the motif is also a climactic instance of overdetermination that finds a parallel in the *Iliad*.

As noted in Chapter 2, though the suitors, in their violations of hospitality, offend Athena in Book 1 (*Od.* 1.227–9), and by the norms of theoxeny already earn their deaths, the epic postpones their destruction until Odysseus returns. The *Odyssey* thus extends the close teamwork between the hero and the goddess even to the actual destruction of the suitors. Commentators tend to maximize revenge as a factor in Odysseus' destruction of the suitors,[32] and minimize, if not entirely ignore, the divine involvement and teamwork. Revenge is an element, Odysseus' reaction to the abuse he suffers at the suitors' hands, and their multi-year depredation of his holdings. But the slaughter of the suitors is initiated and demanded by Athena (*Od.* 13.375–81, 393–6), long before Odysseus returns to Ithaka. He receives no abuse from them in person until Book 17. In Books 17–20 he warns them of coming retribution, and shows them that the door is open; they could cease their offensive behavior, leave the palace, and so avoid the coming destruction (discussed in Chapter 11 as *The wicked ignore prophets' warnings of the consequences of their behavior*). As Athena's agent he slays the suitors as those who violated the sacred institution of hospitality, much as the Greeks have Zeus' support in the sacking of Troy because of Paris' violation of hospitality, as well as earlier acts by Laomedon, and breaking the oaths sworn in Book 3.[33] Words that are occasionally translated as "revenge," such as ποινή (*Od.* 23.312), τίσις (*Od.* 2.76), and forms of the verb τίω / τίνω (*Od.* 3.206, 8.348, 20.121, 20.169, 22.218, 24.352), all actually suggest less emotion-centered ideas than "revenge," and might be better rendered as "retribution," or "recompense." When Laertes is persuaded that Odysseus has really returned and slain the suitors, he regards their deaths as proof that the gods exist, in accord with a principle of just retribution (*Od.* 24.351–2).

The *Odyssey* uses the same combination of motives – Odysseus acting out of revenge, and as agent of divine punishment – in the encounter with Polyphêmos.[34] From the outset the episode suggests a connection with

---

[32] E.g., de Jong (2001: 336): "The function of the bloodthirstiness she displays...is to legitimize Odysseus' ruthless revenge"; cf. 334, 337.
[33] On the Trojans' many forms of misconduct offensive to the gods, see Louden (2006: 183–201).
[34] Cf. de Jong (2001: 233) on Odysseus' defeat of Polyphêmos as a combination of his revenge and Zeus' divine punishment of the Cyclops.

divine retribution in its emphasis on the Cyclopes' lawlessness (*Od.* 9.112–14, 175–6, and especially 9.189: ἀθεμίστια ᾔδη).[35] The entire encounter is further subordinated under the rubric of hospitality,[36] as Odysseus' interaction with the suitors is subordinated under the rubric of negative theoxeny. When he realizes what danger he is in, Odysseus invokes Zeus as the protector and avenger of guests (*Od.* 9.269–72). After the Cyclops has eaten four of his crew, Odysseus wonders how he might "pay him back/requite/punish" (τισαίμην: *Od.* 9.317), so Athena would grant him glory. After blinding him, and saving the rest of his crew, Odysseus declares to the monster that Zeus and the other gods have punished him for his desecration of hospitality (*Od.* 9.479), implying he acted as Zeus' agent.[37] When Polyphêmos cries out in pain, even the other Cyclopes assume Zeus is responsible for his sufferings (Reece 1993: 139–40). There are extensive thematic parallels between Polyphêmos and the suitors in their violations of hospitality. As Reece notes (1993: 173), they demonstrate a "lack of regard for both religious and secular institutions." Both have no fear of Zeus (p. 174). Both attempt to strike Odysseus by hurling objects at him (p. 174). Both are punished by him.

There are further specific parallels less associated with hospitality. Odysseus' strategy of suppressing his real name, and presenting himself instead as "Nobody" (*Od.* 9.364–7), anticipates his use of disguise as a beggar, another kind of "nobody," among the suitors. In both episodes Apollo is indirectly involved. The divine wine, crucial to Odysseus' defeat of Polyphêmos, parallels and prefigures Apollo's involvement in the destruction of the suitors at a feast sacred to him. As Odysseus relates, in sacking Ismaros he spared Apollo's priest, Maron, who in gratitude gave him a divinely potent wine (*Od.* 9.196–212), with which Odysseus temporarily incapacitates Polyphêmos.[38] As explored in Chapter 12 (*The king's pivotal confrontation with his enemies falls on a religious festival*), Odysseus defeats the suitors, mainly through his skill at archery, on a day sacred to Apollo. Though not onstage in either episode, Apollo's role, if indirect, is nonetheless crucial in each case. In the *Cyclopeia*, Apollo's wine suggests the role Athena and the angels play in the negative theoxenies: she temporarily incapacitates the suitors in Book 2 and Book 20, as the angels blind the

---

[35] Cf. Reece (1993: 134), on *Odyssey* 9.275–78, "This response clearly places Polyphemus outside the bounds of normal heroic society."
[36] For analysis of the whole episode as an instance of hospitality, see Reece (1993: 123–43).
[37] Cf. Heubeck (1989: 38), on the same passage, "the moral justification of his actions (τίσις): he feels himself to be the agent of the vengeance of Zeus ξείνιος, in whose name he had requested hospitality."
[38] Reece (1993: 138): "this strong brew will inebriate him and facilitate his blinding."

mob at Genesis 19:11. Or, if we omit the gods, in both episodes those who have violated hospitality have their judgment impaired by alcohol before Odysseus defeats them. In all these particulars the *Odyssey* uses its version of the combat myth, Odysseus' defeat of Polyphêmos by blinding him with a pike made of olive, sacred to Athena, to prefigure the apocalyptic destruction of the suitors.

EXODUS 32'S INNOVATION ON CONTAINED APOCALYPSE

After Moses talks Yahweh out of slaying *all* the Israelites, he himself directs the destruction of a smaller number. When Aaron recounts the events that culminated in the perverse religious ritual, Moses asks who is on Yahweh's side (Exod. 32:21–6). When the Levites rally to his call, he issues a grim directive:

"Arm yourselves, each of you, with his sword. Go through the camp from gate to gate and back again. Each of you kill brother, friend, neighbor." The Levites obeyed, and about three thousand of the people died that day. (Exodus 32: 27–8)

As his participation in the adapted divine council has Moses serve a role usually filled by a god, the same holds for the gruesome destruction. Moses directs the Levites in the destruction required by the contained apocalypse here, much as Athena directs Odysseus in the destruction of the suitors, as that contained apocalypse demands.

In a key difference with the *Odyssey*, however, one that also holds for Genesis 19, the destruction in Exodus 32 seems indiscriminate, not necessarily directed at those who took part in the offensive ritual.[39] Propp notes the basic inconsistencies (2006: 563):

Were only 3,000 of the 600,000 adult men (or two to three million individuals) guilty? One has the impression that almost the whole people was implicated in the Calf worship. If so, then the death of a few is a *pars pro toto* punishment – with the potential of more deaths to follow.

Even more problematic, Aaron, who parallels Eurylochos on Thrinakia as the leader and conductor of the perverse ritual, and thus bears more responsibility for the events than anyone else, is not slain. In the *Odyssey* Eurylochos perishes, not only as the member of the crew who instigates and executes the sacrifice of Helios' sacrosanct cattle, but as part of a series of three parallel figures which also includes Euryalos, the abusive Phaiakian

---

[39] Cf. Propp (2006: 563): "Moses and Yahweh appear to have ordained an indiscriminate slaughter of the entire nation, in accordance with 22:19 and similar proscriptions on apostasy... In the event, only about 3,000 of the two to three million Israelites die."

athlete who insults Odysseus when he declines to compete in their games, and Eurymachos, one of the two ringleaders of the suitors. Each figure, marked by a parallel name formation Eury – lochos, – alos, – machos (Louden 1999: 19–20), having first provoked fractious confrontation with Odysseus, perishes in each of the *Odyssey*'s three contained apocalypses. Aaron's clear kinship with such a figure should require his death in Exodus 32. As Propp notes (2006: 568), Deuteronomy 9:20 recounts a slightly different version of the myth in which an incensed Yahweh would have killed Aaron, had Moses not intervened on his behalf, leading Propp to conclude (*ibid.*), "I think it likely that in a version of the Gold Calf story more complete than that preserved in Exodus, Levite followers of Aaron also fell in the purge."

The reason for Aaron's surprising survival, however, may well lie in the events of a much later period retrojected back upon the myth. Using evidence in a number of passages, commentators have concluded that Israelite culture engaged in a fierce struggle over what constituted a legitimate priest, as Propp summarizes (2006: 567):

> In Second Temple Judaism and afterward, only those claiming Aaronic pedigree were considered legitimate priests... The earlier situation was far more fluid... in protohistorical times, it seems that the entire tribe of Levi was the priestly caste.[40]

If at a later period only those descended from Aaron could serve as priests, then in the ancient myth Aaron clearly has to survive the apocalyptic destruction he helps provoke in Exodus 32. We earlier noted a similar instance of the accommodation of a subgenre of myth to serve an etiological function in the birth of Isaac within Abraham's positive theoxeny. While theoxeny has no necessary connection with the birth of a child (though the motif is also present in Ovid's tale of Hyrieus, *Fasti* 5.493–544), since Abraham has to have male offspring if he is to become the first Israelite patriarch, OT myth adapts positive theoxeny, in which the disguised immortal traditionally rewards the host who has demonstrated his piety, by using it as the vehicle to provide him with a son.

THE *ODYSSEY*'S INNOVATION ON CONTAINED APOCALYPSE

The conclusion of Book 24, the *Odyssey*'s most criticized book,[41] innovates, employing a further variation on contained apocalypse. Book 24's final episode (*Od.* 24.413–548), the aftermath of the destruction of the suitors,

---

[40] For more complete discussion, see Propp (2006: 567–74).
[41] E.g., see Heubeck's notes (1992: 356–8, 381–2, and 406). See also Stanford (1962, Vol. 2: 409–10). For a defense of Book 24, see de Jong (2001: 566–7, 583, etc.).

is a postponed continuation of Book 22. The slaying of 108 men and their retainers, most of the aristocrats from the surrounding area, prompts significant repercussions. But between these two thematically connected sections, the *Odyssey* interposes its conclusion of romance, Odysseus' intricate recognition scenes and reunions with Penelope (Book 23), and Laertes (*Od.* 24.205–412). The intervening episodes, belonging to an entirely different subgenre of myth, and the problematic critical reception of all of Book 24, have prevented accurate understanding of how Book 24's final episode necessarily continues and completes Book 22.

When word of the suitors' deaths spreads through Ithaka, and families have retrieved the corpses of the slain, the relatives gather in an assembly to debate their options. Antinoös' father, Eupeithes, proposes revenging their sons by attacking Odysseus (*Od.* 24.413–37).[42] His entire speech is built on specious reasoning. He incorrectly assigns to Odysseus the blame for the crew's deaths, contrary to the poem's explicit portrayal of them perishing through their own recklessness. He mistakenly assumes Odysseus now intends to flee (*Od.* 23.430–2), whereas the audience knows he is sharing a meal with his father, celebrating their reunion. Eupeithes' motive for retaliation is chiefly how the relatives would *appear* to others should they not avenge their sons' deaths, as opposed to any larger sense of right and wrong, or what the gods would deem correct. Medon, eyewitness to the suitors' destruction, and Halitherses, reprising his role from the Book 2 assembly (*Od.* 2.157–76), both speak against Eupeithes' rash suggestion, pointing out that a god openly aided his defeat of the suitors, and that they earned their destruction through their own recklessness. Nonetheless, a majority of those present are persuaded by Eupeithes, an ironic wordplay as Heubeck notes (1992: 410, on 24.465–6: ἀλλ' Εὐπείθει / πείθοντ').

The incipient crisis, threatening destruction beyond that required by the negative theoxeny, prompts a divine council between Athena and Zeus (*Od.* 24.472–87). Commentators (e.g., Heubeck 1992: 405, 411; Stanford 1962, Vol. 2: 428) usually compare this divine council to that at *Odyssey* 1.26–96, on the grounds that the same two speakers appear in each, and that the two scenes serve as an instance of ring composition. But the divine council at *Odyssey* 5.3–43 also has the same two speakers, Athena and Zeus, which suggests the speakers' identity *per se* is not a sufficient criterion for demonstrating parallels between two divine councils. Furthermore, the

---

[42] Retaliation in the form of a counter-attack may echo the retaliation by the Kikkones and their neighbors at *Odyssey* 9.47–63 (though the outcome of that episode was disastrous for Odysseus, whereas this instance is not).

dialogues at *Odyssey* 24.472–87 and 1.26–96 deal with entirely different topics. I argue instead that 24.472–87 belongs to an entirely different subtype of divine council than 1.26–96, and should be seen as paralleling the *Odyssey*'s other two divine councils that mediate a wrathful god's level of destruction, Zeus and Helios (*Od.* 12.376–88), and Zeus and Poseidon (*Od.* 13.125–59).

Chapter 1 demonstrated that most divine councils feature the sky father deliberating with either the mentor god, or the wrathful god, which distinction, based on a deity's function, divides divine councils into two distinct subtypes. In the divine councils in Books 1 and 5, Athena clearly functions as the mentor deity, steering each council to its focus on Odysseus, and expressing concern for his plight. By contrast, the divine councils in Books 12 and 13, Zeus deliberating respectively with Helios (*Od.* 12.376–88) and Poseidon (*Od.* 13.125–59), clearly feature the latter gods as respective instances of the wrathful god, though angry less with Odysseus than with the respective body of fractious young men, his crew and the Phaiakian crew.

On the basis of verbal formulas, additional parallels, and the larger trajectories of the *Odyssey*'s plot, in this divine council (*Od.* 24.472–87) Athena functions as the wrathful god, angry at the suitors and their party, as the final consequence from their role in the negative theoxeny initiated in Book 1 (*Od.* 1.227–9; cf. 13.393–6). Athena asks Zeus whether he will prompt further fighting between the two factions or establish friendship between them, clearly aligning their discussion with other instances in which the sky father mediates a subsequent level of destruction, as at *Odyssey* 12.376–88 and 13.125–59 (cf., *Il.* 7.443–64). A specific verbal formula occurs here, often found in other instances of divine councils featuring the wrathful god. After Athena raises the two options, further fighting, or peaceful reconciliation, Zeus says she may do as she pleases (*Od.* 24.481: ἔρξον ὅπως ἐθέλεις), the same formula as when he mediates Poseidon's wrath, when the latter initially wants to destroy the entire city of the Phaiakians (*Od.* 13.145: ἔρξον ὅπως ἐθέλεις). The *Odyssey* employs the formula in specific constraints, in parallel contexts. The *Iliad* offers a close variant when Zeus gives Athena permission to cause Hektor's death (*Il.* 22.185: ἔρξον ὅπῃ δή τοι νόος ἔπλετο). In the *Iliad*'s complex divine economy, Athena functions as the wrathful god from Hektor's perspective (Louden 2005: 92–3). As noted in Chapter 1, the Ugaritic epic *The Aqhat* features a similar remark by El, the respective sky father, to Anat, the wrathful goddess who wishes to destroy the title character, "Lay hold of what you desire, carry out what you wish," CTA 18.i.18. Zeus goes on to specify what he would do, which is the less violent of the two options, just as in *Odyssey* 13, with Poseidon, and at *Iliad* 7.459–63, again with Poseidon.

After Odysseus, Laertes, Telemachos, Dolios, and his six sons arm, and the two factions prepare to face each other, Athena breathes great force into Odysseus (*Od.* 24.520: μένος). In the *Iliad* she instills *menos* in a hero as prelude to his *aristeia* (as at *Il.* 5.1–2), his slaying of a number of opposing warriors. Book 24 briefly proceeds as if that were the case, with Athena also breathing *menos* into Laertes (*Od.* 24.520), and instructing him to hurl his spear. When his spear strikes and kills Eupeithes, Odysseus' faction attacks, their momentum underscored in a pivotal contrafactual:

> And now they would have destroyed them all, taken away their return,
> had not Athena, Maiden of aegis-bearing Zeus,
> cried out in a booming voice, restraining all the warriors.
>
> *Odyssey* 24.528–30

Odysseus threatens to expand the level of destruction beyond that of a contained apocalypse to that of the middle degree, destruction of most of the city's inhabitants. The suitors' deaths were mandated by their violations of hospitality, but their relatives have committed no such offence. Much as the *Odyssey*'s presentation of virtual theoxeny (Books 17–22) blurs the line between hero and god, with Odysseus serving as if he were a god in disguise, here too the *Odyssey* has Odysseus act like a wrathful god in desiring a higher level of destruction, who needs to be restrained by Athena.[43] The *Odyssey* innovates not only in having Odysseus act in such a way, but in the chronology of events: usually a divine council mediates the angry god's wrath and determines the level of destruction *before* the apocalypse occurs. Here, however, the scene with Zeus and Athena, and Odysseus' subsequent confrontation with the suitors' relatives, are set a full book and a half *after* the destruction of the suitors, largely because the *Odyssey* first concludes its use of romance with the long-expected recognition scenes with Penelope and Laertes.

GENESIS 18–19'S INNOVATION ON CONTAINED APOCALYPSE

In both contained apocalypses under consideration, Exodus 32, and *Odyssey* 22, human agents carry out the destruction. In Genesis 19, like *Odyssey* 22, destruction that concludes a negative theoxeny, Yahweh himself brings

---

[43] Cf. de Jong (2001: 586): "Athena's peace mission starts off as an 'if not'-situation, which subtly suggests that if not for Athena, Odysseus and his men would have gained a full victory."

about the more extensive devastation of middle-level apocalypse, raining fire and brimstone (Gen. 19:24). The adapted divine council between Yahweh and Abraham in Genesis 18 violates the traditional sequence of such events, as in *Odyssey* 24 with Zeus and Athena. As noted above, Yahweh and Abraham have their adapted divine council *before* the myth depicts mortals performing any acts offensive to the gods. In an additional unexpected variation Yahweh, though requiring the deaths of all inhabitants of the two cities other than Lot and his family, is here less wrathful than in Exodus 32, a contained apocalypse, that results in the deaths of a much smaller number. But Exodus 32 offers an additional parallel with *Odyssey* 13, Poseidon's threatened destruction of all the Phaiakians. Each wrathful god plots the apocalyptic destruction of his own "special" people, angered because their betrayal, as he sees it, is more offensive because of the favor he had shown them.

BREAKING A DIVINE INTERDICTION RESULTS IN PETRIFACTION (GEN. 19, OD. 13)

The apocalypses of Genesis 19 and *Odyssey* 13 are further linked in their use of the specific motif of the petrifaction of mortals who offend the gods. When Lot and his family leave, an angel tells them not to look back (Gen. 19:17), a traditional divine interdiction extant in other myths (e.g., Orpheus and Eurydice, *Metamorphoses* 10.50–9). Lot's unnamed wife does so nonetheless, and is turned into a pillar of salt for her transgression of the prohibition (Gen. 19:26). Her metamorphosis should be taken as an only slightly modified instance of a motif common in Greek myth, a mortal turning into stone as punishment from the gods (e.g., Niobe, *Il.* 24.617; cf. *Il.* 2.319).[44]

Petrifaction of mortals is also the outcome of Poseidon's wrath against the Phaiakian crew. After Zeus mediates his wrath down to a lower level of destruction, Poseidon turns the offending crew and ship into a stone so they will cease ferrying mortals across the seas (*Od.* 13.125–59).[45] Long before ferrying Odysseus home, the Phaiakians knew an ancient prophecy that one day Poseidon would be angry with them for their escorts (*Od.* 8.565–9 = 13.173–7), that his wrath would threaten the entire city

---

[44] The *Aeneid*'s Creusa, unable to make it out of the apocalyptic destruction of Troy, though her husband and offspring do, much as Lot and his daughters do, clearly seems to be an instantiation of the same traditional figure, though without a divine interdiction involved.

[45] Cf. de Jong (2001: 319–20): "Zeus reacts by setting out what he thinks best ... he asks Poseidon to petrify the ship."

(*Od.* 8.569 = 13.177). The prophecy could be understood as an implicit divine interdiction, "do not ferry everyone home with ease (and certainly not Odysseus, object of my wrath)."[46] When he tells Zeus of his threatened course of action, Poseidon uses *ekhô* (ἔχω), which can mean "cease from" (*Od.* 13.151–2) as Stanford renders in his translation (1962, Vol. 2: 204), "that they may now stop and cease from," the consequence of which equals a negative command, "do not." As in Genesis 19, the petrifaction clearly serves as an etiology for a rock formation, whether one in the "real world," or one only in the world of the poem.[47] In myth a god uses metamorphosis as a reward or punishment. Baucis and Philemon become trees, a living metamorphosis that serves as reward for their exemplary behavior in receiving the disguised Jupiter and Mercury. Petrifaction, for Lot's wife and the Phaiakian crew, is metamorphosis as punishment for mortals who violate the gods' behests. Causing petrifaction as conclusion to an apocalypse is a further specific motif shared by Poseidon and Yahweh. What has struck many commentators as the indiscriminate, arbitrary quality of Poseidon's destruction of the Phaiakian crew is paralleled in Genesis 19 in Yahweh's destruction of all the inhabitants of Sodom and Gomorrah. As noted above, the description in the *Works and Days* (240–1) of a city being destroyed because of the actions of one immoral man is a further instance of a similarly problematic kind of divine punishment.

One divine interdiction marks the conclusion of Odysseus' return from Scheria, another marks his approach to it. Implicit in Leukothea's careful commands to him just before his approach to Scheria is a divine interdiction not to turn around, not to look back. Once he has used her divine veil to secure his safety, he is to throw it in the ocean and turn away (αὐτὸς δ' ἀπονόσφι τραπέσθαι: *Od.* 5.350). Though not expressed as a negative command, the expression functions as if it were one, just as Poseidon's formulation for preventing the Phaiakians from further ferrying. Leukothea's prohibition is a clear equivalent of the angel's command to Lot and his company (Gen. 19:17), "don't look back." In a further link, both instances of the motif mark consecutive appearances by Poseidon, suggesting a form of ring composition. Except for his appearance in Demodokos' song (*Od.* 8.344–58), outside of the *Odyssey*'s present-time plot, Poseidon is not onstage between *Odyssey* 5.381 and 13.125.

---

[46] Cf., Louden (1999: 18).
[47] Cf., de Jong (2001: 321): "Thus we are dealing with a negative *aition*, such as is also found in *Iliad* 7.445–64 + 12.9–35 (explanation of why the wall around the Greek camp is no longer visible in the time of the narrator)."

For the Phaiakians, petrifaction of the ship and crew constitutes a boundary around their culture. They will no longer escort mortals home, and thus lose their status as consummate seafarers. As a consequence they will be more removed and isolated from all other mortals, perhaps sealed off from them hereafter. We noted briefly in Chapter 6 that the Clashing Rocks serve a similar function.[48] The end of their escort for mortals thus marks not only a boundary between different ages, but resembles the end of a kind of paradise; their heretofore intimate relations with Poseidon are now ruptured, and will never be quite the same. The same dynamic is present in the Genesis creation myth after Adam and Eve violate the divine interdiction against eating from the tree of knowledge. Yahweh banishes them from Eden that they may not eat from the tree of life, stationing the cherubim and a flashing sword to bar any future return to Eden (Gen. 3: 23–4). Arguably, "don't go back" implicitly underlies Yahweh's acts, and, as such broadly resembles Poseidon's intent for the Phaiakians, "don't go back to providing escort."

THE ONE JUST MAN (LOT, AENEAS, AND ODYSSEUS)

Though the Phaiakian crew all perish, petrified by Poseidon, Odysseus safely reaches Ithaka. He is also the lone survivor of Zeus' destruction of his own crew off Thrinakia. In both contexts Odysseus instantiates a traditional figure, the *one just man* who survives the apocalypse. Amid a community that offends god is a lone man (and his immediate family) who does not violate the divine interdiction, or other specific commands, and is rewarded with surviving the god-sent destruction. Full-scale apocalypse has such a figure in Utnapishtim/Noah and Deukalion, lone survivors of the great deluge, while middle and contained apocalypses have Dardanos (*Aen.* 6.650), Baucis and Philemon (*Metamorphoses*), Enoch (Gen. 5:24), and, in instances more closely related to the *Odyssey*, Aeneas, and Lot. Both Aeneas and Lot escape middle degree apocalypse, destruction of an entire city.[49] Odysseus escapes not one but two instances of contained apocalypse, both set at sea (Jonah, discussed below, offers a partial parallel). Both Aeneas and Lot lose their wives fleeing apocalyptic destruction, but each nonetheless becomes a patriarch, founder of a people. Odysseus escapes his destructions to return to his wife, and restore order to his kingdom. In the *Odyssey*'s virtual theoxeny in Books 17–22, Odysseus as the mysterious beggar, a Christ-like king abused in his own kingdom, also instantiates the same

---

[48] Cf., M. L. West (2005: 42).   [49] Discussion in Louden (2006: 235–8).

traditional figure. If he had not been able to talk Yahweh down to a lower level of destruction, Moses himself would have been a *one just man*, father of a nation like Aeneas, as is evident in Yahweh's angry threat, "Now let me alone to pour out my anger on them, so that I may put an end to them and make a great nation spring from you" (Exod. 32:10).

In several respects Lot is a parodic version of the traditional figure.[50] While Odysseus reunites with Penelope shortly after surviving his apocalypses, and Aeneas wins Lavinia's hand to become progenitor of the Roman people, Lot commits incest with his two daughters (Gen. 19:30–8), their sons becoming patriarchs of two peoples, the Moabites and the Ammonites (Gen. 19:37–8). The daughters get him drunk to manipulate him into having sex with them. While commentators find positive interpretations of the incident,[51] they resort to extra-textual conjectures to do so.[52] I see evident parody in Lot's drunkenness, in his being unaware initially that he serves this pivotal role as father of two nations. The episode offers parallels with two other unusual scenes in Genesis. After being credited with inventing viticulture, Noah gets drunk and passes out, lying naked in his tent. When his son Ham sees him naked he summons his other brothers to look at their father in such a state (Gen. 9:21–7). The encounter parallels Lot's episode in how his child takes advantage of him while he is drunk, and also serves a larger etiological function, assigning subservient status to Ham's offspring, the Canaanites.[53] Like Lot, Jacob is tricked into having sex with Leah, the sister of his intended bride, but compelled to marry her as a consequence (Gen. 29:16–28). Lot, though surviving his apocalypse, concludes his myth in a bizarre variant that undercuts his status as the *one just man*.

Jonah also suggests a parodic inversion of *the one just man* in yet other ways. The many particulars of his myth, the fantastic voyage and storm at sea, object of a divine wrath while at sea, suggest rough parallels with the *Odyssey* as noted in Chapter 7. We also noted that the threatened apocalyptic destruction of Nineveh suggests affinities with the threatened apocalyptic

[50] Cf., Carr (1996: 191, n. 27): "Lot functions consistently throughout as a negative contrast to Abraham."
[51] Alter (2004: 96) suggests the story "may draw on old … traditions in which the supposed origins of these two peoples in incest were understood as evidence of their purity, or their vitality"; cf. Speiser, who, while raising the possibility of ethnic humor, immediately dismisses it (1962: 145), "As they are here portrayed, Lot and his two daughters had every reason to believe that they were the last people on earth … The young women were concerned with the future of the race, and they were resolute enough to adopt the only desperate measure that appeared to be available."
[52] E.g., the narrative does not support Speiser's contention that Lot's daughters are concerned with the future of the race, though archetypal apocalyptic conventions support such a view.
[53] The episode is notoriously confused. See discussion in Speiser (1962: 61–3). For further discussion of parallels between Lot and Noah see Carr (1996: 190–1).

destruction of the Phaiakians' city in *Odyssey* 13. But the protagonists could hardly be more different. Disobedient to and in flight from god, the one member of the crew who looks as though he will not survive, the one mortal *disappointed* when the threatened apocalyptic destruction does *not* come to pass (Jonah 4:1), in his myth Jonah is essentially the one *unjust* man.

NT MYTH: APOCALYPSE POSTPONED

Though starting its negative theoxeny in Book 1, the *Odyssey* postpones its inevitable outcome, the slaying of the suitors, until Odysseus returns to carry it out. By de Jong's reckoning (2001: 588), Odysseus slays the suitors thirty-nine days after they offend Athena (*Od.* 1.227–9). Genesis 19, on the other hand, depicts the destruction of the mob the same night that they threaten Lot's guests, as Exodus 32 depicts the destruction of the rebellious Israelites the same day as their ritual. The *Odyssey*, Genesis 19, and Exodus 32 all depict their apocalypses in present time, each forming a climax, and at least partial conclusion of their respective narrative units. NT myth, though repeatedly referring to a climactic apocalypse, a combined divine wrath and Day of Judgment, does not depict it in present time, but postpones it until the future. As noted above, Hesiod offers a precedent and parallel for NT myth's postponed, not-depicted apocalypse in his comments about how Zeus will destroy his own era, the Iron Age (*Works and Days*: 137–40).

Christianity came into being in a historical-religious context in which eschatological apocalypticism was a dominant form of belief, a dominant way of interpreting the world. Consequently, NT myth has perhaps the strongest apocalyptic orientation of any of the traditions considered in this study. However, consensus is elusive as to the nature of NT apocalypse. I take the position that Christ and Paul are both depicted believing that a large-scale apocalypse is imminent,[54] whether triggered by the crucifixion of Christ and/or the destruction of the Temple in Jerusalem,[55] that Christ's Second Coming involves a Day of Judgment,[56] thought of as "the 'last day,' the end of the present world" (Mosca 1993: 136), on which he passes sentence

---

[54] On the imminence for Paul and early Christians of the Second Coming, and consequently the Day of Judgment, see Travis (1993: 685, in Metzger and Coogan): "Both here (Mark 13:30) and elsewhere (Rom. 13:11–12; 1 Pet. 4:7) the nearness of Christ's coming is stressed . . . He will come to pass judgment on the whole human race (Matt. 25:31–46; 1 Cor. 4:5)."
[55] For discussion of other interpretations of NT apocalypse, see Allison (2000), Horsley (2000), de Boer (2000), Collins, Adela Yarbro (2000), and Frankfurter (2000).
[56] On the Day of Judgment in NT myth, see Mosca (1993: 156–7 in Metzger and Coogan).

over the entire world. NT myth's term for the divine wrath that leads to apocalypse is *orgē* (ὀργή). Relevant passages include Luke 21:23; 1 Thessalonians 1:10; Romans 1:18, 2:5; Revelation 6:17, 11:18, 16;19. The Septuagint also uses ὀργή for divine wraths that lead to apocalyptic destruction in OT myth. Relevant to our analysis and discussion are instances at Exodus 32:10, 11, 12; Numbers 1:1, 10, 14:34, 16:22, 46, 25:4; Lamentations: 1:12, 2:1, 21; Jonah 3:9; and Zechariah 7:12.

NT myth tends to make the traditional motifs it inherits *universal*. Hence its apocalypse is not to be contained, as in Exodus 32 and *Odyssey* 12, 13, and 22, nor averted, as in Jonah, but is full scale, the largest degree. When these texts were written, Christianity was a small, persecuted minority, in transition from its origins as a small subset of Judaism. Those non-Christians who will be destroyed (Mosca 1993: 157: "the destruction of the godless"), those condemned to eternal death, depending on which apocalyptic scenario one takes as dominant, will therefore constitute the vast majority of all mortals. Those who will survive are an extension of the traditional figure of *the one just man*. Now *the one just people*, those who believe in Christ (a tiny percentage of mortals in the first century), will survive the worldwide apocalyptic destruction and divine judgment. Christians, the *one just people*, will be judged as good, and survive the apocalypse.

In spite of the difference in degree, there is a close link between one of the *Odyssey*'s contained apocalypses and NT myth's full-scale apocalypse, as noted in Chapter 2. In Matthew theoxeny serves as the litmus test applied in the Judgment to determine who is saved or destroyed in the apocalypse (Matt. 25:31–46). The mortals who will be judged favorably are those who extended hospitality to Christ. Those who will not receive favorable judgment are those that denied him hospitality:

> For when I was hungry, you gave me food; when thirsty, you gave me drink;
> when I was a stranger (ξένος), you took me into your home.
>
> Matthew 25:35

> For when I was hungry, you gave me nothing to eat; when thirsty, nothing to
> drink; when I was a stranger (ξένος), you did not welcome me.
>
> Matthew 25:42–3

Christ, a god (*theos*) in the guise of a guest (*xenos*) needing hospitality, here instantiates negative theoxeny.[57] However, unlike the *Odyssey*, Genesis

---

[57] Cf. Taylor (2007: 121–2).

19, and Ovid's account of Baucis and Philemon, NT myth postpones the resultant destruction beyond the present time of its narrative, alluding to it only within a prophetic account. The *Odyssey* itself, in depicting the suitors violating theoxeny and offending Athena in Book 1 (*Od.* 1.225–9), but postponing their destruction until Book 22, offers a model for NT myth in delaying the consequent apocalyptic destruction until much later than the occasion that triggers it. But Hesiod in the *Works and Days* (174–201) more closely anticipates NT myth in both postponing full-scale apocalyptic destruction and projecting it into the future beyond the present time of the narrative.

In a further instance of NT myth's tendency to make traditional motifs universal, the difference in outcomes, between moral and immoral behavior in the two opposite types of theoxeny, is also greater. The outcomes of both forms of behavior – correct observance that results in the host being saved, violation of hospitality that results in being destroyed through a divine wrath – are extended into eternity. Those who were hospitable will receive not merely a miraculous survival, but eternal life. Those who failed to be hospitable will not only be destroyed, but will receive eternal punishment (Matt. 25:46). In an additional expansion and extension of the mythic genre, Christ also declares that anyone who acted this way toward one of his followers will be so judged (Matt. 25:45). In so doing he figures all of his followers in virtual theoxenies, mortals acting as the disguised immortal testing their hosts' hospitality and morality. In Matthew's version of the apocalypse, then, as with Odysseus in the *Odyssey*, and to a lesser extent, Elijah and Elishah in OT myth, mortals themselves, now Christians as a specific subset, may themselves provoke a negative theoxeny should they be mistreated by their hosts.

Conclusion

This study demonstrates how the *Odyssey combines* separate, distinct genres of myth, all of which are also extant in Near Eastern cultures. Though parallels were noted in several traditions, Mesopotamian (especially *Gilgamesh*), Egyptian, and Ugaritic, Old Testament myth offers far the greatest number. The parallels provide contexts for the *Odyssey* on three different levels. While revealing interconnections between the *Odyssey* and Near Eastern myths, and a more specific inter-relation with OT myth, they demonstrate sustained parallels between the *Odyssey* and Genesis. This is true of small-scale narratives such as Menelaus wrestling with Proteus, which finds a parallel in Jacob wrestling with Yahweh (Gen. 32:22–32), as well as the *Odyssey*'s three larger genres of myth, romance, theoxeny, and Argonautic myth, all of which appear in Genesis (Gen. 37–47, 18–19, and 27–31, respectively).

In a Mesopotamian link, the *Odyssey*'s most well known episode, Odysseus' encounter with Polyphêmos, employs several motifs prominent in Gilgamesh's defeat of Humbaba. Both episodes are instances of the well-attested genre the combat myth; each occurs at a similar point in the larger epic; each brings the hero fame, but prompts a divine wrath; both heroes' companions try to prevent them from committing a reckless act. Comparison suggests the *Odyssey* innovates, imposing changes upon the basic encounter by adding its thematic concern with hospitality, the fantastic voyage, and the use of cunning to defeat brute force, none of which are concerns in *Gilgamesh*.

Awareness of the *Odyssey*'s favored subtype of divine council, in which Zeus mediates a wrathful god down to a lower level of destruction, employed three times, to conclude three different genres of myth, serves as a hermeneutic for two unusual scenes in OT myth. Genesis and Exodus feature instances of the same subtype, to conclude two of the same genres of myth as in the *Odyssey* (Gen. 18 for negative theoxeny, as in *Odyssey* 24; and Exod. 32, *The people disobey their leader and rebel against god*, as in

Odyssey 12). OT myth here innovates, incorporating this most polytheistic mythic type within its larger monotheistic polemic, by inserting a privileged mortal, Abraham/Moses, in place of the second god in dialogue. These *adapted divine councils*, as we have called them, further innovate in that the privileged mortal functions in the role usually taken by the sky father (Zeus, Anu), mediating the lesser god's wrath, in which position Yahweh surprisingly serves. The *Odyssey* presents the more traditional form of the mythic genre.

In Jonah OT myth offers a fruitful parallel to Odysseus' fantastic voyages. Here and in the larger Exodus myth, Yahweh suggests closer parallels to Poseidon than to Zeus.[1] His threatened but averted destruction of Nineveh (Jonah 3) closely matches Poseidon's threatened but averted destruction of the Phaiakians' city (*Od.* 13.78–164). Both gods send storms against the protagonist (Odysseus, Jonah), preventing him from crossing the sea to his desired destination; both are thought to send sea monsters against him. In the larger myth of the Exodus, Yahweh's wrath functions very like Poseidon's in the *Odyssey* as the main factor behind the extraordinary delay in the protagonists reaching their goal (forty years for Moses and the Israelites, ten for Odysseus and crew). Both gods also act out the traditional motif of a god complaining of a lack of respect, Yahweh in Exodus (see Propp 2006: 555), Poseidon at *Odyssey* 13.127–45.

In Books 14–22, as Odysseus proceeds disguised as a poor wanderer, the *Odyssey* prefigures the modality and central characteristics of New Testament myth. Featuring slaves and swineherds as examples of moral behavior, the *Odyssey* thematically depicts the wealthy suitors as immoral and as abusing power. Unrecognized in his own kingdom, associating with slaves, abused by the power elite, Odysseus' position offers considerable overlap with the gospels' depiction of Christ. Repeatedly offending the gods by abusing hospitality, the suitors provoke Athena's wrath, and, though warned by Theoklymenos of coming apocalyptic destruction, suffer divine judgment.

The *Odyssey*'s two different endings, the suitors' destruction, and the recognition scenes with Penelope and Laertes, should be understood as the *necessary* and *expected* conclusions of the two different genres of myth, both also in Genesis, negative theoxeny in the suitors' case, and romance for the family members. The destruction of the suitors is required as a form of societal justice. The sanctity of hospitality ensures that mortals are

---

[1] I repeat E. L. Brown's (2000) tantalizing, but conjectural, argument that the -daon of Posei-daon (Homeric) is related to Dagon, the Philistines' main god according to OT myth.

able to travel; it allows different communities to exchange information. The destruction of the suitors is a public sign that the gods reward correct behavior and punish those who violate their decrees. A man reuniting with his wife is a more personal form of justice: the gods reward an individual for his pious life.

Within their respective treatments of romance the *Odyssey* and Genesis both use the particular subtype of recognition scene, rare in other romances, postponed recognition, in which the protagonist subjects his relatives to tests, makes them break down and cry, but refrains from disclosing his identity until a later scene. By contrast, in Euripides, Apollonius, and Shakespeare, neither character is usually aware of the other's identity. In their treatments of theoxeny, Genesis and the *Odyssey* present both types, positive and negative, virtually adjacent to each other (Gen. 18 and 19, *Od.* 1 and 3; cf. Matt. 25: 31–46).

OT myth's account of Jacob winning Rachel offers more complex parallels with Argonautic myth. Here the OT develops the respective genre to some length, fleshing it out with a number of incidents. The hostile father-in-law is a common figure in Greek myth, whereas Laban seems unique within OT myth. While household gods are mentioned elsewhere in OT myth,[2] only here are they stolen (though cf. Judg. 18:20). Rachel, Laban's *daughter*, as the thief, animates a figure common in Greek myth, Medea, Ariadne, and certain features of Nausikaa and Kirke. In aggressively stealing her father's household gods (which, for instance, Rahab does not consider doing, though her Greek counterpart, Theano, does), Rachel seems closer to Medea than is usual for women of OT myth. Jacob's journey to obtain a wife offers a homology for four principal characters in Jason's quest for the Fleece (Aietes: Laban; Rachel: Medea; Hera: Rebecca; Jacob: Jason). Rebecca parallels Hera not only as the powerful female who advises Jacob on his quest in Argonautic myth, but in her deception of Isaac, when he wants to bestow his blessing on his favorite son Esau. Homeric epic employs this same genre of myth in the *Iliad*, when Hera deceives Zeus as he intends to bestow his blessing upon his favorite son, Herakles (*Il.* 19.96–133).[3] It is intriguing, to say the least, that Rebecca parallels Hera in two separate myths, in two Homeric epics.

Jacob is the single character in OT myth with the most in common with the *Odyssey*. He participates in three different genres of myth that

---

[2] In addition to the passages involving Laban, Speiser (1962: 245) gives: 1 Samuel 19:13, 16; Ezekiel 21:26; Zechariah 10:2; cf. Judges 17:5, 18:14 ff.; Hosea 3:4.
[3] NT myth offers a similar instance of a father foolishly deceived when he attempts to bestow a blessing in the account of Herodias' daughter and Herod (Mark 6:21–9).

the larger *Odyssey* tradition employs for three *separate* characters. As the male protagonist in Argonautic myth, his winning of Rachel thematically parallels facets of Odysseus' encounters with Nausikaa and Kirke. As the stealer of livestock able to disguise his herds and their tracks, he parallels Autolykos in extra-Homeric accounts, and Hermes in his *Homeric Hymn*. As the man who wrestles god at the water's edge and receives a prophecy and blessing, he parallels Menelaus with Proteus at Pharos.

These and other extensive parallels the *Odyssey* exhibits with Near Eastern mythic traditions challenge the paradigm that it is defined by an Indo-European inheritance. Near Eastern myth in general, but OT myth, Genesis in particular, repeatedly offers the most relevant and the greatest number of specific parallels. Homerists should embrace OT myth as a valuable hermeneutic tool.

Discerning the different genres of myth in the *Odyssey* offers new perspectives on episodes in the poem, without adducing comparative materials. Though commentators often see little distinction between Kalypso and Kirke,[4] in our analysis they participate in different genres of myth. Kirke interacts with Odysseus in Argonautic myth. Kalypso interacts with Odysseus through three very different genres of myth. In the lush secluded space that is Ogygia, the *Odyssey* suggests the influence of creation and paradise myths. In her offer to make Odysseus her husband, as Ishtar does Gilgamesh, the *Odyssey* draws on what we have called *The hero rejects the goddess' offer to be her consort*. In the many covert associations Book 5 makes between Ogygia and the underworld, the *Odyssey* appears to be drawing on a genre of myth in which a male is figured as marrying a Death goddess.

The distinct genres of myth also account for perceived discordances (diverse modalities, differing characterizations of Odysseus, discrete value systems) in operation in different parts of the *Odyssey*. In some genres Odysseus should be seen as the pious mortal who honors the gods, and earns their help, in accord with the morality also seen in OT myth's depictions of Abraham, Moses, and others. In other genres Odysseus' wily qualities, though seen by some as his acting only in his own self-interest, are also closely paralleled in OT myths' depictions of Jacob, and Joseph, in his recognition scenes with his brothers and his father. OT myth also exhibits a similar inconsistency of value systems at times in conflict between one narrative and another. For its relevance to the *Odyssey*, I repeat Carr's observation (1996: 13) that the transmission history of Genesis reflects "often discordant voices now combined into a complex whole."

---

[4] For discussion of their differences, however, see Louden (1999: 104–29).

Though this study is mainly concerned with how instances of the same genres of myths provide a *context* for each other, we briefly consider possible means of interaction between the Greeks and Near Eastern cultures in general, or Israelite culture in specific, that resulted in the parallels we have observed.[5] Teodorsson, building on the work of others, argues for Cyprus as the location where the Greeks became acquainted with the Phoenician alphabet some time between 1000 and 800 BCE (2006: 172), "Cyprus was certainly the most natural meeting-place and station for transit-trade between the Aegean and the Levant." He considers commercial forces the likely motivation (172):

... merchants carrying on commercial interchange with Phoenician colleagues in Cyprus that, after a fairly long period of study of their script, decided to use it for writing Greek. The purpose was obviously, as Puijgh rightly points out, solely commercial.[6]

Finkelberg (2005: 57) notes a specific connection between Cyprus and Phoenician culture with intriguing implications, "Another Cypriot script... was used during the Late Bronze Age both in Cyprus and in nearby Ugarit."[7] Cyprus and the Phoenicians are likely candidates for transmission to the Greeks not only of the alphabet, but of narratives.

Among many factors, including location, Cyprus maintained a unique continuity of Mycenaean culture (Woodard 1997: 218–24), as well as a unique continuity of literacy through the so-called Dark Ages (*ibid.* 224).[8] Powell (2002: 193–4) includes Cyprus among a shortlist of likely locales where a mixing of Greek and some form of Semitic culture provided the conditions necessary for an evolving Greek epic tradition, "In Cyprus, Euboea, Boeotia, and perhaps Italy bilingual Greek/Semitic speakers transmitted story themes, which Greek singers reshaped." Phoenician, Israelite, and Ugaritic cultures are all members of the same language subgroup, West Semitic. Greek culture had extensive interaction with at least one member of this group, possibly with more than one.[9]

---

[5] On general parallels between Greek and Israelite narrative traditions, and the possibility of contact between them, see Lord (1960: 156–8).
[6] But cf. Powell (1991).   [7] Cf. Woodard (1997: 218), Powell (1991: 89, 90, n. 41).
[8] Cf. Palaima (2005: 12–14).
[9] On possible Phoenician contact, see Beye (1966: 16): "This diffusion shows that *Gilgamesh* was widely known in the second millennium... which some scholars believe was imported by the Phoenicians into Greek lands and there served as a model for the *Iliad* and *Odyssey*... The common elements probably derive from a time in the second millennium when the Minoans and Mycenaeans had considerable contact with Asia Minor and the Levant." Cf. Malkin (2008: 266–7): "closer to the region of Greek-Phoenician acculturation oral Ugarit epics were being written down as early as the fourteenth century along the coast of Syria opposite Cyprus." Also Finkelberg (2005: 63): "Thus the evidence

Conclusion

The *Odyssey* depicts various forms of commercial interaction between Greeks and Phoenicians,[10] and Cyprus, in the false accounts Odysseus gives before revealing his identity. In the first (*Od.* 14.199–359), he is a member of a Cretan contingent that fought at Troy, who returns home victorious with his winnings, but a month later decides to take part in an expedition against Egypt (discussed below). That encounter concluded, a *Phoenician* man entices him to join forces. But after getting a year's worth of hard work out of him, the Phoenician deceitfully sells him into slavery (*Od.* 14.257–86), suggesting both the Aietes/Laban figure and motifs central to Joseph's myth. Odysseus later gives a very similar account of a reckless attack on Egypt that results in his being sold into slavery, this time onto Cyprus itself (*Od.* 17.442–4).[11] Earlier, Menelaus tells Telemachos that he wandered to Cyprus and the Phoenicians, among others, suffering pains but also bringing home fabulous goods (*Od.* 4.83–5),[12] stressing a commercial side to the encounter.[13]

In Odysseus' "fictive" accounts, the Phoenicians and Cyprus are not only links between blocks of narrative, motifs of a sort, but instances of cultural interaction and exchange, in a commercial and narrative sense. While usually carrying a negative connotation, as "Egypt" does in OT myth, Phoenicians and Cyprus, and Greek interfaces with them, serve to link the various parts of Mediterranean culture with which records and material remains connect them. "Odysseus" here sold into slavery, becoming a commodity, as well as turning into a narrative, suggests the Phoenicians' likely role in the transmission of narratives ("from there [Cyprus] I have now come here," says the disguised Odysseus: *Od.* 17.444).

I think it best to keep an open mind as to *when* such contacts could have occurred. There may very well have been multiple periods of contact. Exchanges between Greeks and Phoenicians on Cyprus are clearly likely from 900 BCE on, but I see no reason to rule out possible earlier contact, whether in the Levant or in the Greek world, from 1200 on (a possible means is discussed below). It is increasingly clear that influence

---

of linguistics, of archaeology and of Greek tradition coincide in that they show unequivocally that the proper place of Bronze Age Aegean civilisation is in the cultural context of Western Asia... the cultural interaction between the Aegean and Western Asia must have run much deeper than the loan words, floating motifs and other piecemeal borrowings that normally result from casual commercial encounters between strangers."

[10] On which, see also Dougherty (2001).
[11] See also Palaima (2005: 12–13) on mention of Cyprus in Homeric epic.
[12] In his *aristeia* in the *Iliad*, Agamemnon goes into battle bearing a shield that Kinyras of Cyprus gave him (*Il.* 11.20–1).
[13] Malkin (2008: 73) considers the possibility that Temesa (*Od.* 1.184), in Athena-as-Mentes' speech to Telemachos, is Tamassos in Cyprus.

could occur in *both* directions, as Finkelberg (2005: 56) notes of the earlier period, "[W]e can no longer claim unreservedly that the cultural contacts that took place in the Bronze Age proceeded invariably in one direction, from east to west." The earlier the contact, in terms of possible exchange of narrative, the more likely it seems that Ugarit, or Ugaritic culture, would somehow have been involved, given the city's complex role in Near Eastern literature and literacy.[14] The earlier the contact, the higher the chances that a given narrative form may have moved from the Near East to the Greeks, since earlier familiarity with writing in those cultures often ensures that the first known instance of a given mythic genre is in a Near Eastern text. The later the contact or influence, the more likely the relevant narrative type moves from the Greeks to the Near East, and that the authors/redactors of OT myth are influenced by narratives they encounter in a world with ever increasing Greek influence. Until there has been more sifting of the evidence, from a variety of perspectives, using a variety of techniques, it seems unwise to limit ourselves to a single hypothesis as to date, place, or means, but to view the interconnections between Greek and Near Eastern myth as dialogic (influence between the cultures going in both directions), and diachronic. Distinctions between East and West were not as pronounced in the Bronze Age as they would later become (Finkelberg 2005: 167).

Why does Genesis exhibit so many parallels with the *Odyssey*? From a Greek perspective the Pentateuch resembles a *nostos*. With a focus on a *people*, instead of an individual, and a chronology spanning decades, as opposed to a few days for Nestor or Agamemnon, or Odysseus' ten years, Genesis chronicles the events that cause the Israelites to be held in an exotic land (Egypt), while Exodus-Deuteronomy recount their return to the homeland Abraham established. In this sense Genesis corresponds to the *Odyssey*'s back-story, providing an account of how the "protagonist" became isolated from home. Greek and Israelite culture would both naturally employ some of the same genres of myth to depict the typologically similar circumstances. The parallels between the *Odyssey* and Genesis (differences notwithstanding between the heroic modality of the former as opposed to the focus on patriarchs in the latter) are, in fact, closer than those between the returns of Odysseus and Agamemnon, Aias, Nestor, Diomedes, or Teukros, all of whom are usually thought to have some form of a *nostos*. I suspect, but cannot prove, that this indicates diffusion, one culture

---

[14] For a recent assessment of Ugarit's unique importance in the development of writing, alphabets, and the transmission of ancient myth, see Powell (2002: 102–9 especially, cf. 34–8). See also Webster (1958: 66): "The discovery of a Cypro-Minoan tablet in Ugarit may show that the chief intermediaries between the Mycenaeans in Ugarit and the mainland of Greece were the Mycenaeans in Cyprus."

borrowing from the other. The parallels strike me as too numerous to be explained by mere generic resemblance.

If we contemplate which characters would have been more well known between, say, Odysseus or Joseph, Hera or Rebecca, Herakles or Esau, Jason or Jacob, throughout Mediterranean cultures, it would seem far likelier that OT myth is influenced by some form of Greek myth, than vice versa. When we consider which language, Greek or Hebrew, had the greater number of speakers, which culture, Greek or Israelite, was spread over a larger area, which people, by virtue of its maritime facility, was in contact with the greater number of other peoples, the odds grow far greater that Greek culture would have exerted influence, direct or indirect, on Israelite culture, rather than vice versa.

Greek influence on Israelite myth is evident in additional ways this study has not addressed. Finkelstein argues such is the case in the Samson myth (2002: 147):

Homeric influence... makes perfect sense against the background of a seventh-century (or later) reality, when Greeks became part of the eastern Mediterranean scene... Greek mythology is strongly represented also in other stories related to the Philistines (mainly the cycle of Samson)... The Deuteronomistic Historian seems to have borrowed this genre from Greek legends and tales which were perhaps popular in Philistia. This may have been done intentionally in order to give the tales related to the Philistines a Greek air and thus symbolizes their Aegean origin.

Carr notes a further possible instance of the influence of Greek culture on the Torah. Noting there is no explicit attribution of the Pentateuch to Moses (though modern audiences often take it for granted) until the Hellenistic period, Carr (1996: 21, n. 69) repeats B. Mack's (1982) argument that the assertion of Mosaic authorship resulted from "the direct influence of and in response to Greek concepts of authorship and authority."

Considering how separate genres of myth function together in the *Odyssey* opens the door to a very different understanding of Genesis, and other books of the Bible, Old and New Testament. The workings of oral tradition behind Homeric epic result in a collage of references to different time periods, more of which refer to the world contemporary with the bard than with the period in which a given myth is set.[15] The same is true of OT myth. Sparks notes the tendency in Near Eastern myth in general,

---

[15] Cf. Finkelberg's assessment of Homeric epic (2005: 10), "Nobody today would deny that at any given moment historical myth functions as a cultural artifact representative of the period in which it circulates rather than the one which it purports to describe."

adducing specific instances in OT myth that this study earlier addresses (2005: 303):

> [I]t is clear enough from the Near Eastern evidence that many legends were designed to look much older than they were... modern scholars suspect that many of the Bible's stories concerning priestly or cultic legitimacy were composed late in Israel's history but were written or edited to make them appear very old, in many cases creating the impression that the story went back to the earliest days of Israelite history. Possible examples might include... Jacob's dream at Bethel in Gen. 28 (an origin legend of Bethel sanctuary), the story of the Golden Calf in Exod. 32 (legitimizing Levites but critiquing the Aaronid priesthood).[16]

Though occasional *passages* in the OT are quite early (e.g., Deborah's song in Judg. 5), much of Genesis clearly postdates the *Odyssey*,[17] particularly the Abraham narratives, and those parts that link the myths of Jacob and Joseph to the Abrahamic blessing model (Carr 1996: 205).

The *Odyssey* often employs the more traditional form of a given genre of myth than that in the OT. The unusual dialogues between Yahweh and Abraham, and Yahweh and Moses, are clearly modeled on the specific subtype of divine council in which the sky father mediates the anger of a wrathful lesser god to arrive at the appropriate level of destruction for a group of mortals who have committed offence. Both scenes make surprising innovations on the traditional subtype not only in having Abraham and Moses take part in a dialogue that normally occurs between two gods, but in having Yahweh play the role traditionally assigned to the wrathful lesser god, while Abraham and Moses attempt the mediation the chief god normally performs. The dialogue in Genesis 18 offers a further innovation in that the mediation is unsuccessful. Only here, in all the many instances of this subtype, does the "divine council" fail to mediate the wrathful god's intended destruction. The *Odyssey* clearly employs the more traditional form of the divine council, also extant in *Gilgamesh* (VI.81–114 in George 2003), in the corresponding divine councils between Zeus and Helios (*Od.* 12.376–88) and Zeus and Athena (*Od.* 24.472–87).

Genesis radically innovates in its use of romance, when Joseph's family members come to *him*, in the exotic land in which he has been detained for twenty years, for the climactic recognition scenes. Subsuming romance under its larger narrative agenda of providing an etiology for the Israelites' presence in Egypt, Genesis inverts one of the most central thrusts of

---

[16] Cf. Finkelstein (2002: 132): "[M]uch of the material in the Deuteronomistic History should be read from the point of view of the theology and political ideology of the time of writing."

[17] Carr (1996: 222): "Almost no one would date the core of the overall Deuteronomistic history earlier than the seventh century, and most would date its various redactions across the sixth century."

Conclusion

romance, the protagonist's return home. Joseph's *descendants* will instead have a *nostos*, delayed for years by the events depicted in Exodus 32, much as Odysseus' own return is delayed by the typologically equivalent events on Thrinakia.

Finkelberg (2005) notes a further episode in Genesis that suggests an origin in Greek tradition. In Chapter 8 we noted the elliptic account of the Nephilim (Gen. 6: 2–4):

> The sons of the gods saw how beautiful these daughters were, so they took for themselves such women as they chose... In those days as well as later, when the sons of the gods had intercourse with the daughters of mortals and children were born to them, the Nephilim were on the earth; they were the heroes of old, people of renown. (Genesis 6: 2–4)

Finkelberg sees similarities with the *Homeric Hymn to Aphrodite* 247–53, which, in offering an explanation for the discontinuance of unions between gods and women, supplies an implicit etiology for the end of the heroic age, as Clay argues (1989: 166):

> The final upshot of Zeus's intervention is to make Aphrodite cease and desist from bringing about these inappropriate unions between the gods and mortals, which, in turn, will mean the end of the age of heroes.

Finkelberg relates both passages to the wave of destruction that engulfed Aegean cultures at the end of the Bronze Age, perhaps implying Israelite tradition has been influenced by a Greek version of a myth relating that end (2005: 162–3):

> This seems to indicate that versions of the myth of the destruction of the Race of Heroes, probably a reflection of the historical cataclysm that accompanied the end of the Bronze Age, circulated not only in Greece but also in wider regions of the Eastern Mediterranean.[18]

In these respects, and others,[19] Genesis may be seen in a dialogic relation with the *Odyssey* and other Greek myth.

Lord (1960: 156) and others have argued that, as Malkin suggests (2008: 266–7), "[T]he very idea of writing down a great epic could also have come from the Near East, where epic poetry was being written long before the Greeks had thought of using the alphabet to write down the Homeric epics." Malkin continues (267):

---

[18] Cf. Alter (2004: 38–9) on how Gen. 6:2–4 overlaps with Greek myth.
[19] On the basis of parallels discussed in Chapter 6, I strongly suspect, but cannot prove, that the myth of Jason, Medea, Aietes, and the Golden Fleece, is earlier than that of Jacob, Rachel, Laban, and his household gods.

The Near Eastern evidence of written epic and other poetry as early as the third millennium B.C. is still in need of reassessment by classicists, who . . . have not yet recognized how much they have to learn from Near Eastern studies about the development of epic tradition.

The parallels, and the divergences, suggest to me both that the *Odyssey*, in some form, served as a model for individual parts of Genesis (particularly the myth of Joseph), and that, like the *Odyssey*, the redactors of Genesis linked together many different genres of myth to forms parts of a larger *nostos*, return story.

The Philistines, in OT myth, in Egyptian records of the Ramesside Period, and in ongoing archeological discoveries in the Levant, present a further, under-explored, interface between Homeric epic and Near Eastern cultures. In OT myth the Philistines take part in acts that closely parallel incidents in Homeric epic, though, since Israelite myths are set on land, the OT Philistines resemble the *Iliad* more than the *Odysssey*. They are a possible key to a form of cultural diffusion in the Bronze Age.[20]

Aegean archeologists commonly see the Philistines as *Mycenaean* émigrés who first settled on Cyprus, and from there expanded operations to Egypt and the Levant.[21] The first discovered link connecting them with Mycenaean material culture was their pottery (Mycenaean IIIC: 1B), as Finkelberg summarizes (2005: 154):

[S]tudies of the Philistine ware, especially those by W. A. Heurtley in the 1930s and A. Furumark in the 1940s, showed that in this specific respect at least the Philistine settlements in Canaan not only properly belonged to the Mycenaean world but in fact remained the only place where the ceramic traditions of this world were still being perpetuated after they had ceased to exist everywhere else, including Cyprus.

Further discoveries broadened and strengthened the web of connections (Finkelberg, 2005: 153–4):

[I]f the people who arrived in the Levant at the end of the Bronze Age brought with them not only the Mycenaean pottery but also the technology of its production, it is difficult to avoid the conclusions that the people in question could have been

---

[20] On the Philistines and the *Iliad*, see Louden (2006: 170–9, 276–9, 289–90).
[21] Mazar (1985: 104–5): "I would not hesitate to see in the Philistine immigration part of the same wave of civilized immigrants from the Mycenaean world that settled in Cyprus in the early twelfth century BCE."

none other than the Mycenaeans... Yet, although not a few students of the ancient Near East have in fact admitted as much, most Hellenists seem still unaware of this development.[22]

Finkelberg (*ibid.*) cites the Dothans (1992) who argue that because Late Mycenaean pottery style continues in Philistia, after potters elsewhere in the Mycenaean world had switched to different techniques, the Philistines functioned as an isolated remnant maintaining Mycenaean traditions that had ceased to exist elsewhere.[23]

There is evidence of Philistine influence on Near Eastern cultures. Raban notes the ashlar stone-cutting and construction technique used to construct the submerged landing stage at Tel Dor (1988: 272–6), dated to around 1200 BCE, and a rectangular well, using techniques similar to others on Cyprus and in eastern Crete (pp. 276–80). As Raban notes, the innovative techniques by "whether they be called Achaeans, Mycenaeans, or Sea Peoples" (p. 273) were subsequently adopted in Ugarit and elsewhere. Raban (pp. 284–8) also reviews the composite anchors found in Ugarit, Kition, various Phoenician sites, and elsewhere, arguing, on the basis of the incised markings that some of them bear, that they are of Cypro-Mycenaean origin. He sums up the evidence (p. 293) pointing to influence from the West onto the East, "new people came from the west and brought with them new technologies, high standards of urban ways of life, and a rather sophisticated maritime heritage." He suggests the Greeks, Philistines, Cypro-Mycenaeans, or whatever name is most accurate, prompted the later emergence of the Phoenicians as a sea power (p. 294), serving as "perhaps the real trigger for the rapid emergence of a new culture of what may have been the greatest maritime civilization in history – the Phoenicians."

If the Philistines should be seen as Mycenaeans who influenced the material culture of the people who would become the Phoenicians, it is certainly possible that they may also have influenced the Phoenicians' narrative traditions. Though this study has focused on connections between the *Odyssey*'s final form[24] and Near Eastern myth, and pointed out likely influence of the former upon Genesis, we should, I suggest, remain open to the possibility that some Greek narratives or narrative forms also influenced Near Eastern cultures at an earlier date than is usually thought.

---

[22] Cf. Niemeier (1998: 48): "[T]he evidence for the existence of the Mycenaean kitchen kit, of Mycenaean industries and of Mycenaean religious and cult patterns, form criteria which appear to point to actual Mycenaean settlement in Philistia."

[23] Dothan T. and M. Dothan (1992: 51–2). [24] I subscribe to Janko's dating of *Cd.* 700 BCE.

The *Odyssey*'s most intriguing connection with the Philistines lies in how the disguised Odysseus' tale of a failed attack on Egypt (*Od.* 14.258–72 = 17.427–41) corresponds to Egyptian records of an attack by the Philistines, and other Sea Peoples.[25] The records, at Ramses III's temple at Medinet Habu in Thebes, dated to 1175 BCE (Raban 1988: 262), consist of verbal accounts and visual renderings of a battle on sea and one on land.[26] The former features an attempt by the Philistines and other Sea Peoples to invade Egypt by entering the mouth of the Nile (*ANET* 262–3):

> Those who came forward together on the sea, the full flame was in front of them at the river-mouths, while a stockade of lances surrounded them on the shore.... Those who entered the river-mouths were like birds ensnared in the net... Their leaders were carried off and slain.

A similar description follows a little later (*ANET* 263):

> They penetrated the channels of the river-mouths... They are capsized and overwhelmed where they are. Their heart is taken away, their soul is flown away. Their weapons are scattered upon the sea. His arrow pierces whom of them he may have wished, and the fugitive is become one fallen into the water.

Raban, analyzing their maritime techniques, and composite anchors, concludes (p. 265):

> Most scholars would agree that the battle scene actually shows the fleet of the Sea people caught by surprise, while mooring... The textual description of the Egyptian ships blocking the river entrances and "catching the enemy like birds in a net."

In Eumaios' hut the disguised Odysseus relates (*Od.* 14.192–359) how, having led a Cretan contingent at Troy alongside Idomeneus, a month later he took part in an unsuccessful invasion of Egypt. Leading nine ships, reaching Egypt on the fifth day, "Odysseus" has them moor their ships on the Nile (*Od.* 14.258), advising the others to guard them, maintaining watches. But the men are insubordinate, "yielding to their arrogance" (*hubris*: *Od.* 14.262), in not following Odysseus' recommendations.[27] They

---

[25] Hoekstra (1989: 210) raises but quickly dismisses the possibility, "The raid has been thought to recall the attacks on the Nile delta known from Egyptian records from the times of Merheptah and Rameses III"; but (211) argues for historical reference in *Odyssey* 14.257–8, "our line might express the knowledge of the early historical period or of Mycenaean times." See Bierling (1992: 52–3) for a review of Egyptian records of the Sea Peoples.

[26] For discussion of the visual renderings, see Raban (1988: 262–5) and Bierling (1992: 53–9).

[27] Stanford (1962, Vol. 2: 227) "'Yielding to arrogance' refers not to the act of piracy... but their neglect of suitable precautions against a reverse." Hoekstra (1989: 211): "It [14.262] refers to the fact that the men who had been left to guard the ships neglected their duty and threw caution to the winds."

then ravage the fields, taking Egyptian women and children captive, slaying the men. But at dawn an Egyptian force counterattacks, surrounding them, slaying many, capturing the rest for forced labor.

In its unsuccessful outcome the circumstances are reminiscent of the events at Ismaros, and resultant counterattack by the Ciccones (*Od.* 9.43–61),[28] the crew similarly insubordinate and reckless. In Egypt they ignore his recommendation to stay near and guard their ships. At Ismaros they ignore his recommendation to leave. In both episodes, after the Achaians have seized their wives and possessions, the Ciccones and Egyptians counterattack, both times overwhelming Odysseus' forces. At Ismaros Odysseus and crew are able to escape, but only after losing six men from each ship. Odysseus' Egyptian narrative thus depicts very similar events, but in a more realistic, less heroic mode. In both episodes the Achaians, invading from the sea, are caught by surprise.

Even closer to the Egyptian raid, in several respects, are the dynamics and the outcome of the Laistrygones episode (*Od.* 10.121–5), though depicted in a mythical modality. Their unusual harbor is described in some detail (*Od.* 10.87–94), particularly its narrow entrance, the *mouth* (*stomati*: *Od.* 10.90). The Achaians are easily trapped, partly by the harbor's mouth, much as the Sea Peoples are caught within the mouth of the Nile. As at Ismaros and Egypt, Odysseus' more cautious behavior contrasts with the crew's recklessness. As they enter the Laistrygones' harbor Odysseus moors his ship in a safer position, much as he advised caution, and guarding the ships in Egypt. Though they make no attempt to sack the Laistrygones' city, the Achaians are quickly overwhelmed by their sudden attack, paralleling the Egyptians' actions in Book 14, and in the Ramesside accounts of the Sea Peoples' attack. The Laistrygones overwhelm them, pelting them with rocks, "as if they were spearing fish" (*Od.* 10.124); the Egyptians overwhelm the Philistines and other Sea Peoples, "Those who entered the river-mouths were like birds ensnared in the net" (*ANET* 263).

Parallels between Odysseus' Egyptian account, and the episodes involving the Ciccones and the Laistrygones, may be regarded as a natural consequence of Homeric epic's thematic style. But that does not explain the multiple points of resemblance with the Ramesside account. Does this reinforce the possibility that some of the *Odyssey*'s plot refracts a kernel of historicity, Finkelberg's (2005) "reflection of the historical cataclysm that accompanied the end of the Bronze Age"? Could the disastrous encounters

---

[28] de Jong (2001: 353) regards Odysseus' Egyptian narrative as "an allomorph of the Ciconian adventure."

with the Ciccones and Laistrygones be modeled on the Egyptian narrative, rather than the other way around? More meaningful exploration of the extent of Homeric epic's relationship with Philistine culture requires the combined resources of scholars from several disciplines.

The *Aeneid* offers a relevant conceptual model for understanding the formation of Genesis, and, possibly, of the *Odyssey*. In the *Aeneid*'s case we can, in a sense, watch the larger epic come together from once independent narratives. The *Iliad* establishes Aeneas as a suitably heroic figure, son of a goddess, as a survivor of Troy's apocalyptic destruction (*Il.* 20.297–305). By Vergil's time, foundation stories, in which Aeneas originally had no part, perhaps modeled on tales of Greek colonization, had also become attached to him, as Weinfeld argues (1988: 354):

Since the *Aeneid* is modeled upon foundation stories prevalent in Greek colonies, the so-called *Ktisissagen*, I saw in the patriarchal stories, with their promises for the inheritance of the land of Canaan, a reflection of the same genre.

Separate stories, separate genres of myth, come together over time, coalescing around his central figure. We earlier noted OT scholarship that argues for a similar process behind David's duel with Goliath, that it was originally independent, not part of David's myth, but later came within his gravitational field, so to speak.

Weinfeld argues the post-*Iliad* Aeneas is typologically quite similar to Abraham. Aeneas comes from the highly developed culture that is Troy, Abraham from Ur, both conforming to Weinfeld's figure (1988: 355), "A man leaving a great civilization charged with a universal mission." Weinfeld assumes Greek influence on the Abrahamic myths (353–4), "this kind of story telling, including the David Court Story, crystallized in the David period when there were contacts with elements which originated in the Greek sphere." Both the David, and Samson, cycles of myths, are set against the Philistines.

I suspect the *Odyssey* came together in a partly analogous fashion. Odysseus is a figure who, like Aeneas, is already guaranteed a future beyond the *Iliad*, in its sly allusions to his role in the destruction of Troy (discussion in Louden 1996). To the cunning figure who sacks Troy, accrued a form of Argonautic myth, already in existence as a mythic type, to articulate his encounters with other peoples, and increase his own heroic dimension and potential. To articulate his successful return to his family and home, romance, already in existence as a mythic type, perhaps originating in Egypt, was combined with tales of the wanderings of Mycenaean warriors to Cyprus, Egypt, and the Levant. To depict the troubles he finds at home after his long absence, troubles that may reflect the social upheavals accompanying the end of the Bronze Age, theoxeny, already in existence as a mythic type, was added to his tale to depict his initial reception, and how he subsequently restores his rule. Divine councils that mediate the destruction required by the *Odyssey*'s three wrathful gods, the specific subtype already present in *Gilgamesh* (VI.81–114 in George), direct the outcomes of the poem's use of Argonautic myth and romance, while Athena directs the negative theoxeny beginning with her theophany to Odysseus (*Od.* 13.287–439), a type-scene also already extant in *Gilgamesh*.

Bibliography

Abusch, Tzvi (1986). "Ishtar's proposal and Gilgamesh's refusal: an interpretation of *The Gilgamesh Epic*, Tablet 6, Lines 1–79," *History of Religions* 26: 143–87.
  (1990). *Lingering over Words: Studies in Ancient Near Eastern Literature in Honor of William L. Moran*, (eds.) Abusch, John Huehnergard, and Piotr Steinkeller. Atlanta: Scholars Press.
  (2001). "The epic of Gilgamesh and the Homeric epics," in Whiting (2001), pp. 1–6.
Ackerman, James S. (1987). "Numbers," and "Jonah," in Alter and Kermode (eds.), pp. 78–91, 234–43.
Albright, W. F. and Mann, C. S. (1971). *The Anchor Bible: Matthew. Introduction, Translation, and Notes*. Garden City, New York: Doubleday.
Allan, William (2006). "Divine justice and cosmic order in early Greek epic," *Journal of Hellenic Studies* 126: 1–35.
Allison, Dale C. Jr. (2000). "The eschatology of Jesus," in John J. Collins (2000a), pp. 267–302.
Alster, Bendt (1990). "Lugalbanda and the early epic tradition in Mesopotamia," in Abusch, pp. 59–72.
Alter, Robert (1981). *The Art of Biblical Narrative*. New York: Basic Books.
  (1999). *The David Story: A Translation with Commentary of 1 and 2 Samuel*. New York: W. W. Norton.
  (2004). *The Five Books of Moses: A Translation with Commentary*. New York: W. W. Norton.
Alter, Robert and Kermode, Frank (eds.) (1987). *The Literary Guide to the Bible*. Cambridge: The Belknap Press of Harvard University Press.
Anderson, William S. (1972). *Ovid's Metamorphoses Books 6–10: Edited, with Introduction and Commentary*. Norman: University of Oklahoma Press.
  (1997). *Ovid's Metamorphoses Books 1–5. Edited with Introduction and Commentary*. Norman: University of Oklahoma Press.
Annus, Amar (2001). "Ninurta and the son of man," in Whiting, pp. 7–17.
Austin, Norman (1975). *Archery at the Dark of the Moon: Poetic Problems in Homer's Odyssey*. Berkeley: University of California Press.

Bachvarova, Mary R. (2005). "The Eastern Mediterranean epic tradition from *Bilgames* and *Akka* to the Song of Release to Homer's *Iliad*," *Greek, Roman, and Byzantine Studies* 45: 131–53.

Baikouzis, Constantino and Magnasco, Marcelo O. (2008). "Is an eclipse described in the *Odyssey*?" *Proceedings of the National Academy of Sciences of the United States of America*. Vol. 105, no. 26: 8,823–8.

Bakker, Egbert J. (2001). "The Greek *Gilgamesh*, or the immortality of return," (Proceedings of the 9th International Symposium on the *Odyssey*). *Eranos*, Ithaca.

(2002). "Epos and Mythos: language and narrative in Homeric epic," *Arethusa* 35: 63–81.

(2005). *Pointing at the Past: From Formula to Performance in Homeric Poetics*. Washington, DC: Center for Hellenic Studies.

Barnes, Jonathan (1984). *The Complete Works of Aristotle. Vol. 2*. Princeton University Press.

Barnouw, Jeffrey (2004). *Odysseus, Hero of Practical Intelligence: Deliberation and Signs in Homer's* Odyssey. Lanham: University Press of America.

Basinger, Jeanine (1987). *The It's a Wonderful Life Book*. New York: Alfred A. Knopf.

Beck, Deborah (2005a). "Odysseus: narrator, storyteller, poet?" *Classical Philology* 100: 213–27.

(2005b). *Homeric Conversation*. Washington, DC: Center for Hellenic Studies.

Beltz, Walter (1983). *God and the Gods: Myths of the Bible*. Trans. Peter Heinegg. Penguin Books.

Beye, C. R. (1966). *The Iliad, The Odyssey, and the Epic Tradition*. Garden City, New York: Doubleday.

Bierling, Neal (1992). *Giving Goliath His Due: New Archaeological Light on the Philistines*. Grand Rapids: Baker Book House.

Block, Elizabeth (1985). "Clothing makes the man: a pattern in the Odyssey," *TAPA* 115: 1–11.

Bloom, Allan (1968). *The Republic of Plato: Translated, with Notes and an Interpretive Essay*. New York: Basic Books.

Bolin, Thomas M. (2004). "The role of exchange in ancient Mediterranean religion and its implications for reading Genesis 18–19," *JSOT* 29: 37–56.

Boling, Robert G. and Wright, Ernest G. (1982). *Joshua: Translation, Notes, and Commentary* (The Anchor Bible). Garden City, New York: Doubleday.

Bollinger, Robert (2001). "The ancient Greeks and the impact of the ancient Near East: Textual evidence and historical perspective (ca. 750–650 BC)," in Whiting, pp. 233–64.

Brann, Eva (2002). *Homeric Moments: Clues to Delight in Reading the Odyssey and the Iliad*. Philadelphia: Paul Dry Books.

Bremmer, Jan (1999). "Paradise: from Persia, via Greece, into the *Septuagint*," in Luttikhuizen, pp. 1–20.

(2004). "Don't look back: from the wife of Lot to Orpheus and Eurydice," in Noort and Tigchelaar, pp. 131–45.

Brown, Edwin L. (2000). "The roots of Poseidon in the Levant." Paper given at the April 8 meeting of the Classical Association of the Middle West and South, Knoxville, Tennessee.

Brown, John Pairman (1995). *Israel and Hellas (Beihefte zur Zeitschrift für die alttestamentliche Wissenschaft, Band 231)*. Berlin: Walter de Gruyter.

(2000). *Israel and Hellas: Volume II, Sacred Institutions with Roman Counterparts (Beihefte zur Zeitschrift für die alttestamentliche Wissenschaft, Band 276)*. Berlin: Walter de Gruyter.

Brown, Raymond B. (1966). *The Gospel According to John (i–xii): Introduction, Translation, and Notes. The Anchor Bible*. Garden City, New York: Doubleday.

(1970). *The Anchor Bible: The Gospel According to John (xiii–xxi). Introduction, Translation, and Notes*. Garden City, New York: Doubleday.

Brug, John F. (1985). "A literary and archaeological study of the Philistines," diss. Bar International Series 265.

Bryant, John and Springer, Haskell (eds.) (2007). *Moby Dick: A Longman Critical Edition*. New York: Longman.

Bryce, Trevor R. (1986). *The Lycians in Literary and Epigraphic Sources*. Copenhagen: Museum Tusculanum Press.

(2006). *The Trojans and Their Neighbours*. London: Routledge.

Burgess, Jonathan (1999). "Gilgamesh and Odysseus in the otherworld," *Classical Views/Echos du monde classique* 43: 171–210.

(2001). *The Tradition of the Trojan War in Homer and the Epic Cycle*. Baltimore: The Johns Hopkins University Press.

Burkert, Walter (2005). "Near Eastern connections," in Foley, pp. 291–301.

Burnett, Anne Pippin (1970). "Pentheus and Dionysus: host and guest," *Classical Philology* 65: 15–29.

Burton, Ernest De Witt and Goodspeed, Edgar Johnson (1920). *A Harmony of the Synoptic Gospels in Greek*. The University of Chicago Press.

Byre, Calvin S. (1994). "The rhetoric of description in *Odyssey* 9.116–41: Odysseus and Goat Island," *The Classical Journal*. 89: 357–67.

Cancik, Hubert (2000). "The end of the world, of history, and of the individual in Greek and Roman antiquity," in John J. Collins (2000a), pp. 84–125.

Carr, David M. (1996). *Reading the Fractures of Genesis: Historical and Literary Approaches*. Louisville: Westminster John Knox Press.

Carter, Jane B. and Morris, Sarah P. (1995). *The Ages of Homer*. Austin: The University of Texas Press.

Chadwick, John (1976). *The Mycenaean World*. Cambridge University Press.

Chantraine, P. (1990). *Dictionnaire étymologique de la langue grecque*. Paris: Editions Klincksieck.

Clay, Jenny Strauss (1983). *The Wrath of Athena: God and Men in the Odyssey*. Princeton University Press.

(1989). *The Politics of Olympus: Form and Meaning in the Major Homeric Hymns.* Princeton University Press.
Clements, Ronald E. (1972). *The Cambridge Bible Commentary: Exodus.* Cambridge University Press.
Clifford, Richard J., SJ (2000). "The roots of apocalypticism in Near Eastern myth," in John J. Collins (2000a), pp. 3–38.
  (ed.) (2007). *Wisdom Literature in Mesopotamia and Israel.* Atlanta: Society of Biblical Literature.
Coats, George W. (1999). *Exodus 1–18.* Grand Rapids: William B. Eerdmans.
Cody, Aelred, OSB (1993). "Aaron," in Metzger and Coogan, p. 3.
Cogan, Mordechai (2001). *1 Kings: A New Translation with Introduction and Commentary. The Anchor Bible.* Garden City, New York: Doubleday.
Collins, Adela Yarbro (2000). "The Book of Revelation," in John J. Collins (2000a), pp. 384–414.
Collins, Derek (1998). *Immortal Armor: The Concept of Alkê in Archaic Greek Poetry.* Lanham, MD: Rowman & Littlefield.
Collins, John J. (2000a). *The Encyclopedia of Apocalypticism; Volume 1: The Origins of Apocalypticism in Judaism and Christianity.* New York: Continuum.
  (2000b). "From prophecy to apocalypticism: the expectation of the end," in John J. Collins (2000a), pp. 129–61.
Coogan, Michael D. (1998). *The Oxford History of the Biblical World.* Oxford University Press.
Cook, Erwin F. (1995). *The Odyssey in Athens: Myths of Cultural Origins.* Ithaca: Cornell University Press.
  (2004). "Near Eastern sources for the palace of Alkinoos," *American Journal of Archaeology* 108: 43–77.
Crane, Gregory (1988). *Calypso: Backgrounds and Conventions of the Odyssey.* Frankfurt am Main: Athenäum.
Crenshaw, James I. (1993). "Jonah, the book of," in Metzger and Coogan, pp. 380–1.
Cross, Frank Moore (1973). *Canaanite Myth and Hebrew Epic: Essays in the History of the Religion of Israel.* Cambridge: Harvard University Press.
Crotty, Kevin (1982). *Song and Action: The Victory Odes of Pindar.* Baltimore: The Johns Hopkins University Press.
Cunliffe, Richard John (1963). *A Lexicon of the Homeric Dialect.* Norman: University of Oklahoma Press.
Dahoud, Mitchell, SJ (1968). *The Anchor Bible: Psalms II 51–100. Introduction, Translation, and Notes.* Garden City, New York: Doubleday.
Dalley, Stephanie (1991). *Myths from Mesopotamia.* Oxford University Press.
de Boer, M. C. (2000). "Paul and apocalyptic eschatology," in John J. Collins (2000a), pp. 345–83.
Dee, James H. (2000). *Epitheta Hominum apud Homerum: The Epithetic Phrases for the Homeric Heroes; A Repertory of Descriptive Expressions for the Human Characters of the Iliad and the Odyssey.* Hildesheim: Olms-Weidmann.
  (2001). *Epitheta Deorum apud Homerum.* Hildesheim: Olms-Weidmann.

de Jong, Irene J. F. (2001). *A Narratological Commentary on the Odyssey*. Cambridge University Press.
Dekker, Annie F. (1965). *Ironie in de Odyssee*. Leiden: E. J. Brill.
Dell, Katharine J. (2001). "Wisdom literature," in Perdue, pp. 418–31.
Demsky, Aaron (1997). "The name of the goddess of Ekron: a new reading," *JANES* 25: 1–5.
Detienne, Marcel and Vernant, Jean-Pierre (1974, 1991). *Cunning Intelligence in Greek Culture and Society* (trans. Janet Lloyd). University of Chicago Press.
de Vaux, Roland (1971). *The Bible and the Ancient Near East*. Garden City, New York: Doubleday.
Dimock, George E. (1989). *The Unity of the Odyssey*. Amherst: The University of Massachusetts Press.
Dodds, E. R. (1960). *Euripides Bacchae, edited with introduction and commentary*. Oxford: Clarendon Press.
Dothan, Trude (1982). *The Philistines and Their Material Culture*. New Haven: Yale University Press.
Dothan, Trude and Moshe (1992). *People of the Sea. The Search for the Philistines*. New York: Macmillan.
Dougherty, Carol (2001). *The Raft of Odysseus: The Ethnographic Imagination of Homer's* Odyssey. Oxford University Press.
Drury, John (1987). *Mark*, in Alter and Kermode, (eds.), pp. 402–17.
Edelstein, Emma J. and Ludwig (1998). *Asclepius: Collection and Interpretation of the Testimonies*. Baltimore: The Johns Hopkins University Press.
Emlyn-Jones, Chris (1984). "The reunion of Penelope and Odysseus," *Greece & Rome* 30: 1–18.
Felson-Rubin, Nancy (1994). *Regarding Penelope: From Character to Poetics*. Princeton University Press.
Fenik, Bernard (1974). *Studies in the Odyssey* (Hermes Einzelschriften Heft 30). Wiesbaden: Franz Steiner Verlag.
Fernández-Galiano, Manuel (1992). Books XXI–XXII, in Russo, Fernández-Galiano and Heubeck (eds.).
Finkelberg, M. (2000). "The *Cypria*, the *Iliad*, and the problem of multiformity in oral and written tradition," *Classical Philology* 95: 1–11.
  (2005). *Greeks and Pre-Greeks: Aegean Prehistory and Greek Heroic Tradition*. Cambridge University Press.
Finkelberg, M. and Stroumsa, Guy G. (eds.) (2003). *Homer, the Bible, and Beyond: Literary and Religious Canons in the Ancient World*. Leiden: Brill.
Finkelstein, Israel (2002). "The Philistines in the Bible: a late-monarchic perspective," *Journal for the Study of the Old Testament* 27: 131–67.
Fitzmyer, Joseph A. (1981). *The Gospel According to Luke (I–IX): Introduction, Translation, and Notes. The Anchor Bible*. Garden City, New York: Doubleday.
  (1985). *The Anchor Bible: The Gospel According to Luke (X–XXIV)*. Garden City, New York: Doubleday.
Foley, John Miles (1999). *Homer's Traditional Art*. University Park: The Pennsylvania State University Press.
  (2005). *The Blackwell Companion to Ancient Epic*. Oxford: Blackwell.

Fontenrose, Joseph (1959). *Python: A Study of Delphic Myth and Its Origins*. Berkeley: University of California Press.
Ford, J. Massyngberde (1975). *Revelation: Introduction, Translation and Commentary. The Anchor Bible*. Garden City, New York: Doubleday.
Foster, Benjamin R. (2005). *Before the Muses: An Anthology of Akkadian Literature*. Bethesda: CDL Press.
Frankfurter, David (2000). "Early Christian apocalypticism: literature and social world," in John J. Collins (2000a), pp. 415–53.
Friedrich, Rainer (1987). "Thrinakia and Zeus' ways to men in the *Odyssey*," *GRBS* 28: 373–400.
  (1991). "The Hybris of Odysseus," *JHS* 111: 16–28.
Frye, Northrop (1976). *The Secular Scripture: A Study of the Structure of Romance*. Cambridge, MA: Harvard University Press.
Gainsford, Peter (2003). "Formal analysis of recognition scenes in the *Odyssey*," *JHS* 123: 41–59.
Gaisser, Julia Haig (1968). "A structural analysis of the digressions in the *Iliad* and the *Odyssey*," *HSCP* 73: 27–31.
  (1983). *Bryn Mawr Commentaries: The Homeric Hymn to Hermes*. Bryn Mawr College.
Gantz, Timothy (1993). *Early Greek Myth*. Baltimore: The Johns Hopkins University Press.
Garvie, A. F. (1994). *Homer, Odyssey: Books VI–VIII*. Cambridge University Press.
George, A. R. (2003). *The Babylonian Gilgamesh Epic. Introduction, Critical Edition and Cuneiform Texts. Vols. I & II*. Oxford University Press.
Gerber, Douglas E. (1999). *Greek Elegiac Poetry: From the Seventh to the Fifth Centuries B.C.* Cambridge, MA: Harvard University Press.
Giesecke, Annette Lucia (2007). "Mapping utopia: Homer's politics and the birth of the polis," *College Literature* 34.2: 194–216.
Gitin, A., Mazar, A. and Stern, E. (eds.) (1998). *Mediterranean Peoples in Transition. Thirteenth to Early Tenth Centuries BCE*. Jerusalem: Israel Exploration Society.
Glenn, Justin (1971). "The Polyphemus folktale and Homer's Kyklôpeia," *TAPA* 102: 133–81.
Gordon, Cyrus H. (1965a). *The Ancient Near East*. New York: W. W. Norton.
  (1965b). *The Common Background of Greek and Hebrew Civilizations*. New York: Norton.
Gray, John (1979). "The blood bath of the goddess Anat in the Ras Shamra texts," *Ugarit-Forschungen* 11: 315–24.
Grottanelli, Cristiano (2001). "The story of Combabos and the *Gilgamesh* tradition," in Whiting (2001), pp. 19–27.
Hainsworth, Bryan (1993). *The Iliad: A Commentary. Vol. III: Books 9–12*, gen. ed. G. S. Kirk. Cambridge University Press.
  (1988). Books V–VIII," in Heubeck, West, and Hainsworth (eds.).
Hall, Edith (2006). "No man's lands: modern myths of the Cyclops," *The Times Literary Supplement*, No. 5382 (May 26): 14–15.

Hallo, William W. (2003). *The Context of Scripture: Canonical Compositions from the Biblical World*. Leiden. E. J. Brill.
Halpern, Baruch (2001). *David's Secret Demons: Messiah, Murderer, Traitor, King*. Grand Rapids: William B. Eerdmans.
Hamilton, A. C. (ed.) (1997). *The Spenser Encyclopedia*. University of Toronto Press.
Hankey, Robin (1985). "Eumaeus and the moral design of the Odyssey," in *Essays in Honour of Agathe Thornton*, (eds.) R. Hankey and D. Little, pp. 26–34. University of Otago Press.
Hansen, William (2004). *Classical Mythology: A Guide to the Mythical World of the Greeks and Romans*. Oxford University Press.
Hard, Robin (1998). *Apollodorus: The Library of Greek Mythology. Translated with an Introduction and Notes*. Oxford University Press.
Harris, Rivkah (1990). "Images of women in the Gilgamesh epic," in Abusch, pp. 219–30.
Hatch, Edwin and Redpath, Henry A. (2005). *A Concordance to the Septuagint: And the Other Greek Versions of the Old Testament (Including the Apocryphal Books)*. Grand Rapids: Baker Academic.
Haubold, J. (2002). "Greek epic: a Near Eastern genre?" *Proceedings of the Cambridge Philological Society* 48: 1–19.
Hauge, Martin Ravndal (2001). *The Descent from the Mountain: Narrative Patterns in Exodus 19–40 (Journal for the Study of the Old Testament Supplement Series 323)*. Sheffield Academic Press.
Heitman, Richard (2005). *Taking Her Seriously. Penelope & the Plot of Homer's Odyssey*. Ann Arbor: University of Michigan Press.
Heltzer, M. and Lipinski, E. (1988). *Society and Economy in the Eastern Mediterranean (c. 1500–100 B.C.)*. Leuven: Uitgeverij Peeters.
Heubeck, Alfred (1988). *A Commentary on Homer's Odyssey*. Vol. 1: Introduction and Books i–viii. eds. Heubeck, Stephanie West, and J. B. Hainsworth. Oxford: Clarendon Press.
  (1989). "Books IX–XII," in *A Commentary on Homer's Odyssey*, eds. A. Heubeck and A. Hoekstra. Vol. 2. Oxford: Clarendon Press.
  (1992). "Books XXIII–XXIV" in *A Commentary on Homer's Odyssey*, eds. J. Russo, M. Fernández-Galiano and A. Heubeck. Vol. 3. Oxford: Clarendon Press.
Hindson, Edward E. (1971). *The Philistines and the Old Testament*. Baker Studies in Biblical Archaeology. Grand Rapids, Michigan: Baker Book House.
Hoekstra, A. (1989). "Books XIII–XVI," in *A Commentary on Homer's Odyssey*, (eds.) A. Heubeck and A. Hoekstra. Vol. 2. Oxford: Clarendon Press.
Hoffner, Harry A. (1998). *Hittite Myths*. Atlanta: Scholars Press.
Hollis, A. S. (1990). *Callimachus Hecale, edited with Introduction and Commentary*. Oxford: Clarendon Press.
Holm, Tawney L. (2005). "Ancient Near Eastern literature: genres and forms," in *A Companion to the Ancient Near East*, ed. Daniel C. Snell, pp. 269–88. Oxford: Blackwell Publishing.

Hölscher, Uvo (1988). *Die Odyssee: Epos zwischen Märchen und Roman.* Munich: Verlag C. H. Beck.
Horsley, Richard A. (2000). "The kingdom of God and the renewal of Israel: synoptic gospels, Jesus movements, and apocalypticism," in John J. Collins (2000a), pp. 303–44.
Hunter, R. L. (1989). *Apollonius of Rhodes: Argonautica, Book III.* Cambridge University Press.
Irvin, Dorothy (1978). *Mytharion: The Comparison of Tales from the Old Testament and the Ancient Near East.* Kevelaer: Butzon & Bercker.
Jacobsen, Thorkild (1987). *The Harps That Once... Sumerian Poetry in Translation.* New Haven: Yale University Press.
   (1990). "The Gilgamesh epic: romantic and tragic vision," in Abusch 1990, pp. 231–49.
Janko, Richard (1992). *The Iliad: A Commentary. Vol. IV: Books 13–16*, gen. ed. G. S. Kirk. Cambridge University Press.
   (1998). "The Homeric poems as oral dictated texts," *Classical Quarterly* 48: 1–13.
Jones, D. M. (1954). "Ethical themes in the plot of the *Odyssey*," inaugural lecture, Westfield College, London.
Kakridis, H. J. (1963). *La notion de l'amitié et de l'hospitalité chez Homère.* Salonika.
Kapelrud, Arvid S. (1969). *The Violent Goddess: Anat in the Ras Shamra Texts.* Oslo: Universitetsforlaget.
Karavites, Peter (Panayiotis). (1986). "*Philotes*, Homer and the Near East," *Athenaeum* 64: 474–81.
   (1992). *Promise-Giving and Treaty-Making: Homer and the Near East.* Leiden: E. J. Brill.
Katz, M. A. (1991). *Penelope's Renown: Meaning and Indeterminance in the Odyssey.* Princeton University Press.
Kearns, E. (1982). "The return of Odysseus: A Homeric theoxeny," *CQ* 32: 2–8.
Kelly, A. (2006). "Homer and history: *Iliad* 9.381–4," *Mnemosyne* LIX: 321–33.
Kirk, G. S. (1974). *The Nature of Greek Myths.* Harmondsworth: Penguin Books.
Koraka, Katerina (2001). "A day in Potnia's life. Aspects of Potnia and reflected 'Mistress' activities in the Aegean Bronze Age," in Laffineur, pp. 15–26.
Kugel, James (1990). "The case against Joseph," in Abusch, pp. 271–87.
Laffineur, Robert and Hägg, Robin (eds.) (2001). *Potnia: Deities and Religion in the Aegean Bronze Age* (Proceedings of the 8th International Aegean Conference, Göteborg, Göteborg University 12–15 April 2000). University of Texas at Austin.
Larson, Jennifer (2005). "Lugulbanda and Hermes," *Classical Philology* 100: 1–16.
Lateiner, Donald (2002). "Pouring bloody drops (*Iliad* 16.549): the grief of Zeus," *Colby Quarterly* 38: 42–61.
Lefkowitz, Mary (2003). *Greek Gods, Human Lives: What We Can Learn from Myths.* New Haven: Yale University Press.
Levine, Amy-Jill (1998). "Visions of kingdoms: from Pompey to the First Jewish Revolt," in Coogan, pp. 467–516.

Levine, Baruch A. (1993). *Numbers 1–20: A New Translation with Introduction and Commentary. The Anchor Bible.* Garden City, New York. Doubleday.
Levine, Daniel B. (1983). "Theoklymenos and the apocalypse," *CJ* 79: 1–7.
Lichtheim, M. (1973). *Ancient Egyptian Literature, Vol. 1: The Old and Middle Kingdoms.* Berkeley: University of California Press.
Lloyd-Jones, Hugh (1996). *Sophocles, edited and translated by Hugh Lloyd-Jones. Vol. 3, Fragments.* Cambridge, MA: Harvard University Press.
Lonsdale, Stephen (1988). "Protean forms and disguise in *Odyssey* 4," *Lexis* 2: 165–78.
Lord, Albert B. (1960). *The Singer of Tales.* Cambridge, MA: Harvard University Press.
  (1990). "*Gilgamesh* and other epics," in Abusch, pp. 371–80.
Louden, Bruce (1993). "Pivotal contrafactuals in Homeric epic," *Classical Antiquity* 12: 181–98.
  (1995). "Categories of Homeric wordplay," *TAPA* 125: 27–46.
  (1996). "Epeios, Odysseus, and the Indo-European metaphor for poet," *The Journal of Indo-European Studies* 24, nos 3 and 4: 277–304.
  (1999). *The Odyssey: Structure, Narration, and Meaning.* Baltimore: The Johns Hopkins University Press.
  (2005). "The gods in epic, or the divine economy," in Foley, pp. 90–104.
  (2006). *The Iliad: Structure, Myth and Meaning.* Baltimore: The Johns Hopkins University Press.
  (2007). "Reading through *The Alcestis* to *The Winter's Tale*," *Classical and Modern Literature*, 27.2.
  (2009). "The *Odyssey* and Frank Capra's *It's a Wonderful Life*," in *Reading Homer: Film and Text*, ed. Kostas Myrsiades, pp. 208–28. Madison: Fairleigh Dickinson University Press.
Lowe, N. J. (2000). *The Classical Plot and the Invention of Western Narrative.* Cambridge University Press.
Luttikhuizen, Gerard P. (1999). *Paradise Interpreted: Representations of Biblical Paradise in Judaism and Christianity.* Leiden: Brill.
Lyons, William John (2002). *Canon and Exegesis: Canonical Praxis and the Sodom Narrative (Journal for the Study of the Old Testament Supplement Series 352).* London: Sheffield Academic Press.
MacDonald, Dennis R. (2000). *The Homeric Epics and the Gospel of Mark.* Yale University Press.
Mack, B. (1982). "Under the shadow of Moses: authorship and authority in Hellenistic Judaism," *SBLSP* 21: 299–318.
Malkin, Irad (2008). *The Returns of Odysseus: Colonization and Ethnicity.* Berkeley: University of California Press.
Mann, C. S. (1986). *The Anchor Bible. Mark: A New Translation with Introduction and Commentary.* Garden City, New York: Doubleday.
Margalith, Othniel (1994). *The Sea Peoples in the Bible.* Wiesbaden: Harrassowitz.

Maronitis, D. N. (2004). *Homeric Megathemes: War-Homilia-Homecoming*. Trans. David Connolly. Lanham: Lexington Books.
Martin, Richard P. (2005). "Epic as genre," in Foley, pp. 9–19.
Mazar, A. (1985). "The emergence of the Philistine material culture," *Israel Exploration Journal* 35: 95–107.
McCarter, P. Kyle, Jr. (1985). *The Anchor Bible: I Samuel: A New Translation with Introduction, Notes & Commentary*. Garden City, New York: Doubleday.
McKenzie, John L. (1968). *The Anchor Bible: Second Isaiah: Introduction, Translation, and Notes*. Garden City, New York: Doubleday.
Metzger, Bruce M. and Coogan, Michael D. (eds.) (1993). *The Oxford Companion to the Bible*. Oxford University Press.
Meuli, Karl (1921). *Odyssee und Argonautika: Untersuchungen zur griechischen Sagengeschichte und zum Epos*. diss. Universität Basel.
Michalowski, Piotr (1990). "Presence at the creation," in Abusch, pp. 381–96.
Miller, Patrick D., Jr. (1973). *The Divine Warrior in Early Israel*. Cambridge, MA: Harvard University Press.
Mills, Donald H. (2003). *The Hero and the Sea: Patterns of Chaos in Ancient Myth*. Wauconda: Bolchazy-Carducci Publishers.
Mondi, Robert (1983). "The Homeric Cyclopes: folktale, tradition, and theme," *TAPA* 113: 17–38.
Morris, Sarah P. (1992). *Daidalos and the Origins of Greek Art*. Princeton University Press.
  (1995). "The sacrifice of Astyanax," in *The Ages of Homer*, (eds.) Jane B. Carter, and Sarah P. Morris, pp. 221–45.
  (2001). "Potnia Aswiya: Anatolian contributions to Greek religion," in Laffineur, pp. 423–34.
Mosca, Paul G. (1993). "Day of judgment," in Metzger and Coogan, pp. 156–7.
Moscati, Sabatino (1960). *The Face of the Ancient Orient: Near Eastern Civilization in Pre-Classical Times*. Mineola, NY: Dover Publications.
Mühlestein, H. (1987). *Homerische Namenstudien*, Beiträge zur klassischen Philologie 183. Frankfurt am Main: Athenäum.
Mullen, E. Theodore Jr. (1980). *The Divine Council in Canaanite and Early Hebrew Literature*. Chico: Scholars Press.
Munck, Johannes (1967). *The Anchor Bible: The Acts of the Apostles. Introduction, Translation and Notes*. Revised by William F. Albright and C. S. Mann. Garden City, New York: Doubleday.
Muraoka, T. (2002). *A Greek-English Lexicon of the Septuagint*. Louvain: Peeters.
Murnaghan, S. (1987). *Disguise and Recognition in the Odyssey*. Princeton University Press.
Nagy, Gregory (1979). *The Best of the Achaeans*. Baltimore: The Johns Hopkins University Press.
  (2005). "The epic hero," in Foley, pp. 71–89.

Nakassis, Dimitri (2004). "Gemination at the horizons: east and west in the mythical geography of archaic Greek epic," *Transactions of the American Philological Association* 134: 215–33.

Nardelli, Jean-Fabrice (2004). *Le motif de la paire d'amis héroïque à prolongements homophiles: Perspectives odysséennes et proche-orientales.* Amsterdam: Adolf M. Hakkert.

Nelson, William B., Jr. (1993). "Eschatology," in Metzger and Coogan, pp. 192–4.

Niditch, Susan (1993). *War in the Hebrew Bible: A Study in the Ethics of Violence.* Oxford University Press.

(2005). "The challenge of Israelite epic," in Foley, pp. 277–87.

Niemeier, W.-D. (1998). "The Mycenaeans in Western Anatolia and the problem of the origins of the Sea Peoples," in Gitin, Mazar and Stern, pp. 17–65.

Nightingale, Andrea Wilson (2004). *Spectacles of Truth in Classical Greek Philosophy: Theoria in Its Cultural Context.* Cambridge University Press.

Noegel, Scott B. (2005). "Mesopotamian epic," in Foley, pp. 233–45.

Noort, Ed (2004). "For the sake of righteousness. Abraham's negotiations with YHWH as prologue to the Sodom narrative: Genesis 18:16–33," in Noort and Tigchelaar, pp. 3–15.

Noort, Ed and Tigchelaar, Eibert (2004). *Sodom's Sin: Genesis 18–19 and its Interpretations.* Leiden: E. J. Brill.

Olson, S. Douglas (1995). *Blood and Iron: Stories and Storytelling in Homer's Odyssey.* Leiden: E. J. Brill.

Orgel, Stephen (1996). *The Winter's Tale,* The Oxford Shakespeare: Oxford University Press.

Page, Denys (1955). *The Homeric Odyssey.* Oxford: Clarendon Press.

(1972). *Folktales in Homer's Odyssey.* Cambridge, MA: Harvard University Press.

Palaima, Thomas D. (2005). *The Triple Invention of Writing in Cyprus and Written Sources for Cypriote History* (2004 Annual Lecture for The A. G. Leventis Foundation). Nicosia: Leventis Municipal Museum.

Perdue, Leo G. (ed.) (2001). *The Blackwell Companion to the Hebrew Bible.* Oxford: Blackwell Publishing.

Petegorsky, Dan (1982). *Context and Evocation: Studies in Early Greek and Sanskrit Poetry.* Ph. D. dissertation, Berkeley: University of California Press.

Pitt-Rivers, Julian (1977). *The Fate of Shechem, or The Politics of Sex: Essays in the Anthropology of the Mediterranean.* Cambridge University Press.

Plass, Paul (1969). "Menelaus and Proteus," *Classical Journal* 65: 104–8.

Powell, Barry B. (1977). *Composition by Theme in the Odyssey.* Meisenheim am Glan: Verlag Anton Hain.

(1991). *Homer and the Origin of the Greek Alphabet.* Cambridge University Press.

(2002). *Writing and the Origins of Greek Literature.* Cambridge University Press.

Pritchard, James B. (ed.) (1969). *Ancient Near Eastern Texts Relating to the Old Testament.* Princeton University Press.

Propp, William H. C. (1998). *Exodus 1–18: A New Translation with Introduction and Commentary (The Anchor Bible).* Garden City, New York: Doubleday.

(2006). *Exodus 19–40: A New Translation with Introduction and Commentary (The Anchor Bible)*. Garden City, New York: Doubleday.

Pucci, Pietro (2002). "Theology and poetics in the *Iliad*," *Arethusa* 35: 17–34.

Raban, Avner (1988). "The constructive maritime role of the Sea Peoples in the Levant," in Heltzer, pp. 261–94.

Race, William H. (1993). "First appearances in the *Odyssey*," *TAPA* 123: 79–107.

(ed. and trans.) (1997). *Pindar: Olympian Odes, Pythian Odes*. Cambridge, MA: Harvard University Press.

Reardon, B. P. (ed.) (1989). *Collected Ancient Greek Novels*. Berkeley: University of California Press.

Redford, Donald B. (1970). *A Study of the Biblical Story of Joseph (Genesis 37–50)*. Leiden: E. J. Brill.

Reece, Steve (1993). *The Stranger's Welcome: Oral Theory and the Aesthetics of the Homeric Hospitality Scene*. Ann Arbor: University of Michigan Press.

(1995). "The three circuits of the suitors: a ring composition in *Odyssey* 17–22," *Oral Tradition* 10: 207–29.

Richardson, N. J. (1983). "Recognition scenes in the *Odyssey* and ancient literary criticism," *Papers of the Liverpool Latin Seminar* 4: 219–35.

(1993). *The Iliad: A Commentary, Volume VI: books 21–24*. Cambridge University Press.

Richardson, Scott (2007). "Conversation in the Odyssey," *College Literature* 34.2: 132–49.

Ricoeur, P. (1973). "The hermeneutic of distanciation," *Philosophy Today* 17: 129–41.

Rose, Gilbert P. (1969). "The unfriendly Phaeacians," *Transactions of the American Philological Association* 100: 387–406.

Rouse, Wh. H. D. (1940). *Nonnus: Dionysiaca II*. Cambridge, MA: Harvard University Press.

Russo, J. (1992). Books XVII–XX, in Russo, Fernández-Galiano and Heubeck, (eds.).

Russo, Joseph, Fernández-Galiano, Manuel, and Heubeck, Alfred (eds.) (1992). *A Commentary on Homer's Odyssey*, Vol. 3. *Books xvii–xxiv*. Oxford: Clarendon Press.

Rutherford, R. B. (1992). *Homer, Odyssey: Books XIX and XX*. Cambridge University Press.

Sarna, Nahum M. (1991). *The JPS Torah Commentary: Exodus. The Traditional Hebrew Text with the New JPS Translation Commentary by Sarna*. Philadelphia: The Jewish Publication Society.

Sasson, Jack M. (1990). *The Anchor Bible, Jonah: A New Translation with Introduction, Commentary and Interpretation*. Garden City, New York: Doubleday.

(2005). "Comparative observations on the Near Eastern epic traditions," in Foley, pp. 215–32.

Schmiel, Robert (1972). "Telemachus in Sparta," *TAPA* 103: 463–72.

Scodel, R. (1998). "The removal of the arms, the recognition with Laertes, and narrative tension in the *Odyssey*," *Classical Philology* 93: 1–17.
Scott, R.B.Y. (1965). *The Anchor Bible: Proverbs; Ecclesiastes*. Garden City, New York: Doubleday.
Simpson, William Kelly (1972). *The Literature of Ancient Egypt: An Anthology of Stories, Instructions and Poetry*. New Haven: Yale University Press.
Sinclair, T. A. (1966). *Hesiod: Works and Days*. Hildesheim: Georg Olms Verlagsbuchhandlung.
Smith, Mark S. (1990). *The Early History of God: Yahweh and the Other Deities in Ancient Israel*. San Francisco: Harper Collins.
  (1995). "Anat's warfare cannibalism and the West Semitic ban," in *The Pitcher is Broken: Memorial Essays for Gösta W. Ahlström*, (eds.) Steven W. Holloway and Lowell K. Handy, pp. 368–86. Sheffield Academic Press.
  (2001). *The Origins of Biblical Monotheism: Israel's Polytheistic Background and the Ugaritic Texts*. Oxford University Press.
Sparks, Kenton L. (2005). *Ancient Texts for the Study of the Hebrew Bible*. Peabody, Mass: Hendrickson Publishers.
Speiser, E. A. (1962). *The Anchor Bible: Genesis, Introduction, Translation, and Notes*. New York: Doubleday.
Stager, Lawrence E. (1998). "Forging an identity: the emergence of ancient Israel," in Coogan, pp. 123–75.
Stanford, W. B. (1961). *The Ulysses Theme in Literature*. Oxford University Press.
  (1962). *The Odyssey of Homer*. 2 vols. London: St Martin's Press.
Steinrück, Martin (1992). "Der Bericht des Proteus," *QUCC* 42: 47–60.
Stewart, Douglas J. (1976). *The Disguised Guest: Rank, Role, and Identity in the Odyssey*. Lewisburg: Bucknell University Press.
Stroumsa, Guy G. (2003). "Early Christianity – a religion of the book?" in Finkelberg, pp. 153–73.
Sturdy, John (1976). *Numbers*. Cambridge University Press.
Suggs, M. Jack, Sakenfield, Katharine Doob and Mueller, James R. (1992). *The Oxford Study Bible*. Oxford University Press.
Surtz, Edward S. J. and Hexter, J. H. (1965). *The Complete Works of St. Thomas More. Volume 4*. New Haven: Yale University Press.
Talon, Philippe (2001). "*Enuma Elish* and the transmission of Babylonian cosmology to the West," in Whiting, pp. 265–77.
Taylor, John (2007). *Classics and the Bible: Hospitality and Recognition*. London: Duckworth.
Teodorsson, Sven-Tage (2006). "Eastern literacy, Greek alphabet, and Homer," *Mnemosyne* 59: 161–87.
Thalmann, William G. (1998). *The Swineherd and the Bow: Representations of Class in the Odyssey*. Ithaca: Cornell University Press.
Thomas, Carol G. and Wedde, Michael (2001). "Desperately seeking Potnia," in Laffineur, pp. 3–13.
Thornton, Agathe (1970). *People and Themes in Homer's Odyssey*. London: Methuen.

Tigay, Jeffrey H. (2002). *The Evolution of the Gilgamesh Epic*. Wauconda: Bolchazy-Carducci Publishers.
Travis, Stephen H. (1993). "The second coming of Christ," in Metzger and Coogan, pp. 685–6.
Tsagarakis, Odysseus (2000). *Studies in Odyssey 11* (Hermes-Einzelschriften Heft 82). Stuttgart: Franz Steiner Verlag.
VanderKam, James C. (2000). "Messianism and apocalypticism," in John J. Collins (2000a), pp. 193–228.
Vawter, Bruce (1955). "The Canaanite background of Genesis 49," *The Catholic Biblical Quarterly* 17: 1–18.
Vlahos, John B. (2007). "Homer's *Odyssey*, Books 19 and 23: early recognition; a solution to the enigma of ivory and horns, and the test of the bed," *College Literature* 34.2: 107–31.
von Kamptz, H. (1982). *Homerische Personennamen*. Göttingen: Vandenhoeck & Ruprecht.
Walsh, Thomas R. (2004). *Fighting Words and Feuding Words*. Lanham: Rowman & Littlefield.
Webster, T. B. L. (1958). *From Mycenae to Homer*. London: Methuen.
Weinfeld, Moshe (1988). "The promise to the patriarchs and its realization: an analysis of foundation stories," in Heltzer and Lipinski, pp. 353–69.
  (2001). "The roots of the Messianic idea," in Whiting, pp. 279–87.
Wender, Dorothea (1978). *The Last Scenes in the Odyssey*. Leiden: E. J. Brill.
West, Emily (2008). "Review of Louden (2006)". *Classical Journal* 103: 312–15.
West, M. L. (1966). *Hesiod Theogony: Edited with Prolegomena and Commentary*. Oxford: Clarendon Press.
  (1978). *Hesiod: Works and Days*. Oxford: Clarendon Press.
  (1997). *The East Face of Helicon: West Asiatic Elements in Greek Poetry and Myth*. Oxford: Clarendon Press.
  (2003). *Homeric Hymns, Homeric Apocrypha, Lives of Homer*. Cambridge, MA: Harvard University Press.
  (2005). "*Odyssey* and *Argonautica*," *Classical Quarterly* 55: 39–64.
  (2007). *Indo-European Poetry and Myth*. Oxford University Press.
West, S. (1988). Books I–IV, in Heubeck, West and Hainsworth (eds.).
Westenholz, Joan Goodnick (1997). *Legends of the Kings of Akkade: The Texts*. Winona Lake: Eisenbrauns.
Westermann, Claus (1994). *Genesis 12–36: A Continental Commentary*, trans. John J. Scullion, S.J. Minneapolis: Fortress Press.
Whiting, R. M. (2001). *Mythology and Mythologies: Methodological Approaches to Intercultural Influences (Melammu Symposia II)*. Helsinki: The Neo-Assyrian Text Corpus Project.
Whitman, Cedric H. (1958). *Homer and the Heroic Tradition*. New York: W. W. Norton.
Williams, James G. (1987). "Proverbs and Ecclesiastes," in Alter and Kermode, pp. 263–82.
Williams, R. D. (1977). *The Aeneid of Virgil: Books 1–6*. London: St. Martin's Press.

Woodard, Roger D. (1997). *Greek Writing from Knossos to Homer: A Linguistic Interpretation of the Origin of the Greek Alphabet and the Continuity of Ancient Greek Literacy*. Oxford University Press.

Woodhouse, W. J. (1930). *The Composition of Homer's Odyssey*. Oxford: Clarendon Press.

Wyatt, Nicolas (1998). *Religious Texts from Ugarit*. Sheffield Academic Press.

Yadin, Azzan (2004). "Goliath's armor and Israelite collective memory," *Vetus Testamentum* 54/3: 373–95.

Yasur-Landau, Assaf (2001). "The mother(s) of all Philistines? Aegean enthroned deities of the 12th–11th century Philistia," in Laffineur, pp. 329–43.

Index locorum

Apollonius
  Argonautica
    2.1–97 119
    3.66–73 145
    3.400–21 146, 149
    3.619–27 144
    3.845–66 147
    3.1,282 140
    4.212–14, 228–36 159
    4.228–35 146

Bible
  Acts
    10
      37–8 271
    14
      8–20 55
  Amos
    8
      9 292
  2 Corinthians
    1
      21 271
  Daniel
    5
      1–4 291
  Deuteronomy
    28
      28–9 254
  Exodus
    2
      12–15 138
      15b–21 136
    3
      17 224
    4
      14 230
      21 252
    5
      20 227
    7
      20–1 231
    9
      12 52
    12
      23 279
    16
      3 227
    17
      1–7 228
    20
      3–5 233
      23 233
      25–31 229
    32 25, 222, 260, 286, 287, 302
      1–5 232
      6 233
      7–10 237
      7–14 237, 290
      10 310
      11–14 237
      17–18 236
      27–8 239, 302
  Ezekiel
    32
      7–8 293
  Genesis
    1
      26 127
    1–6
      4 2
    2
      10–14 125
    3
      22 23, 127
      23–4 309

Bible (cont.)
  Genesis (cont.)
    6
      1–4 182
      2–4 127
      5–8.22 286
    9
      21–27 310
    11
      7 23
      15 290
    17
      1–22 290
    18 25, 26, 36
      1–15 38
      20 289
      20–3 288
      23–32 289
    19 32, 36, 44, 45, 46, 281, 302
      4 289
      8 49
      9 50
      11 289, 302
      14 51
      17 308
      17–26 227
      26 307
      30–8 310
    22
      13–15 118
    24
      10–61 136
      15–21 137
      17 140
      26–8 137
    28
      11–15 117
    29
      1–20 136
      7–10 138
      11–12 138
      15 146
      16–28 310
    30
      14 147
      32 101, 148
      37–9 101
    31
      1 149
      7 149
      19–35 149
      26–30 152

    32
      22–4 114
      26 118
    34 102
    37
      6–9 65
    39
      6–7 68
      6–20 62
      23 71
    41
      16 97
    42
      6–8 92
      13 72
      16–24 93
      21–2 72
    42–5 92
    44
      7–13 93
      31 95
    45
      3 94
      12 94
  Isaiah
    13
      10 293
    14
      9 256
    34
      2–4, 6 299
    63
      2–3, 6 43, 298
  Jeremiah
    7
      11 268
  Job
    1
      6–8 24
    2
      1–7 24
      12 91
  Joel
    2
      31 292, 293
  John
    3
      19 263
    12
      1–8 270
      9–11 267
      19 267
      42 267
      49 262

Index locorum

Jonah
  1
    7 173
    12 173
  3
    4–10 178
  4
    1–3 179
Joshua
  2 106
1 Kings
  3
    5–15 131
  10
    1 131
  17 52
  17–19, 21 44
  22
    19–22 24
2 Kings
  1–8 44
  2
    23–4 250
  4
    8–17 53
  6
    18 47, 254
Lamentations
  1
    12 312
Luke
  1
    53 263
  4
    18 263, 270
  5
    1–11 263
  7
    36–50 270
  9
    22 276
    34–5 265
  16
    14 268
  18
    32 41
  19
    45–8 268
  20
    9–19 272
  21
    1–4 268
    23 312
  22
    24–30 281
    44 281
    49–50 278
    63–4 276
  23
    18–25 274
Mark
  3
    22 273
  8
    31 276
  9
    3 265
  12
    1–2 272
  14
    3 270
    21 277
    65 276
  15
    6–15 274
    17–19 276
  16
    5 262
Matthew
  1
    5 110
  4
    18–22 263
  12
    40 176
  16
    21 41, 276
  17
    1–2 266
    2 265
  21
    12–17 268
    13 268
    33–46 272
  24
    29 271
  25 54
    31–46 312
    45 313
  26
    7 270
    14–16 278
    24 280
    37–8 281
    67–8 276
  27
    16–26 274
Numbers
  11 241

Bible (cont.)
Numbers (cont.)
13
   32–3   183
14   241
21
   4–7   242
Proverbs
1
   11–18   250
   27   249
2
   18   256
5
   22–3   253
7
   22   257
9
   7   248
   18   257
11
   5   253
24
   5–6   245
Psalms
10
   7   249
68
   21–3   299
73
   8–9   249
Revelation
4
   1   219
11
   18   312
   12   285
1 Samuel
4
   11   111
9
   11–14   142
15
   1–3   198
   22–3   198
17
   4   183
   51   189
28   197
   3   199
   15   96
   16–18   202
   19   203
2 Samuel
22
   15   279

Euripides
Bacchae
   272–4, 516–17   267
Medea
   478–82   156

Gilgamesh
2.217–29   185
4.201–3   187
5.1–9   186
5.86–7   188
5.103–4   190
5.137–41   189
5.184–6   194
5.244–5   192
5.255–7   195
5.257   206
5.291–6   191
5.300–1   196
6.3–4   287
6.81–114   322
12.90–153   206
12.11–78   206
12.79–84   206
12.87   206
12.102, 104, 106, 108, 110, 113, 115, 117, 132, 134, 144, 146, 148, 150, 152
12.102–15   206, 207
12.144–5   207
12.150–3   207

Hesiod
Theogony
   142–4   187
   805–6   132
   861–7   190
Works and Days
   17–26   246
   47–174   2
   85–7   232
   94–5   232
   127–37   247
   137–40   286, 311
   174–201   286, 313
   180   272
   238–41   247
   240–1   19, 287
   251   247
Homer
Iliad
   1.497   214
   3.205–24   112
   4.1–73   290
   5.348–51   23
   6.56–60   103
   6.268   295

Index locorum 349

6.297–311 111
7.443–63 22
7.446–53 21
7.459–63 306
8.1–37 290
8.363–9 197
10.482–97 113
13.15 122
13.44 122
13.624–5 30
14 124
16.431–58 196
16.459 281
17.446–7 52
18.509–40 295
19.91–133 98
19.96–133 145, 316
19.100–13 25
20.14 122
20.147 166
20.297–305 328
21.441–57 146
21.455 46
22.166–86 23
22.166–329 295
22.185 305
22.325–7 35
23.65–108 206
23.700–39 118
24.163–5 91
24.334–5 132
24.617 307

Odyssey
1.1–3 215
1.1–4 192
1.6–8 226
1.26–96 16
1.32–4 228
1.32–95 17
1.34 253
1.39 244
1.45–7 33
1.62–3 96
1.65–7 224
1.68–75 185
1.99–101 35, 295
1.115–17 35
1.225–9 313
1.227–9 21, 34
1.257–64 34
1.405–11 48
2.66 248
2.85–128 249
2.93–110 266
2.110–28 266
2.161–6 253

2.171–6 261
2.187–93 266
2.244–51 249
2.345–80 85
2.377–8 85
2.393–8 297
2.394–6 47, 255, 289
3.14–28 224
3.31–384 32
3.48 37
3.218–24 37
3.230–1 38
3.274 235
3.421–38 235
4.83–5 319
4.242–58 77
4.244–64 106
4.285–8 77
4.289 85
4.342–4 118
4.360–3 225
4.450 122
4.667–72 250
4.770–1 50
5.3–42 18
5.28–43 127
5.70–1 125
5.121–28 129
5.129–36 129
5.135 129
5.135–6 130
5.151–8 126
5.154–5 68, 133
5.173–91 130
5.286–90 25
5.350 308
5.377–9 25
5.419–22 164
6.21–40 138
6.244–5 140, 142
6.255–315 140
6.273–84 141
6.321–8 142
7.19–78 136
7.257 129
7.311–15 142
8.73–82 119
8.100–98 141
8.132–51 157
8.457–68 155
8.509 235
8.548–9 156
8.565–9 307
9.43–61 226
9.67–81 66

Homer (cont.)
  Odyssey (cont.)
    9.79–81 64
    9.116–41 181, 186
    9.196–212 301
    9.224–9 190
    9.269–72 301
    9.270–71 30
    9.316–28 189
    9.320–8 188
    9.364–7 301
    9.387–94 189
    9.391–3 190
    9.464–5 191
    9.523–5 193
    9.525 64, 193
    9.528–35 194
    9.534–5 31
    10.29–45 226
    10.29–55 280
    10.50–1 173
    10.82–5 160
    10.105–8 159
    10.110–11 159
    10.114 159
    10.115–32 159
    10.121–3 160
    10.206–7 174
    10.266–9 174
    10.429–45 227
    10.441 230
    10.492–5 201
    11.23–4 231
    11.51–83 220
    11.71–8 207
    11.100–137 62
    11.101–3 202
    11.104–13 202
    11.107–13 234
    11.107–15 227
    11.121–34 203
    11.134 122
    11.134–7 203
    11.139–51 209
    11.210–14 210
    11.216–22 210
    11.223–4 210
    11.235–332 136, 162
    11.287–97 161
    11.328–32 210
    11.330–84 220
    11.335–41 198, 210
    11.336–41 84
    11.363–6 156
    11.489–90 213
    12.69–72 135
    12.98–100 169
    12.137–41 227
    12.258–9 168
    12.266–76 227
    12.267–76 234
    12.297–302 227
    12.313–15 225
    12.333–4 228
    12.333–8 280
    12.340–2 228
    12.340–7 232
    12.346–7 223, 234
    12.348–51 234
    12.357–63 233
    12.366–9 236
    12.376–88 287, 305
    12.377–83 287, 292
    12.382–3 20, 236
    12.385–8 20
    12.405–25 66
    12.408–19 165
    12.447–8 165
    13.78–164 165
    13.125–58 178, 287
    13.125–59 305
    13.128–9 21
    13.130 120
    13.145 305
    13.149–52 21
    13.154–8 21
    13.179–87 178
    13.221–360 76
    13.287–440 290
    13.296–9 42
    13.310 275
    13.335–6 75
    13.387 42
    13.393–4 42
    13.394–5 294
    13.395 42
    14.36–534 77
    14.56–8 264
    14.83–8 248
    14.152 261
    14.199–359 319
    14.258–72 326
    14.283–4 30
    14.457 293
    15.20–3 83
    15.225–56 254
    15.226–38 161
    15.242–4 161
    15.403–84 77

15.420–2 82	19.478–9 255
16.108–9 50	19.505 269
16.166–220 78	19.535–53 97
16.173–4 265	19.572–80 278
16.174–6 265	19.589–90 86
16.179–80 265	20.6–16 49
16.187–8 79	20.25–30 274, 280
16.220–1 79	20.215 248
16.371–86 251	20.318–19 50
17.204–54 44	20.345–9 47, 255
17.217–32 44	20.345–70 233
17.233–4 275	20.347–70 268
17.248–53 248	20.348 291
17.290–327 80	20.354 297
17.300 291	20.356–7 272, 291
17.360–3 45	20.360 255, 273
17.360–4 251	20.392 280
17.364 45	21.152–62 253
17.377 45	21.188–227 86
17.415–44 248, 271	21.360–7 267
17.442–4 319	22.139–52 277
17.444 319	22.308–9 297
17.446–52 248	22.402 294
17.460–88 267	22.473–6 278
17.479–80 46	23.1–232 86
17.483–7 31, 46	23.48 87
17.494 278	23.205 89
18.1–116 217	24 256
18.15–31 248	24.205–350 90
18.43–9 251	24.240 90
18.100 274	24.306–7 90
18.114–16 275	24.315–17 91
18.125–50 51, 271	24.323–4 91
18.154–6 52	24.351–2 300
18.274–303 268	24.413–37 304
18.276–82 252	24.413–548 303
18.317 217	24.451–65 261
18.325 49	24.472–86 21
18.327 273	24.472–87 304
18.346–8 251	24.472–88 287
18.353–5 249	24.473–6 22
18.357–86 246	24.478–86 64
18.414–15 246	24.481 305
19.34–40 217	24.528–30 306
19.53–251 81	*Homeric Hymn to Aphrodite*
19.75–88 271	247–53 323
19.87–8 49	*Homeric Hymn to Demeter*
19.211–12 81	310–13 286, 290
19.329–34 246	
19.353–505 85	*Mahabhârata*
19.363–9 85	2.72.8–10 255
19.363–91 269	
19.393–466 85	Ovid
19.395–8 98	*Fasti*
19.406–9 98	5.493–544 33, 40, 53, 303

Ovid (*cont.*)
  Metamorphoses
    1.5–88 2
    3.281–309 99
    8.611–724 32, 33
    8.679–80 53, 55
    8.689–97 41
    10.50–9 307

Plato
  Republic
    516d5–6 212
    517 a5 216
    Book 7 261

Rig Veda
  1.92.1 4, 12, 14 292

Vergil
  Aeneid
    2.163–8 113
    2.604–20 208
    5.604–745 242
    5.664–99 243
    6 208
    6.509–34 113
    6.650 309
    6.724–51 210
    6.756–853 209
    8.193–265 132

Subject index

Aaron 222, 230, 239, 302, 303
Abraham 14, 25, 26, 32, 38, 39, 40, 288, 290, 307, 322, 328
Adam 125
Adapa 2
Aeneas 113, 243, 309
Agamemnon 103
Aietes 144, 146, 149, 151, 241
Aigisthos 27, 31, 33, 58, 244
Aiolos 172
Alkinoös 119, 142, 155, 177
Allan, William 14
Amphinomos 52, 251
anabasis 218, 229
Anat 23, 29, 42, 87, 195, 295, 296, 297, 299, 305
Anchises 208
angels in Genesis 19
  parallels with Athena 46
anointing 109
Antikleia 204, 208, 209, 211
Antinoös 32, 44, 45, 48, 50, 248, 249, 250, 266, 275
Antiphates 159
Anu 17, 18, 23, 196, 287, 290
apocalypse 164
apocalyptic myth 18, 19, 176, 285, 286
  contained apocalypse 20, 22, 26, 272
Apollo 46, 278, 301
Apsyrtos 151
Apuleius 170, 179
Aqhat 18, 23, 25, 28, 305
Arete 84, 210, 211
Argonautic myth 14, 135, 153, 158, 161, 288, 314, 316, 317, 328
Argos 80
Ark 111
atasthala 51
Athena 17, 27, 32, 35, 42, 45, 47, 48, 70, 85, 138, 248, 251, 252, 254, 262, 280, 281, 288, 294, 295, 305

Atrahasis 27
Autolykos 98, 99

Baal 18, 28
Baal Cycle 284, 295, 297
ban, the 107, 198
Barabbas 274, 275
Baucis and Philemon 43, 45, 281, 287
Benjamin 93, 94
betrothal type-scene 136
Bible
  Exodus
    32 15
  Ezekiel 25
  Genesis 14, 314, 320, 321, 323
    19 19, 260
  Numbers
    16 242
  Proverbs 245, 247
  Revelation 218, 283, 284, 285
  Zechariah 219
bifurcation 153
Bolin, Thomas M. 30
Buñuel, Luis
  The Exterminating Angel 50

Carr, David M. 3, 23
catabasis 197, 199, 212
Catalogue of Women 162, 198, 204, 210
Charybdis 167, 168
Christ 216, 219, 258, 259, 267, 268, 270, 275, 276, 315
Cicero
  "Scipio's Dream" 198, 205, 217
Collins, John J. 3
combat myth 285
creation myth 2, 124
Cyprus 318, 319, 324

Dagon 237
Danel 18, 25

353

Dante
  Inferno 198
Deïphobos 113
Dinah 102
Diomedes 111
Dionysus 258, 259, 260, 267
divine council 126, 304, 314, 329
  adapted 237, 240, 287, 288, 290, 307, 315
divine interdiction 130, 227, 232, 307, 308
divine wrath 16, 17, 21, 23, 34, 35, 120, 130, 131, 171, 178, 189, 198, 202, 241, 243, 271, 284, 286, 312
dreams 64, 65, 70, 96

eclipse 291, 292, 294
El 18, 23, 28
Elijah 44, 52, 259
Elisha 44, 53, 249, 250, 254, 259
Ellil 18, 27
Elpenor 207
Enki and Ninmah 2
Enkidu 17, 18, 185, 206
Enlil 183, 195
Enoch 309
Enuma Elish 2, 284
Eos 67, 129, 134
epic triangle 17
Esau 98, 145, 146
euangelion 261
Eumaios 43, 77, 83, 95, 247, 263
  his hounds 44
Euripides 103
  Alcestis 74, 132, 259
  Bacchae 259, 282
  Helen 59, 74
  Ion 59, 65, 74
  Iphigenia in Tauris 74
  Medea 147
Euryalos 119, 143
Eurybates 84, 110
Eurykleia 77, 84, 85, 263, 269, 270
Eurylochos 173, 174, 222, 226, 229, 239, 241, 277, 281
Eurymachos 217, 246, 249, 255, 266, 267
Eurystheus 98
Eve 126

fantastic voyage, the 164
Frye, Northrop 1, 70

genres of myth 2, 107
Gilgamesh 8, 17, 18, 20, 21, 23, 35, 67, 121, 124, 126, 205, 236
  12 205

Golden Fleece 144, 149
Goliath 183, 189, 328

Halitherses 253, 261, 266, 304
Hamor 102
Helen 105, 108
Helios 20, 21, 153, 154, 161, 222, 236, 240, 286, 288, 292
Hephaistos 120
Hera 25, 98, 99, 145, 316
Herakles 25, 99, 146, 197, 259
Hermes 18, 27, 69, 100, 127, 148, 200, 244, 317
Hesiod
  Works and Days 19, 245
Homer
  Iliad 6
  20 17
Homeric Hymn to Aphrodite 129
Homeric Hymn to Demeter 20
Homeric Hymn to Hermes 100
hospitality 49, 106, 109, 248
hospitality myth 9
household gods 136, 144, 149, 316
hubris 246, 247
Humbaba 181, 185, 187, 188
Hyrieus 33, 40

irony 34, 37, 44, 72, 85, 231, 246, 250, 255, 275, 276, 278, 279, 304
Iros 248, 273
Isaac 98, 145
Ishtar 17, 18, 20, 67, 68, 69, 124, 128, 194, 196, 236, 287
It's a Wonderful Life 59, 198

Jacob 14, 98, 100, 114, 316
Jericho 106
Jeroboam I 240
John the Baptist 261
Jonah 170, 172
Joseph 6, 9, 14, 92, 96
Joshua 105
Judas 267, 270, 277, 278

Kalidasa
  Shakuntala 6, 59, 73, 74
Kalypso 8, 61, 66, 68, 69, 124, 129, 317
Kirke 67, 153, 160, 200, 317
Kirta 18, 28
Kothar 23
Kronos 18

Laban 100, 137, 146, 149, 151, 316
Laertes 75, 90, 95, 300

Subject index

Laistrygones 158, 327
Laodamas 155
Laomedon 46, 146
Lazarus 259, 267, 270
Leah 146
Leodes 253
Levi 103
Leviathan 285
Lot 14, 36, 44, 47, 48, 49, 51, 309, 310
Lovecraft, H. P. 169
Lowe, N. J. 1, 4, 7

magic 147, 148
Mahabhârata 117, 162
mandrake 147, 148
Medea 136, 143, 316
Melampous 161, 162, 259
Melanthios 44, 248, 249, 267, 277
Melantho 49, 81, 249, 273
Menelaus 14, 113, 118, 317
Mentes 33
Mentor 32
mentor god 16, 17, 18, 23, 24, 28, 145, 189, 196
Milton
  Paradise Lost 2
Moses 25, 138, 222, 224, 237, 286, 302, 310

Nausikaa 71, 138
Nausithoös 177
Nephilim 182, 323
Nestor 9, 14, 32, 37, 39, 40, 123
New Moon 292, 293
Nineveh 177
Noah 286, 310
nymphs 44

Ogygia 125, 165
one just man 286, 309, 312
opis 247, 248
overdetermination 52, 252, 278, 300
Ovid
  Metamorphoses 36

Palladium 111
Parable of the Vineyard Owner 272
paradise 125
Passover 270, 275, 278
Peisistratos 37, 40
Pelias 145
Penelope 245, 255, 256, 266, 268
Persephone 132, 134

Perses 246, 247
petrifaction 307, 308, 309
Pharaoh 252
Pharisees 267, 268, 270, 277
Philistines 199, 321, 324, 325, 326
Philoitios 263
Philomeleïdes 118, 120
Phoenicians 10, 318, 319
Planktai 154
plazô 47, 64, 91, 171, 297
Polyphêmos 64, 66, 180, 185, 187, 285, 300, 301
Poseidon 15, 17, 21, 22, 25, 38, 46, 47, 64, 118, 120, 121, 122, 158, 164, 166, 172, 175, 193, 195, 237, 242, 288, 307, 309, 315
Potiphar's wife 62, 65, 68, 69
Proteus 113, 115

Queen of Sheba 131

Rachel 136, 138, 149
Rahab 105, 106, 108, 112
Rebecca 98, 136, 137, 145
recognition scenes 73, 316
  delayed 75, 78, 85
  immediate 75, 80
  postponed 75, 81, 92
  reversed 75, 76, 87
Roman Empire, The 267
romance 245, 306, 315, 328

Sadducees 267
Samuel 201, 203
Sargon 223
Satan 278
Saul 198, 203
"Scipio's Dream" 198, 205, 217
sea-monsters 166, 175
self-control 130, 238
Septuagint 12, 13, 48
Shakespeare
  Pericles 70, 74
  The Winter's Tale 66, 70, 74
Shamash 17, 18, 35, 42, 189, 191, 195, 196, 206
Shamhat 126
Shechem 102, 103
Shipwrecked Sailor, The 61, 165, 175
Sibyl 208
Simeon 103
Sirens 166
skotos 293
Skylla 167
Solomon 131
Sophocles 111, 112, 147
Sparks, Kenton L. 2, 5, 8, 10

suitors 33, 47, 48, 49, 97, 266, 272, 275, 291, 315
  destruction of 45
  parallels with crew 43
  parallels with mob in Genesis 19 46, 50
Swift, Jonathan
  Gulliver's Travels 214

Tale of Sinuhe 60
Tale of the Two Brothers 62
Teiresias 64, 122, 197, 201, 203, 209
Telemachos 9, 14, 28, 32, 33, 38, 47, 50, 263
Theano 111, 150, 297, 316
Theoklymenos 44, 171, 204, 253, 259, 273, 276, 280, 291, 293
theoxeny 245, 312, 329
  negative 32, 281, 294, 315
  positive 32
  virtual 43, 45, 52, 313

Thrinakia 209, 222
Tithonos 134
Typhoeus 190, 285

Ugaritic culture 318, 320
Ugaritic myth 6, 11, 23

Venus 208
Vergil
  Aeneid 328
vision, the 198, 204, 218, 229

West, M. L. 6

Yadin, Azzan 12
Yahweh 24, 25, 43, 175, 237, 252, 286, 289, 298, 315

Zeus 16, 22, 23, 25, 30, 63, 145, 290, 301